George Lansing Raymond

Proportion and harmony of line and color in painting, sculpture, and architecture:

An essay in comparative sthetics

George Lansing Raymond

Proportion and harmony of line and color in painting, sculpture, and architecture:
An essay in comparative sthetics

ISBN/EAN: 9783337810061

Printed in Europe, USA, Canada, Australia, Japan

Cover: Foto ©ninafisch / pixelio.de

More available books at **www.hansebooks.com**

PROPORTION AND HARMONY

OF

LINE AND COLOR

IN

PAINTING, SCULPTURE, AND ARCHITECTURE

AN ESSAY IN

COMPARATIVE ÆSTHETICS

BY

GEORGE LANSING RAYMOND, L.H.D.

PROFESSOR OF ÆSTHETICS IN PRINCETON UNIVERSITY ; AUTHOR OF "ART IN THEORY,'
"THE REPRESENTATIVE SIGNIFICANCE OF FORM," "POETRY AS A REPRESENT-
ATIVE ART," "PAINTING, SCULPTURE, AND ARCHITECTURE AS REPRESENT-
ATIVE ARTS," "THE GENESIS OF ART-FORM," "RHYTHM AND
HARMONY IN POETRY AND MUSIC," "THE ESSENTIALS
OF ÆSTHETICS," ETC.

SECOND EDITION REVISED

G. P. PUTNAM'S SONS
NEW YORK AND LONDON
The Knickerbocker Press

COPYRIGHT, 1899
BY
G. P. PUTNAM'S SONS
Entered at Stationers' Hall, London

The Knickerbocker Press, New York

PREFACE.

IN many important regards the conceptions and conclusions of this volume differ from those ordinarily presented with reference to the subjects of which it treats. When considering, for instance, the first of the two general topics discussed, the view expressed in Gwilt's " Encyclopedia of Architecture," and still quite prevalent, to the effect that proportion is " but a synonym for fitness," is entirely ignored. This is not because of any undervaluation of the æsthetic importance of fitness, but because it is recognized that this latter characterizes many other artistic arrangements of form, as those of rhythm, tune, and color; and because it is recognized also that no amount of mere fitness could cause, or even suggest, that which is generally meant not only by artists but by people in general when they speak of proportion. When using this term in any strict or technical sense they almost invariably refer to an effect of measurements indicating a certain mathematical relationship between the parts of a product as compared with one another and with the whole.

This effect of proportion thus interpreted is further limited in this book by being ascribed to measurements that are *apparent* as distinguished from *actual*. It is shown that we judge of the proportions of the parts of a body or of a building when viewing each from a distance, not when examining it near at hand. This conclusion is reached and emphasized by pointing out the difference between proportion and perspective. It is shown that perspective, to which several chapters are devoted, has to do with the methods of arranging real outlines and with them, of course, measurements, so as to have them produce a certain desired visual result, whereas proportion has to do with the measurements as they appear in the result after perspective has produced it.

Again the effect of proportion is attributed in this volume to the mind's *conscious* as distinguished from *unconscious* measurements. This distinction is the logical result of a conception of an essential correspondence between proportion and rhythm. In the latter the mind is always consciously able to count, if it choose, the notes, syllables, feet, bars, lines, phrases—in other words the measures or measurements—which cause the effect. This is the same as to say that proportion in the arts of sight is not, as has been almost universally supposed (see Chapter III.), the analogue of harmony in the arts of sound. Harmony is produced in these arts whenever the number of vibrations *per second* determining the pitch of one tone sustains a certain ratio to the number of vibrations *per second* determining the pitch of another tone. But only the investigations of science have been able to discover that this is the reason for the effect. The mind cannot count the vibrations. It is not conscious of them; but only of an agreeable thrill or glow in case they coalesce, as they do when they sustain to one another the required harmonic ratio. Now if we go upon the supposition that the measurements determining the effects of proportion are perceived just as are those determining the effects of harmony, it is evident that we must suppose ourselves dealing with factors of which the mind is unconscious; and must remain ignorant until science has come into possession of certain data not yet discovered. Is it any wonder that those accepting this supposition who have tried to explain the effects, have either held that they cannot be explained at all, or have made attempts at explanation which may be said in a general way to have failed to prove convincing ? Is it any wonder that, even when acknowledging that the Greeks once had a knowledge of the subject, very many in our own times, after seeking for this knowledge in wrong directions, have conceived of the subject as hidden in almost impenetrable mystery,—as involving principles which it is wellnigh useless for present artists to attempt either to understand or to apply ?

Once more, artistic proportion is based in this volume, as all acknowledge rhythm to be, upon the principle of *comparison*. It is held that, fundamentally, measurements go together because they appear to be exactly alike, that is, as 1 : 1; and that the mind accepts the ratios of certain small numbers that are not alike, like 1 : 2 or 2 : 3, because it is able to recognize in the first that which corresponds to 1 : 1 + 1, and in the second that which corresponds to 1 + 1 : 1 + 1 + 1. Finally, connected with this, it is shown that as rhythm starts by putting together similar small parts such as feet and lines, and produces the general effect of the whole as a result of the combined effects of these parts, so does artistic proportion. For instance, the height of the front of the Parthenon is to its breadth as 4 : 9. But we need not consider the architect as aiming primarily at this proportion; or that it is any more than a secondary, though, of course, a necessary result of the relations, the one to the other, of the different separate measurements put together in order to form the whole.

The distinctions thus made seem important theoretically, not merely because of their rendering logically consistent, according to the principles of comparative æsthetics, the correspondences indicated between proportion and rhythm on the one hand, and between color and tone on the other; but also because of their rendering comprehensible the particular art-effects to which they are applied. But the distinctions seem equally important practically. Only as the effects of proportion are separated from those of perspective, and the limitations of each are perceived and determined, can the methods underlying each be successfully applied to products. There may be a simplicity of result in the conclusions reached, reminding the reader of the story of the egg which Columbus, by smashing on a table, made to " stand on its end." But simplicity is the door through which alone intelligence can enter into the complex. As indicated in either opinion or production, the artistic intelligence of our own time has, as yet, scarcely an apprehension, and no comprehension whatever, of that which is acknowledged to have formed the chief visual excellence of Greek art. The author is convinced that this fact is owing almost wholly to a misunderstanding of the aims of proportion, together with a confounding of it with perspective.

Besides treating of these two subjects, this volume contains, as applied to measurement, or size, as well as to what is termed harmony of outline, or shape, several deductions not noticed in other works, which it is thought will in a new way emphasize the importance as well as interpret the meaning, as used in the wholes or parts of contours, of the curved line, and especially, as suggested by the phenomena of binocular vision, of that of the circle, the ellipse, and the parabola.

In dealing with that much-disputed subject, the harmony of color, the author has been careful to incorporate enough that has been said by others to give the reader a general conception of such opinions as may be considered the most trustworthy and authoritative. As influencing practice, his own conclusions will be found to coincide with these. As influencing theory, his method of reaching his conclusions will be found in several regards to be different. For this fact, no apology need be offered. The musical notes harmonized by Pythagoras do not differ essentially from those harmonized by Helmholtz. But no one who thinks, questions the philosophic value of the very different reason for thus using the notes which is given by the latter. In the volume of this series entitled " Rhythm and Harmony in Poetry and Music," each of the art-methods mentioned in the chart on page 3 was shown to exert an influence in securing the general effect of harmony of tone; and in this book the same methods are shown to exert a corresponding influence in securing harmony of color. But, in connection with this fact, it seemed æsthetically desirable to show that, in particular, the physiological effect which is most essential to harmony —the effect which, in these volumes, has been termed consonance—is in both sound and color similarly conditioned. In sound, we know it to be a result of vibrations produced in the ear by external sound-waves which are related to one another according to certain ratios. In color why should it not be a result of external light-waves similarly related ? More weight is attached in this book to this supposition than some may deem warranted. Perhaps the most important objection to the theory is the phenomenon of the two complementary colors which are invariably produced, at least potentially, wherever one color is produced. To this phenomenon, at first thought, there seems to be no actual correspondence among the sounds. But certain facts are adduced to show that there is more of a correspondence than at first appears; and that, even though it were lacking, this circumstance would not necessarily lessen the possibility of a correspondence between the methods of operation of the waves of sound and of light. The complementary colors may be attributed solely to the eye's organism. This may be supposed to be so constituted that, when a wave of light is divided into two parts, as it always is potentially when a given color is produced, each particular organ of perception influenced by light is also divided into two parts, and in such a way that the mind is directly conscious of only the effect produced in that part which is nearest the optic nerve-fibre. In the eye, each of the organs which we know to be particularly instrumental in recognizing color is found to have an outer separated from an inner limb, the one nearer the optic nerve-fibre than the other. Moreover, of these organs themselves, there are two different kinds — rods and cones. Whether we consider the two limbs, or the two organs containing them, therefore, the conditions just indicated as presumably necessary to the effects of complementary color are present. In the text, certain reasons are given why the rods may be supposed to be affected mainly by light in general, or atmosphere, and the cones by what is termed local color. But whether this be the case or not, both, of course, according to the supposition just advanced, must manifest complementary hues; and both, as will be noticed, have two limbs, and therefore can realize the condition indicated as necessary for the two results.

PREFACE. ix

However, when treating of a problem which so many far abler investigators have failed to solve satisfactorily, it will not do for one to be too confident. Perhaps, the most that can be claimed for this theory is that, practically, it can do no harm; that, philosophically, it is logical; that, physiologically, it is supposable, and that, æsthetically, the facts concerning the subject ought to develop along the lines suggested.

In the last chapter of this volume will be found indicated the connection between the thought unfolded in it and in the other volumes of this series.

The author wishes to express his sense of obligation to his colleagues, Dr. Allan Marquand, Professor of Archæology and the History of Art, for the use of books in his valuable library, to Dr. Elmer H. Loomis, Professor of Physics, for his kindly reading of certain portions of the text; also to three volumes to which in the latter part of the work almost constant reference seems to have been made—Professor Ogden N. Rood's " Modern Chromatics," Professor Joseph Le Conte's " Sight," and Professor Wilhelm Von Bezold's " Theory of Color," translated by S. R. Koehler.

PRINCETON, N. J., August, 1899.

CONTENTS.

I.

CORRESPONDENCE BETWEEN THE ELEMENTS OF FORM
   IN THE ARTS OF SOUND AND OF SIGHT . 1–7

Object of the Present Volume—Connection between the Subjects Treated in it and the Requirements of Beauty—Similarity of these Requirements in the Arts of Sound and of Sight—Chart of the Methods of Art-Composition—Sounds are Perceived in Time, Sights in Space—Sounds are Separated by Silences or Pauses, Sights by Lines or Outlines—Sounds may Differ in Duration, Force, Quality, and Pitch; Sights in Extension, Light and Shade, and in Quality and Pitch of Color—Respective Correspondences between Effects in Sound and in Sight—Combined Influences of these Effects as Manifested in Rhythm and also in Proportion, as well as in Harmony, whether of Sound or of Sight.

II.

MEANING OF PROPORTION AND THE RECOGNITION
   OF IT IN ART AND NATURE . . . 8–19

Proportion as Meaning Measurement, and a Comparison of Measurements, either Absolute or Relative—As Indicating Relationships or Ratios of Measurement, or Likeness or Equality of these—Tendency of the Mind to Make Relative Measurements of Spaces Illustrated—Historical Evidences of the Existence of this Tendency—Primitive Ornamentation—Later Ornamentation—Additional Examples—The Same Tendency as Manifested in Reproductions of Objects Imitated—Proportion as Manifested in Nature as a Whole and in its Parts—The Subject Important and Complex—Its Analogy to Rhythm—Ratios Used in Poetry and Music—In the Longer Rhythmic Divisions of both Arts—Rhythmic Ratios are Represented by Small Numbers, and thus Rendered easily Recognizable—Same Principle Applicable to Proportion—Proportion may be Recognized without a Recognition of the Exact Ratio Causing it—The Use by the Greeks of Ratios Represented by Small Numbers.

III.

EFFECTS OF PROPORTION AS WRONGLY CONFOUNDED WITH THOSE OF PERSPECTIVE . . . 20-31

Difficulties Experienced in Applying Principles of Proportion—If ever Understood they can be Understood to-day—Necessity, to Rid the Subject of Complexity, of Separating Two Processes in Perception—First, the Unconscious Physical Recognition of Appearances; Second, the Conscious Mental Measurement of them—As Applied to Sounds, the First Process Determines Effects of Harmony; the Second, Effects of Rhythm—So in Sights, not the First, but the Second, Determines Effects of Proportion—This Results from the Conscious Measurement of Appearances after and as they have been Perceived, whereas the Unconscious Physical Process Determines Effects of Perspective—The Two Processes are easily Confounded, with Resulting Difficulties in Theory and Practice—The Two Supposed to have been Confounded by the Greeks—This Supposition not wholly Tenable—Yet at the Basis of Modern Theories which Correlate Proportion to the Effects of Musical Pitch upon the Ear, as do the Theories of Legh and Zeising—Of Hay, Fergusson, Penrose, and Lloyd—Impossibility of any Theoretic or Practical Understanding of Proportion according to this Conception of it.

IV.

PROPORTION AS BASED UPON COMPARISONS OF APPARENT MEASUREMENTS: STRAIGHT LINES AND RECTANGULAR FIGURES . . . 32-47

Proportion and Perspective Both to be Studied, but Separately—Perspective Considers the Difference between Subjective Effects and Objective Arrangements Occasioning them—Proportion Considers Appearances, Perspective the Method of Producing them—Comparison or Likeness is the Basis of Proportion—Illustrations—Small Numbers Necessary to the Recognition of Ratios—Outlines Indicating Like Subdivisions an Aid to this Recognition — The

Principle Applicable to Comparisons between both Rectilinear and
Rectangular Measurements—Between Adjacent Figures as Wholes
—Hay's Theory.

V.
PROPORTION AS BASED UPON COMPARISONS OF MEASUREMENTS IN CURVED AND COMPLEX FIGURES. 48-72

Complex and Irregular Figures Shown to be in Proportion by
Comparing each with some Simple and Regular Figure—Regular
Figures as Compared with Rectangles— Importance of Having
the Rectangles Visible—The Choir of Ely Cathedral—Illustrating
the Influence of Suggestion in Outlines—The Use of Figures
not Rectangular as Standards of Comparison between Complex
Figures—Aid Afforded by Straight Lines to the Perception of
Proportion in Complex Curves—Illustrations—Intimate Connection between Proportion as thus Manifested and Harmony of
Outline—Curved Circles, Ellipses, Used as Standards of Comparison between Complex Figures—Application of this Method to
the Human Figure.

VI.
PROPORTION IN LANDSCAPES, PLANTS, ANIMALS, AND THE SURROUNDINGS OF HUMAN FORMS . 73-84

Outlines and Figures Used as Standards of Comparison in Measurements—Can be Used even in Connection with Accurate Imitation
of Nature—Application of the Principle to Landscape—To Forms
of Vegetable and Animal Life—To the Arranging of the Surroundings of the Human Form—In Stained-Glass Windows—
In Clothing—Neglect of this Opportunity—The Mind's Satisfaction in a Partial Application of the Principle — Surrounding
Arrangements in Connection with no Clothing.

VII.
PROPORTIONS OF THE HUMAN FIGURE THEORETICALLY CONSIDERED 85-114

Proportion as Suggested by Imaginary as well as Real Lines
Drawn through the Form—Illustrated in the Case of the Face—
Of other Parts of the Body—The Fact that Æsthetic Judgments
of the Form are Based on Comparative Measurements—The

xiv   CONTENTS.

Standards of Measurements Determined by Observation—Observation of Nature Essential to Successful Art—Especially to Representations of the Human Form — Opportunities for Observing this in Greece—Proof that the Excellence of Greek Sculpture was Influenced by this Opportunity—The Conventionality of the Face on Greek Sculpture no Argument against this—Other Reasons why the Greek Face was Conventional—The Greek Statues not Literal Imitations—But their very Differences Show the Influence of the Study of Nature—Connection between Form and Significance in all the Arts— Especially of those Representing the Human Form—Physiological Basis for this View—An Objection to it—Disguising Concealment of the Form in Civilized Clothing —Disenchanting Exposure of it in Conventional Art—The Mean between these Extremes—Different Proportions as Appealing to Different Tastes, and as Vehicles of Different Vibratory Spiritual Influences.

VIII.

PROPORTIONS OF THE HUMAN FIGURE PRACTICALLY
    CONSIDERED 115-143

Standard of Measurement in Rhythm and Proportion as Fixed by Congruity—Repetition and Alternation—Repetition or Likeness of Measurements—Reason for Satisfaction in Effects of Proportion—Not the Usual Explanation—But not Inconsistent with the Conceptions of the Greeks—Criticism of Statements with Reference to them—Difference between an Apparent and a Real Measurement—Exact Value of the Statements of Vitruvius—How to Find the True Greek Theory—Quotation from Vitruvius—What it Implies—The Ratios to be Considered a Result of Likeness— Measurements of the Head and Face—The Greek Type of Face not the only one Manifesting Effects of Proportion—Nor are the Methods of Subdividing it the Ones usually Adopted—Or Necessary to the Recognition of Beauty—More Minute Like Measurements in the Front Face—In the Side Face—In the Form when Fronting One—Effects of High Civilization on the Wedge-Shape of the Form—The Lower Limbs from the Front—From the Side—Other Related Measurements—Measurements according to Curvilinear Standards—Similar Circumferences Describing Many Different Outlines—Elliptical Figure as Described about the Form as a

CONTENTS. xv

PAGE

Whole—Significance as Represented in the Form of a Man and of a Woman—Principles of Proportion not Creative, but Guides to the Selection of Models—Affording Aid in Determining the Pose —Proportion merely an Application to Measurements of the Art-Methods on Page 3.

IX.

PROPORTION IN ARCHITECTURE 144-161

The Study of Proportion is still more Essential to the Architect than to the Painter or Sculptor—Ways in which a Building may be Given Expression and Character—The Essential Condition of Form is the Grouping of Factors that in Part are Alike— Architectural Likeness by Way of Congruity—Of Repetition, Alternation, Consonance, Interchange, Gradation, etc.—All these Methods may be Applied to Measurements—Ratios of Measurements Recognizable when Expressed in Small Numbers—This Fact as Applied to an Exterior—To Interiors—Relative Measurements Need to be Apparent—Apparent Measurements Differ with Circumstances—Effects Produced by Apparent Subdivisions— Horizontal Subdivisions as Indicated by Outlines—Vertical Subdivisions—Horizontal as Related to Vertical Subdivisions—Influence of Subdivisions as Counteracting Real Dimensions by Apparent Ones.

X.

PROPORTION IN ARCHITECTURE (CONTINUED) . . 162-176

The Mind Takes Satisfaction, not in Ratios, but in the Repetition of Measurement Indicated by them—This Form of Repetition Illustrated—Repetitions of Measurements and Shapes Go together —Illustration of an Absence of both Forms of Repetition—Alternation of Measurements—Consonance as Applied to Shapes—Interchange as Applied to Shapes—A Unique Illustration of it— Consonance and Interchange as Applied to Measurement—An Illustration of them and of Complication—Gradation of Shapes and Measurements—Complement and Balance of Shapes and Measurements—Proportion an Application to Measurements of the Art-Methods Mentioned on Page 3.

xvi CONTENTS.

XI.

PROPORTION IN GREEK ARCHITECTURE . . . 177-199

Greeks Pre-eminent in Architecture—The Secret of their Methods of Proportion Involves more than the Study of Measurements—The Mind is Conscious of Ratios in Proportion—It has Reasons for Using them—The Reasons of the Greeks may have been Different from what we Suppose—To Understand the Reasons we must Judge their Buildings as we do Other Art-Products, by their General Effects—And Draw our Conclusions from Many Specimens—The Authorities Consulted in the Measurements to be Quoted in this Book—The Greek Temple Composed of Different Sets of Factors, each Set Having the Same Measurements—To Show this we are to Start with Factors of Small Dimensions—Same Height in the Abacus and Corona of Horizontal and Raking Cornices, the Ovolo, Cyma Recta, etc.—Measurements of these Parts in Different Temples—Variations and Explanations—Like Proportions of all the Parts just Mentioned to the Height of the Capitals, and of both the Cornices and the Steps—Ratios of 1 : 2 Sustaining this Statement—Of 1 : 3—Of 2 : 3—Like Ratios of the Parts just Mentioned to the Height of the Architrave, Frieze, and Raking Cornice with Cymatium—Also to Upper Diameter of Shafts and Width of Metopes—Explanations—Ratios of 1 : 2—Of 1 : 3—Remarks—Like Ratios of the Parts just Mentioned to the Height of the Entablature, Tympanum, and Width of Upper Inter-Columnation—Confirmation—Insufficiency of Data with Reference to the Tympanum and Pediment—Like Ratios of the Height of Entablature and Pediment Spaces, Differently Divided, to the Height of Column-Space—The Different Methods of Dividing these Gave Opportunity for Originality Exercised in Conformity to Law.

XII.

THE LARGER DIVISIONS OF THE FRONT OF THE DORIC TEMPLE 200-214

The Column-Space and the Method of Principality—Proportion on the Flanks of Height of Columns to the Entablature—Variety of Exact Proportions on the Front might Arise from a Desire to Have Similar Apparent Proportions—Difficulty of Determining the

Line of Separation between the Tympanum, Entablature, and Column-Spaces—Illustrated in the Temple at Ægina—How its Tympanum and Entablature each can be Made to be to Columns as 1 : 3—How Pediment and Entablature, Including Capital, each can be Made to be to Shaft as 1 : 2—How Rectangles of Front in Foundation, Columns, Entablature, Pediment, etc., are all in Proportion—Triangle of both Tympanum and Pediment are in Proportion to Spaces under them—These Arrangements Illustrate the Complexity of Harmony, but are Analogous to those of Rhythm, not Pitch—Illustrated from Temple at Bassæ—Entablature, Pediment, and Columns—Proportions of the Rectangles Formed by the Front Spaces—Temples in which the Abacus is Treated as Part of the Entablature Space—Proportions of the Rectangles of the Front in Propylæa and the Theseum—The Parthenon at the Beginning of a Transition—Departure in it from Former Methods—How these, nevertheless, Conform to the Principles here Unfolded —Other Subordinate and Complementary Proportions—All Tending to Produce General Harmony of Effect.

XIII.

OTHER GREEK ARCHITECTURAL MEASUREMENTS AND GENERAL CONCLUSIONS 215–228

Unusual Size of the Tympanum of the Parthenon—Reasons for this—Proportions of the Rectangles of the Front of the Parthenon —Same Principles Revealed in the Measurements of Other Temples—Exact Squares Formed by the Width and Height of Three Adjacent Columns in Many Temples—Proportion between the Diameters and Heights of Many Columns—Measurements from Twenty-three Doric Temples Verifying the hitherto Unverified Statements in Chapters X. and XI.—Why the Doric Temples are Chosen for Illustrations—After Experiment had Determined the Laws of Proportion, Art Imitated and Degenerated—Because Artists no longer Followed out the Natural and Instinctive Art Tendency Founded upon Comparison — This Tendency Apparent in that which Originated the Gothic and Renaissance Styles— No Great Architecture without it—Possibilities of Architecture not Exhausted but must be Developed from the Principle of Comparison.

XIV.

HARMONY OF OUTLINE : PERSPECTIVE . . . 229-253

Outlines and Colors, the Respective Analogues of Words and Tones—Form-Harmony is less Essential than Significant Representation, yet Important—In Poetry Harmony is Owing to Apparent Like Effects as in Alliteration, etc., and also to Subtle Effects Adapted to Ease of Auditory Action—Analogous Conditions in Arts of Outline : The Perspective and Circumspective—Perspective Relates all Objects to a Centre of the Field of Sight : Lines, Directed toward this Centre, Converge—Appearance of Horizontal Lines—Of Vertical Lines—Both Lines as Represented in Painting and Architecture—Optical Illusions in Triangles—In Horizontal with Crossing Vertical Lines—Exact Explanation of these Illusions not as Important as to Recognize that they Exist—Analogy Drawn from Effects of Color Remote and Near—Failure in our Time to Recognize the Fact as Applied in Architecture—A Building was once Judged by its General Effect as Seen from a Distance—Proof of this Furnished by Discoveries in Egypt and Greece by Pennethorne, Hofer, Schaubert, and Penrose—By Goodyear—His Special and General Contribution to the Subject—Some Measurements of Penrose—To be Interpreted as Related to Perspective, not to Proportion—Differences in Measurement Accord with this Interpretation—Greek Architects Experimented with their Products as Artists do in other Arts.

XV.

HARMONY OF OUTLINE : PERSPECTIVE AS DETERMINING ENTASIS AND IRREGULARITY IN GREEK ARCHITECTURE 254-265

Upward Curves in apparently Horizontal Architectural Lines Ascribed to Effects of Pediment—To the Formation of the Eye—An Explanation of Vitruvius—Ascribed to a Desire to Increase Apparent Size—To a Desire to Represent Relationship to Other Lines—Forward Leaning of apparently Perpendicular Lines—Inward Leaning and Tapering of the Columns—Designed Physically to Meet Requirements of the Eye and Artistically to Suggest Height—The Same is True of the Outward and Inward Curving of the Column's Sides—Laws of Vitruvius with Reference to

Columns—Differences in the Measurements of Different Greek Columns—Difference between the Greek and Roman use of Principles—Columns and Spaces at the Corners of Colonnades—Sizes of Columns as Determined by their Position Exterior and Interior—General Conclusion.

XVI.

HARMONY OF OUTLINE: BINOCULAR VISION . . 266–295

Curvature—The Field of Vision for both Eyes not the Same—The Horopter which both Eyes See—At either Side of the Horopter Something else Seen by but One Eye: Its Influence on the Recognition of Relief in Form—This Fact as Developed in Stereoscopy—Other Illustrations—Perception of Relief at the Sides of an Object through Unconscious though Constant Movement of the Eyes—As a Result of no Movement—Seeing the Sides of an Object Important to Gaining a Conception of its Form—Shape of the Eyes' Field of Sight, for each Eye and for both Eyes—The Horizontal Shape Seen with the Least Effort is Rounded Backward—The Perpendicular Shape is Elliptical—Convergence of Axis, and a Lack of it as Applied to Near and Distant and to Many and Few Details—Practical Experiments Evincing Ease of Perception of all Outlines in an Elliptical Shape—To Perceive Outlines of this Shape, no Conscious Movement of the Eye's Lens is Necessary—Therefore they Realize the Condition Required by Visual Rest, Enjoyment, Beauty—This Fact may Explain the Use of the Ellipse in Art—The Ellipse in General—In Vases, Leaves, Birds, Animals, Fishes—Human Form—Its Like Curves are Accommodated to the Least Expenditure of Visual Effort—The General Method through which, when the Eye's Axis Changes, we can Look from One to Another Line with the Least Visual Effort.

XVII.

ARTISTIC COLORING AS INFLUENCED BY SCIENTIFIC
    METHODS 296–308

Imitative and Decorative Use of Color—The Two Connected —Scientific Study of Color Important—Art can Advance beyond the Discoveries of Science—Yet in every Age is Helped by them

—Artistic Invention as Related to Scientific Investigation of
Effects of Color—Illustrated from History of Greek Painting—
Roman — Christian — Italian — Spanish and Dutch — English—
French—German—Modern—Need of Learning from Experience
and Experiment.

XVIII.

EFFECTS OF COLOR AS DISCOVERED BY SCIENTIFIC
EXPERIMENTS 309-324

Newton's Discovery of the Colors of the Spectrum—They are
Contained only in White Light—The Diversity and Brilliancy of
the Spectrum's Colors Dependent on the Amount and Intensity of
the Light—Brightness and White Making all Colors Pale ; Darkness and Black Making them the Opposite—Names of the Chief
Colors—The Terms: Hues, Full, High, Dark, Light, Pale,
Broken, Shades, Tints, Tone, Local, Positive, Neutral, Warm,
Cold, Primary, Secondary—Colors Transmit and Reflect Rays of
Like Color with themselves—Practical Bearing of this upon the
Kind of Light with which Objects are Illumined, Lamps, Sun, etc.
—Shows why Colors are most Vivid when Illumined by Light of
their own Color—Why White Objects Reflect the Color Illumining them—What are the Actual Colors of Nature—Of Foliage—
Of Water—Of the Atmosphere—Of Objects in External Nature
in Light or Shade, when the Sun is on the Horizon—Especially
at a Distance—When the Sun is in the Zenith—Colors of the Same
Objects in Cloudy Weather ; the Terms Cold and Warm—Effects
of Light and Shade within Doors—Cold and Warm Colors in the
Representation of Distance—These Effects Dependent on the
Degrees of Light—Difference of Opinion with Reference to Certain Deductions Made from Acknowledged Facts of Aërial Perspective—The Apparent Truth with Reference to the Subject.

XIX.

BASIS OF COLOR-HARMONY 325-336

The Tendency in Natural Color for Like to Go with Like in
Analogy with the Same Tendency in Natural Language—Differences of Opinion Regarding the Essential Requirements of Color-Harmony—Some Truth in all these Opinions, but only so far as
Certain Principles are Fulfilled—Those of Unity, Variety, Com-

plexity, Order, Confusion, Counteraction, Grouping—Like with Like in the Colors of Nature, is the Basis for the Same Arrangement by Way of Comparison and Contrast—Colors Called the Contrasting or Complementary Colors not All that really Contrast—The Complementary Colors—What they are as Determined by Dividing the Rays of Light—As formerly Determined by Mixing Pigments—Proof of the Erroneousness of the Latter Method—Von Bezold's Color Chart—As One Complementary Becomes Brighter, the Other Becomes Darker—Wide Differences in the Complementaries of Different Shades of Green.

XX.

PHYSICAL AND PHYSIOLOGICAL CORRESPONDENCES BETWEEN HARMONY IN MUSIC AND PAINTING. 337–351

Study of Color-Effects in the Eye itself—Not as far Advanced as the Study of Sound-Effects in the Ear; Facts Known with Reference to the Effects of Amplitude and Rate of Sound-Waves—Of their Form—Compound Waves—Determining Quality—Partial Tones—Their Influence upon Harmony, Simultaneous and Successive—Correlation of Rhythm and Harmony; the Latter's Physiological Effect—Foster's Explanation—Correspondences between Vibratory Effects in the Ear and in the Eye—Differences between them—Inferences from the Minuteness of Color-Waves—Two Main Questions Involved in the Discussion of Color-Harmony.

XXI.

GENERAL EFFECTS OF COLOR IN PAINTINGS CONSIDERED AS WHOLES 352–369

Artistic Harmony not Imitated from Nature—Field-Theory with Reference to the Method of Securing it—Physiological Objection to it—Psychological—Principality, Subordination: Tone—Harmony, whether Due to Similarity, as in Tone, or to Variety, an Exemplification of Similar Physiological Requirements—Analogy from Music and the Key-Note—Balance and Organic Form—Their Effects both Psychical and Physiological—Congruity as Representing Conceptions and Conditions—Incongruity, Comprehensiveness, Central-Point, Setting, and Parallelism — Symmetry—

xxii CONTENTS.

PAGE

Repetition—Alteration, Alternation—Massing, Breadth, or Chiaroscuro—Its Relation to Principality and Balance—And Other Methods—Interspersion, Complication, and Continuity.

XXII.

SPECIAL EFFECTS OF COLORS WHEN PLACED SIDE BY
SIDE. 370-388

Consonance—Importance of this Subject—Colors Placed Side by Side Produce Subjective Effects in the Eye—Successive Contrast or After-Image of Complementary Colors Following Colors suddenly Obscured—A Similar Phenomenon among Sounds—Explanation of Differences between the Phenomena—Ordinary Explanation of the After-Images—Simultaneous Contrasts as in Shadows—Suggested Insufficiency of Reasons ordinarily Given for Successive and Simultaneous Contrast—Suggestions with Reference to the Perception of Color—Nothing in the Organism to Throw Doubt upon these Suggestions—The Principle Involved Explains the Main Difference between Successive and Simultaneous Contrast—Colors Impart about them Tints of their Complementaries—These Effects on Light and Shade or on Light and Dark Neutral Surfaces as Produced by Warm and Cold Colors—By Different Tints and Shades—Same Effects as Produced on Colored Surfaces—Three Ways of Using Contrast to Relieve Objects from their Background.

XXIII.

COLOR-SCALES 389-405

Object of this Chapter—Colors can be Used together that Differ either Slightly or Greatly—Theory that Two, Three, or More can be Used together if they Make White—Theory Based on Construction of Color-Scales: Von Bezold's of Twelve Colors—Rood's Summary of Combinations of Colors Founded on Experience—Combinations Determined as in Musical Harmony by Ratios between the Numbers of Vibrations a Second Causing the Colors—All the Colors can Represent only the Ratios Possible to a Single Scale—Compensating Possibility of Variety in each Color—Correspondences Need to be Found only between the Ratios Underlying the Harmonic Notes and the Harmonic Colors—The Ratio

CONTENTS. xxiii

PAGE

Expressive of the Two Chief Harmonics of Music aside from that of the Octave, which has no Analogue in Color—The Same Ratio as Applied to Color—The Tonic and Dominant Harmonize all the Notes of the Scale as the Two Complementaries Contain all the Colors of the Spectrum—The Tonic and Dominant Represent the Same Ratios as the Complementaries – Reasons for Apparent Exceptions—Ratios Expressive of the Three Harmonics in the Major Triad of Music—Same Ratios Applied to Triads of Colors —Recapitulation—A Fourth Color would Naturally Correspond to the Seventh in Music, a Result Approximating that Reached by Von Bezold—The Reason why Notes and Colors thus Related Satisfy the Senses—Similarity of Method in Determining Consonance either in Sound or Color.

XXIV.

ADDITIONAL ART-METHODS CAUSING COLOR-HARMONY 406–412

Dissonance and Interchange—Criticism by Sir Joshua Reynolds—Gradation—Suggested by Nature—Physiological Explanation of—Abruptness—Transition and Progress.

XXV.

THE FOREGOING PRINCIPLES AS APPLIED TO DECORATIVE PAINTING . . . 413–418

Differences between the Use of Color in Pictorial and Decorative Art—Differences between Classes of Forms to which Colors are Applied and Classes of Like Colors that are Applied to Like Forms—Monochromatic and Polychromatic Decoration—Color on the Exteriors of Buildings—Possibility of New Styles of Architecture in our Age—Modern Development of Mineral Resources and Facilities of Transportation and their Influence on the Shapes of Buildings—But Especially on their Sizes and their Colors as Produced both by Pigments and by the Materials Used—Errors to be Avoided in Attempting Originality, but Possibility of Success.

XXVI.

RECAPITULATION OF RESULTS REACHED IN THESE
VOLUMES ON COMPARATIVE ÆSTHETICS . 419-439

Introductory Statement—Examination of Facts and Opinions in
"Art in Theory"—Method Adopted in Volumes Following it—
In "The Representative Significance of Form"—Art Developed
from Natural Forms of Expression—The Methods of their Development—Elements of Representation in Arts of Sound, as
Analyzed in "Poetry as a Representative Art" and in "Music as
a Representative Art"—As Combined, according to the Same
Essays, in Poems and Musical Compositions Considered as Wholes
—Elements of Representation, as Analyzed in "Painting, Sculpture, and Architecture as Representative Arts"—As Combined,
according to the Same Volume, in Paintings, Statues, and Buildings Considered as Wholes—Form in General as Treated in "The
Genesis of Art-Form"—Form in Particular as Treated in
"Rhythm and Harmony in Poetry and Music," and in "Proportion and Harmony of Line and Color in Painting, Sculpture,
and Architecture"—This Series of Volumes Traces All Art-
Developments, whether of Significance or Form, to a Single Principle—This Done with a Practical as well as Philosophic Aim—
The Acknowledgment of No Standards Leads either to Imitation
or Eccentricity in Production and in Critical Judgment—The
Possibility of Finding Standards—These Need not Interfere with
Originality—Necessity for the Study and Knowledge of Standards
in our own Age and Country—Unavoidable Limitations in a
Philosophic and Technical Treatment of the Kind Attempted in
these Volumes.

INDEX 441-459

ILLUSTRATIONS.

	PAGE
1. THE VITRUVIAN SCROLL	12

From photograph of an engraving. Mentioned on pages 12, 40.

2. THE GREEK FRET 12

From photograph of an engraving. Mentioned on pages 12, 40.

3. TRIGLYPHS AND METOPES, FROM A GREEK TEMPLE . . 12

From photograph of an engraving. Mentioned on pages 12, 40, 168.

4. ILLUSTRATION OF THE FORMATION OF AN IMAGE ON THE RETINA, 22

From Le Conte's "Sight." Mentioned on pages 22, 23, 234.

5. THE CAVITY OF THE EYE 22

From the same. Mentioned on pages 21, 22.

6. A MAORI FESTIVAL, NEW ZEALAND 33

From Cassell's "Isles of the Pacific." Mentioned on pages 40, 162, 174.

7. KAFFIR STATION, AFRICA 34

From Cassell's "Races of Mankind." Mentioned on pages 40, 162.

8. TYPE OF AN ASSYRIAN SQUARE 35

From Cassell's *Magazine of Art*. Mentioned on pages 40, 43, 44, 162.

9. MEDIÆVAL CASTLE 36

From Cassell's "Land of Temples." Mentioned on pages 40, 145, 162.

10. TEMPLE OF THESEUS, ATHENS 36

From Lübke's "History of Art." Mentioned on pages 40, 44, 116, 156, 163, 164, 168, 170, 175, 188, 189, 193, 196, 201, 210, 211, 218, 219, 220, 221, 224, 252.

11. ST. STEPHEN'S CAEN, NORMANDY 37

From Fergusson's "History of Architecture." Mentioned on pages 42, 44, 154, 163, 166, 170, 175, 226.

12. CANTERBURY CATHEDRAL, FROM SOUTHWEST 38

From a photograph. Mentioned on pages 42, 163, 175, 226.

13. CENTRAL CONGREGATIONAL CHURCH, BOSTON, MASS. . . 39

From Cassell's "The World, its Cities and its People." Mentioned on page 42.

ILLUSTRATIONS.

		PAGE
14. WILLESDEN CHURCH, NEAR LONDON, ENGLAND		40

From Cassell's "Greater London." Mentioned on pages 42, 154.

15. CHICHESTER CATHEDRAL, ENGLAND 41
    From Cassell's "Our Own Country." Mentioned on pages 42, 43, 158, 163, 165.
16. LINES IN PROPORTION 42
    From a drawing. Mentioned on pages 42, 43.
17. LINES SUBDIVIDED TO INDICATE PROPORTION 43
    From the same. Mentioned on page 43.
18. FIGURES WITH LINES SUBDIVIDED TO INDICATE PROPORTION . 44
    From the same. Mentioned on pages 44, 263.
19. RECTANGLES IN PROPORTION 45
    From the same. Mentioned on page 45.
20. HAY'S METHOD OF DETERMINING PROPORTIONAL RELATIONS
    OF RECTANGLES 45
    From D. R. Hay's "Science of Beauty and Laws of Geometric Proportion." Mentioned on page 46.
21. HAY'S RECTANGLES CORRESPONDING TO THE MUSICAL SCALE . 46
    From the same. Mentioned on page 47.
22. FIGURES RELATED BECAUSE INSCRIBABLE IN THE SAME SQUARE, 49
    From drawings. Mentioned on page 49.
23. FIGURES RELATED BECAUSE INSCRIBABLE IN THE SAME RECTANGLE 49
    From the same. Mentioned on page 49.
24. FIGURES RELATED BECAUSE INSCRIBABLE IN THE SAME OR A
    RELATED FIGURE 49
    From the same. Mentioned on pages 49, 50.
25. FIGURES RELATED BECAUSE INSCRIBABLE IN FIGURES IN PROPORTION 50
    From the same. Mentioned on pages 50, 51.
26. RELATIONSHIP OF FIGURES, AS INDICATED AND AS NOT INDICATED 50
    From the same. Mentioned on page 50.
27. CHÂTEAU DE RANDAU, VICHY, FRANCE 51
    From a photograph. Mentioned on pages 51, 149, 164, 166.
28. CHENONCEAU CHÂTEAU, FRANCE 53
    From Lübke's "History of Art." Mentioned on pages 52, 166.
29. WALKER MUSEUM, CHICAGO UNIVERSITY 54
    From the *Cosmopolitan Magazine*. Mentioned on page 52.

ILLUSTRATIONS. xxvii

	PAGE
30. CHOIR OF ELY CATHEDRAL, ENGLAND	55

From Fergusson's " History of Architecture." Mentioned on pages 52, 56, 57, 163, 166.

31. LINES AND CURVES INDICATING PROPORTIONS OF A HUMAN FORM. FRONT VIEW 57

Drawn about an illustration in Putnam's "Art Hand-Book of Figure Drawing." Mentioned on pages 15, 58, 59, 69, 72, 85, 87, 118, 120, 130, 131, 135, 137, 138, 290, 291, 295.

32. BACK VIEW OF THE SAME 58

Drawn about the same. Mentioned on pages 15, 58, 59, 69, 85, 87, 118, 120, 130, 131, 135, 137, 290, 295.

33. CURVE EXEMPLIFYING GRADATION 60

From Ruskin's " Modern Painters." Mentioned on pages 59, 69, 294.

34. CURVE EXEMPLIFYING GRADATION 61

From the same. Mentioned on pages 59, 69, 294.

35. CIRCLES DRAWN ABOUT A MAN'S FORM. SIDE VIEW . . 70

Added to an illustration in Putnam's " Art Hand-Book of Figure Drawing." Mentioned on pages 15, 59, 69, 87, 134, 135, 141, 290, 294, 295.

36. CIRCLES DRAWN ABOUT FORM OF D. R. HAY'S IDEAL MAN . 71

Added to illustration in Hay's "Geometric Beauty of the Human Figure." Mentioned on pages 15, 59, 69, 72, 87, 133, 134, 135, 295.

37. CIRCLES DRAWN ABOUT FORM OF HAY'S IDEAL WOMAN . 72

Added to an illustration in the same. Mentioned on pages 59, 69, 72, 87, 134, 295.

38. THE CANAL, COROT 75

From a photograph. Mentioned on pages 74–77, 363, 365, 369.

39. RADIATION IN NATURAL FORMS 78

From Ruskin's " Elements of Drawing." Mentioned on pages 78, 288.

40. STAINED GLASS OF THE FOURTEENTH CENTURY . . . 79

From Cassell's *Magazine of Art*. Mentioned on page 79.

41. COSTUMES DIVIDING THE HUMAN FORM PROPORTIONATELY . 80

From a drawing by C. C. Rosenkranz. Mentioned on pages 81, 82.

42. COSTUMES NOT DIVIDING THE HUMAN FORM PROPORTIONATELY, 81

From the same. Mentioned on pages 81, 82.

43. A NEW GUINEA CHIEF 82

From Cassell's " Picturesque Australia." Mentioned on pages 83, 130, 131, 132, 133, 141.

44. THE APOLLO BELVEDERE 84

From Lübke's " History of Art." Mentioned on pages 83, 84, 98, 99, 102, 131, 132, 141.

ILLUSTRATIONS.

		PAGE
45.	FRONT FACE DIVIDED PROPORTIONATELY BY LINES	86

Drawn over an illustration from Putnam's "Art Hand-Book." Mentioned on pages 15, 59, 86, 87, 105, 120, 125, 126, 128, 129, 134, 141, 295.

46. EAR AND EYE PROPORTIONATELY DIVIDED BY STRAIGHT LINES,   86
From the same. Mentioned on pages 87, 141.

47. VENUS DE' MEDICI, STATUE OF 92
From Mitchell's "History of Sculpture." Mentioned on pages 92, 97, 99, 102, 141.

48. FARNESE HERCULES, STATUE OF 94
From the same. Mentioned on page 97.

49. DIADUMENOS, BY POLYCLEITUS, STATUE OF 95
From Cassell's "Greek Archæology." Mentioned on pages 97, 132, 141.

50. DISCOBOLUS OR QUOIT THROWER, BY MYRON, STATUE OF . 96
From Turner's "Short History of Art." Mentioned on pages 97, 141.

51. PALLAS OF VELLETRI, FROM THE LOUVRE, PARIS . . . 97
From Viardot's "Wonders of Sculpture." Mentioned on page 97.

52. THESEUS OF THE PARTHENON, STATUE OF 98
From Abbott's "Pericles." Mentioned on pages 97, 141.

53. FAUN, BY PRAXITELES, STATUE OF 99
From Lübke's "History of Art." Mentioned on pages 97, 99, 141.

54. HERMES, BY PRAXITELES, STATUE OF 100
From Cassell's "Gods of Olympus." Mentioned on pages 97, 99, 102, 132, 141.

55. GROUP OF NIOBE, SCULPTURE 101
From Müller's "Denkmaler der Alten Kunst." Mentioned on pages 59, 98.

56. MELEAGROS, STATUE IN THE VATICAN 102
From Cassell's "Gods of Olympus." Mentioned on pages 99, 141.

57. GANYMEDE, AFTER LEOCHARES, STATUE OF 103
From the same. Mentioned on pages 99, 132, 141.

58. APOLLO SAUROCTONOS, BY PRAXITELES, STATUE OF . . 104
From Cassell's "Gods of Olympus." Mentioned on pages 99, 141.

59. VENUS ASCRIBED TO STYLE OF PRAXITELES, STATUE OF . 105
From Cassell's *Magazine of Art,* Mentioned on pages 99, 102, 141.

60. MEPHISTOPHELES AS DEPICTED IN ART . . . . . 106.
From Well's "New Physiognomy." Mentioned on page 106.

61. CONTEMPT AND ANGER AS DEPICTED IN THE COUNTENANCE . 106
From the same. Mentioned on page 106.

62. WHOLE HUMAN FORM AS RELATED TO THE CIRCLE . . 121
From Cassell's *Magazine of Art.* Mentioned on pages 15, 59, 121, 130, 132, 133, 141.

ILLUSTRATIONS. xxix

		PAGE
63.	WHOLE HUMAN FORM AS RELATED TO THE SQUARE	122

From the same. Mentioned on pages 15, 59, 122, 130, 131, 141.

64. FACE PROPORTIONATELY DIVIDED BY STRAIGHT LINES . . 126

Drawn over a photograph in the *Dramatic Mirror*. Mentioned on pages 116, 126, 127, 128, 130.

65. FACE PROPORTIONATELY DIVIDED BY STRAIGHT LINES . . 126

From the same. Mentioned on pages 116, 126, 127, 128.

66. FACE PROPORTIONATELY DIVIDED BY STRAIGHT LINES . . 127

From the same. Mentioned on pages 116, 126, 127, 128.

67. FACE PROPORTIONATELY DIVIDED BY STRAIGHT LINES . . 127

From the same. Mentioned on pages 116, 126, 127, 128.

68. FACE PROPORTIONATELY DIVIDED BY STRAIGHT LINES . . 127

From the same. Mentioned on pages 116, 126, 127, 128, 130.

69. SIDE FACE DIVIDED BY LINES 128

Drawn over illustration in Putnam's "Art Hand-Book of Figure Drawing." Mentioned on pages 15, 59, 126, 128, 129, 130, 135.

70. LEG AND FOOT 133

From Duval's "Artistic Anatomy." Mentioned on pages 132, 133.

71. CLOTHING PROPORTIONAL IN PARTS 134

From a drawing by C. C. Rosenkranz. Mentioned on pages 82, 130, 133.

72. WOMAN'S FORM ENCLOSED BETWEEN CIRCLES . . . 136

From a drawing. Mentioned on pages 59, 138, 270, 291, 295.

73. MAN'S FORM ENCLOSED BETWEEN CIRCLES 137

Drawn about D. R. Hay's ideal man in "Geometric Beauty of the Human Figure." Mentioned on pages 15, 59, 72, 87, 135, 137, 138, 290, 291, 295.

74. WOMAN'S FORM ENCLOSED IN LIKE CIRCLES 139

Drawn about a model-figure in the same, prepared for D. R. Hay. Mentioned on pages 15, 59, 72, 87, 135, 138, 290, 295.

75. FIGURE FROM NAUSICA, BY E. J. POYNTER 142

From Cassell's "History of Art." Mentioned on pages 59, 133, 141, 369.

76. UNIVERSITY AT SYDNEY, AUSTRALIA 147

From Cassell's "Picturesque Australia." Mentioned on pages 146, 158, 163, 165, 175, 226.

77. PAVILION OF RICHELIEU, LOUVRE, PARIS 150

From Cassell's "The World, its Cities and Peoples." Mentioned on pages 42, 44, 149, 152, 154, 158, 160, 162, 163, 175.

78. ARCH OF SEPTIMIUS SEVERUS 152

From Fergusson's "History of Architecture." Mentioned on pages 152, 163, 175.

xxx ILLUSTRATIONS.

	PAGE
79. ARCH OF AUGUSTUS AT AOSTA	153

From a drawing. Mentioned on pages 152, 163.

80. TEMPLE OF THEMIS, AT RHAMNUS 153
From a drawing. Mentioned on pages 152, 154, 163, 164, 168, 175.

81. COLOGNE CATHEDRAL, FAÇADE 155
From a photograph. Mentioned on pages 42, 44, 153, 154, 156, 157, 160, 163, 165, 175, 226, 236, 237.

82. ST. SULPICE, PARIS 156
From Fergusson's "History of Modern Architecture." Mentioned on pages 42, 43, 44, 154, 158, 160, 161, 166, 175.

83. ST. SULPICE MODIFIED 157
Mentioned on page 161.

84. ST. SULPICE MODIFIED 159
Mentioned on page 161.

85. AN AMERICAN CHURCH 163
From Fergusson's "History of Modern Architecture." Mentioned on pages 164, 166.

86. OPERA HOUSE, PARIS 167
From the same. Mentioned on pages 15, 166, 167, 170, 175, 226.

87. SAINT ÉTIENNE DU MONT, PARIS 169
From Cassell's "Paris." Mentioned on pages 167, 168.

88. GERMAN SPIRE AT KUTTENBERG 171
From Fergusson's "History of Modern Architecture." Mentioned on page 172.

89. STEEPLE OF BOW CHURCH, LONDON 171
From the same. Mentioned on page 172.

90. STREET AND BELFRY AT GHENT 172
From Cassell's "The World, its Cities and Peoples." Mentioned on page 172.

91. TOWER OF BORIS, KREMLIN, MOSCOW 173
From a drawing. Mentioned on pages 172, 173.

92. DOME OF CHIAVAVALLE IN ITALY 174
From a drawing. Mentioned on page 173.

93. COLUMN AND ENTABLATURE OF THE TEMPLE AT ÆGINA . 182
From a drawing. Mentioned on pages 183, 185, 187, 188, 191, 192, 203, 219.

94. GREEK DORIC TEMPLE OF ÆGINA, FAÇADE 183
From Fergusson's "History of Architecture." Mentioned on pages 42, 170, 183, 185, 186, 187, 188, 189, 191, 192, 196, 197, 204, 207, 224.

95. ACROPOLIS, ATHENS, RESTORATION OF WEST END OF . . 186
From White's "Plutarch." Mentioned on pages 186, 190, 210, 211, 216, 219, 252, 259.

ILLUSTRATIONS. xxxi

	PAGE
96. PARTHENON AT ATHENS, THE	190

From Fergusson's "History of Architecture." Mentioned on pages 15, 186, 190, 201, 211. *See* index.

97. IONIC PILLAR AND ENTABLATURE 204

From Cassell's "Manual of Greek Archæology." Mentioned on pages 203, 219, 220.

98. CORINTHIAN CAPITAL OF PILLAR 220

From the same. Mentioned on pages 203, 220.

99. PANTHEON AT ROME, THE 223

From Cassell's "The World, its Cities and its Peoples." Mentioned on page 224.

100. ST. PAUL'S, COVENT GARDEN, LONDON 225

From Fergusson's "History of Modern Architecture." Mentioned on page 224.

101. ST. SOPHIA, CONSTANTINOPLE 226

From Lane-Poole's "Turkey." Mentioned on page 226.

102. EFFECT OF DISTANCE ON MAGNITUDE, LIGHT, CONTRAST, AND DETAIL 235

From J. W. Stimson's "Principles and Methods in Art Education." Mentioned on pages 13, 47, 234, 237, 241, 329, 369, 412.

103. GREEK TEMPLE INSCRIBED IN CIRCLES REPRESENTING HORIZON LINES 236

From a drawing. Mentioned on pages 234, 237, 239, 251, 255, 257, 258.

104. OPTICAL ILLUSIONS CAUSED BY LINES ARRANGED AS IN PEDIMENTS 240

From the *Architectural Record.* Reproduced from Thiersch's "Optische Täuschungen auf dem Gebiete der Architectur." Mentioned on pages 240, 241, 242, 250, 254, 256.

105. OPTICAL ILLUSIONS WITH TWO PARALLEL HORIZONTAL LINES, 241

From the same. Mentioned on page 241.

106. OPTICAL ILLUSIONS WITH THREE PARALLEL HORIZONTAL LINES 242

From the same. Mentioned on pages 242, 243.

107. MAISON CARRÉE, SHOWING CORNICE CURVE 245

From the same, drawn by J. W. McKechnie. Mentioned on pages 246, 249, 250, 251, 252, 255, 258.

108. PHOTOGRAPHIC EFFECT OF THE SAME CORNICE . . . 247

From the same, drawn by the same. Mentioned on pages 239, 246, 249, 250, 251, 255, 258.

xxxii   *ILLUSTRATIONS.*

109. PHOTOGRAPHIC EFFECT OF CURVED STYLOBATE AND COLUMN OF PARTHENON 251
From the same. Mentioned on pages 250, 255, 258, 260.

110. FINGERS, ONE BEHIND THE OTHER, AS SEEN WITH EACH EYE 269
From Le Conte's "Sight." Mentioned on page 269.

111. THE SAME FINGERS AS SEEN WITH BOTH EYES . . . 269
From the same. Mentioned on pages 269, 278, 279, 280.

112. SAME OBJECT AS SEEN DIFFERENTLY BY EACH EYE . . . 272
From Le Conte's "Sight." Mentioned on pages 271, 272, 274, 280.

113. PARTS OF OBJECTS AS SEEN WITH NEAR AND DISTANT BACK-GROUNDS 272
From the same. Mentioned on pages 234, 268, 273, 280.

114. LENS OF EYE ADJUSTED TO NEAR AND DISTANT OBJECTS . 273
From the same. Mentioned on pages 231, 273, 323.

115. FIELD OF VIEW OF BOTH EYES 278
From Foster's "Text Book of Anatomy." Mentioned on pages 276, 277, 278, 279.

116. FIELD OF DISTINCT VISION FOR BOTH EYES TOGETHER . 278
From a drawing. Mentioned on pages 277, 280, 288.

117. EGYPTIAN VASE AND DOLL 283
From Wilkinson's "Ancient Egyptians." Mentioned on pages 284, 295.

118. PRIZE VASES FOR ATHENIAN GAMES 283
From Lübke's "History of Art." Mentioned on pages 284, 295.

119. BUILDING ENCLOSED BY CIRCLES 284
From a drawing. Mentioned on page 284.

120. VASES, OUTLINES BY ELLIPSES AND SEGMENTS OF CIRCLES . 285
Drawn about forms suggested in Hay's "Ornamental Geometric Designs," etc. Mentioned on pages 68, 286, 287, 295.

121. CURVED LINES AS OUTLINED BY ELLIPSES 287
From a drawing. Mentioned on page 287.

122. BEASTS, FISHES, AND BIRDS AS OUTLINED BY ELLIPSES . 289
From D. R. Hay's reproduction from Jardine's "Naturalist's Library." Mentioned on pages 78, 288, 295.

123. OUTLINES OF CURVES AS DETERMINED BY CHANGES IN BACK-GROUNDS 293
From a drawing. Mentioned on pages 292, 293, 294, 295.

ILLUSTRATIONS.   xxxiii

		PAGE
124.	BREAKING UP A RAY OF WHITE LIGHT	310
	From Cassell's "Science for All." Mentioned on page 310.	
125.	FORMATION OF COMPLEMENTARY COLORS	330
	From Von Bezold's "Theory of Color." Mentioned on page 331.	
126.	FORMATION OF COMPLEMENTARY COLORS	331
	From the same. Mentioned on page 331.	
127.	COLOR CHART	334
	From the same. Mentioned on pages 333–336, 390–393, 398, 403, 414.	
128.	CONES AND RODS IN DIFFERENT PARTS OF THE RETINA	350
	From Le Conte's "Sight." Mentioned on pages 349, 350, 381.	
129.	THE DESCENT FROM THE CROSS: RUBENS	359
	From a photograph. Mentioned on pages 59, 303, 358, 363, 365, 367, 369.	
130.	SECTION OF RETINA	380
	From Le Conte's "Sight." Mentioned on pages 349, 380, 383.	
131.	GENERALIZED SECTION OF RETINA SHOWING INNER AND OUTER RODS AND CONES	381
	From Foster's "Text-Book of Anatomy." Mentioned on pages 349, 381, 383.	

The author wishes to express his sense of obligation to the various artists, publishers, and authors to whom he is indebted for kind permission to insert in this book such illustrations as are owned by them, or are protected by their copyrights, especially to *The Architectural Record*, and to Messrs. D. Appleton & Co., Dodd, Mead & Co., Charles Scribner's Sons, Fowler & Wells, and the F. A. Stokes Co. of New York, Cassell & Co. and John Murray of London, and Ebner & Seubert of Stuttgart.

PROPORTION AND HARMONY OF LINE AND COLOR IN PAINTING, SCULPTURE, AND ARCHITECTURE.

CHAPTER I.

CORRESPONDENCES BETWEEN THE ELEMENTS OF FORM IN THE ARTS OF SOUND AND OF SIGHT.

Object of the Present Volume—Connection between the Subjects Treated in it and the Requirements of Beauty—Similarity of these Requirements in the Arts of Sound and of Sight—Chart of the Methods of Art-Composition—Sounds are Perceived in Time, Sights in Space—Sounds are Separated by Silences or Pauses, Sights by Lines or Outlines—Sounds may Differ in Duration, Force, Quality, and Pitch; Sights in Extension, Light and Shade, and in Quality and Pitch of Color—Respective Correspondences between Effects in Sound and in Sight—Combined Influences of these Effects as Manifested in Rhythm and also in Proportion, as well as in Harmony, whether of Sound or of Sight.

THE mental and material origin of the methods of art-composition, the manner and order of their development, and the correspondences between their effects as manifested in the very different elements entering into form in the different arts, were unfolded in the volume of this series of essays entitled " The Genesis of Art-Form." A summary of the results attained in that volume is printed on page 3 of this one; and from time to time references will be made to them, sufficiently explicit, it is hoped, not only to recall to those who have read the previous discussion, but to interpret to those who have not, the connection between the line of thought pursued then, and to be pursued now. This connection is that between the more generic and the more specific. We need to know not merely how, in all the different arts, the methods of composition correspond, but also how, in each art and each product of it, the different methods operate conjointly.

This latter is a subject which, at first thought, the reader may be inclined to underrate, supposing it to be subordinate, in some way, to certain other æsthetic considerations. But in Chapter XIV. of the opening volume of this series, "Art in Theory," it was shown that the methods to be discussed here can never be wisely slighted, because material to effects not merely of art-composition but also of all beauty, whether perceived in art or in nature. Accordingly this book, in the degree in which it attains its end, will reveal not only the requirements of proportion and harmony in line and color, but also, at the same time, as a consequence of its general subject, the requirements of any visible art-form when so composed as to produce an effect of beauty.

The volume entitled "Rhythm and Harmony in Poetry and Music" was written to apply the principles to be unfolded in this book to audible products; and, as one object of these essays has been to indicate the correspondences between the arts, the first chapter of that work was devoted to indicating how the factors entering into rhythm may be correlated to those entering into proportion; as well as how the factors entering into harmony of tone may be correlated to those entering into harmony of line or color. For the benefit of readers who

METHODS OF ART-COMPOSITION.

	Mainly Conditioned upon the Requirements of the Mind.		
Mainly conditioned upon	*Mind.*	*Matter.*	*Mind and Matter.*	*Mind and Matter.*
Mind.	UNITY.	VARIETY.	COMPLEXITY.	GROUPING.
Matter.	Order,	Confusion.	Counteraction.	

Mainly Conditioned upon the Requirements of Matter.

Mind.	COMPARISON.	CONTRAST.	COMPLEMENT.	ORGANIC FORM.
Matter.	Principality.	Subordination.	Balance.	

Mainly Conditioned upon the Requirements of the Product.

Mind.	CONGRUITY.	INCONGRUITY.	COMPREHENSIVENESS.	SYMMETRY.
"	Central Point.	Setting.	Parallelism.	
Matter.	REPETITION.	ALTERATION.	ALTERNATION.	CONTINUITY.
"	Massing.	Interspersion.	Complication.	
Mind and Matter.	CONSONANCE.	DISSONANCE.	INTERCHANGE.	PROGRESS.
	Gradation.	Abruptness.	Transition.	

Right-side bracketed groupings:

{ ORGANIC FORM } → DURATION IN TIME. / EXTENSION IN SPACE. } RHYTHM AND PROPORTION.

{ SYMMETRY / CONTINUITY } → ACCENT IN STRESS AND LINE.

{ PROGRESS } → QUALITY AND PITCH IN NOTE AND COLOR. } HARMONY IN NOTE AND COLOR.

have not had access to that volume, a brief recapitulation of what was said there will not be out of place here.

The first fact that was noticed there was that poetry and music are composed of elements of sound appealing to the ear in the order of time, and that painting, sculpture, and architecture are composed of elements of sight appealing to the eye in the order of space.

A second fact noticed was that, as a condition for constructing a form whether appealing to the ear or eye, one must be able to apprehend and use more than one sound or one object of sight. A sound single in the sense of manifesting neither alteration nor cessation, would soon come to convey no more intelligence to the ear than absence of sound; and a single hue of the same shade from nadir to zenith would soon convey no more intelligence to the eye than absence of hue. In order to be understood and used by a man who cannot conceive of time or space except as it is divided into parts, that which is heard must be interrupted by periods of silence and that which is seen must be separated from other things by outlines. This is the same as to say—and here we may refer to the chart on page 3—that what we hear must have a certain limit of *duration* indicated by pauses in the sound; and that what we see must have a certain limit of *extension* indicated by lines. How shall the artist determine what these limits shall be? Fortunately, in the more important regards, nature herself has determined them. As for poetry and music, they are both developed primarily from methods of using the human voice,—in the one case in speech, in the other in song; and, secondarily, from methods in which sounds external to man are produced. But whenever the human voice is used, pauses are used, both at comparatively short intervals, after separate words and notes, and also at longer intervals where it is necessary for the lungs to draw in air; and whenever sounds that are not produced by the human voice are heard, they too are separated by intervals of silence. Painting, sculpture, and architecture, again, are developed from the methods in which men use or perceive objects in the external world. All of these reveal outlines not only separating them from other objects, but generally also separating their own constituent parts from one another. What more natural than that the artist should accept such arrangements of everything heard or seen in nature, and should let them determine, according to methods of imitation, the relative duration or extension that shall be manifested in his works? As a fact, we know that this is exactly what he does do.

Duration and *extension*, however, are not the only conditions that the artist must consider. As shown in " Poetry as a Representative Art," Chapter III., sounds may differ not merely in duration or the quantity of time that they fill; but in force, or the stress with which they are produced, making them loud or soft, abrupt or smooth, etc.; also in quality, making them sharp or round, full or thin, aspirate or pure, etc.; and in pitch, making them high or low, or rising or falling in the musical scale. Sights, too, may differ in analogous ways; *i. e.*, not merely in extension or the quantity of space that they fill, which is the same thing as size; but in contour, which is the same thing as shape, and is shown by the appearance of forcible or weak lines of light and shade; also in quality of color, which has to do with their tints and shades and mixtures; and in pitch of color, which is determined by the hue.

In addition to merely stating these facts, it may be

well to enlarge upon one or two of them. Notice, for instance, how true it is that *force* which gives emphasis to sounds, rendering them more distinct from one another than would be the case without it, corresponds to *light and shade*, which emphasize and render more distinct the contour through which one portion of space having a certain shape is clearly separated from another. Notice, also, that accented and unaccented syllables or notes, as they alternate in time, perform exactly analogous functions to those of light and shade, as they alternate in space. The impression of form, for instance, which, so far as it results from metre, is conveyed by varying force and lack of force in connection with divisions made in time, is the exact equivalent of that impression of form which, so far as this results from shape, is conveyed by varying light and shade in connection with divisions made in space. Notice, again, that *quality* and *pitch* are terms almost as much used in painting as in music, quality in colors depending, in a way analogous to quality in sounds, on the mixture of hues entering into the general effect; and pitch in colors depending on the subdivision of light to which each color is due. Undoubtedly, too, it is owing partly to a subtle recognition of the correspondences just indicated that to certain effects in the arts both of sound and of sight the more general terms, *tone* and *color*, have come to be applied interchangeably.

Later on, in connection with the various divisions and subdivisions under which will be treated the different phases of form to be considered, it will be shown in what way each phase is influenced by the different methods which, on page 3, are represented as instrumental in its development. Here it is sufficient to say that *duration*, limited by pauses in connection with force, as applied to the accents of syllables or notes, gives rise to *rhythm;* that *extension,* limited by outlines in connection with light and shade, as applied to contour or shape, gives rise to *proportion;* that *quality* and *pitch* of tone taken together furnish the possibility of developing the laws of the *harmony of sound;* and that *quality* and *pitch* of color furnish the same possibility with reference to the laws of the *harmony of color.* It is important to notice, too, that *force* or *accent,* while having to do mainly with rhythm, has a certain influence also upon tone—in poetry upon the tunes of verse, and in music upon the melodic suggestions of different degrees of animation ; also that, in the same way, *light and shade,* while having to do mainly with outline and proportion, have a certain influence also upon color. They change it in order to interpret the meaning which a colored surface is intended to convey, as, for instance, whether it is to represent what is flat or round. They suggest, too, the vitality characterizing nature. Correspondingly, also, it is important to notice that quality and pitch of sound are often necessary for the full effects of force as applied to *rhythm;* and that the same elements of color are often necessary for the full effects of light and shade as applied to *proportion.* In fact, when used in the same art, the different special effects that enter into the general effects of proportion and harmony which are now to be considered are none of them produced exclusively according to one method or to one combination of methods, but more or less according to all of them when operating conjointly.

CHAPTER II.

MEANING OF PROPORTION AND THE RECOGNITION OF IT IN ART AND NATURE.

Proportion as Meaning Measurement, and a Comparison of Measurements, either Absolute or Relative—As Indicating Relationships or Ratios of Measurement, or Likeness or Equality of these—Tendency of the Mind to Make Relative Measurements of Spaces Illustrated—Historical Evidences of the Existence of this Tendency—Primitive Ornamentation—Later Ornamentation—Additional Examples—The Same Tendency as Manifested in Reproductions of Objects Imitated—Proportion as Manifested in Nature as a Whole and in its Parts—The Subject Important and Complex—Its Analogy to Rhythm—Ratios Used in Poetry and Music—In the Longer Rhythmic Divisions of Both Arts—Rhythmic Ratios are Represented by Small Numbers, and thus Rendered easily Recognizable—Same Principle Applicable to Proportion—Proportion may be Recognized without a Recognition of the Exact Ratio Causing it—The Use by the Greeks of Ratios Represented by Small Numbers.

THE term proportion, when used in a non-technical sense, signifies frequently little more than measurement. When we say that a house has the proportions of a palace, or a growing boy the proportions of a man, we mean merely that the one is as large as the other, or has the same general measurements. In addition to this, however, there is often connected with the term, when carefully used, a conception of a comparison of measurements. When we say of a man that his feet are out of proportion, or of a copy of a Greek temple, that its pediment is out of proportion, we are probably recalling a normally developed man or an ancient Greek temple. If so, we mean that, in the specimen before us, the measurements of the parts mentioned are not the same as in the specimen of which we are thinking.

There may be two reasons why these measurements are not the same: one reason, because they are absolutely larger or smaller than in this specimen; the other reason, because they are relatively so, a hand or a limb being said to be in proportion because its measurements, whether large or small, bear the same relation to the parts or to the whole of a body that they do in the typical man which is supposed to be the artist's model.

But proportion has still another meaning. From this, any conception of imitation, whether or not suggested by any particular model, is absent; and a part is said to be in proportion because of the relationship which its measurements sustain to the measurements of other parts or to the whole of a product. This seems to be the meaning when we speak of the proportions of the human figure, irrespective of any references to attempts to copy any particular model; and it certainly is the meaning when we speak of the proportions of a building in a style such as has never before had existence. Evidently, too, this latter use of the term is the one which we need chiefly to consider in this volume, our main object being not to show how certain standards of proportion can be imitated, but what there is in them that makes them worthy of imitation; and in what way, in the case of architecture at least, new forms, by being constructed according to the principles exemplified in the old, may be made to manifest the old characteristics. Notice also that, in this sense, proportion includes the ideas, both of ratios or relationships, as in $1:2$, and also of likeness or equality in ratios, as in $1:2::3:6$.

Observe, too, the connection between what has just been said and what was said in the last chapter, viz., that proportion is to effects in sight what rhythm is to effects in sound. Just as, in rhythm, pauses separate syllables or notes, and, aided by the absence or presence of force in the accents, divide the whole duration of a series of sounds into like parts or multiples of parts; so, in proportion, it is possible for lines to separate objects of sight, and, aided by light and shade revealing their shapes, to divide the whole extent of space covered by a series of forms into like parts or multiples of parts, all of which may be shown thus to have measurements exactly related to one another or to the whole.

But if it be possible to divide spaces thus, is it probable that any or many will care to do this? The moment that the question is asked, it will be found to admit of but one answer. Such a method of measuring spaces is not only probable but inevitable. Apparently the mind, in arranging different objects of sight, or in judging of their effects as it finds them arranged, cannot avoid making these measurements. None of us can look at windowpanes, doors, or façades of buildings, without comparing the lengths and breadths of each. It is true that we do not always compare them consciously. But if one dimension be greater than another, we usually perceive the fact, and form an estimate as to how much greater it is. After a most limited glance at a building, we describe it to others by saying that it is two or three times, as the case may be, longer than it is high. Or, to notice the tendency when exemplified in action, between which and the mental processes necessitated in art the correspondence is more complete, suppose that one be framing an engraving occupying the centre of a sheet, about which centre there must be a margin on all sides. Even if he have never seen a picture framed before, forty-nine times out of fifty he will place the engraving so that, intervening between it and the frame, there shall seem to be, to his eyes, an equal amount of space on every side of it, or, at least, on opposite sides of it. Or, if the picture must be hung on a wall between two doors, he will hang it so that, to his eyes, there shall seem to be an equal distance between the frame and each door. Even children, if building houses of blocks, will select blocks of similar sizes to be put in corresponding places at different sides of the same windows and porches.

An analogous fact is true universally, and always has been true. There is no primitive kind of ornamentation, no matter how barbarous the race originating it, of which one characteristic, perhaps the most marked, is not an exact division or subdivision of spaces, the mind, apparently, deriving the same sort of satisfaction from rude lines of paint and scratchings upon stone, made at proportional distances from one another, that it does from the rhythmical sounds (see Fig. A) drummed with feet, hands,

(A)

or sticks to accompany the song and dance of the savage. In fact, an arrangement, as in the staves and bars that follow, might be used as preparatory either for writing music or for decorating with color—*i. e.*, for the purpose of representing either rhythm or proportion. (See Fig. B.)

(B)

The same tendency is illustrated in the two following figures (Figs. 1 and 2). They are very ancient forms of

FIG. 1.—VITRUVIAN SCROLL.
See pages 12, 40.

FIG. 2.—GREEK FRET.
See pages 12, 40.

decoration used in pottery, goldsmith's work, and architecture, but, for the reason, apparently, that they are perfectly conformed to the requirements of the mind, they are used to-day almost as extensively as ever. Notice the same tendency, too, in the triglyphs and metopes which adorned the frieze of the Greek Doric temple (Fig. 3); also in various parts, which need not be pointed out, in the forms in Figs. 6 to 12, on pages 33 to 38.

FIG. 3.—TRIGLYPHS AND METOPES.
See pages 12, 40, 168.

These figures indicate that equal divisions of spaces satisfy mental demands of which all men, whether young or old, cultivated or uncultivated, are conscious. It is not only because it is convenient, but because it is artistically satisfactory, that in all sorts of decorative work, whether upon stone, wood, paper, or cloth,—from the finishing upon the ridge-pole of a roof to the lace and fringe upon a window-curtain,' and the patterns upon carpets and wall-papers,—outlines, sometimes subdivided with great variety, but nevertheless covering like spaces, are put together.

Nor is this tendency exhibited in merely those departments of art in which the mind works upon forms originated almost wholly by itself. It is found also in forms which, with more or less literalness, are copied from nature. Just as poetry can take words and phrases, actually heard in conversation, and rearrange them in such ways as to fulfil the requirements of rhythm, so painting and sculpture can take outlines perceived in nature, and rearrange them in such ways as to fulfil the requirements of proportion.

Of course, this could not be the case unless, to some extent, the requirements of proportion were fulfilled in nature. In Chapter II. of " Rhythm and Harmony in Poetry and Music" it was shown that rhythm is a characteristic of natural forms. Notice now that the same is true of proportion. Take nature as a whole. The sky and earth always divide the possible field of vision, approximately at least, into two equal and complementary parts. When the painter composing his picture according to the laws of perspective (see Chapter XIV., page 233, and Fig. 102, page 235) decides upon the places for his horizon, his vanishing point, and his principal figures, and upon the distances of these from one another, and from the margins on either side of his composition, as well as upon the sizes and shapes of his trees, houses, men, animals, considered in themselves or in connection with other objects near them or remote from them, he makes his decisions as a result of relative measurements, mental or actual. And so with reference to the different members and the general shape of the human form, or of the forms of animals, trees, plants, or of any objects, in fact, that are transferred from nature to canvas or marble by way of imitation,—it is as a result of a certain comparison of measurements between part and part, that one can say that certain of these forms are or are not in proportion. Take, for instance, a very heavy body, either of flesh or of foliage, supported by very slight limbs ; should we not say at once that the parts were out of proportion ? Or take the case of limbs jointed, as at the elbow or knee, and one of them very much longer than the other ; should we not say at once that the two were out of proportion ? Even of such small details as eyes, ears, hands, and nostrils we should make a similar affirmation, in case discrepancies in measurements were apparent. And though the relative sizes of parts differ greatly in individual instances, they are always in the same body expected to be so related, each to each, and to other members, as to show an effect that can be recognized only as a result of comparing measurements.

At first thought, the action of the mind in making these comparisons may seem to be of little importance, scarcely worthy of the serious attention which evidently we are about to give it. But, in this life, it usually takes very little to start that which may develop into very much. Rhythm, too, is apparently of little importance. If one knew nothing about art, what could appear more absurd than for an intelligent man to think it worth while, when wishing to say something, to count the syllables that he utters, so that they shall reveal exact divisions and subdivisions of time, such as the negro makes when he beats his hands and feet for dancers? Yet it is out of this simple method of counting, that art has developed the most important element in the form of poetry, as well as an element extremely important in the form of music. When we come to examine the different combinations of effects attributable to rhythm, we find that we are by no means dealing with a subject so simple as at first appeared. The same is true of proportion. Before deciding, for instance, that a foot or a nose is disproportionately large or small, it must be compared not only with other feet and noses, but with the sizes of all the other surrounding features in the animal or man in which it appears. The same feature may look too large with small surroundings, and too small with large ones. Indeed, the number and variety of measurements that any extensive knowledge or application of proportion involves are almost incalculable. When we try to determine exactly what it is that causes its results to be satisfactory, in the human form, for instance (see Figs. 31, page 57; 32, page 58; 35, page 70; 36, page 71; 45, page 86; 62, page 121; 63, page 122; 69, page 128; 73, page 137; and 74, page 139), or in buildings like the Parthenon (see Fig. 96, page 190; also pages 211 to 214), or the Grand Opera House at Paris (see Fig 86, page 167; also pages 170 and 171), then we begin to perceive that this characteristic, as is true of every other entering into the effects of beauty (see page 160 of " Art in Theory "), is capable of complexities as well as possibilities almost infinite.

The best way of beginning to understand the complexities of any method of expression is by trying to understand its elementary processes. Elementary proportional processes may be rendered most intelligible, perhaps, by dwelling for a little upon the correspondences, already many times suggested, between proportion and rhythm. In the volume entitled "Rhythm and Harmony in Poetry and Music" rhythm was shown to result from the mind's endeavor, in the element of time or duration, to arrange the features of form in such a way as to be able to conceive of them as a *unity*. (See the note beginning on page 61.) It was pointed out that it is in order to accomplish this end that the mind divides the composition as a whole into equal or approximately equal parts determined by the duration of each part. These parts in poetry, as we know, are feet, measures, lines, verses, couplets, triplets, stanzas, cantos, etc., and in music are measures, motives, phrases, sections, periods, etc. Now notice that in poetry, in the smallest of these divisions,—feet, or measures as they are also called,—there are never more than one, two, three, four, or, at most, five syllables. That is to say, as measured by the syllables, the successive feet, so far as concerns their duration, are to one another as 1 to 1, 1 to 2, 1 to 3, 1 to 4, 1 to 5, 2 to 3 (2 to 4, which is the same as 1 to 2), or as 3 to 4. As may be seen by referring to pages 11 to 13 and 26 to 37 of "Rhythm and Harmony in Poetry and Music," these ratios represent all that are used in poetic measures. In music the measures are filled with a certain fixed number of notes, or rests corresponding to them. Of these, the longest note ordinarily used is the whole note, to which, as a rule, is given the same duration as to two half notes, four quarter notes, eight eighth notes, sixteen sixteenth notes, and thirty-two thirty-second notes, *e. g.*:

(c)

All these notes, however, whether we express their ratios by the numbers 1 to 2, 1 to 4, etc., or by 2 to 4, 2 to 8, etc., represent comparatively little variety. Each is simply the ratio 1 to 1 with one or both of its factors multiplied by a small even number. Occasionally also three notes, like those in the measures marked 3 in the music on page 11, can be given the same time as would ordinarily be given to two notes of the same length as themselves, or to one note twice as long. In the same way six notes, like those marked 6 in the same music, and, now and then, five notes, marked 5, can be given the same time as four notes of the same length as themselves, or two notes twice as long. It is possible, therefore, through the combined effects of measures and notes used in order to produce musical rhythm, to have represented the following ratios, or the same with one of their factors multiplied by a small even number, viz.: 1:1, 1:2, 1:3, 1:4, 1:5, 1:6, 2:3, 2:5, 3:4, 3:5, 4:5, and 5:6. From these ratios, 2:4, 2:6, 3:6, and 4:6 are omitted because they are already expressed in the ratios 1:2, 1:3, and 2:3.

Still less variety characterizes the ratios representing the relations, each to each, of the larger divisions made in these two arts. In the majority of cases, successive poetic lines, couplets, and stanzas, or musical motives, phrases, sections, and periods are of identical length, *i. e.*, as 1 : 1. Even when the numbers of syllables or measures in successive lines or phrases differ, these are usually made to have a similar general effect by a pause in poetry, or a prolongation in music, at the end of the shorter of the lines, thus causing all to seem to be uttered in the same time (see Fig. D, page 17.)

The longest line used in poetry without being virtually a double line, and one as long as any usual phrase in music, contains eight measures, *e. g.*:

"Comrades, leave me here a little, while as yet 't is early morn."
—*Locksley Hall: Tennyson.*

Were this to be alternated with a line containing seven measures we should have as a ratio representing the largest possible numbers in poetic rhythm 7 : 8, but in reading such lines we should invariably pause after the shorter line in such a way as to cause the effects of the two lines together to appear to be as 1 : 1. Accordingly, we may say that the effects of rhythm are produced by subdivisions whose relations to one another can be represented by ratios confined to small numbers. It is evident, too, that the fact that they are small is that which enables the mind to recognize the likeness between the parts, and thus to perceive a *unity* in general effect notwithstanding *variety* and *complexity* in certain details. (See page 3, also the note beginning on page 61.) Were poetic measures composed of from five to seven syllables, or poetic lines of from eight to thirteen measures, we should very often be unable to recognize either the character of the metre or its existence.

Evidently the same principle ought to be illustrated in proportion. It is natural to suppose that just as the mind, when listening through the ear, takes satisfaction in sounds so divided and subdivided as to duration that all can appear to be parts of a unity, because all can be measured according to some clearly recognized standard of comparison (see note on page 61); so the same mind, looking through the eye, takes satisfaction in objects of sight so divided and subdivided as to extension, *i. e.*, as to size or shape, that these also can be measured and compared. Notice, too, that they can be compared with ease in the degree in which they can be perceived to measure exactly the same, *i. e.*, to be as $1:1$; or, if not so, can reveal their relationships to $1:1$, as can $1:2$ or $1:3$, because it means $1:1+1$; or $1:1+1+1$. As will be shown hereafter, this is a condition underlying the effects of proportion which is fundamental, and must be recognized before the subject can be fully understood.

Notice, again, that proportion, as it is thus attributed to measurements that are compared, is merely a statement of a fact; nor is it essential that the mind, before stating this fact, should recognize what the ratio is, only that it has existence. The same principle applies here as in rhythm. To experience the effects of this, we do not need to be able to tell what the metre is—whether long or short, iambic or trochaic—only that there is a metre. But while this is true, the metre must be capable of being analyzed; and we must feel that it is so, although, perhaps, we ourselves do not actually go through with the analytic process.

What has been said will show us a good reason, too, why, as affirmed by W. W. Lloyd in his "Memoir on the Systems of Proportion," published with Cockerill's "Temples of Ægina and Bassæ," p. 64, "the Greek architects attached great value to simple ratios of low natural numbers." Of course, the simpler the ratio, and lower the number, the more easily could each be recognized.

CHAPTER III.

EFFECTS OF PROPORTION AS WRONGLY CONFOUNDED WITH THOSE OF PERSPECTIVE.

Difficulties Experienced in Applying Principles of Proportion—If ever Understood they can be Understood to-day—Necessity, to Rid the Subject of Complexity, of Separating Two Processes in Perception—First, the Unconscious Physical Recognition of Appearances; Second, the Conscious Mental Measurement of them—As Applied to Sounds, the First Process Determines Effects of Harmony; the Second, Effects of Rhythm—So in Sights, not the First, but the Second, Determines Effects of Proportion—This Results from the Conscious Measurement of Appearances after and as they have been Perceived, whereas the Unconscious Physical Process Determines Effects of Perspective—The Two Processes are easily Confounded, with Resulting Difficulties in Theory and Practice—The Two Supposed to have been Confounded by the Greeks—This Supposition not wholly Tenable—Yet at the Basis of Modern Theories which Correlate Proportion to the Effects of Musical Pitch upon the Ear, as do the Theories of Legh and Zeising—Of Hay, Fergusson, Penrose, and Lloyd—Impossibility of any Theoretic or Practical Understanding of Proportion according to this Conception of it.

IF, as shown in Chapter Second, the principles underlying proportion be simple in character as well as similar in effect to those of rhythm, it would seem to follow that, like those of rhythm, they should be comparatively easy to interpret and to produce. Why, then, are they usually treated as if this were not the case? Why are they sometimes attributed to laws of vision with which the Greeks alone of all human beings have been acquainted, which laws, as understood by them, it is in our day next to impossible to discover or to apply?

In endeavoring to answer this question, let us begin by recalling the fact that, if a subject, however complex, have once been made to appear intelligible, it can presumably be made to appear so again. It need not be supposed to be a mystery wholly impenetrable. It probably can be seen through, and this in accordance with the workings of the powers of observation and reflection allotted to the ordinary man of one's own generation.

Another fact that it is well to recall is, that, in the degree in which any subject appears complex, it does so because the elements connected with it have not been completely analyzed. How is it with those connected with proportion? Let us see. What are these elements? —First of all, a preliminary effect whereby an image is impressed on the retina. Dr. Henry D. Noyes, in his "Diseases of the Eye," gives a picture of the eye of a dead rabbit in which are seen, photographed, as it were, parallel bars that had been held in front of the eye just before the animal was killed. The experiment is shown in proof of the theory that form is impressed upon the visual organs in connection with the chemical action of the fluids, producing effects analogous to those produced upon the negative of a photograph. Aside from what the experiment indicates with reference to this theory, it certainly shows that the eye has in it a picture of the form as a form. Indeed, merely by looking into the eyes of our fellows, we can sometimes see in them an image of the external world as perfect as a reflection in a mirror. "A camera and an eye," says Le Conte in his "Sight," "are both contrived for the same purpose, viz., the formation of a perfect image on a screen properly placed. Look into the camera from behind, and we see the inverted image on the ground-glass plate; look into the eye from behind, and we see also an inverted image on the retina. [See Fig. 4.] "The camera is a small, dark chamber, open

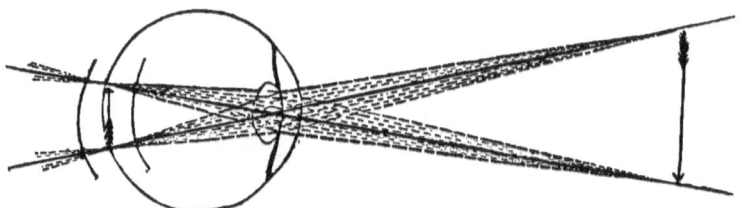

FIG. 4.—ILLUSTRATION OF THE FORMATION OF AN IMAGE ON THE RETINA.
See pages 22, 23, 234.

to the light only in front, to admit the light from the object to be imaged. It is coated inside with lamp-black, so that any light from the object to be imaged, or from other objects, which may fall on the sides will be quenched, and not allowed to rebound by reflection, and thus fall on the image and spoil it. So the eye also is a very small, dark chamber, open to light only in front, where the light must enter from the object to be imaged, and lined with a dark pigment to quench the light as soon as it has done the work of impressing its own point of the retina, and thus prevent reflection and striking some other part and thus spoiling the image. Both camera and eye form their images by means of a lens or a system of lenses." (See Fig. 5, above.) The way in which the rays of light pass through the crystalline lens

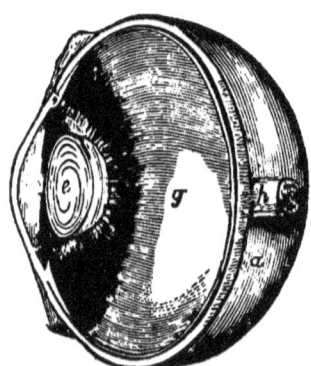

FIG. 5.—THE CAVITY OF THE EYE.

a, outer layer; *e*, crystalline lens; *g*, retina; *h*, optic nerve.

See pages 21, 22.

of the eye and impress upon the retina an inverted but exact image of the thing seen is illustrated in Fig. 4, page 22. But notice now that the production of this image is not all that is necessary in order to produce the impression of proportion. Besides being made to perceive the image, the mind must perceive the relative measurements of different parts of the image.

Manifestly the first of these effects involves a very different process from the second. The first is wholly dependent upon the operation of physical laws, an operation in which the organs of sight take care of themselves, through processes of which the mind is wholly unconscious. The second of the effects is wholly dependent upon mental action, as much so as that of a man determining with a tape-measure the relative dimensions of an image in a mirror. These dimensions cannot be recognized as sustaining certain relations to one another except as the mind, as a result of comparison, forms judgments with reference to them.

In Chapters VII. to XV. of the volume entitled "Rhythm and Harmony in Poetry and Music," it was shown that effects of harmony, as developed in poetry or in the scales and chords of music, are determined by the action of the physical organs of hearing, irrespective of any conscious action of the mind; and in Chapters II. to VI. of the same book, it was shown that effects of *rhythm*, as developed in either art, are determined by the conscious action of the mind when comparing the measurements of different syllables, notes, feet, or phrases—that is to say, it was shown that, before recognizing or constructing rhythm, the physical organs of hearing report to the mind certain sounds; and afterwards that the mind, by purely psychological and conscious processes, measures the different lengths of different sounds, or the different degrees of their intensity, and thus estimates or arranges their rhythmic possibilities.

Now with these facts concerning sounds in mind, let us consider again the two elements underlying the perception of external objects. Here, also, we shall find physical processes of which the mind is unconscious, as a result of which an image of different shadings or colors is made to appear on the retina. Is it not clear that these processes correspond to those resulting from the physical actions of the ear, which, while preparatory to rhythm, do not themselves produce or determine it? And, if so, is it not logical to infer that these processes in the eye, while preparatory to proportion, do not themselves produce or determine it?

What then does determine it?—what but the conscious action of the mind judging of the relative measurements of the different parts of this image? Notice the phraseology here—of this *image*. Every painter knows that colors and shadows as examined close at hand in the external world often differ greatly from what they appear to be to one who judges of them by the image on the retina. To him an actually checkered surface may appear to be of a single color, and a color, owing to the influence of surrounding hues, may appear unlike that which it actually is. The same fact is true with reference to outlines. The eye is rounded and therefore the mind behind it sees everything through a rounded surface. If one look into a convex mirror he will find all of the dimensions of the natural world slightly altered. As a rule, for instance, the straight upward lines of a square object with its base on the middle line of the mirror will appear not to be parallel but to approach one another. The effects in the mirror merely exaggerate the effects already exerted upon nature by the rounded formation of the eye. As applied to natural surroundings, we become accustomed to these effects and never judge lines to be curved or lacking in parallelism merely because they are so in the image on the retina. On the contrary, unless they were so in this image, we should judge the lines to be neither straight nor parallel. Accordingly, when men try, as in drawing a picture, to reproduce the appearance of such an image, it becomes important for them to carry out what are termed the laws of linear perspective. These are laws, as will be explained in Chapter XIV., in accordance with which all the outlines of an artificial image, whether drawn, painted, carved, or constructed, or however changed in size, are made among other things to sustain somewhat the same relations as in an image naturally produced on the retina.

Notice, moreover, that to fulfil these laws of perspective so as to make this artificial image correspond to the image in the eye is one thing; and that to make the respective dimensions of this image appear to fulfil, each to each, the laws of proportion is another thing. Yet it is quite easy and natural to confound the two. We need not be surprised, therefore, to find them almost invariably confounded in theories of proportion, especially in those which have had most influence in causing men to think that the subject is too complex and mysterious for solution. Those who have advanced these theories have failed to recognize that the analogue of proportion is not harmony but rhythm. Moreover, as rhythm is an effect of the conscious action of the mind, its general principles are comparatively easy to ascertain; and, by carrying out the analogies suggested by them, the explanation of the effects of proportion may be rendered comparatively easy. But the processes through which the ear becomes cognizant of the harmonic relations between musical notes and chords are difficult to ascertain, for the very reason that the mind is not conscious of these processes. No wonder, therefore, that a theory identifying with them those of proportion by which the mind, through the eye, becomes cognizant of the relations existing between spaces, should involve difficulties. Such a theory starts out with the supposition that effects of proportion end in the physical senses, whereas they are recognized only by the mind. Afterwards, when the theory goes on to explain these effects, of course it can do this only so far as it can explain other physiological effects. But these cannot be explained except through hypothesis.

Yet this theory, as has been said, is the one that is usually advanced. It is true, too, that it is supposed to have been derived from the Greeks; and that the Greeks are acknowledged to have had a more thorough understanding of the subject than any other people. But is the theory derived from the Greeks? Is it certain that the expressions of the Greeks with reference to the matter have been properly interpreted? The Latin writer Vitruvius tells us in his " De Architectura," book iii., chapter i., that they called proportion not harmony but analogy (ἀναλογία). To this it may be answered, of course, that Pausanias, in chap. xii. of the Arcadia, speaking of the beauty of the stone of which the " Theseum was composed, and its harmony throughout," employs the word harmony (ἁρμόνιος), and that Plato, too, in his Republic, says that, " as the eyes seem to be fitted for the harmonious proportions of the celestial orbits, so the ears seem to be fitted for the harmony of musical intervals; and these seem to be sister sciences; as the Pythagoreans, indeed, affirm, and we must accord with them."

This use of terms, however, does not necessarily mean all that is attributed to it. There is nothing corresponding to what we, at least, term proportion in the effects of the celestial orbits, or, if there were, did we ourselves choose to use the word harmony not in its more restricted technical sense as applied in modern times merely to note or color, but, as the Greeks themselves did, as meaning any unity whatever produced by a blending of parts or multiples of parts according to mathematical ratios, then we too could ascribe harmony not only to note or color but also to rhythm; and if to rhythm, of course, to proportion.

But it has generally been supposed that the Greeks meant more than this, that, reversing, to say the least, the natural order of investigation, they determined what should be the conscious action of the mind in measuring spaces from an examination of what will be shown, in Chapter XX. of this volume, to be its unconscious action as affected by conditions underlying the effects of note and color. This conception of the Greek method is at the basis of the theory in Peter Legh's " Music of the Eye "; as well as of that in Adolf Zeising's work "On the Law of Proportion which Rules all Nature." In the latter, the relations of harmonic tones in music are used as a basis for the construction of a " Golden Section," as it is called. This may be described as a measure divided into parts, each of which is related to all the other parts, according to some simple ratio; and the whole is represented as furnishing a standard of related measurements for all beautiful proportions. The theory is suggested by a not wholly warranted interpretation given to an obscure passage in Plato's " Timæus," in which there is mention, indeed, of divisions of a string as determining proportions; but also, a little farther on, of angles and figures as determining them. It is noteworthy, too, that in making practical tests of this golden rule, the author finds fault with the Parthenon because it does not conform to his requirements. But the Greeks would hardly have esteemed this building so highly, had it not fulfilled their own architectural principles.

D. R. Hay, again, attributes to suggestions from the ancients the whole of the very ingenious and interesting theory in his essay on a "System of Geometric Proportion"; and he bases this theory upon the same hypothesis, namely, that "the division of space into an exact number of equal parts will æsthetically affect the eye in the same way that the division of the time of vibrations [by which he means the vibrations determining the pitch of notes] in music into an exact number of equal parts æsthetically affects the mind through the medium of the ear." James Fergusson, also, in his "History of Architecture," vol. i., pt. i, bk. iii, chap. ii, sanctions this view. In speaking of the effects of the ratios employed by the Greeks, he says: "Many would be inclined to believe they were more fanciful than real. It would, however, be as reasonable in a person with no ear or no musical education, to object to the enjoyment of a complicated concerted piece of music experienced by those differently situated, or to declare that the pain musicians feel from a false note was mere affectation. The eyes of the Greeks were as perfectly educated as our ears. They could appreciate harmonies which are lost in us, and were offended at false quantities which our dull senses fail to perceive. But in spite of ourselves we do feel the beauty of these harmonic relations, though we rarely know why." Nor does Fergusson attempt to explain the reason.

F. C. Penrose, also, in his work on "The Principles of Athenian Architecture," implies, in many expressions, his adherence to this theory. So too does W. W. Lloyd in the very valuable Appendix accompanying that work as published by the Society of Dilettanti, as well as in his equally valuable one accompanying C. R. Cockerill's "Temples at Ægina and Bassæ." While Lloyd does this, however, he makes an important concession. "In response to what is implied in these expressions," he says (Penrose's "Prin. of Athen. Arch.," Appendix, p. 111), "the speculative have not been remiss in asserting for architectural harmony as close a dependence on mathematics as has been so long established for musical. Admitting the justness of the presumption so far, I may say, at once, that my own conclusions are quite at variance with what is often the next presumption, that the ratios of the diatonic scale have any special value as realized in architectural forms."

What ratios do have value in the Parthenon he tells us in the following language (*idem*, p. 112): "It will be observed that the ratios 2 : 7, 4 : 9, and 9 : 14 have respectively the common difference between their terms of 5. In the recited order the terms approach towards equality, and the series may be extended by insertion of intermediate and other ratios having the same characteristic. Thus 1 : 6, 2 : 7, 3 : 8, 4 : 9, 5 : 10, etc. It will be found that several of these ratios are repeated with marked intention." And what if they are? What if we learn even so important a fact as that, in the Parthenon, the width of the column was to that of the whole breadth of the front as 5 : 81 ; or, as Penrose informs us in his "Principles of Athenian Architecture," that the ratio of the architrave to the step was 89 : 90? It is evident that, for any practical purpose, unless something more be discovered—unless some deeper principle be unfolded which apparently these surface-facts have suggested not even as a possibility to these writers—an architect of our own time can derive no benefit from them. Years ago, when the author of this book was in college and studying mechanics, a subject that was taught by compelling the class to learn by rote long series of intricate formulæ, a classmate—John H. Denison—came around one morning and declared that now he understood, as never before, the object of our study. He said that he had had a dream. In this, he had found himself in an oriental country. They were erecting a gigantic building. But, to complete it, they needed to raise from the ground an enormous stone with which to crown its summit. The king and his ministers and all the people had assembled to see this done. But all efforts were in vain. Finally, impelled by a happy inspiration, he himself shouted at the top of his voice the longest of these formulæ that he had been learning. Instantly, lifted by the magic of this, which proved to be an incantation, the great stone ascended to its place, while all the people prostrated their forms before the man who had shouted the formula, and the heiress to the throne was led forward to be presented to him in marriage. As ordinarily conceived, the connection between the ratios used by the Greeks and the practical applications of them to æsthetic requirements is about as close as was that between formulæ and performance in the conception of the students for whose benefit this dream was told. As has been intimated, the fundamental reason for such a lack of connection is a misunderstanding of the nature of the effects of proportion, arising from allying them with those at the basis not of musical rhythm but of harmony. Of course, as already intimated, there is an analogy between the mathematical ratios that determine results in harmony and in rhythm or proportion ; and this fact may at times render plausible, often apparently conclusive, each of the various theories mentioned in this chapter. But the point is that all these theories fail to take into consideration a fact which modifies the effects of their strict application. This fact is the difference between actual measurements and apparent measurements, between measurements as they are in an external object and as they seem to be to the eye perceiving them from a distance.

CHAPTER IV.

PROPORTION AS BASED UPON COMPARISONS OF APPARENT
MEASUREMENTS: STRAIGHT LINES AND
RECTANGULAR FIGURES.

Proportion and Perspective Both to be Studied, but Separately—Perspective Considers the Difference between Subjective Effects and Objective Arrangements Occasioning Them—Proportion Considers Appearances, Perspective the Method of Producing them—Comparison or Likeness is the Basis of Proportion—Illustrations—Small Numbers Necessary to the Recognition of Ratios—Outlines Indicating like Subdivisions an Aid to this Recognition—The Principle Applicable to Comparisons between both Rectilinear and Rectangular Measurements—Between Adjacent Figures as Wholes—Hay's Theory.

TO say that proportion is one thing, and perspective another thing, does not free the man who would have an intelligent view of the former subject from the necessity of paying attention to the latter. It merely makes it imperative for him to separate the two, and study each by itself. This we shall now proceed to do, devoting Chapters IV. to XIII. to proportion, and those immediately following them to perspective. Meantime, before unfolding further the latter subject, enough has been said to indicate to the reader that, when treating of proportion, we are treating of effects produced upon the mind by conditions that appear to exist in the object perceived, but which do not necessarily exist there in reality. That is to say, though in nature the measurements of an object may fulfil the requirements of proportion, they may not, owing

FIG. 6.—A MAORI FESTIVAL, NEW ZEALAND.
See pages 40, 162, 174.

to the operation of the laws of perspective, fulfil them in the image which this object produces on the retina; and, *vice versa*, though in nature the measurements may not fulfil the requirements of proportion, they may, neverthe-

FIG. 7.—KAFFIR STATION, AFRICA.
See pages 40, 162.

less, owing to the operations of the laws of perspective, fulfil them in this image. In short, as applied to proportion as to many other artistic features, a work of art,

PROPORTION AND PERSPECTIVE. 35

whether a painting, a statue, or a building, has to be judged by what may be termed, and is, in this sense, its subjective effect after it has begun to influence the eye and mind.

FIG. 8.—TYPE OF AN ASSYRIAN SQUARE.
See pages 40, 43, 44, 162.

Is it necessary to argue that this truth is not generally recognized? When a man with a yardstick is measuring, close at hand, the parts of the Parthenon, then, according to the generally accepted representation, he is studying proportion. But he is really doing nothing of the sort. He is studying proportion, when he is standing at a distance from the building and noticing the parts of it, which, from that distance, appear to fulfil the requirements of those comparative measurements which proportion necessitates. When he is close against the building with his yardstick, he is more apt to be learning the differences between measurements as they are, and as, from a distance, they appear to be, the consideration of which differences and the methods of obviating them furnish the subject-matter not of proportion but of perspective. In the case of the Greeks, too, as we shall find, the principles of the latter were applied in order to produce distant appearances of proportion not only, but also of height, breadth,

FIG. 9.—MEDIÆVAL CASTLE.
See pages 40, 145, 162.

FIG. 10.—TEMPLE OF THESEUS, ATHENS.
See pages 40, 44, 116, 156, 163, 164, 168, 170, 175, 188, 189, 193, 196, 201, 210, 211, 218, 219, 220, 221, 224, 252.

straightness, parallelism, and other effects, which, in addition to those of proportion, were deemed desirable. As

PROPORTION AND PERSPECTIVE. 37

said in the last chapter, a chief reason why the require-

FIG. 11.—ST. STEPHENS, CAEN, NORMANDY.
See pages 42, 44, 154, 163, 166, 170, 175, 226.

ments of proportion are supposed to be involved in impenetrable mystery, and why, therefore, the neglect of them in our own day is supposed to be excusable, is traceable to this confounding of these two entirely different objects of inquiry.

Now with a clear apprehension that, at present, we are to consider merely proportion, which has to do with the

FIG. 12.— CANTERBURY CATHEDRAL, FROM SOUTHWEST.
See pages 42, 163, 175, 226.

measurements which the mind makes of appearances; and that only by and by are we to consider perspective, which has to do with the arrangements producing appearances, let us confine attention for a time to the former subject. In proportion, it is the apparent measurements of certain divisions and subdivisions of objects that are compared. As was said in the last chapter, these measure-

PROPORTION MARKED BY LIKE SUBDIVISIONS. 39

ments could not be compared unless they were related to one another according to ratios expressible in small numbers. To illustrate this fact further, as well as to indicate why it is a fact, let us suppose ourselves to be judging of the relative lengths of different lines or sur-

FIG. 13.—CENTRAL CONGREGATIONAL CHURCH, BOSTON.
See page 42.

faces, or of different divisions of the same line or surface. Our task will evidently be easiest when the numbers are smallest ; *i. e.*, when the two lengths compared are as 1:1, or are exactly alike. We see, therefore, why this relationship should be historically the earliest form and, even in our own day, the most universal in which the tendency to proportion manifests itself. Notice, as already indicated in Chapter II., the equal spaces in Figs. 1, page 12, 2, page 12, and 3, page 12. In Fig. 6, page 33, notice the equal spaces between the platforms. In Fig. 7, page 34, notice the rude but similarly equal divisions of heights. In the specimen of early civilized architecture, in Fig. 8, page 35, observe the equal height of each storey and

FIG. 14.—WILLESDEN CHURCH, NEAR LONDON, ENGLAND.
See pages 42, 154.

the equal width of each panel. In Fig. 9, page 36, observe the equal divisions in the tower considered perpendicularly. In Fig. 10, page 36, observe that the columns divide the sides considered horizontally into approximately equal divisions, as do also the foundation, entablature, and pediment of the front (see Fig. 94,

FIG. 15.—CHICHESTER CATHEDRAL, ENGLAND.
See pages 42, 43, 158, 163, 165.

page 183) considered perpendicularly. Observe, too, the perpendicular divisions of the towers in Fig. 11, page 37, and the horizontal divisions caused by the buttresses in Fig. 12, page 38. Fig. 13, page 39, shows an imitation of this last method, but with the number of spaces of exactly the same width, too small to produce the desired rhythmic or proportional effect. Figs. 77, page 150, 81, page 155, 82, page 156, show like measurements both vertical and horizontal. In Fig. 15, page 41, the ornamentation of the spire divides it so that each part of it seems to be of the same height as the upper part of the tower beneath it, and in Fig. 14, page 40, the tower seems to be of the same width as the church. This universal use of the ratio 1 : 1 has been illustrated thus fully, because it is important for the reader to understand that it is the elementary relationship which is recognized in proportion, and, as such, is at the basis of all its developments.

If, however, the relationship be not that of 1 : 1, the next easiest to recognize is that of 1 : 2, as between the first of the upper and lower lines at the left of Fig. 16.

FIG. 16.—LINES IN PROPORTION.
See pages 42, 43.

Nor is it difficult to recognize the relationship of 1 : 3, as between the second pair of lines in this figure, or of 2 : 3, as between the third pair. But it is evident that as the values of the numbers representing the ratios increase, these become less recognizable; as, for instance, when they are as 4 : 5 or as 5 : 7, as between, respectively, the fourth and fifth pairs of lines in this Fig. 16. When, at last, we get to a relationship that can be expressed only by large numbers like 10 : 11, or 15 : 16, the mind is no longer able to recognize even its existence.

There is a way, however, in which one may be made to recognize it, even when represented by comparatively large numbers. This is when, in accordance with the elementary process in proportion of putting like with like, the wholes of the forms that are to be compared are measured off into like subdivisions. For instance, it is far more easy to recognize the relationship of 4 : 5, or at least that there is such a relationship, when it is expressed as in Fig. 17, below, than when it is expressed as in lines like those in Fig. 16, page 42. Accordingly, like subdivisions when they are indicated as in Fig. 17 may show not

FIG. 17.—LINES SUBDIVIDED TO INDICATE PROPORTION.
See page 43.

only the relationship that each subdivision sustains to each other subdivision that measures the same as itself, but the relationship also that whole series of subdivisions sustain to other series of them, which, as series, do not measure the same. Thus, the panels in the lower storey in the Assyrian tower in Fig. 8, page 35, show that the whole length of each storey sustains a certain definite relationship to the whole length of each other storey. So, too, the ornamental divisions in the spire in Chichester Cathedral (Fig. 15, page 41) show that the whole spire sustains an exact relationship of 3 : 1 to the square part of the tower visible below it; and the divisions in the towers of St. Sulpice. Fig. 82, page 156, suggest that their whole height sustains a relationship of 2 : 1 to the height of the central part of the building.

We are told by W. W. Lloyd in his "Memoir on the Systems of Proportion," published with Cockerill's "Temples of Ægina and Bassæ," page 64, that all the architectural quantities as made proportionate were estimated by the Greeks chiefly in two ways: by rectilinear proportions, or by divisions of one continuous straight line; and by rectangular proportions, or a comparison of length and breadth, height and width, etc., at right angles. We have considered the first of these ways. In considering the second, we can expect, of course, no change in principle. In case the lines to be compared form adjacent sides of a rectangle, the ratio between the lines must be recognizable in the degree in which it can be expressed in small numbers, 1 : 2, 2 : 3, 3 : 4, etc. Or, if comparatively large numbers be necessitated, they can still be recognized in the degree in which certain marks suggest them to the eye; or, if not the numbers themselves, at least the fact that they exist and represent ascertainable ratios. Notice this Fig. 18, representing

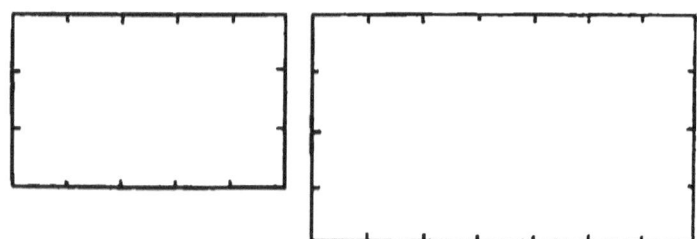

FIG. 18.—FIGURES WITH LINES SUBDIVIDED TO INDICATE PROPORTION.
See pages 44, 263.

3 : 5 and 4 : 7. As applied in actual construction also, observe Fig. 8, page 35; and the like horizontal or vertical divisions in Figs. 10, page 36, 11, page 37, 77, page 150, 81, page 155, and 82, page 156.

RECTILINEAR AND RECTANGULAR PROPORTIONS. 45

Of course, this method of making lengths and breadths seem in proportion in the same figure can make them seem so in adjacent figures; in other words, it can make one figure as a whole seem in proportion to another figure. If, in such cases, the figures be rectangles, they may be similar in width, and then their relationships may be determined by the ratios of their heights, as in the first three rectangles at the left of Fig. 19. Or if the rectangles be similar in height, their relationships may be determined by the ratios of their widths, as in the fourth, fifth, and sixth rectangles in the same figure Or, if the

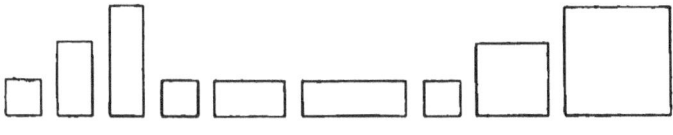

FIG. 19.—RECTANGLES IN PROPORTION.
See page 45.

rectangles be similar neither in width nor in height, their relationships may still be determined by the ratios, each to each, of both these respective dimensions, as in the seventh, eighth, and ninth rectangles in Fig. 19.

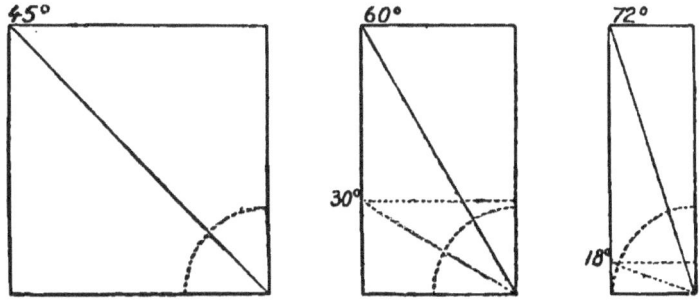

FIG. 20.—HAY'S METHOD OF DETERMINING PROPORTIONAL RELATIONS
OF RECTANGLES.
See page 46.

D. R. Hay, in his "Science of Beauty and Laws of Geometric Proportion," makes the proportions of rectangles to one another depend upon the ratios of the angles described by lines drawn from corner to corner as in Fig. 20, page 45. There may be something in this; but mainly

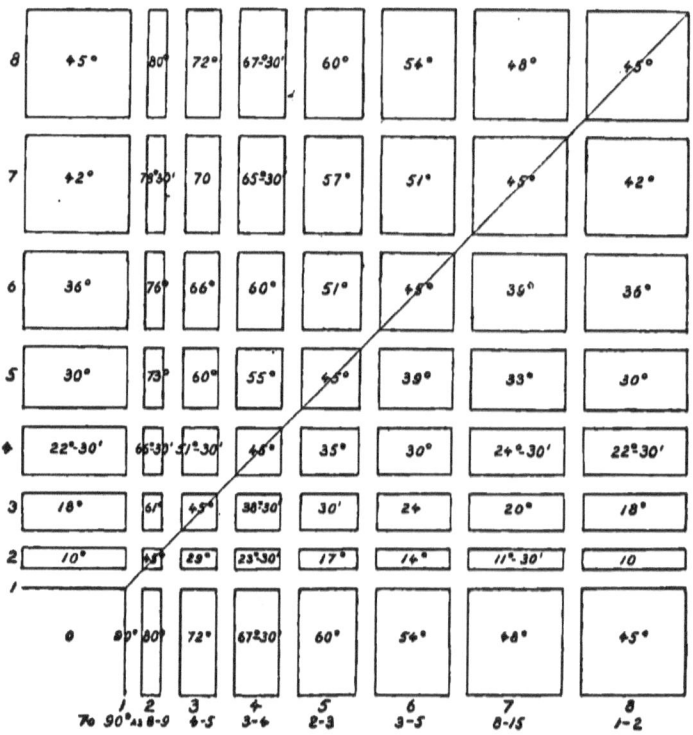

FIG. 21.—HAY'S RECTANGLES CORRESPONDING TO THE MUSICAL SCALE.
See page 47.

for a reason which Mr. Hay does not state. This is the influence which, in all acts of vision, angles of this kind have, owing to the way in which, according to the laws of perspective, the straight lines are brought together at a vanishing point. See page 233, also Fig. 102, page 235. It is possible that, in order to cause lines on a rounded retina to appear to be of like lengths, we should compare them by comparing the angles to which they are similarly related, not at one corner of the figure, as Mr. Hay does, but—what would practically produce the same result— at the centre of the figure. Mr. Hay, carrying out the theory mentioned on page 28, holds that all rectangles, as well as all figures that may be regularly described in such rectangles, are harmonious, in case the angles that he mentions bear the same relations to one another as do the strings of musical notes that form harmonics ; in other words, if these angles be to one another as 1 : 2, 2 : 3, 3 : 4, 4 : 5, 5 : 6, etc. According to him, the rectangle in Fig. 21, page 46, indicated by *1*, corresponding to *do* of the musical scale, would form an harmonic with that marked *3*, or *5*, or *8*, corresponding respectively to *me*, *sol*, and *do* of the musical scale. So the rectangles marked *4*, *6*, and *8* would form harmonics, because corresponding respectively to the *fa*, *la*, and *do* of the musical scale.

CHAPTER V.

PROPORTION AS BASED UPON COMPARISONS OF MEASUREMENTS IN CURVED AND COMPLEX FIGURES.

Complex and Irregular Figures Shown to be in Proportion by Comparing each with some Simple and Regular Figure—Regular Figures as Compared with Rectangles—Importance of Having the Rectangles Visible—The Choir of Ely Cathedral—Illustrating the Influence of Suggestion in Outlines—The Use of Figures not Rectangular as Standards of Comparison between Complex Figures—Aid Afforded by Straight Lines to the Perception of Proportion in Complex Curves—Illustrations—Intimate Connection between Proportion as thus Manifested and Harmony of Outline—Curved Circles, Ellipses, Used as Standards of Comparison between Complex Figures—Application of this Method to the Human Figure.

SO far we have considered only straight lines and rectangular figures. Of course, there are other figures, and they form a vast majority, that are not composed of straight or rectangular or even regular outlines. It is evident that to compare these figures together, especially when for different reasons they differ, is extremely difficult; not only so but that it is impossible, unless all can be shown to be allied to some simpler and more regular figure which can serve as a standard of measurement. This simpler figure, which is just as essential to the determining of like space-dimensions in shape as a yardstick is to the determining of like lengths, may be either actually outlined at the time of comparing the measurements or only ideally imagined. But whether actually outlined or not, on the principle that things equal to the same thing are equal to one another, all other figures inscribed in this simpler figure and that touch all its sides can, for this reason, be recognized as being related. See Figs. 22, 23, and 24.

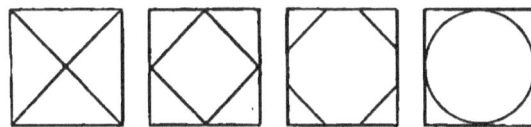

FIG. 22.—FIGURES RELATED BECAUSE INSCRIBABLE IN THE SAME SQUARE.
See page 49.

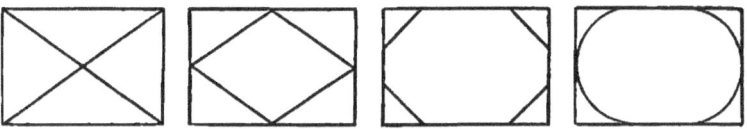

FIG. 23.—FIGURES RELATED BECAUSE INSCRIBABLE IN THE SAME RECTANGLE.
See page 49.

FIG. 24.—FIGURES RELATED BECAUSE INSCRIBABLE IN THE SAME OR A RELATED FIGURE.
See pages 49, 50.

There is a deduction from this fact made by Mr. Hay, which well illustrates the erroneous influence of an untenable theory, his theory being, as stated on page 28, that "the division of space into an exact number of equal parts will æsthetically affect the eye in the same way that the division of the time of vibrations [*i. e.*, the vibrations determining pitch] in music into an exact number of equal parts æsthetically affects the mind through the medium of the ear." He says that any regular figures inscribable in one rectangle are related to other figures inscribable in another rectangle precisely as the two rectangles themselves are related. Thus the same relation that the first and second drawings in this Fig. 25, sus-

FIG. 25.—FIGURES RELATED BECAUSE INSCRIBABLE IN FIGURES IN PROPORTION.
See pages 50, 51.

tain each to each, is respectively sustained also by the third and fourth, the fifth and sixth, and the seventh and eighth. With reference to this, it will be observed that the statement, however accurate in certain cases, does not include that which is essential to render it accurate in all cases. As was said on page 24, proportion is an effect of a comparison of measurements made through, but not by, the physical organs of sight. It is made by the mind. The statement that two things are in proportion being a statement of what seems a fact, because apparent to the mind, it is evident that any surrounding arrangements which render the results of the measurements apparent, and thus interpret them, are very important factors in producing the effect. Certainly, the first three forms in Fig. 26, when they are separated from the rectangles in

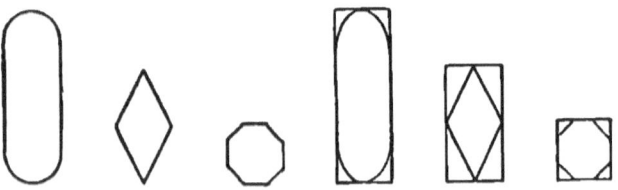

FIG. 26.—RELATIONSHIP OF FIGURES AS INDICATED AND AS NOT INDICATED.
See page 50.

PROPORTION IN IRREGULAR FIGURES.   51

which, in the last three forms, they are shown to be inscribable, do not suggest any relationship to one another. Nor would the fifth and sixth or the seventh and eighth forms in Fig. 25, page 50, were it not for the rectangles in the first and second, with which the figure shows them to be connected. Or, to indicate the practical bearings

FIG. 27.—CHÂTEAU DE RANDAU, VICHY, FRANCE.
See pages 51, 149, 164, 166.

upon art of this remark, it is conceivable that the different triangles described by the pitch of the gable-windows, roofs, and turrets in Fig. 27, above, would all be found to be exactly inscribable in rectangles which, according to what was said on page 48, are in proportion to one another. But because the rectangles are not visible, and, in the circumstances, cannot be made visible, the different triangles do not seem to be either in proportion or in harmony. In this regard, they have a much less artistic effect than the like triangularity of the shapes, and consequent parallelism of the lines, in the arrangements connected with the roofs and turrets in Fig. 28, page 53. Notice, too, how the rectangular framings into which are set the arched doors and windows in the middle of the front of the building in Fig. 29, page 54, redeem the whole from an effect of incongruity and disproportion which, otherwise, might characterize it.

In fulfilment of the same principle, it will be observed that the like rectangular spaces in the ornamentation in the screen behind the upper seats in Fig. 30, page 55, reveal that both the rounded outlines in its lower section and the pointed outlines in its upper section are in proportion. Notice also the correspondence between the width of these rectangular spaces and the width of each of the divisions in the under part of the window just below the ceiling, indicating a relationship of 1 : 1 to these divisions, as well as of 1 : 2 to the divisions in the middle large arch below it. Notice, also, the apparently like measurements in the width of these same rectangular spaces above and behind the seats and in the height of the mouldings over the two large arches rising toward the ceiling, as well as in the height of the string-courses, or cornices, immediately above these mouldings; and also in the height of the ornamentation which is immediately in front of the higher seats. Notice again, sustaining a general ratio of about 3 : 1 to the measurement just mentioned, like measurements of height in that which is between the lower edge of the ornamentation in front of the higher seats and the floor of the cathedral; also between the upper edge of this ornamentation and each highest point reached by each of the small arches above it; also between this latter and the highest point reached by the screen behind the stalls; also between this and the lower edge of

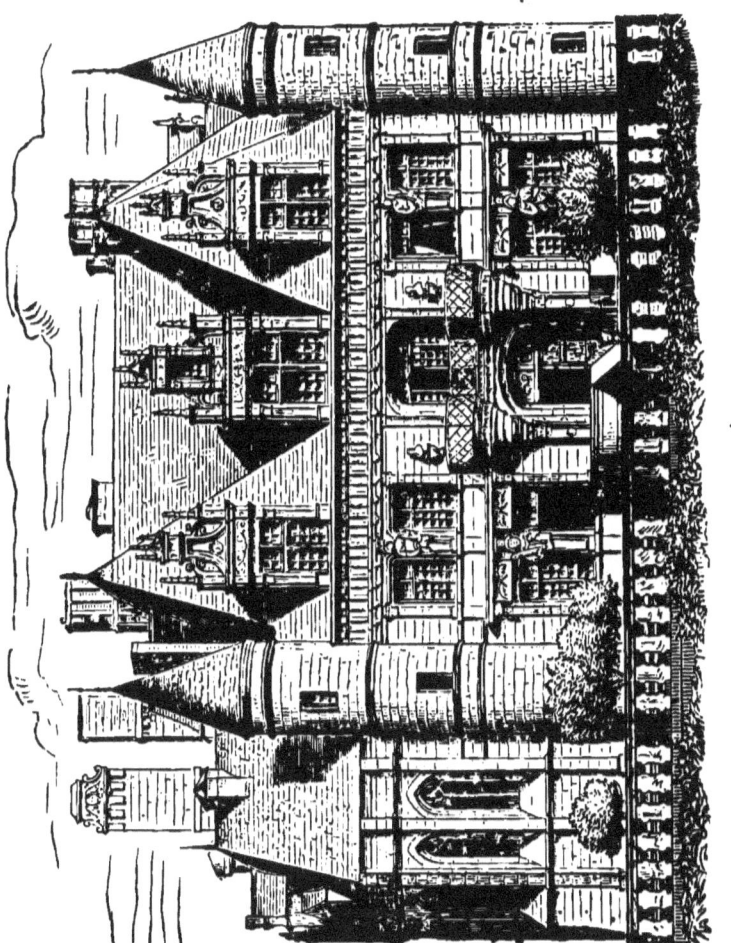

FIG. 28.—CHENONCEAU CHÂTEAU, FRANCE.
See pages 52, 166.

the mouldings over the lower large arch; also—but only approximately—between the upper edge of these mouldings and the capital of the column from which the middle large arch springs; also between this last and the lower edge of the mouldings above the middle large arch; and also—but here too only approximately—between the

FIG. 29.—WALKER MUSEUM, CHICAGO UNIVERSITY.
"COSMOPOLITAN MAGAZINE."
See page 52.

upper edge of these mouldings and the place from which the arch of the upper window springs. Two of these divisions have been indicated as being only approximately of the same height as the rest. With reference to this it may be suggested, first, that to one looking upward from below, as alone these divisions can be seen, the difference indicated would not be distinguishable, and, second, that probably few looking at the plan, as it lies before one in the figure, will not feel that, as a whole, it would be more satisfactory were these divisions, instead of being approximately the same, actually the same; will not feel, in other words, that the general arrangement would seem

FIG. 30.—CHOIR OF ELY CATHEDRAL, ENGLAND.
See pages 52, 56, 57, 163, 166.

more satisfactory, were the space between the lower string-course and the middle arch slightly higher, and the ceiling higher above the upper window, and rounder In addition to what has been said, it is scarcely necessary to point out the almost infinite instances of like measurements in the minute details of the ornamentation in Fig. 30; or how often these details are made to fit exactly two, three, four, or five times, as the case may be, into some larger feature of which they are constituent members. It is enough to remark that, while it is sometimes supposed to be otherwise, careful observation will detect that the beauty of Gothic as well as of Greek architecture is virtually inseparable from the minutest fulfilment, on the part of their architects, of these elementary principles of proportion.

This Fig. 30, page 55, may be made to illustrate two other facts. If the reader will glance along the upper part of the ornamentation over the stalls he will see that in many places, where there are no actual horizontal lines, the outlines are so arranged as to suggest these, and, therefore, through them, to suggest spaces with like measurements. It has been pointed out that, when two figures are related because of their relationships to related rectangles, it is desirable to have the lines of these rectangles indicated. Of course, in many cases this cannot be done. But, though not indicated, they may often be suggested, as in the outlines just noticed. At other times, as in the outlines of plants and animals, it may seem as if even suggestion were impossible. But, as we shall find, such is not the case as frequently as might be supposed.

The other fact which Fig. 30 may be made to illustrate is this. It will be observed that the different out-

PROPORTION IN THE HUMAN FORM.   57

lines and divisions in the large arches are made to seem in proportion because these arches themselves, in which they are framed, are in the main alike. In other words, figures of various outlines can be made to seem to be in proportion, when they are, or can be, framed not only in like

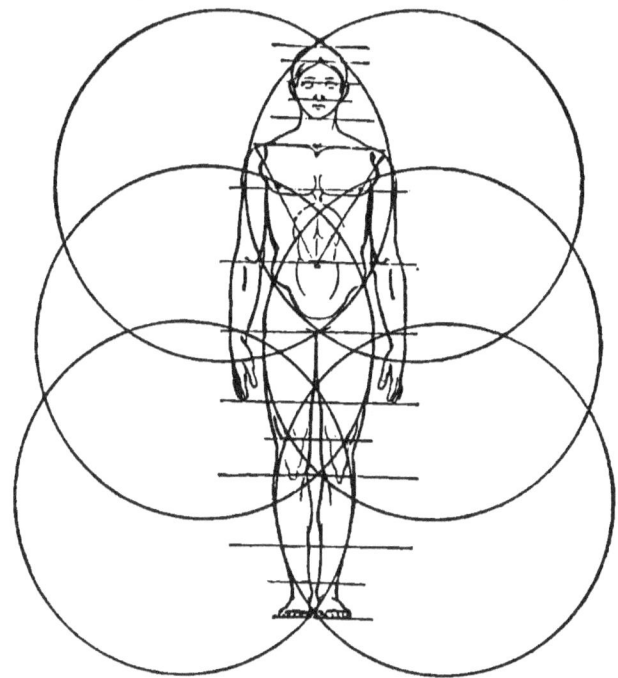

FIG. 31.—LINES AND CURVES INDICATING PROPORTIONS OF A FORM TAKEN FROM PUTNAM'S HANDBOOK.

See pages 15, 58, 59, 69, 72, 85, 87, 118, 120, 130, 131, 135, 137, 138, 290, 291, 295.

rectangles, but in any like figures whatever. The rectangle is used as an actual or ideal standard of comparison merely as a matter of convenience. It is comparatively easy to recognize whether or not straight lines, such as form its sides, are of the same lengths, or are the same distances apart, or have, in other regards, other measurements that are in proportion. It would be a mistake, however, to suppose that the standard of measurement is, or, in all cases, can be rectangular. Take the human form. It is ordinarily divided into equal parts by hori-

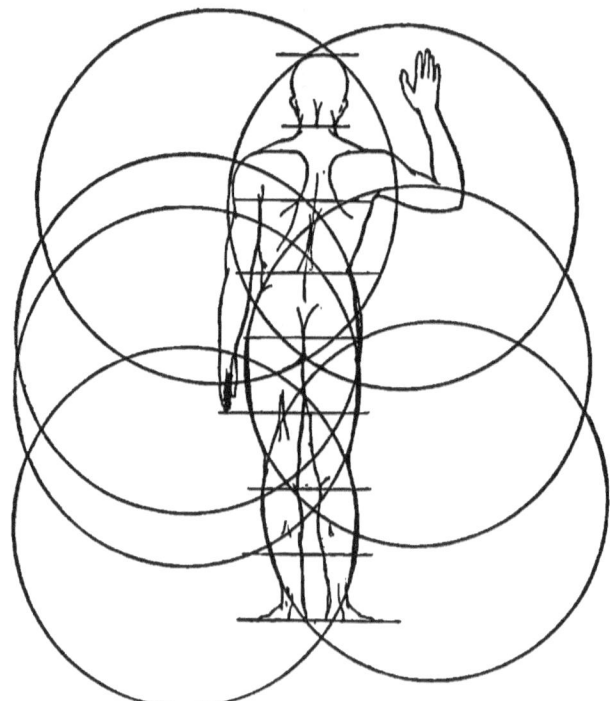

FIG. 32.—LINES AND CURVES INDICATING PROPORTIONS OF A FORM TAKEN FROM PUTNAM'S HANDBOOK.

See pages 15, 58, 59, 69, 85, 87, 118, 120, 130, 131, 135, 137, 290, 295.

zontal lines, such as may be seen in Fig. 31, page 57, and Fig 32; and these lines are undoubtedly an aid in determining the proportions. But, as will be shown on page 68, effective aid may be afforded by circles also, such as, in this book, are drawn about the forms in these figures not only, but also in Figs. 35, page 70; 36, page 71; 37, page 72; 45, page 86; 62, page 121; 72, page 136; 73, page 137; and 74, page 139; as well as by curves of a more varied character described on pages 60, 61, and 292. Notice also how the contours of all the human forms in the products represented in Figs. 55, page 101; 75, page 142; and 129, page 359, are arranged along lines of like curvature. Segments of curves, like those drawn about the figures mentioned in the sentence before the last, are almost always suggested to the mind when looking at the human figure; and it is mainly, perhaps, by likeness in these that the impression is conveyed—so important to æsthetic effects—of the fufilment of similar principles both in shape and in measurement.

But while this is true, it does not render less true the fact that the relationships of irregular figures are rendered much more easy to recognize, when so arranged that the measurements of their parts can be compared, each to each, with those resulting from the use of straight lines. Notice how the straight lines drawn about or through the outlines in Figs. 31, page 57; 32, page 58; 45, page 86; 62, page 121; 63, page 122; 69, page 128, facilitate the recognition of like divisions of spaces in these outlines.

A very interesting illustration of the aid afforded by straight lines to the perception of the fact that like is put with like, may be observed in Fig. 33, page 60, and Fig. 34, page 61. These figures contain the curve which Ruskin, in his "Modern Painters," vol. iv., chapter xvii., page 5, declares to be the most common in nature. It is the curve, too, certain like segments of which, as indicated in the paragraph before the last, furnish us with a standard for judging of shape and proportion in the human form. It is the curve which, outlining limbs of different lengths and breadths, gives a suggestion of similarity to the effects of the contours of the arms from shoulders to elbows, and from elbows to wrists; of the legs from hips to knees, and from knees to ankles, as well too as of larger parts of the frame, as from shoulders to heels, and also from hips to heels. The curve is one so described as to show a constant tendency to become straight, although never becoming straight. In Fig. 33,

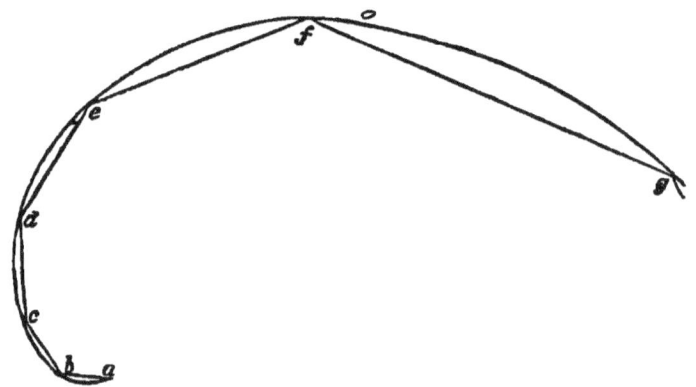

FIG. 33.—CURVE EXEMPLIFYING GRADATION.
See pages 59, 69, 294.

the angles at a, b, c, d, and e are in each case the same, but the line a—b becomes regularly shorter than b—c, and so on. In the direction of g, the curve a—g evidently inclines more and more to differ from the requirements of a circle, and to approximate a straight line. In Fig. 34, page 61, the distance between the lines A—a and B—b and C—c, etc., is the same, but the curved line a—b becomes regularly shorter than b—c, and so on. It is evident that in this figure the curve a—g, while constantly approaching the form of a straight line, can never become one. In "The

PROPORTION IN CURVES. 61

Genesis of Art-Form," page 283, it was asked why curves of this kind are seen so frequently in nature, and why, when they are seen, they are considered especially satisfactory? The answer suggested was that such curves necessarily fulfil the requirements of the methods developed from *comparison*,¹ as indicated in the chart on page 3. In the first figure, the angles at *a*, *b*, *c*, etc., are the same, and in the second figure the distances between the lines *A—a*, *B—b*, *C—c*, etc., are the same, while the differences in the divisions of lines in both figures are increased or diminished according to the same degrees or ratios. The principle of putting like measurements with like, therefore, enters into the formation of these curves, notwithstanding the constant tendency that they show toward a deviation from it. Each of the curves, too, is so constructed that any given part of it may be magnified so as to represent exactly *f—g*. There is therefore a sense in which these curves are formed in accordance with the methods indicated in the chart on page 3, under the heads not only of *comparison* and *repetition* but also of *gradation, transition,* and *progress.*¹

¹ There may be some who would like to have indicated here the exact way in which each of the methods of composition mentioned on page 3 can contribute to the effects of proportion. In "The Genesis of Art-Form," all these methods were said to result from the effort of the mind to reduce, in order to understand and use, the *variety* and *complexity* of nature to some form of *unity*. (Notice that, in this note, the words which are the same as the terms used for the art-methods in the chart on page 3 are italicized.) The means of attaining this *unity* was said to be classification, which is a

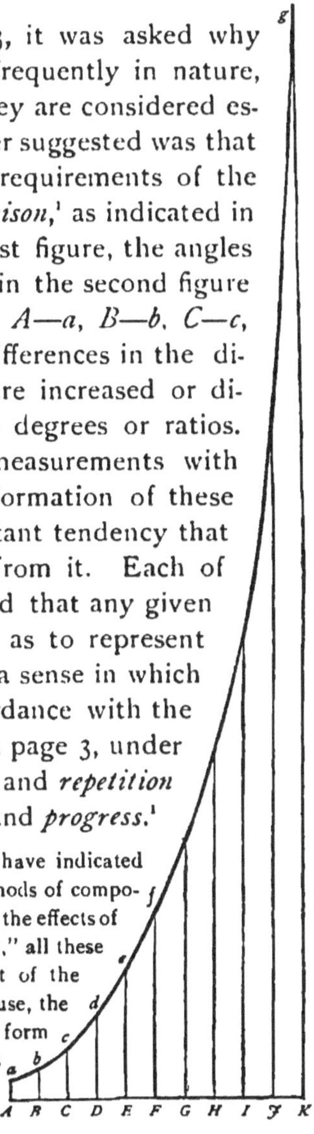

FIG. 34.—A CURVE EXEMPLIFYING GRADATION.

See pages 59, 69, 294.

As said at the beginning of the last paragraph, this illustration with its many straight lines will suggest the influence of these lines in causing a recognition of the fulfilment of the principle of proportion even in very subtle and complex curves. It cannot fail to be observed, however, that these straight lines, as drawn here,

process of putting into the same groups unlike complex wholes on the ground that they are alike in part. Dogs and wolves, for instance, are not alike as wholes, but they are in part. So scientific zoölogy puts them together. Buddhism and Christianity are not alike as wholes, but they are in part. So scientific religion puts them together. Art deals with external appearances. So in it, partially similar sounds or shapes are put together. But if they must be put together in such ways that they may be recognized to be in part alike, it is necessary, first of all, that they be arranged in accordance with some principle of *order* exercised sufficiently, at least, to cause the *confusion* of mere *variety* to be *counteracted* by the *grouping*. As applied to objects of sight, this would mean that no artistic effects can be produced by any number, say, of eyes, ears, fingers, feet, columns, capitals, steps, whatever they may be, when lying about in a disarranged condition. Their effects as related to proportion, for instance, would be impossible to determine before, by means of *orderly grouping*, the eyes, ears, fingers, feet, columns, capitals, or steps had been put into the places for which they were designed. Such a *grouping*, moreover, can be effective in revealing the proportions so as to be easily recognized in the degree only in which it is conducted on the principle of putting like factors side by side in such a way as to facilitate an exercise of *comparison*. That which enables the mind to perceive that one feature is not larger or smaller than it should be, and is, therefore, in proportion, is the fact that it is of the same measure as another feature, or as a part of some other feature with which, owing to the place in which it is *grouped*, it can readily be *compared*.

This is the *fundamental fact with reference to proportion*. That it has not been brought to light and emphasized, is little less than marvellous. But whether we look at an animal, a man, or a building, we recognize its members to be in proportion in the degree only in which we find large numbers of them that have like measurements, and others that are exact multiples of these. It is ordinarily supposed that we have discovered the proportions, as they are termed, when we have found one or two factors related to one another, say as $4:9$, or $7:12$, or $9:14$. This is an error. As has been already shown, we have not discovered the proportions,

are an afterthought, and that the connection between them and the effect of this kind of a curve is of a more occult character than that which has been said to be ascribable to proportion. That is to say, it is not of a character which can be considered to be distinctively apparent. But, in connection with this thought, the

until we have found not one or two but many factors, each of which is related to many others, and all of which are often related to all the others by the same or multiples of the same ratios.

Even when this has been done, however, inasmuch as no object is composed of features all of which are absolutely alike, there is necessarily involved a recognition of *contrast* also. In fact it is largely because of contrast in substances, as when wood is used together with stone, or in qualities, as when red color is used together with blue, that it is important that features should compare in shapes, sizes, or quantities, as in proportion. Just as in the arts appealing to the ear, the mind can perceive a reason why sounds compare, though produced by very different instruments and at very different degrees of pitch,—including, sometimes, the very inharmonious effects of drums and cymbals,—if only all these sounds together seem to be constituent factors of one general form of rhythm, so with the various effects appealing to the eye, in case they seem factors of one general form of *proportion*. The mind can readily recognize a basis of *comparison* between them, in case they be grouped so that like measurements are apparent. But in measurements there are often *contrasts* too. In such cases, as in others like them mentioned in Chapters II. to V. of "The Genesis of Art-Form," effects of *unity* may still be secured by grouping the factors in such ways that the contrasting features, where they cannot compare with others, shall *complement* them,—as, for instance, the head of a turtle complements its tail, and the head of a man his feet, or his arms his legs, or the roof of a house its foundation. It must not be forgotten, however, that, as *comparison* is the fundamental method, *principality* must in all cases be given to this method, while *subordination* must be given to the method of *contrast*. At the same time *balance* may be applied to many such features as have been mentioned, as well as to like eyes, ears, hands, feet, and windows and towers. These, though they cannot be placed together in the centre of a product, may all be grouped so as to occupy corresponding places at either side of the centre, and thus may all be made to be essential factors entering into the general *unity* of its *organic form*.

These statements are enough to indicate briefly in what sense proportion

reader needs to be reminded that the developments resulting from putting like with like according to the methods indicated in the chart on page 3, are manifested not only in rhythm and proportion but also in harmony, whether of sound or sight, the difference between the first two and the latter being that in the former we are con-

is a development of the earlier of the methods treated in "The Genesis of Art-Form," and mentioned in the chart on page 3. But let us go on. The three methods in which, according to the discussion in that book, *comparison* manifests itself, are by way of *congruity*, of *repetition*, and of *consonance*. As applied to proportion, comparison by way of *congruity* would lead to having the like divisions of spaces, large or small, or tending to either extreme, representative of the sentiment. By this is meant, as explained in Chapters III. to VI. of "Painting, Sculpture, and Architecture as Representative Arts," that such qualities as weight, importance, firmness, dignity, or nearness, whether in an animate or inanimate form, would be indicated by relative largeness; and that such qualities as lightness, unimportance, flexibility, grace, and remoteness, would be indicated by relative smallness. The thick wrists, ankles, fists, feet, and neck of a pugilist, or the heavy columns and entablatures of a Greek temple, mean one thing, and the slight wrists, ankles, fingers, feet, and neck of a dancer, or the light shafts and pointed arches of a Gothic cathedral, mean another thing.

Owing to the *variety*, however, always characterizing every object in nature, there are frequently delicate features,—eyes, ears, nose, mouth, fingers, and limbs, as the case may be, even upon a pugilist; as well as delicate carvings and mouldings amid the weightier effects of a Greek temple; while opposite characteristics may be seen in the form of the dancer or of the Gothic temple. These exceptions, though introducing *incongruity*, may nevertheless, by similarity in measurements, in a single direction, as in length alone, or in breadth alone, be *in proportion*, and together with the features which are wholly *congruous*, enhance the proportional *comprehensiveness* of the general result.

When assuming postures, to suggest thought through a representation of arrested motion, as well as to meet the requirements of the laws of perspective, the forms of men and animals, as also, for other reasons, those of landscapes and buildings, have to be arranged, as explained in Chapters X. and XI. of "The Genesis of Art-Form," with reference to one *central-point* of view. Vitruvius, in his "De Architectura," tells us that, with the Greeks, "every posture of action, as in walking, wrestling, boxing, was mathemati-

scious of the elements that are put together, and in the latter we are not conscious of them, and can only become aware of them as a result of scientific demonstration. At the same time, there are both sounds and sights which are in the border-land, as we may term it, between these two conditions. For instance, in the deepest bass-note of the

cally studied ; and the line of the centre of gravity was carefully marked ; whèh the position of each limb and the breadth of each portion of the whole frame, first conceived to be located in a circumscribed circle or square, and then in an enclosed cube or square, was measured with the greatest accuracy " ; and we shall find in Chapter XIV. that an analogous method was practised by the same people in determining the proportions of architecture. These facts are noteworthy because it is evident that, while such arrangements about a *central-point*, in connection with the extremities, treated as in what is called in the chart on page 3 *setting*, do not change the necessity for like measurements or multiples of measurements, they do change, decidedly, the actual measurements. A foreshortened limb represented as thrust forward toward us from a picture must be actually drawn much shorter than another of exactly the same size in nature. Otherwise we should say that the foreshortened limb was out of proportion. Thus we see that proportion has to do with *central-point* and *setting;* and an analogous connection will be shown in Chapter XIV. to exist between it and the same principles of perspective as applied to architecture.

Again, when members, especially those connected with organized life as in animals and human beings, are arranged in accordance with the requirements of *central-point* and *setting*, it is evident that the recognition of likeness in measurements or multiples of measurements, may be greatly facilitated through the method of *parallelism*. Even when a body is in repose, similar general lines of direction, either horizontal, as in those of the eyes, mouth, and shoulders, or vertical, as in those of columns or of window sides, enable us easily to compare their measurements. The method is needed still more when objects are not in repose, when limbs are apparently thrust out at all angles from a body, or when roofs and spires project from a building. Then, only *parallelism* between two or more directions can enable us readily to estimate the relative measurements ; and only many instances of *parallelism* in the features at either side of a form, can enable us to perceive clearly that these are well balanced. And it is only when *parallelism*, as thus revealing *balance*, has had its perfect work, that we can say that a form is *in proportion* in the sense in which we use the word when we refer

organ we can distinguish vibrations allying its effects to those of rhythm almost as clearly as we can distinguish pitch allying them to those of harmony. So in the case of this particular curve, a reason for the use of which is indicated here in accordance with the principles of propor-

to what is termed its *symmetry*. See Chapters X. and XI. of "The Genesis of Art-Form."

The connection between proportion and comparison by way of *repetition*, *alteration*, *alternation*, hardly needs to be mentioned. By-and-by it will be shown how many like measurements there are both in bodies animate and inanimate, and in buildings, facilitating thus the recognition of proportion not only by way of *repetition* but of *massing*. Of course, however, few of these features do not manifest also *alteration*. Moreover, as many of them are absolutely unique like noses and mouths amid eyes and ears, or doors amid windows, and spires amid roofs, they exemplify *interspersion*. Frequently, too, as do fingers and columns with their intervening spaces, they exemplify *alternation*, and, less frequently perhaps, as intertwining limbs in active figures, and as interlacing arches and groinings of roofs, they exemplify *complication*, and, when lines, though interrupted, are continued, they exemplify *continuity*. See " The Genesis of Art-Form," Chapter XIV. In connection with none of these methods, however, can the different features composing the form be said to be in proportion, except so far as in length or in breadth or in some other regard they apparently manifest like measurements or like multiples of these.

Features are said to be in proportion, in the sense of fulfilling the method of *consonance*, when they exemplify like principles of formation. These are exemplified when like measurements or multiples of these appear to separate or determine different parts of their shapes. If, for instance, there be a similarity of shape between the upper line of the eyebrows and the lower line of the hair on the forehead, we admire what we term the proportions of the forehead. Or if, in postures, there be given from a side view a similar bend to the elbow and to the hip, or to the wrist and to the knee, a bend, *i.e.*, of such a kind that many curves and angles seem similar, and many lines seem parallel—in this case too we admire what we term the proportions, by which we mean the similar or symmetrical measurements of the spaces between the respective curves, angles, and lines ; and an analogous principle evidently applies to square, round, or angular window-caps, arches, and gables. Even where there is not consonance but *dissonance*, proportion may still appear to be a characteristic, in case the products manifest the

tion,—this explanation will not prevent another, and perhaps a better one, which will be given on page 292, and which ascribes it to the principles underlying harmony of outline.

Figs. 31 to 34 have shown how, when of equal length

same general measurements between the features, even though, specifically considered, these be differently shaped, as is the case where there is the same distance from the hair of the forehead to the middle of the eye-space, that there is from the latter to the nostrils, or from the nostrils to the tip of the chin. See page 86. So too with the façade of a building in which the forms considered in themselves are unlike. They may, nevertheless, be separated by like spaces. See Chapters IX. and X. The same likeness of spaces may cause proportion where there is *interchange*, as when, descending from the two eyes and ears through the one nose but with two nostrils, a *transition* is made to a single feature, the mouth and chin; or when, descending from arched windows in an upper storey of a building through straight window-caps but an arched doorway in a lower storey, a *transition* is made to uniformly straight window-caps and door-caps in a basement. *Interchange*, as thus interpreted, and also as explained in Chapter XVII. of "The Genesis of Art-Form," is merely one of a general series of links that we have in *gradation*; but, as related to proportion, this last method, as well as that of *abruptness*, has chiefly to do with arrangements through which, by means of curves or angles (see "The Genesis of Art-Form," pages 282-9), a *transition* is made in the *progress* of the general outline from one measurement or series of measurements to another or others. No artist hesitates to speak of the proportions of the human figure as determined not merely by measurements, as is the case primarily, but also (see Chapter VIII.) by the curves or angles through which a member with a certain form is made to pass into one with another, as, for instance, the breast into the waist, the waist into the hips, the calf into the ankle, or the ankle into the foot; and the same is true of the phrases used in order to express the way in which columns are made to pass into arches, and arches into groinings, or into other ornamental features of a ceiling above them. Inasmuch, also, as light and shade and color have to do with producing the apparent effects of form upon the eye,—that is, in causing them to appear as curves, angles, or squares,—it will be seen, as was said on pages 6 and 7, that just as there is a virtually inseparable connection between rhythm and harmony as appealing to hearing, so too there is a similar connection between proportion and harmony as appealing to sight.

or separated by equal distances, straight lines drawn about or through forms facilitate the recognition of the fact that certain segments of curved outlines are in proportion. As has been said, these straight lines with or without rectangles are used for this purpose as a matter of convenience. It is hardly necessary to add that the same conditions might sometimes cause the standard for judging of the proportions of adjacent outlines to be something else than straight lines, or than any combinations of them, as in squares, triangles, or rectangles. As applied, for instance, to almost all curved lines, this standard would be some regular curve, as in an ellipse or a circle. Of these two, the latter may be said to furnish in some regards a standard of comparison the most satisfactory of any. The circle is more regular, and thus more in accordance with the fundamental principle of proportion than is even the square. Every segment of a regular circumference illustrates a like degree of curvature, and is at a like distance from the centre, as well as from a segment of the circumference exactly opposite itself. The ellipse, too, though not so regular as the circle, is sufficiently regular for practical purposes. See the dotted lines especially in the two upper drawings in Fig. 120, page 285. In the ellipse the opposite sides, though illustrating *contrast* by way of direction, illustrate *comparison* also by way of *complement*. See the chart on page 3. Besides this, as D. R. Hay says in his "Ornamental Geometric Diaper Designs as Applied to the Decorative Arts," the ellipse " possesses that essential constituent of beauty, variety. Its outline being formed by two radii, one of which is continually decreasing while the other is increasing, it imperceptibly varies from an oblate to an acute curve,"— a method of variation not essentially different in principle, as will be noticed, from that which was shown on page 61, to be fulfilled in the curves in Figs. 33 and 34. For the reasons just stated, either the circle or the ellipse may be made a standard of comparison by which to judge of the relative measurements, or—what is the same thing —the proportions of contours drawn about it or within it; and, of course, in case outlines are curved a curved standard is much more satisfactory than one that is rectangular. Attention has already been directed to the suggestions of like segments of circles such as are made to describe the chief curves in the foremost outlines of the human form in Figs. 31, page 57, and 32, page 58. There is a reason for the use of these circles as a standard of measurement derived from the physiological requirements of the eye, especially in binocular vision. This reason will be found unfolded in Chapter XVI. Here it is sufficient to say that the circumference of each of the two circles in the same horizontal plane represents the sphere of the distinct—not entire—vision of one eye, and that when all the circumferences of the circles described about the same figure are the same, the eyes are supposed to be focussed for distinct vision at exactly the same distance. At a certain distance from the form, for instance, all the circles are of one size, but nearer than this all of them are of another size.

All, too, are attached in this book to figures drawn not by the author but by others to represent what they supposed to be approximately perfect proportions. Is it not remarkable that such like circles outline so many general features of the contour when viewed from the distance represented in Figs. 35, page 70, and 37, page 72, and also so many particular features of the same when viewed from the distance represented in Fig. 36, page 71? Similar circles would have been described about the statues depicted in this volume, had not the pose of these been necessarily such as in most cases to throw the limbs slightly out of an upright position. But any one who will go over any representations of the human figure with

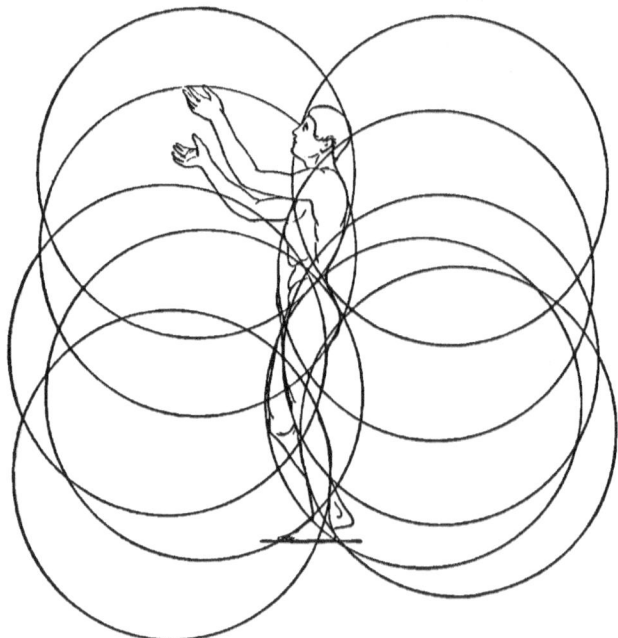

FIG. 35.—CIRCLES DRAWN ABOUT A FORM TAKEN FROM PUTNAM'S HANDBOOK. SIDE VIEW.

See pages 15, 59, 69, 87, 134, 135, 141, 290, 295.

compasses will be surprised to find how large a part of a segment of exactly the same circle fits either the bend of the calf, forearm, thigh, abdomen, chest, or back. If then his experience—say at a bathing-place—causes him to recall the æsthetic influences of such formations as a long arm or leg combined with great leanness, or a small chest combined with an abnormally large abdomen, he will find upon reflection that the effects of disproportion, while attributable partly to association, are also attributable partly to a recognition of an absence of like curves. Or, to illustrate this fact from a contrary condition, everybody admires a small ankle and a good-sized calf. Yet the moment the calf becomes so large proportionately as to interfere with the suggestions of a like curve in this, and in the outlines of the hip, almost everybody is conscious of receiving a suggestion of disproportion. With reference to these circles drawn about the forms, it will be noticed too that in the case of a man there is a like degree in which the two horizontal circumferences separate, being as much nearer

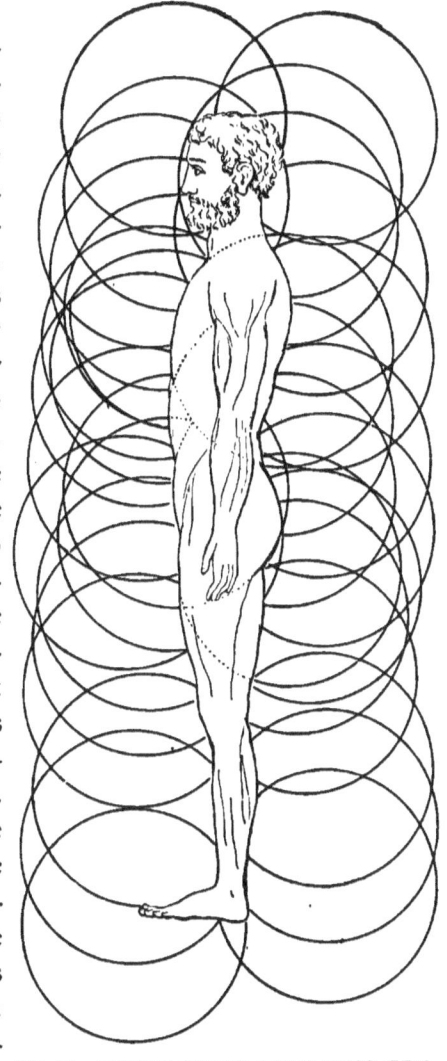

FIG. 36.—CIRCLES DRAWN ABOUT HAY'S IDEAL MAN. SIDE VIEW.

See pages 15, 59, 69, 72, 87, 133, 134, 135, 290, 295.

72   PROPORTION AND HARMONY.

together at the shoulders than at the hips as they are nearer together there than at the calves. (See Figs. 31, page 57; 36, page 71 ; and 73, page 137.) In the case of a woman, the circles seem to be very nearly at the same distance apart at the hips as at the shoulders. (See Fig. 37; and Fig. 74, page 139.) Whatever the arrangements may be, however, it is evident that, as applied to these as well as to

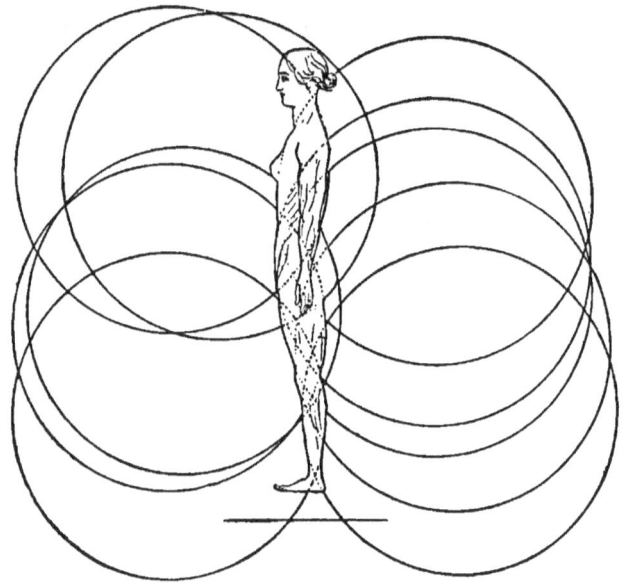

FIG. 37.—CIRCLES DRAWN ABOUT HAY'S IDEAL WOMAN. SIDE VIEW.
See pages 59, 69, 72, 87, 134, 295.

others that will be mentioned hereafter, we may draw the general conclusion that the proportions of human figures and, probably, of all natural figures, may be said to conform to certain straight, rectangular, or circular standards of measurement which, or the ratios between which, may be conveniently compared.

CHAPTER VI.

PROPORTION IN LANDSCAPES, PLANTS, ANIMALS, AND
THE SURROUNDINGS OF HUMAN FORMS.

Outlines and Figures Used as Standards of Comparison in Measurements—Can be Used even in Connection with Accurate Imitation of Nature—Application of the Principle to Landscape—To Forms of Vegetable and Animal Life—To the Arranging of the Surroundings of the Human Form—In Stained-Glass Windows—In Clothing—Neglect of this Opportunity—The Mind's Satisfaction in a Partial Application of the Principle—Surrounding Arrangements in Connection with no Clothing.

IN the preceding chapter it was shown that simple outlines and figures, such as characterize regularly constructed triangles, squares, rectangles, circles, ellipses, etc., may be used as standards of comparison through which to determine the relative space-dimensions of complex and more or less irregular outlines and figures. It was said also that these simpler outlines and figures described through or about the more complex ones may be either actually outlined or merely ideally imagined. Of course, in all cases they can be actually outlined by the artist during the preparatory stages of his work. But it is not of these that we are now speaking, but of their results and of the methods of recognizing the proportions in the product, which is often a complex and more or less irregular figure. In forms imitating nature, as represented in painting and sculpture, it might be supposed that any simpler outlines or figures revealing the proportions must, in every case, be left to be imagined. In other words, it might be supposed that no such outlines or figures could be made apparent in connection with the representations of hills, valleys, rivers, trees, plants, animals, or human beings.

Yet why should this be supposed? Natural speech is not always rhythmical, at least not in that higher sense in which it is also metrical. Yet a dramatic poet, in his artistic representation of speech, may make it so. In the same way, why may not a painter or sculptor, whether or not a form or collection of forms manifest proportion in nature, make it do so in his artistic treatment? The main requisite of proportion, as we have found, is to have some apparently like standard of measurement into which certain parts or sets of parts in an object of sight are divided; and there are innumerable methods, not involving any lack of exactness in imitation, through which this result may be attained. Take a mountain scene. A selection of one point of view only a hundred feet away from another may entirely change the suggestion of like divisions afforded by the lines of distant and nearer ridges, of snow or flora of different characters, and of the borders of lakes or rivers. Or take a scene involving, apparently, much greater irregularity, as in Fig. 38, page 75. Upon first glancing at this, one may think that there is neither need nor evidence of any regard for proportion in it. But if what has been said thus far in this volume be true, effects of proportion, æsthetically considered, are always important; and an absence of them will always exert some influence, even though the spectator may not be conscious of the source of it. With this thought in mind, let us see if we can find any evidence of a regard for proportion in this particular painting. Recalling that

FIG. 38.—THE CANAL BY COROT.
See pages 74-77, 363, 365, 369.

the measurements for which we are in search need to be alike not in the object itself but in the appearance which it presents, and beginning at the right margin, notice the same apparent distance between it and a part of the bush near the bottom of the picture; then the same distance between this bush and the first tree to the left of it; then notice about half this same distance (1 : 2) between this tree and another to the left of it ; then once more notice the whole of the distance first mentioned between this other tree and the next tree to the left ; then the same distance between this last tree and the white form of the man ; also between this and the left side of the bright water-space; also between this last and the left side of the dark water-space ; also between this last and the end of the boat ; then apparently the same distance, at the extreme rear, between the line of tall trees and the darker bank at the left of them ; also the same between the beginning of this darker bank and the beginning of a still darker bank to the left of it ; also the same between this last and one of the two stakes on the river's bank ; then, after an interval of about half this distance (1 : 2), another stake, and finally the same distance as that separating the most of the objects mentioned between this second stake and the left margin. Besides this, notice other subsidiary sets of like distances—for instance, the four and one half like dimensions into which, by the man's form and the water-shadows, the top of the boat seems to be divided ; also the five and one half like distances between the tall trees and the left margin indicated by the general outlines of the small trees at the rear ; again notice another like distance separating the lower margin of the picture from the water-end of the boat, also this latter from the lower water-line of the bank at the rear, and this latter again from the top of the small tree above the bank. Not less apparent is still another like distance separating the lower margin of the picture from the bank at the rear of the water, and this again from the top of the tree a little to the left of the centre of the picture, and this tree-top again from the upper margin. Another like distance can be observed too between the lower margin, the white shoulders of the man, the white line at the top of the foliage, and the white sky appearing under the leaves of the trees. Notice, again, the smaller subsidiary divisions in the arrangements of the banks and their shadows at the rear. Once more as an aid to effects of proportion, because allying the whole to regularity, observe also the parallelism of the trunks of the high trees and the concentration of radiating lines at the left of the centre,—lines formed by shadows, banks, or foliage, but all together entering unmistakably into the general effect. Nor can we consider it without design that the light and dark effects in the picture seem to be distributed in very nearly equal quantities. So much for the evidences of proportion in this picture, which has been selected for the very reason that, at first, it might not be supposed to contain any such evidences. Yet they are there. Nor, in connection with them, is there the slightest suggestion of artificiality. The painting accurately represents nature, and nature deprived of none of its variety. But if the artistic representation did not fulfil the requirements of proportion, it might be no more entitled to be considered a work of art than would be a poem, if devoid of rhythm.

Unlike the outlines of inanimate nature, those of vegetable and animal life are always proportional in themselves. Trees and bushes as wholes, as also their trunks, limbs, and leaves, invariably suggest similar measurements, or, at least, approximately similar measurements, in that they are *balancing*, *complementary*, or *parallel*, as on opposite sides of triangles, squares, circles, ellipses, or their combinations. See the chart on page 3 ; also the note beginning on page 61. This similarity in measurement is sufficiently suggested, as in the shape of a tree and its branches, or of a leaf and its veinings, in Fig. 39, below, and of quadrupeds, birds, and fishes, in Fig. 122, page 289. What most concerns the student of art is the application of the principle to the human form, both because it is this to which, necessarily, artistic representation is mainly confined, and because, being the most complex of all forms, it is the one necessitating requirements of proportion that are the most difficult to explain.

FIG. 39.—RADIATION IN NATURAL FORMS.
See pages 78, 288.

Of the human form, it seems logical to begin by saying that, as usually represented, it is almost always possible to suggest the proportions through a use of outlines surrounding it, as in shrubbery, upholstery, drapery, or clothing. For instance, take the outlining conditions of pictures produced upon stained glass, especially in windows. Such windows are always constructed on a network of bars which cannot be hidden ; and these necessitate dividing whatever is represented on the glass into certain parts. See Fig. 40, on this page. Why has it never occurred to artists to have these bars divide human forms, when crossing them, into parts of like longitudinal dimensions? Straight lines, as intimated on page 58, cannot give us, perhaps, the most important indication of the measurements determining the proportions of the human form. But such lines can give us some indication, and, so far as they do this, the artist, alive to his opportunities, will utilize them, it being an elementary principle in art that its necessary limitations should be made to add to its effectiveness.

These bars in windows of stained glass furnish art exceptional opportunities. Like ones are afforded in almost every other case in which the human form is represented. But how seldom does the thought of utilizing them occur to the painter or sculptor, not to speak of the originator of styles of clothing? It is sometimes supposed that these latter need fulfil no æsthetic principles,—that men will think beautiful any style to which they

FIG. 40.—OLD GLASS OF 14TH CENTURY.
See page 79.

have become accustomed. But they will not think it beautiful—whatever word they may use in order to express their thought of it; at best, they will merely think it fitting, because it is conventional; and for the same reason, too, they may think any other style inappropriate. But in some way, which possibly they cannot explain, perhaps not even recognize, life for them will be deprived of certain legitimate æsthetic influences, the presence of which might enrich their experience. This statement applies not only to the use of form and color, but also of proportion. How easy it would be to cause the cut of the garments to reveal the four, five, six, or eight parts of equal lengths into which the height of the well proportioned body is divisible! A line below the knee, whether of skirt or breeches; a line at the middle, whether of girdle or waistcoat; a line in the centre of the breast, whether of bodice or vest, together with other lines, always divide the figure satisfactorily. These lines, as intimated on page

FIG. 41.—COSTUMES DIVIDING HUMAN FORMS PROPORTIONATELY.
See pages 80, 81.

58, may not indicate that which is most important in the proportions of the human figure. But so far as they go, they furnish a method of representing proportion with which the art of the costumer cannot afford to dispense.

Notice this fact as illustrated in certain universally admired costumes of different periods, as sketched in Fig. 41, page 80. The first figure to the left shows a division into four equal parts; the next figure to the right of it, a division into five equal parts; and the next two figures, divisions into six equal parts. This next Fig., 42, shows

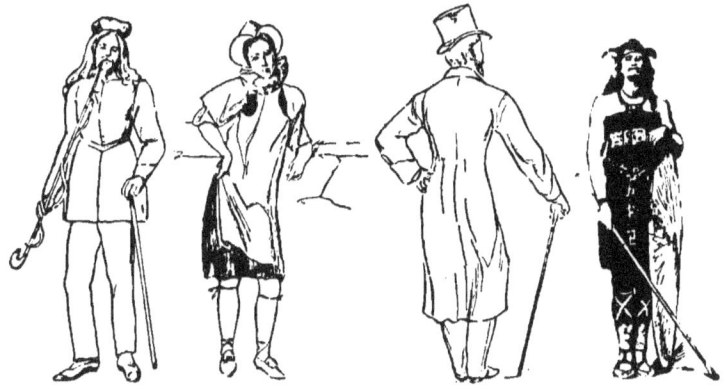

FIG. 42.—COSTUMES NOT DIVIDING HUMAN FORMS PROPORTIONATELY.
See pages 81, 82.

costumes, fashionable and not fashionable, in which there are no suggestions of equal divisions. A glance at the results will be enough to reveal their unæsthetic effects, and that they are due to a lack of likeness in measurements.

Why is the influence of the arrangements just indicated not recognized more frequently? Why do even those who design costumes for the stage disregard them? Why do they not, through a little judicious deceit, if needed, in the use of straight lines and curves, as well as of color, cultivate and satisfy, with reference to less favored forms, one's sense of beauty? In fact, how can either artists or

82   *PROPORTION AND HARMONY.*

costumers afford to neglect, as they almost invariably do, their very great opportunities in these directions?

On the principle that a half-loaf is better than none, the mind, when these like divisions are not revealed in the arrangements of the form as a whole, seems to wish to see them revealed in, at least, a part of it. Thus the like distance suggested between the top of the shoe and the upper shoe-strings, and between the garter and the bottom of the skirt, in the second figure from the left in Fig. 42, page 81, does something, though, of course, very little, to redeem the general lack of proportional effects which the other outlines manifest. So in Fig. 71, page 134, the two equal distances suggested between the ankles and the waistband of the breeches; and the two, unequal to the former, but equal to each other, between the bottom of the coat and the top of the head, and between the shoulder and the tips of the fingers of the left hand; and the three equal distances in the right arm, all afford, so

FIG. 43.—A NEW GUINEA CHIEF.
See pages 83, 130, 131, 132, 133, 141.

far as they go, a certain degree of æsthetic satisfaction. In Fig. 43, page 82, there is no clothing to spare. But observe how greatly that which accidentally happens to be present enhances the artistic interest. First of all, notice that the extremities—by head-gear, wristlets, or anklets—are separated from the rest of the body, and are not included in the equal divisions suggested in it. But aside from the extremities, the form seems to be equally divided above the anklets by the bands about the calves, by the staff, by the girdle, by the ornament on the breast in connection with the bands about the upper arms, and by the band about the neck. It is well to observe, moreover, that the separation of the extremities, necessary to the apparent division of this figure into equal parts, corresponds to a method to which we are all more or less accustomed. We cannot look at a boy in knickerbockers, for instance, without instinctively comparing the distance between the tops of his shoes at the ankles and the bottom of his breeches with a like distance between this point and the bottom of his jacket. Nor can we fail to compare the length of a lady's bare arm between the top of her glove and the elbow with the length from there to the sleeve. In other words, as has been said, when judging of proportions, we instinctively separate from the form the extremities. At the same time, this does not prevent, as shown on pages 130 and 133, our expecting to find ascertainable ratios between the length of the foot below the ankle, or the length of the hand below the wrist, and the measurement of the leg or of the arm above it.

Even when the whole form is exposed, it is possible, as in some of the Greek statues, to suggest, by surrounding arrangements or drapery, these results of like measurements. The Apollo Belvedere, for instance, Fig. 44, page 84, seems to be divided according to the very simple ratios of 1 : 2, 1 : 4, 1 : 8, 2 : 4, 2 : 8, and 4 : 8. The whole height of the body is apparently separated, just at the broadest part of the hips, into two parts, the half below the middle to be separated into two parts at the knees, and the half above the middle to be separated into the same by the lower line of the scarf surrounding the neck, while the chin is just half-way from the bottom of this scarf to the top of the head. The trunk of the tree on which the right hand leans, measures, perpendicularly, — it inclines somewhat, — the same as half the height of the body. So does the scarf from its upper point above the left shoulder to its lower border. The scarf, again, divides into two equal parts, one extending from its extreme outer edge on the right shoulder to its outer edge on the left shoulder, and the other from the latter point to its extreme border on the left. Once more, the measurement from the left side of the scarf below the left shoulder to the tips of the fingers in the right hand appears the same as half the height of the body, and near the right elbow this last measurement again is divided into two equal parts.

FIG. 44.—THE APOLLO BELVEDERE.
See pages 83, 84, 98, 99, 102, 131, 132, 141.

CHAPTER VII.

PROPORTIONS OF THE HUMAN FIGURE THEORETICALLY CONSIDERED.

Proportion as Suggested by Imaginary as well as Real Lines Drawn through the Form—Illustrated in the Case of the Face—Of other Parts of the Body—The Fact that Æsthetic Judgments of the Form are Based on Comparative Measurements—The Standards of Measurements Determined by Observation—Observation of Nature Essential to Successful Art—Especially to Representations of the Human Form—Opportunities for Observing this in Greece—Proof that the Excellence of Greek Sculpture was Influenced by this Opportunity—The Conventionality of the Face on Greek Sculpture no Argument against this—Other Reasons why the Greek Face was Conventional—The Greek Statues not Literal Imitations—But their very Differences Show the Influence of the Study of Nature—Connection between Form and Significance in all the Arts—Especially of those Representing the Human Form—Physiological Basis for this View—An Objection to it—Disguising Concealment of the Form in Civilized Clothing—Disenchanting Exposure of it in Conventional Art—The Mean between these Extremes—Different Proportions as Appealing to Different Tastes, and as Vehicles of Different Vibratory Spiritual Influences.

WHEN we come to consider the human body aside from all possible suggestions afforded by the surroundings, it might be supposed that the influence of such lines as are drawn through it or through parts of it, in Figs. 31, page 57, and 32, page 58, might not be felt because they are not actually present. Nevertheless, because they are ideally present, they have some influence.

If, for instance, a person be facing us, it is almost impossible not to suppose an imaginary vertical straight line drawn from the middle of his forehead to the middle of his chin, as in Fig. 45, below, and if we find this line passing through the middle of his nose, we obtain an impression of regularity which, so far as concerns it alone, is an aid to the agreeableness and consequent beauty of the effect ; but in the degree in which the middle of the nose is out of this vertical line, not only irregularity but ugliness is suggested. A similar tendency of thought causes us to suppose other imaginary vertical straight lines, drawn, as in the same Fig. 45, at equal distances

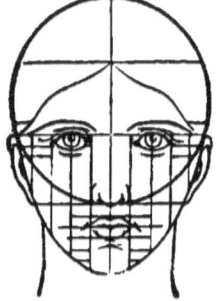

FIG. 45.—FRONT FACE DIVIDED BY LINES.
See pages 15, 59, 86, 87, 105, 120, 125, 126, 128, 129, 134, 141, 295.

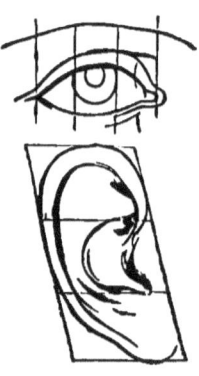

FIG. 46.—EYE AND EAR.
See pages 86, 87, 141.

from this central line ; and from them we may gain an impression of relative regularity by noticing to what extent the lines pass through corresponding sides of the face. Besides this, we are prompted to suppose horizontal lines drawn, as indicated in the same figure, across the forehead, eyes, and mouth ; and from these lines, too, we form judgments with reference to the degrees of regularity. If the hair be farther down on one side of the forehead than on the other, or if the arch of the eyebrows be not symmetrically rounded, or if the sides of the mouth incline downward or upward, or a lip be larger on one side than on the other, we notice the fact. Of course we do this, only so far as we compare the result with that of an imaginary straight line drawn through the feature.

The same is true, too, with reference to lines dividing other parts of the body. If one part of an eye or ear (see Fig. 46, page 86), or if a neck, or hand, or trunk, or leg, be, relatively to other features of the frame, too long, or too short, we perceive the defect almost immediately; but we can only do it as a result of ideally drawing such lines as are in Figs. 45 and 46, and measuring and comparing the distances between them. In the same way, the similarity in curvature suggested by the outer lines of calves, thighs, and shoulders, prompts us to imagine similar curves drawn somewhat as in Figs. 31, page 57; 32, page 58; 35, page 70; 36, page 71; 37, page 72; 73, page 137; and 74, page 139, concerning which see pages 135 to 138; and in case there be any deviation in outline from conformity to a segment of one of these curves, the eye will observe the fact; and the parts of the contours about which they are described will not seem to be constructed on the same lines, as we say, and, therefore, will not seem to be in proportion. So much as to the general principles in accordance with which such lines are made the basis of æsthetic judgments, either because they are actually delineated or are merely imagined.

As for the fact that these æsthetic judgments take place, and that they take place, as was said on page 23, as a result of comparing measurements, this is an almost necessary inference from the phrases used by men when speaking of the subject. Though willing to admit that they cannot exactly define what they mean, all are generally ready to express the opinion that, as compared with other surrounding features, a shoulder, arm, nose, ankle, foot, is or is not in proportion, or that the form, as a whole, is or is not well proportioned. The tendency to form such judgments, too, so far as can be ascertained, has existed from very early times, influencing not only the theory of art, but also its practice. The Egyptians endeavored to embody their conceptions of the methods of determining proportion by dividing the height of the body into fifteen equal sections, and the Greeks, as we shall find presently, into six or eight.

Before deciding which, if any, of these methods is preferable, let us begin by asking, first, how we are to come to a decision. The answer, of course, is by making a study of the human form. But how shall we make this study? In our own day, no one would concede that this could be done except through some method founded upon observation. Readers of this book have probably had their attention drawn to the measurements published by D. A. Sargent, M.D., of Harvard College, in his articles entitled "The Proportions of the Typical Man," "Physical Characteristics of the Athlete," and "Physical Development of Woman," published in "Scribner's Magazine," of the dates, respectively, of July, 1887, November, 1887, and February, 1889. These measurements were the results of the examination of large numbers of subjects, many of whom, by their success in wrestling, running, ball-playing, and other gymnastic work, had shown certain parts of their bodies to be well developed ; and the articles furnish, for estimating the proportions of the typical man, one method, at least, thoroughly scientific. In connection with this, to many parts of the body thus tested the methods of composite photography may now be applied.

Indeed, there is no reason why standards for the guidance of artists should not be furnished in our age far more scientific than any that were ever before conceived.

It must not be supposed, however, that the general recognition of the necessity of observation is, in any sense, peculiar to modern times. Though induction, as a philosophic method, was not formulated till the time of Bacon, it has been practised ever since the origin of the human mind; and in every period of high attainment it has been practised extensively. Nor does the history of art furnish any exception to this statement, though, at many different periods, certain works have been produced in large numbers on the supposition that mere theories of form, originally derived, of course, from nature, but finally held independently of it, could be substituted for continued and careful observation. We find such works among the remains of the arts of Egypt and Assyria, as well as of Greece prior to the time of Dædalus. We find them in the painting and sculpture of the primitive Christians, and of the Middle Ages. We find them in the conventional flowers and leaves wrought into the decorations of the earlier Gothic cathedrals. We find them in many of the figures and landscapes of the arts of China and Japan; and we find them in designs for illustrations of books and for ornamentations on walls, even in elaborately wrought products of the decorative and what is termed the decadent art of our own day; but we find them in the foremost products of no age or style in which art is acknowledged to have been at its best.

What is true of the representation of other appearances in the world about us, is true of that of the human figure. It is as impossible to produce successful pictures or statues of any kind without studying, at every stage, the forms of visible nature, as to produce successful poems without studying, at every stage, the forms of audible speech. Those who imagine that by looking elsewhere than to nature they can find guidance which is a substitute for it, have not read aright the history of art, and do not understand the character of its mission.

If, with this thought in mind, we look farther into the subject, we shall find that never—except, perhaps, in Japan—among a people sufficiently cultivated to avail themselves of their æsthetic advantages, have such opportunities been afforded for observing the human form under the best conditions, whether at rest or in motion, as among the ancient Greeks. Owing to the peculiar nature of their social, civil, and religious habits and observances, they became accustomed, as an every-day occurrence, to gaze upon this form in a state but slightly removed from that of nature. The artist of the present is obliged to make his observations upon a small number who follow the profession of posing in the presence of painters and sculptors only, and, of course, with all the self-consciousness that their employment involves. The artist of Athens could choose from thousands moving about him in the freedom of nature, giving unconscious and unconstrained expression to every motive, and besides this, he could have his own judgments confirmed by the verdicts of an entire populace, one of whose chief delights consisted in criticising and comparing the curve of every limb, and the grace of every movement that was supposed to render one of the favorites of the city more beautiful or attractive than another.

It is such facts as these that warrant the attention that, in modern times, has been given to Greek sculpture. Naturally, too, the excellence of this sculpture, taken in connection with the testimony of Greek and Roman writers, has given rise to the opinion that the result was largely due to a study of proportion in the abstract. But notice that even this study need not involve neglect of the study of nature in the concrete. The human mind being what it is, it is more than likely that the Greek in his circumstances would have used models even more extensively than is done to-day ; and, not only so, but also, on account of his greater opportunities for observation, that he would have used them more judiciously. What if he did form certain theories concerning proportion? Are there any thinking minds, or many, that can practise any profession for any length of time, without developing theories concerning it? The fact that the Greeks had these does not involve their being servile imitators of one another's works, or even believers in one another's conceptions. The painter Eupompus told the sculptor Lysippus (Pliny's Nat. Hist., xxxiv, 19) that "Nature herself is to be imitated, not the artist,"—which opinion possibly underlay that development of the art in the hands of the latter to which Pliny refers when he says: "He added much to statuary by making the heads smaller and the bodies more graceful and less bloated ; through which the height of statues seemed greater." "' That you, Cleito,'" said Socrates, according to the "Memorabilia," iii, 10, 6, "' make different forms, racers, wrestlers, boxers, and experts in all kinds of gymnastics, I see and understand ; but if you wished to bring out the soul of man through the form so that it should appear a living thing, how would you work this into a statue?' When Cleito, looking away, was slow in answering, 'Would you not,' continued Socrates, 'make your work a copy of the appearances of living men?' 'Certainly so,'" was the reply. And in a country in which the artist had such opportunities of studying the appearances of living men, we can scarcely imagine how

FIG. 47.—VENUS DE' MEDICI.
See pages 92, 97, 99, 102, 141.

Cleito could have given a different answer. What need would he have to fall back upon other artists' products or theories? Interested, as he would necessarily be, in the personal charms of those about him, would it not be unnatural for him to do otherwise than reproduce them as they were? Like Raphael, Titian, Shakespeare, Goethe, and innumerable artists since his time, would he not care as much, at least, for humanity as for mathematics? But why need one ask these questions? What were the masterpieces of the painter Apelles and of the sculptor Praxiteles? The first is said to have been the "Venus Anadyomeme;" the second the original of the Venus de' Medici (Fig. 47); and both are said to have been modelled after the form of the Athenian beauty, Phryne (Pliny's Nat. Hist., xxxv, 36, note 59; xxxiv, 19, note 43.)

One fact always affords a strong argument in support of the theory that Greek sculpture was produced mainly by an application of mathematical principles, and this is the conventional character of the face of the statue. With few exceptions, the nose, mouth, eyes, and forehead all show the results of the same relative measurements; and the question is asked very pertinently, If the face were conventional, why was not the form also? To answer this question, makes it necessary to direct attention to something which we moderns find it difficult to understand, yet which nevertheless seems to be a fact, namely, that the impression, or expression, of beauty on the part of the human figure, in the conception of the Greek, had comparatively little to do with the face. Any one who has ever stood, as has the writer, in a narrow street in Constantinople, and, at the risk of offending the authorities, gazed critically at the ladies of the Sultan's harem, when, under the protection of their eunuchs, half a hundred of them, perhaps, were being driven past in their carriages, all forms and faces being concealed with the exception of the eyes, has probably been made to realize, as never before, how much expression there is in the eyes. From these alone, one is able to form a judgment, though, of course, very superficial, of the general characteristics of their owners. If an ancient Greek were to be raised to life in our day and country, he would see, in some cases, human beings with every part of their forms concealed except their hands and faces. This would be a new experience to him, and it probably would be accompanied by a discovery with reference to the capabilities of expression in the human countenance both as regards thought and character, of which he never before had conceived. The fact is, that character and thought are expressed in the whole human figure. Of this, the face forms a very small part. If we are in circumstances where we can see the whole figure, there, by a necessary law of the mind, we think mainly of that which occupies the main part of the field of vision. If we have analyzed our own thoughts, when witnessing a scene in which the clothing of the performers was less ample than that allotted by our standards of civilization,—an athletic exhibition, or the bathing of boys on the seashore,—we shall recall that those with the finest forms and most graceful movements invariably attracted our attention and won our admiration, no matter how ugly may have been their countenances. In such circumstances, we scarcely seem to notice countenances at all. This was the condition and attitude of the Greek. And the fact in his case, and the reason for it, seem to furnish a satisfactory answer to the theories of some modern artists and critics who hold that because, in Greek art, the face, as a rule, is comparatively expressionless, it should be so in modern art. Here is one of those abundant instances in which circumstances alter cases. One reason why Greek art was great is because it was true to Greek life. Modern art can become great only in the degree in which it is true to modern life.

FIG. 48.—FARNESE HERCULES, BY GLYCON THE ATHENIAN.
See page 97.

But now for our main application of what has been said. Many beautiful forms that served as models for the

Greek artists were undoubtedly surmounted by ugly faces. The Greek did not believe in ugliness anywhere; and for this reason, in place of the faces that he found, he may have substituted his conventional face, probably itself a copy of some face which common opinion had pronounced beautiful. Moreover, by using this face and no other, he would avoid giving offence to those who might desire to have him reproduce their countenances as well as forms. Besides this, too, large numbers of his statues represented gods, and it would scarcely have been considered appropriate had he represented these by using a literal portrait of a living person.

Once more, it must not be supposed, even

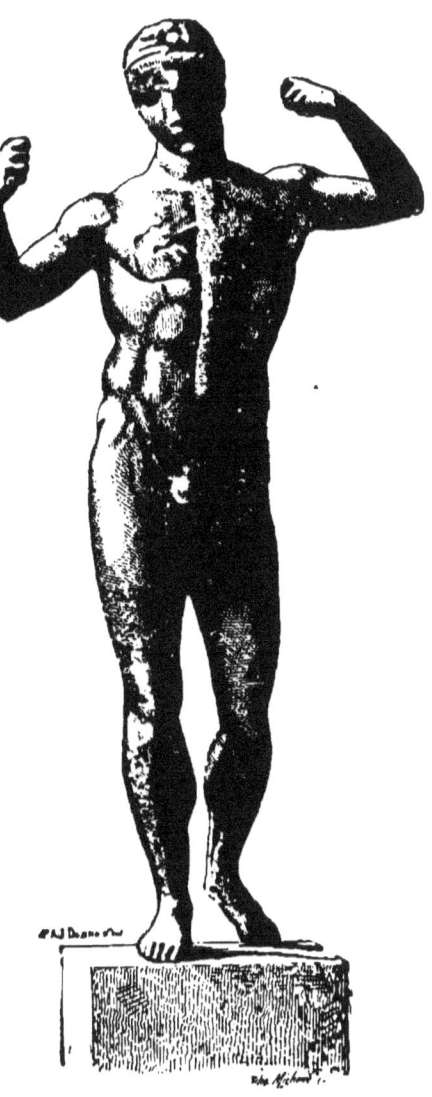

FIG. 49.—DIADUMENOS, BY POLYCLEITUS.
See pages 97, 132, 141.

though it be admitted that the Greek used models freely, that he was often content to have all the parts of any one statue literally reproduce all the parts of any one model.

FIG. 50.—THE DISCOBOLUS, OR QUOIT-THROWER.
See pages 97, 141.

On the contrary, the history of the best period of his art is a record of changes in forms, as these were developed with more or less gradualness, the one from the other. The earliest style is termed muscular and bold, as exemplified in the lost wooden statue of Hercules by the prehistoric

Dædalus. The Farnese Hercules, Fig. 48, page 94, by Glycon, an Athenian sculptor supposed to be of the time of Hadrian, born A.D. 76, is said to represent the characteristics of this Hercules, as copied previously by the portrait-sculptor Lysippus about 372–316 B.C. Next we have the "athletic" style of Ageladas preceding 500 B.C., of which we still have representations in the works of his pupils,—the Diadumenos (Fig. 49, page 95) of Polycleitus, born about 482 B.C., and the Discobolus (Fig. 50, page 96) of Myron, born about 500 B.C. Developed at the same time, but usually described as a little later, by another pupil of Ageladas, we have the more refined "grand" style of Pheidias, born about 500 B.C., and exemplified in his Minerva and Jove and other compositions connected

FIG. 51.—PALLAS OF VELLETRI.
LOUVRE, PARIS.
See page 97.

with the Parthenon. The statue in Fig. 51, is supposed by some to be a literal copy of the Minerva of Pheidias, and the Theseus, Fig. 52, page 98, is itself one of the statues of his Parthenon. Then we have the delicate and "graceful" style of Praxiteles, a pupil of Pheidias, illustrated in the Faun (Fig. 53, page 99), the Venus (Fig. 47, page 92), and the Hermes (Fig. 54, page

100). About the same time as the "graceful" style, there is said to have been developed the "historical" style of the portrait-sculptor Lysippus; and the "impassioned" style, still preserved to us in the group of Niobe and her children (Fig. 55, page 101), supposed to be the work of Scopas, and, a little later, in the Laocoön and other statues

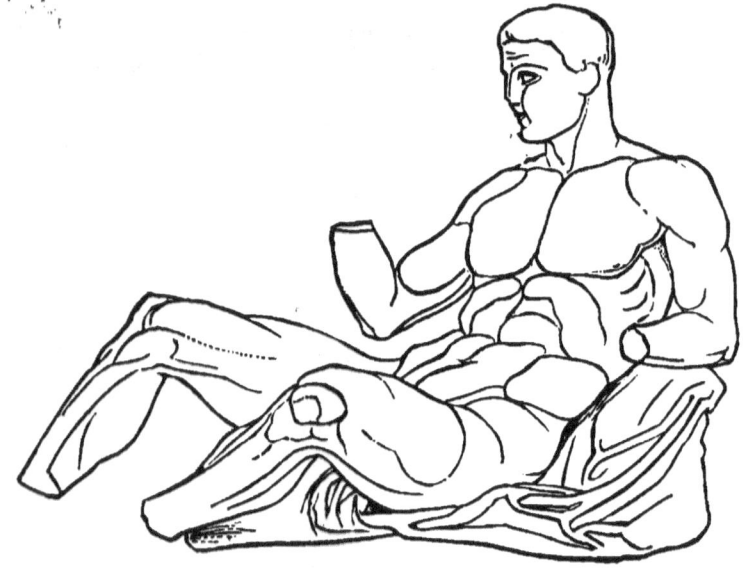

FIG. 52.—STATUE OF THESEUS.
See pages 97, 141.

of the Rhodian School. Finally we hear of the "colossal" style, in which Chares, a pupil of Lysippus, executed the Colossus of Rhodes. But notwithstanding the general fact that these styles were developed one after another, it is also true that many of them were developed at the same period. For instance, the Apollo Belvedere, Fig. 44, page 84, supposed to be a copy of an original by Praxiteles, is as nearly allied to the "grand" style as to the "graceful," of which that sculptor is supposed to be the chief master. Notice, too, the very great differences in form perceptible between Figs. 44, page 84; 56, page 102; and 58, page 104; also between Figs. 47, page 92, and 59, page 105; and also between Fig. 53, and Figs. 54, page 100, and 58, page 104,—all supposed to be copies of statues produced at about the same period. In the "graceful" style, moreover, measurements which in former periods were applied exclusively to the male figure alone, or to the female alone, came to be applied to both conjointly. (Notice again this Fig. 53, and Fig. 57, page 103.) Would this ever have been done, or even thought of, except by artists accustomed to unite in the same form characteristics of different living models? We are told that, when the Holland-English sculptor Ruysbrack was preparing his Hercules, he took for the head of the statue the conventional head of the Greek god, but for the rest of the

FIG. 53.—THE FAUN OF PRAXITELES.
See pages 97, 99, 141.

FIG. 54.—HERMES OF PRAXITELES.
See pages 97, 99, 102, 132, 141.

body various parts of the forms of some half-dozen of the best gymnasts of London. The painter Ellis, for instance, sat for the legs. There are reasons for supposing that certain of the methods of the ancients did not differ essentially from this. They used models, but probably rejected the members of a model that did not conform to accepted standards.

FIG. 55.—FROM GROUP OF NIOBE AT FLORENCE.
See pages 59, 98.

Suggested by the thought in the last paragraph, there is another consideration which, in studying the proportions of the human body, necessitates taking the observation of nature for the point of departure. This is the fact that different forms of men, even when conforming to accepted standards, or conforming sufficiently to be all equally well proportioned, differ in their measurements. Among the Greek statues, for example, the athletes, as contrasted with other men, have broader measurements at the shoulders, as seen both from the front and the sides, and their whole forms taper more decidedly between the shoulders and the ankles; the children have comparatively larger heads, longer trunks, shorter limbs, and smaller feet; while, as contrasted with the men, most of the women, but not all, have a height about one tenth less, and eight times, instead of six times, the length of the foot, and have shoulders relatively narrower, thighs broader, and all outlines, including limbs, hands, fingers, and nails, more perfectly tapered and rounded. Compare Figs. 44, page 84, and 54, page 100, with 47, page 92, and 59, page 105. As shown, too, in Chapter VII. of "Painting, Sculpture, and Architecture as Representative Arts," such variations may be ascribable to differences not only in occupation, age, and sex, but also in temperament,—the mental, the vital, and the motive, which are respectively expressive of very different intellectual and physical traits, each tending to a different general contour.

FIG. 56.—MELEAGROS, IN THE VATICAN.
See pages 99, 141.

FIG. 57.—GANYMEDE, AFTER LEOCHARES, IN THE VATICAN.
See pages 99, 132, 141.

This connection between the contour and the traits represented by it merely carries out an analogy which is true in every form of art. A man, in writing a song or a poem—whether a drama or a lyric—must begin by making it fulfil the requirements of *congruity* (see "The Genesis of Art-Form," Chapter IX.); *i. e.*, by making it conform strictly to a man's natural mode of expressing the emotion or conception intended to be conveyed. Otherwise, all that is excellent in the poem will be virtually wasted. So of all that is excellent in a painting or a statue in the way of proportion. Especially is this true, as related to the human form. One must always bear in mind that its proportions are expressive of significance. All the members, whether connected with forehead, eyes, ears, nose, mouth, chin, neck, shoulders, arms, hands, waist, hips, legs, calves, ankles, feet, are adapted to some purpose ; in our minds they are associated

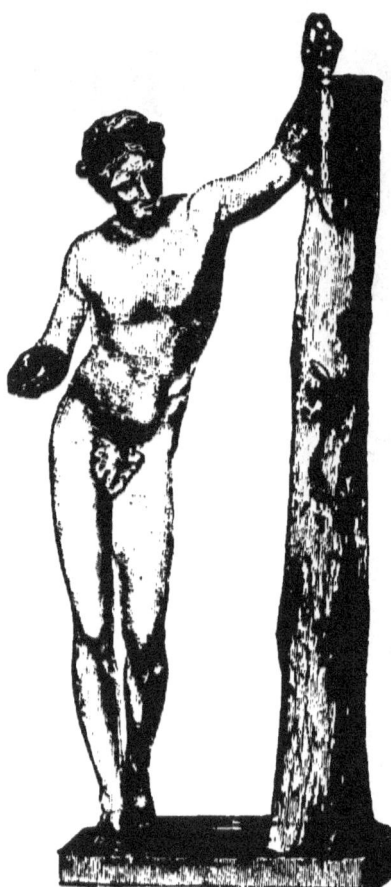

FIG. 58.—APOLLO SAUROCTONOS—
PRAXITELES—VATICAN.
See pages 99, 141.

HUMAN PROPORTIONS RELATIVE TO CHARACTER 105

with this purpose; and seem beautiful or ugly, on account, partly, of the way in which they fulfil it, and, partly, of the deficiency or superabundance of the characteristics supposed to be represented by them, in case they are relatively smaller or larger than is usual. This is true as applied to combinations, the beauty of which is ordinarily judged to be dependent upon form solely. For instance, take those outlines in the countenance composing what are ordinarily described as regular features. When, as in these, after drawing vertical and horizontal lines across the face (see Fig. 45, page 86), the corresponding parts of eyebrows, eyes, nostrils, on the opposite sides of the face, appear to be in exact balance, inasmuch as the whole is outlined by a framework that is exactly square or rectangular, the external arrangement is satisfactory because it seems representative of something internal that is satisfactory; in other words, because we associate these physical conditions with correlated ones that are mental and moral. Because

FIG. 59.—VENUS ASCRIBED TO STYLE OF PRAXITELES.
See pages 99, 102, 141.

the face is square, we judge that the character is square. For instance, Mephistopheles as represented on the stage is always painted with the arch of the eyebrows not in line with the horizontal, but beginning high up on the temples and running downward toward the bridge of the nose (see Fig. 60). This is the way, too, in which even a handsome man looks when contracting his brows under the influence of arrogance, pride, contempt, hatred, and, most of all, of malice (see Fig. 61). With a similar general effect of irregularity, a simpleton on the stage is painted with nostrils and lips which exaggerate the expression of the smile by running too far up at the sides; and a scold, with the sides of the same features exaggerating the expression of the sneer and frown, by running too far down. Or if we consider combinations which almost every one admires, of a comparatively small ankle and large calf, or of a small wrist and large forearm, or of a small waist and broad shoulders, or, in a woman, broad hips; certainly one way of explaining the effects of combinations of this kind is to attribute them to significance. Clumsy joints at the places where the body must bend suggest a lack of flexibility, deftness, and grace; and slender muscles at the places where the body must exert itself suggest a lack of stability, strength, and persistence. Therefore, though the curve

FIG. 60.
MEPHISTOPHELES.
See page 106

FIG. 61.
CONTEMPT AND ANGER.
See page 106.

connecting the ankle with the calf, or the wrist with the forearm, or the waist with the breast or hips, is beautiful, as will be shown by-and-by, because it fulfils a requirement connecting together with ease two outlines in vision, it is beautiful also because it fulfils a requirement connecting together with satisfaction two facts in thought. After all that can be claimed, therefore, for the effects of mere outlines, there remain certain other requisites of beauty for which these never can account. They can be attributed to significance alone, under which general term we may include, for reasons given in Chapter XV. of "Art in Theory," all such suggestions as are contained in conceptions like those of adaptability, fitness, association, symbolism, sympathy, and personality.

Indeed, even upon the supposition that beauty is merely a physiological effect of form, this conclusion is inevitable. As will be brought out in Chapter XX. of this volume, the most subtle conceivable effects of harmony, whether of sound or color, are results of experiencing a regularly recurring series of vibrations causing the nerves to thrill or glow ; whereas effects of discord are results of irregularly recurring series of vibrations causing a sensation of a jar or shock. But whence comes the thrill or the shock, as the case may be? Every physiologist admits that the nerves may be affected not only from the sense-side, but also from the mind-side. A man suffers in spirits and health not only because of influence exerted upon his body from without, but also because of influence coming from his own thoughts and emotions. It is a simple physiological fact, therefore, that, even though the nerves may be agreeably affected by a form, nevertheless if, owing to a lack of adaptability or fitness, or to a failure to meet the mind's requirements of association, symbolism, sympathy, or personality, certain suggestions of the form jar upon one's sense of congruity or propriety, or, as we say, shock one's sensibilities, then even the physiological condition which is the subjective realization of the presence of beauty will not ensue.

The author is aware that to take this ground is to meet with the accusation, on account of the one subject to which the principle is most frequently applied, that he is confounding the æsthetical with the ethical. But this is not so. It seems so because the dictates of conscience are more apt to be the same in all men than those of any other part of one's nature, and because, therefore, that which violates these dictates is that which is most likely to appear distasteful to the largest number. But the principle involved applies to a vast range of subjects which have nothing to do with ethics. A picture untrue to the requirements of history also, or to the scenes of a locality, might have a correspondingly distasteful effect upon the mind of an historian or a traveller; might so jar upon his sensibilities as to counterbalance entirely any possible degree of excellence in form considered merely as form.

As applied to the human figure, and to the expression, through every part of it, of a particular phase of significance, it is apparent that certain legitimate deductions from this principle are often ignored. When this is said, it must be said also, if we are to deal with the subject with perfect truth, that they are ignored almost as much in certain disguising concealments of the form characterizing some of the customs of civilization, as in certain disenchanting exposures of it characterizing some of the conventionalities of art. Viewing the subject not with the prejudice which supposes that whatever is, is necessarily right, and therefore finds fault with straight skirts on a woman merely because others are wearing hoops, and with knickerbockers on a man merely because others are wearing pantaloons; but viewing the subject in a rational way, it may be said that the human form just as it is, is God-made, whereas human clothing is man-made; and that the latter, even though it drag for yards behind the feet, especially if with just enough exposure to suggest a possibility of more exposure, may be in its tendency less humanizing, in a good sense, than a garb disclosing enough, at least, to allow free and natural expression to the soul within. The Hebrew priest [1] was told to sprinkle the blood of a sacrificial victim—representing life that was innocent and therefore spiritual—on the vessels of the temple every time that he had occasion to use them. The people were thus taught that nothing in the world that is material, not even a consecrated implement of the sanctuary, is sacred except when made to represent the presence of spiritual life. Much less is the material clothing of human figures sacred. One might argue that it can never represent spiritual life quite as well as when it faithfully reveals the general outlines of the form which the creative power designed that spiritual life on earth should have. Or—to examine the subject in the light of its practical effects—what artist ever represented a wanton in the scanty short skirts and bare feet of a peasant? What man, so far as form in dress could affect him, would not be conscious of more kindly, tender, generous, and protective impulses awakened in him by the simple clothing of the latter, or of a young girl just entering her teens, than by the trailing silks and laces of the

[1] Ex. 29:20, 21; Lev. 1:5, 11; 3:2, 8, 13; 7:2; 17:6, 11; Num. 18:17; 19:4.

former? Thus much for one of the many mistakes of civilization. No influence is more indirectly exalting than beauty, and no beauty ought to be more exalting than that of the human form. To veil it wholly, as the oriental women do their faces, may impair the charm of life not only, but its chastity. When much that is concealed, might if revealed, put an end both to legitimate curiosity and to purely æsthetic desires, might it not also put an end to much that, when developed, reinforces desires of a less exalted nature? It is certainly a question whether, in such cases, complete satisfaction would not often accompany that which satisfied merely the eye. The Japanese, familiar from childhood with an almost total exposure of the form, and notwithstanding traditionally low standards of conventional morality, are believed by themselves, and by others who have studied them, to be, absolutely considered, more moral by nature, in that they are less prone to morbid and soulless forms of indulgence, than are the Europeans. Is not one proof of this—as it certainly is a proof of the delicacy of their sense of propriety and, for that matter, of beauty—afforded by the fact that, in their higher art, complete nudity is never depicted?

So much for a mistake of conventional fashion. Now a few words with reference to a mistake in an opposite direction made by conventional art. The true principle in art is that it should represent life, and, if dealing with human life, should represent that which is in the highest sense humanizing. But that which is in the highest sense humanizing gives principality to mental and spiritual suggestions, and keeps others subordinate. Can this be said to be done when parts of the body, which even barbarians conceal, are exposed, in conditions, as sometimes happens in modern art, so different from those of natural life that one is forced to the inference that they are exposed for the sole purpose of exposure? In answer to this we are referred to Greek art. But Greek art was true to the conditions of Greek life. The legitimate deduction is that our art should be true to the conditions of our life. Then again we are referred to the use of models by our artists; and this is the sort of argument that makes a sensible man feel faint. A gentleman uses a dressing-room. To prove himself a gentleman need he invite the public to witness his performances in it? Probably, it was merely by a slip of the tongue that one of our artists testified in a police court that, in his opinion, the exhibition not of the finished product of the studio but of the undressed—one might say—skeleton of the studio would be eminently appropriate for a Broadway shop-window. But the remark was an unmistakable manifestation of a tendency. There have been times when it was thought in bad taste, even with reference to things never considered so in themselves, for a man to talk "shop" or to act "shop" or in any way to thrust his "shop" upon public attention. But evidently those times have passed. Even now, however, a logical mind ought to recognize the difference between arguing with reference to what may be necessary to support the life of art, and arguing with reference to how much the remains of that which has been denuded of what might properly be termed its meat can contribute to sanitary effects—to sweetness and enlightenment, when thrown out of the front window onto the public pavement.

The truth is that, in this, as in every other practical possibility, there is no end worth seeking, whether it be the representation of human sentiment or of skill in workmanship, that cannot be attained without going to extremes. When one thinks of this fact, and of the liability, if it be disregarded, of having art lower its aims, or, if not this, having it antagonize, through creating false impressions of its aims, thousands of those in special need of its influence,—in other words, when one thinks how much might be gained to the world, and how little can be lost, by applying in this sphere the same common sense that all men are expected to apply in other spheres, it certainly seems strange that those who wish to make the most of art should pursue a course, in either criticism or production, fitted really to make the least of it.

Before closing this chapter, it may be well to remind the reader that the fact that the whole human form and every part of it owes the beauty which we recognize in it largely to its representation of a certain phase of significance, furnishes the best possible explanation for those discrepancies in taste, which are nowhere more apparent than in the judgments which different persons, equally cultivated, form with reference to precisely the same human proportions. These judgments differ because men differ in their views of adaptability and fitness, and in the recollections which they associate with persons characterized by certain features; but more than all, because they differ in their feelings of companionship with those possessing traits which these features represent. Owing to one or the other of these reasons, there are, for all of us, certain forms so adjusting themselves into the framework of vision and mind that they fit into what men term their ideals as into a vise, and hold sympathy spellbound. Certain movements in these forms seem regulated to such a rhythm that, in unison with it, all our currents of vein and nerve leap from the heart and brain and thrill along their courses. They do so very likely because of the operation of those universal laws of vibration, the connection between which and the effects of beauty was suggested in Chapter XII., and also in Appendix I. of " Art in Theory." But the exact reason lies deeper in nature than any plummet dropped by human means can fathom. We cannot know the cause any more than what, when all conductors are in place, speeds the impulse of an electric current. We only know that a reason exists at all because of the results which we experience. Just as certain organs of the ear or eye respond and glow with a sense of complete freedom and delight in the presence of certain harmonious elements or combinations of sounds or sights, so does the spirit as a whole. There may be some so constituted physically, or so incapable of analyzing what they feel, that they confound this apprehension of beauty, which only we are now considering, with something less pure and elevating. But those who have never made their souls the servants of their bodies, and whose æsthetic as well as ethical natures have, therefore, developed normally, are aware that the influence which flows from beauty and beauty alone is different in kind from anything debasing, and allied to that which is wholly spiritual. It is not without strength in extreme youth, nor lost in old age, and in its power to give delight and even to arouse romance, it is stronger, often, when exerted by man upon man and woman upon woman, than when exerted by one upon another of another sex. These æsthetic effects, when they reveal their sources through the outward forms in which they are expressed and embodied, do this mainly through what we term the proportions. What if these latter in themselves be merely a collection of like or related measurements? Is this not exactly what we should expect of anything the effects of which can be ultimately traced to vibrations? Cannot the same be affirmed not only of the minute waves that underlie results in melody and harmony of tone, but even of the larger waves of rhythm? And, if without rhythm there can be no effective music or poetry, how should there be effective painting or sculpture without proportion?

CHAPTER VIII.

PROPORTIONS OF THE HUMAN FIGURE PRACTICALLY CONSIDERED.

Standard of Measurement in Rhythm and Proportion as Fixed by Congruity—Repetition and Alternation—Repetition or Likeness of Measurements—Reason for Satisfaction in Effects of Proportion—Not the Usual Explanation—But not Inconsistent with the Conceptions of the Greeks—Criticism of Statements with Reference to them—Difference between an Apparent and a Real Measurement—Exact Value of the Statements of Vitruvius—How to Find the True Greek Theory—Quotation from Vitruvius—What it Implies—The Ratios to be Considered a Result of Likeness—Measurements of the Head and Face—The Greek Type of Face not the Only one Manifesting Effects of Proportion—Nor are the Methods of Subdividing it the Ones usually Adopted—Or Necessary to the Recognition of Beauty—More Minute Like Measurements in the Front Face—In the Side Face—In the Form when Fronting one—Effects of High Civilization on the Wedge-Shape of the Form—The Lower Limbs from the Front—From the Side—Other Related Measurements—Measurements according to Curvilinear Standards—Similar Circumferences Describing Many Different Outlines—Elliptical Figure as Described about the Form as a Whole—Significance as Represented in the Form of a Man and of a Woman—Principles of Proportion not Creative, but Guides to the Selection of Models—Affording Aid in Determining the Pose—Proportion merely an Application to Measurements of the Art-Methods on Page 3.

THE rhythm of a musical composition is usually fixed by that of a few notes, definitely suggestive of a certain phase of feeling. These notes comprise the theme, from which the whole is developed; and their measures furnish, as one might say, the standard for the measures of the whole. So the proportions of a whole human figure are usually fixed by those of a few features, furnishing the standard. The vital temperament, for instance, gives a standard measurement, as in the neck, waist, hips, and calves, that in itself has greater width than the standard measurement of the mental temperament. Starting with whatever may furnish the standard, the other measurements in well formed figures will be found to be in proportion to it. This will cause the figures to fulfil perhaps more definitely than any other the art-method of *congruity*, already discussed between pages 104 and 107 of Chapter VII. This art-method, occasioned as it is (see the note on page 61, also the chart on page 3) by the requirements of the mind, will usually reveal important particulars in which the same figures also fulfil the more commonly noticed methods of *unity, order, comparison,* and *principality*. According to the chart on page 3, the primary method connected with the requirements of matter, *i e.,* of the material of which the product is constructed, is *repetition,* and an important development of this, as influenced by the *variety* common to all things in nature, is *alternation*. Concerning this latter something will be said later. At present, it is enough to point out that it is a method of relieving *repetition* of monotony ; and, in its application, it can, at times, without detriment to the *unity* of the general proportional effect, introduce into the same product two apparently different schemes of measurement. For instance, in the front of the Greek temple, Fig. 10, page 36, the width of the columns represents one measurement, and the width of the spaces between them represents another. So the wide spaces between certain of the lines drawn horizontally across the faces in Figs. 64 to 68, on pages 126 and 127, represent one measurement, and the narrower spaces another. In such cases, there is usually a certain recognizable ratio between the different widths, as 1 : 2, or 2 : 3, or 3 : 4. But notice that this ratio need not be expressible in such small numbers as to be readily made out. In a temple, for instance, no matter how the width of one column was related to the width of the space beside it, the relation of the one to the other would be recognized to be precisely the same as the relation of the next column to the next space beyond.

Now let us go back to *repetition*. The main reason why the mind is satisfied when seeing outlines related to one another as 1 : 2, or 2 : 5, is because, in such cases, it recognizes that the first is another expression for 1 : 1+1, and the second another expression for 1+1 : 1+1+1+1+1. In other words, the mind takes satisfaction not in the ratio *per se*, but in that which the ratio enables it to recognize, which is, that in fulfilment of the fundamental art-method, measurements have been put together which are alike as to their parts.

This is not the explanation usually given for effects of proportion. But it is the explanation most consistent with that usually given for effects of rhythm; it is the explanation most consistent with all the methods of art as unfolded in "The Genesis of Art-Form," and represented in the chart on page 3 of this volume ; and, finally, it is the explanation which can render most easy and simple the practical application of the principle to all possible visible effects.

It can readily be shown, too, that this explanation is not inconsistent with the conceptions which the Greeks must have had of the subject. In commenting upon the testimony of the Roman writer Vitruvius, in his " De Architectura," Samson, in his " Elements of Art-Criticism," book iii., chapter i., summarizes certain of these conceptions as follows : "The entire statue was eight heads or ten faces ; and one half the statue was above the os pubis. The breadth of the shoulders was two heads ; of the loins, one head and one nose ; of the thighs, one head and two noses. The length of the arm was three heads, one and one half from the shoulder to the elbow, and one and one half from the elbow to the first knuckles. From the thigh to the knee was two heads, and the same from the knee to the ankle, and the foot was one head and one nose. The depth of the chest was one head and one third of the nose ; of the loins, three and one third noses. The breadth of the upper arm was one and one half noses, front view, and two noses, side view ; of the lower arm, in the thickest part, one and one half noses, and of the wrist, one nose. The depth of the thigh was three noses; of the calf of the leg, two noses ; of the ankle, one nose."

Some of these measurements, as will be noticed, are carried out in Figs. 31, page 57, and 32, page 58. Others, like the last mentioned, are indefinite. The statement is true if the ankle be viewed from the front, but false if it be viewed from the side ; and just the opposite is true with reference to the wrist. The measurements have been quoted here, not so much on their own account, as on account of the testimony which they furnish to the fact that, with the Greeks, all the members of the form were viewed in their relations to a unit,—as stated in this case, to the nose, which to the Greeks represented one third of the face, or one fourth of the head.

As for the details of this statement of Vitruvius, we must be cautious about trusting to them too implicitly. Among the dimensions mentioned, take "the depth of a head and one third of a nose." If the Greeks really made any such law, it may have been because the peculiar shape of the member to which it was applied made it necessary slightly to increase the real dimension in order to manifest a sufficient apparent dimension, one head and one third of a nose in one position appearing no longer than a head alone would in another. It is beyond question, as will be shown in Chapter XIV., that, in applying the principles of proportion to architecture, the Greeks cared less for like measurements than for producing the appearance of them; and probably the same would be true when applying these principles to the human form.

Moreover, it is important to notice that an apparent measurement necessitates, at times, not only a different result from an actual measurement, but also a different conception of what should be measured. As an instance of a different result, consider how the leg between the heel and the place where it separates from the body is apparently divided at the knee into two equal parts. This is not a result of having the half below the knee of the same length as the half above it. Being slimmer, the lower half would appear longer, were it not in reality slightly shorter. Again, as an instance of a different conception, consider the measurement of the ankle. Ordinarily, we should suppose this to be a dimension determined by its circumference. But, when considering effects of appearances, it is not the circumference that concerns us, but the apparent distance from one side of the ankle to its other side, as it is seen from a single point of view.

With this thought in mind let us turn again to the opinions of the Greeks, quoting, in order to suggest what these opinions were, from Vitruvius. He can furnish us with testimony sufficient for our purpose, even though we admit, as we must, that his authority is not the best. He was an architect, not a sculptor. He was a Roman too; and, as has been proved, he was not fully informed with reference to the Greek laws even of architecture. Besides this, the passages in which he refers to the proportions of the human form are introduced into his work as illustrations, the argument being that as the human figure has fixed proportions, so, too, a building should have them. He mentions a few of these proportions, but there is no evidence that he even intended to mention them in any categorical way. These facts show that what is of value in his testimony is less what he says than what he implies,—namely, that there was an opinion in his time, that the Greeks had a theory that the proportions of human figures are determined by comparative measurements, and that they based their practice upon this theory.

But what were these proportions, and what principles did they fulfil? Toward answering this, the statements to be quoted may give us hints. The principles underlying all the art-methods, as unfolded in "The Genesis of Art-Form" and summarized on page 3 of this volume, may interpret these hints; and a tape measure assiduously used upon the existing Greek statues, as has been done by the author, may test the accuracy of the interpretation. "Nature has so fashioned a well formed human figure," says Vitruvius, in book iii., chapter i., of his "De Architectura," as translated by Joseph Gwilt, "that in the face from the tip of the chin to the forehead or to the roots of the hair is a tenth part of the height of the whole body. From the chin to the crown of the head is an eighth part of the whole height [see Figs. 31, page 57, 32, page 58, and 45, page 86], and from the nape of the neck to the crown of the head the same. From the upper part of the breast to the roots of the hair, a sixth; to the crown of the head, a fourth. A third part of the height of the face is equal to that from the chin to the under side of the nostrils; and thence to the middle of the eyebrows, the same; from the last to the roots of the hair, where the forehead ends, the remaining third part. The length of the foot is the sixth part of the height of the body; the forearm, a fourth part; the width of the breast a fourth

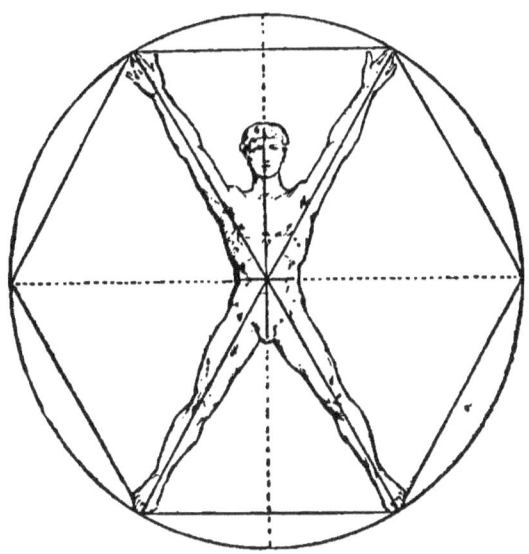

FIG. 62.—WHOLE HUMAN FORM AS RELATED TO THE CIRCLE.
See pages 15, 59, 121, 130, 132, 133, 141.

part. The navel is naturally placed in the centre of the human body, and if, when a man is lying with his face upward and his hands and feet extended, from his navel as a centre a circle be described, it will touch his fingers and toes." (See Fig. 62 above.) " Measuring from the feet to the crown of the head and then across the arms fully extended, we find the latter measure equal the former; so the lines at right angles to each other enclosing the figure will form a square." (See Fig. 63.)

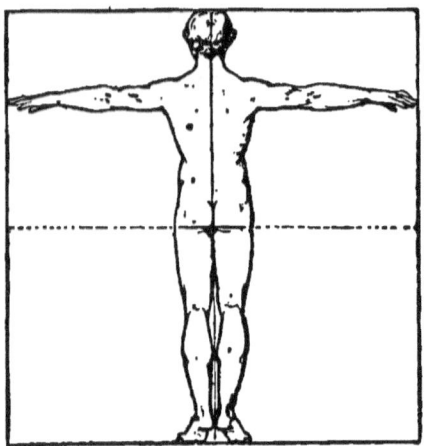

FIG. 63.—WHOLE HUMAN FORM AS RELATED TO THE SQUARE.
See pages 15, 59, 122, 130, 131, 141.

In this quotation, as will be noticed, we again have certain parts of the form taken as standards of measurement, *i. e.*, the face and head, though not, as on page 118, the nose. Notice also the note at the bottom of this page.[1] Neither this quotation from Vitruvius, however,

---

[1] In this connection, the following note xviii. of Sir Joshua Reynolds on Fresnoy's "Art of Painting" may be of interest. From the note a few clauses in which the proportions mentioned are the same as in the quotation from Vitruvius on page 120 are omitted.

VERSE 145.

Learn then from Greece, ye youths, Proportion's law,
Informed by her each just position draw.

Du Piles has, in his note on this passage, given the measures of a human

nor this note, nor any usual method of presenting the subject, seems to get down to the fundamental source of the artistic effect involved, which is the satisfaction derived by the mind from perceiving certain dimensions put with others that are like them, or are exact multiples of them. Nevertheless, that this satisfaction is really the

body, as taken by Fresnoy from the statues of the ancients, which are here transcribed:

"The ancients have commonly allowed eight heads to their figures, though some of them have but seven; but we ordinarily divide the figure into ten faces.[1]

. . . .

From the chin to the pit betwixt the collar-bones are two lengths of a nose.

From the pit betwixt the collar-bones to the bottom of the breast, one face.

From the bottom of the breasts to the navel, one face.[2]

From the navel to the genitories, one face.[3]

From the genitories to the upper part of the knee, two faces.

The knee contains half a face.

From the lower part of the knee to the ankle, two faces.

From the ankle to the sole of the foot, half a face.

A man when his arms are stretched out is from the longest finger of his right hand to the longest of his left as broad as he is long.

From one side of the breast to the other, two faces.

The bone of the arm called the Humerus is the length of two faces from the shoulder to the elbow.

From the end of the elbow to the root of the little finger, the bone called Cubitus, with part of the hand, contains two faces.

From the bone of the shoulder-blade to the pit betwixt the collar-bones, one face.

If you would be satisfied in the measure of breadth, from the extremity of one finger to the other, so that this breadth should be equal to the length of the body, you must observe that the boxes of the elbow with the humerus,

---

[1] This depends on the age and quality of the persons. The Apollo and Venus de' Medici have more than ten faces.—*R*.

[2] The Apollo has a nose more.—*R*.

[3] The Apollo has half a nose more; and the upper half of the Venus de' Medici is to the lower part of the belly, and not to the privy parts.—*R*.

source of the artistic effect is implied in all the quotations that have been used, and will be confirmed by the results of a tape measure tried upon any large number of classic statues.

It has been pointed out that we could not recognize that a nose on a given face was out of proportion, unless in the same face, near the nose, were something with which to compare it. It is equally true that we could not recognize the fact readily, unless there were something with which we could compare the nose exactly, *i.e.*, something which, as a rule, is of exactly the same length. Notice again, now, that we could not recognize the fact as well if there were only one other feature of like length in the face, as if there were many features. The same principle applies to every member of the form. And the readiness with which all people recognize a lack of proportion in any member, proves the presence of many features of like dimensions with the one that is the subject of adverse

and of the humerus with the shoulder-blade, bear the proportion of half a face when the arms are stretched out.

The sole of the foot is the sixth part of the figure.

The hand is the length of the face.

The thumb contains a nose.

The inside of the arm from the place where the muscle disappears, which makes the breast (called the Pectoral muscle), to the middle of the arm, four noses.

From the middle of the arm to the beginning of the hand, five noses.

The longest toe is a nose long.

The two utmost parts of the teats, and the pit betwixt the collar-bones of a woman, make an equilateral triangle.

For the breadth of the limbs, no precise measures can be given, because the measures themselves are changeable, according to the quality of the persons and according to the movement of the muscles."—*Du Piles*.

The measures of the ancient statues by Audran appear to be the most useful, as they are accompanied with the outline of the figures which are most distinguished for correctness.—*K*.

criticism. Ordinarily, no one can tell what these features are, nor which of their dimensions are used as a basis of comparison, but that they exist is beyond question. Otherwise men could not make the comparisons that are so common. The bearing of this upon the subject before us, of course, is that proportion is determined by likeness, of which the ratios are a result, not a cause. Where certain features are as 1 : 1 and 1 : 2, and so on, there we necessarily have conditions that lead to the other simple ratios.

Applying what has been said to the human form, as represented both by the Greeks and by modern artists, and considering, first, rectilinear, and, later, curvilinear measurements, we find that, in spite of the variations already indicated as necessarily existing, there is a general tendency to like measurements or exact multiples of them in the following cases.

To begin with the head and face, Fig. 45, page 86, shows five like horizontal measurements at the level of the eyes, two filled by the eyes themselves, two by the spaces, as seen from the front, between the eyes and the ears, and one filled by the width of the nose. Three other like horizontal measurements may be seen at the level of the mouth, one filled by the main outlines of the mouth,—not including all of them,—and the other two by the spaces on each side between the mouth and the sides of the cheeks. Another like horizontal measurement may be seen also at the nostrils, and still another at the lowest point of the chin. The same figure shows like vertical measurements between the top of the head and the top of the forehead, also between this and the bridge of the nose, also between this and the nostrils, and, again, between these and the chin.

These measurements conform to the Greek type of face, which this figure, and Fig. 69, page 128, are supposed to represent. It must not be inferred, however, that all faces, in order to meet the requirements of proportion, need to be similar. In its way, a dog's face may exemplify proportion as well as a man's; and there is no reason why one human face should not exemplify it as well as another, though differing from it almost radically. This is so because proportion need not always be carried out

FIG. 64.—FACIAL DIVISIONS.
See pages 116, 126, 127, 128, 130.

FIG. 65.—FACIAL DIVISIONS.
See pages 116, 126, 127, 128.

by divisions of exactly the same kind. For instance, none of the spaces in Figs. 64 and 65, or in Figs. 66, 67, and 68, page 127, are vertically divided in the same way as in Figs. 45, page 86, and 69, page 128. Nor, as compared with one another, are all the spaces in Figs. 64 to 68 divided in the same way. Yet they are all divided so that certain measurements in each are like one another. The like measurements, moreover, which are illustrated in Figs. 64, 66, and 67, are such as, probably, half the people in the world, without ever having been aware of it, have been in the habit of perceiving. In other words, they have been in the habit, when looking at a face, of comparing, mentally, the distance between the chief line of the eyebrows and of the eye, with the distance between the nostrils and the mouth, and also of comparing, above and below these narrower spaces, the wider distances between the hair and the eyebrows, the eyes and the nostrils, and the mouth and the chin. These narrower distances are usually to the wider as 1:2, though,

FIG. 66.
FACIAL DIVISIONS.
See pagse 116, 126, 127, 128.

FIG. 67.
FACIAL DIVISIONS.
See pages 116, 126, 127, 128.

FIG. 68.—FACIAL DIVISIONS.
See pages 116, 126, 127, 128, 130.

in accordance with the principle of *alternation* as explained on page 116, it is not absolutely necessary that the ratio between the two should be expressible in just these numbers. All that is necessary is that the third measurements should seem alike, and that the intervening ones should seem sufficiently unlike these others not to confuse the mind by suggesting likeness where it is not supposed to be suggested.

If the reader will examine Figs. 64 to 68, and then recall his own experiences, when judging of faces, he will probably be ready to admit that, much as has been made of the Greek vertical divisions of the face as in Fig. 45, page 86, and Fig. 69, few persons now think of comparing either the height of the forehead, or the length of the nose, with the distance between the nostrils and the chin. Moreover, if they do compare these, and find all of equal measurement, they do not, usually, in case they are Americans, admire the arrangement, and for a very good reason. It fails to represent the face to which they are the most accustomed, or, to go deeper, it fails to represent the characteristics by which they are most attracted. The longer Greek nose (see Chapter VII. of "Painting, Sculpture, and Architecture") represents less emotive susceptibility than a shorter nose, and the shorter Greek chin represents less will-power than a longer chin. As a rule, the American does not admire the degree of moderation—the calculating tact—of the Greek face; but he does admire plenty of will-force, which he calls character and which he supposes to be necessary in order to steady the tendency of a more susceptive temperament.

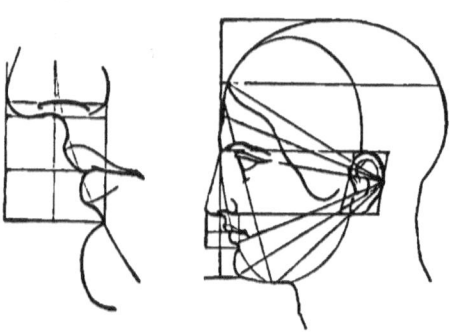

FIG. 69.—SIDE FACE DIVIDED BY LINES.
See pages 15, 59, 126, 128, 129, 130, 135.

For these reasons, when he tells us that he considers the faces in Figs. 64 to 68 more beautiful than those conforming to the Greek type, he is justified. According to the laws of form, properly interpreted, such faces fulfil equally with the Greek—though according to a different method—the principles of proportion. But, besides this, according to the laws of significance, as derived from his association with faces of the ordinary American type, from his deductions with reference to the characteristics manifested by them, and from his sympathy with the persons possessing such characteristics, it is in complete fulfilment of æsthetic principles (see Chapter XIII. of " Art in Theory ") to say that, while as beautiful in form as are the Greek faces, their beauty, to one of the race and country to which they belong, is enhanced on account of its significance.

In many faces, as in Fig. 45, page 86, there are a number of measurements more minute, which a front view of the face will show to be alike; for instance, the vertical distance from the eyebrow to the upper lid of the eye, and then from this across the eye to its lower lid, each of which distances again seems to be one half the horizontal width of the eye (1 : 2). The distance, too, from the nostrils to the opening of the mouth seems to be the same as between this and the dimple under the lower lip; and the ear and the nose, too, are often upon the same level, and of the same length.

If we look at the side of the face, as in Fig. 69, page 128, we find that the eye is back from the bridge of the nose, the nostril back from the point of the nose, and the side of the mouth from its centre just about the same distance, while the eyebrows extend back about twice as far (1 : 2). Other facts which are true of what we Americans consider symmetrical features, but which not only our own artists but also the Greeks, with all their keenness of observation, seem to have entirely overlooked, are that the horizontal lines formed by the front of the eyebrows, by the lower lid of the eye, by the lower line of the nose, and by the mouth are parallel (Figs. 64, page 126, and 68, page 127), and that the downward slope of the ear also is parallel to that of the nose, with which it also corresponds in length. See Figs. 64, page 126; 68, page 127; and 69, page 128. In order to bring out this effect, this latter figure, which was supposed to represent the Greek type, had to be altered when transferred to this book.

Returning to a front view of the body, we find that the whole length of the head is apparently the same as that of the hand, measuring the latter not from the bottom of the palm, but farther up the arm, above the wrist joint, at the place where bracelets are usually worn. See Figs. 31, page 57; 32, page 58; 43, page 82; 62, page 121; 63, page 122; and 71, page 134. This is the place which, when the arms are bare, attracts the attention of the eye, and seems to be the dividing point between hand and arm. The height of the face below the hair is the same as the length of the hand to the bottom of the palm. The inside of the arm from armpit to wrist, as described two sentences above, seems to be twice the length of the hand, as described in the same sentence, *i. e.*, 2 : 1 (Figs. 31, page 57, and 32, page 58.) In a man, the distance from shoulder to shoulder is at times the same as this last measurement of the arm excluding the hand, *i. e.*, as 1 : 1 (Fig. 63, page 122). The inside measurement of the leg from trunk to heel seems to be twice this same measurement of the arm excluding the hand, *i.e.*, as 2 : 1 (Fig. 31, page 57). Or, if we choose, we can look at the outside measurement of the arm from the wrist to the side of the shoulder; and this we shall find to be one half of the outside measurement of the leg from the ankle to the highest point of the hip. Notice, in this connection, what is said in the note on page 123. The dimensions given there do not disagree with those just indicated, but are calculated differently. The inside measurements, however, seem to be the best suited for our purpose. It is they that determine the visible length of each limb when at rest. It is because of them that, when the arms are stretched straight outward and the man stands on tiptoe, there are just eight dimensions of the head or of the hand measured from above the wrist both in the height of the figure and also between the tips of fingers on either side of the body (Fig. 63, page 122). The centre of this height is apparently, but seldom actually, the bottom of the trunk where the legs separate from it. At this place, the width of the body is of course twice that of the legs when they separate (2:1). The waist is about half the distance between this and the armpits, and, in a man, its apparent width is about twice that of each of the legs, when measured at the same distance below the bottom of the lower extremity of the trunk as the waist is above this (Figs. 31, page 57; 32, page 58; and 63, page 122.) Sometimes, as if the arms were merely cut out with curves from the sides of the body, the waist itself appears to be narrower than the shoulders by the widest combined width of the two elbows, each of which sustains to it a simple ratio, and in large numbers of men of our own time, the hips seem to be narrower than the shoulders merely by the width of the two wrists, each of which also sustains a simple ratio to them. See Fig. 31, page 57.

It is interesting, by the way, to notice the effect which high degrees of civilization seem to have upon the forms of men. If we walk on an American street, we can scarcely find one whose form corresponds to that in Fig. 43, page 82, nor many whose forms correspond to that in Fig. 44, page 84. One reason for this, probably, is that, in civilized countries, growing boys exercise their arms less and sit down, as in studying, more. It is worth noticing, too, that, accompanying this physical change, there has come a suggestion—in certain cases, not, of course, in all of them, nor in any of them except in a very general way—of a psychological change. The man acquires a larger number of womanly traits, becoming what is termed a gentleman. How far a corresponding change takes place in a woman, as she becomes more intellectually independent, is a question. But it is a fact that, in the opinion of most American artists, a woman's hips should be of the same breadth as her shoulders, whereas, in the opinion of most English artists, the hip-measurement should be the greater.

There is as much diversity in the measurements of the lower limbs as of the trunk. Viewed from in front, the calf below the knee is often of the same width as is that part of the leg which is just as far above the narrowing of the lower limb below the knee as the calf is below this point. See Figs. 43, page 82; 44, page 84; 54, page 100; and 57, page 103. The width of the calf, as seen in front, is usually twice that of the ankle (2 : 1), which latter is the same as the width of the instep below the ankle-bone, *i. e.,* 1 : 1 (see Figs. 49, page 95, and 57, page 103); and the centre of the foot is usually of the same width as is that part of the leg which is at the same distance as it is from the narrowest part of the ankle (1 : 1) and of the same width also as is the palm of the hand (1 : 1). See Fig. 62, page 121. Viewed from the side (see Fig. 70, page 133), the calf of the leg is usually of the same width as is that part of the leg which is at the same distance above the narrowing of it just below the knee as the calf is below this narrow point; and sometimes the width of the calf is the same as is the diagonal distance from the top of the instep to the heel (1 : 1). This last measurement is very variable; but one reason why a high instep is generally admired, seems to be because it enables the eye to perceive a resemblance between this dimension at the ankle and the dimension at the calf. In the side view again, the width of the ankle is usually as 1 : 1 to that of the distance from the highest point of the instep to the floor. It is about as 2 : 3—though in this Fig. 70 it is represented as 1 : 2—to the width of the calf; and it is as 1 : 2 to the upper length of the foot from the top of the instep to the end of the toes. See Fig. 36, page 71; Fig. 70; and Fig. 75, page 142. The upper length of the foot appears to be the same as that of the hand from the bottom of the palm. The ankle is located a little above the instep, and one wearing bracelets and anklets appears to have extremities, *i. e.*, hands and feet, of equal lengths (1 : 1). See Figs. 71, page 134; also 43, page 82; and 62, page 121. The sole of the foot, excluding the toes, is very nearly the length of the hand, as ex-

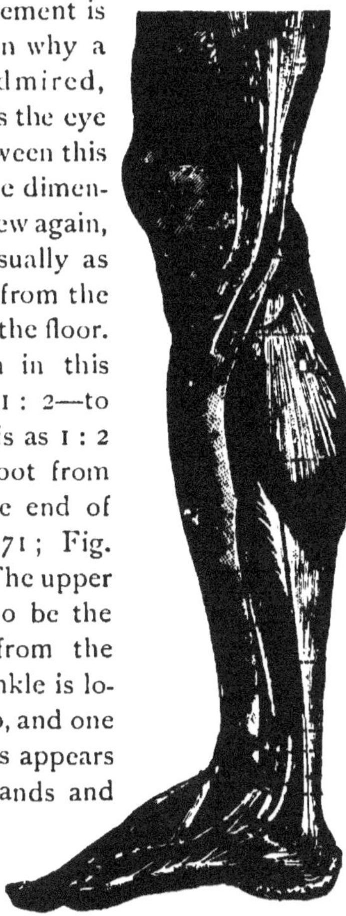

FIG. 70.—LEG AND FOOT.
See pages 132, 133.
From Duval's " Artistic Anatomy."

plained on page 130; and though we are told that according to the Greeks the length of the whole foot of a man was one sixth of the height of the body, we seldom find a foot that is relatively as long as this. From the same side view of the body, we may often notice, too, a like or clearly related width in the neck and certain parts of the legs; also in the head, waist, and a certain part of the thigh; also in the breast and lower trunk, though generally, especially in the male, these dimensions, as related, respectively, each to each, seem gradually lessened as the measurements are applied to a lower part of the form. See Figs. 35, page 70; 36, page 71; and 37, page 72.

FIG. 71.
CLOTHING PROPORTIONAL IN PARTS.
See pages 82, 130, 133.

But we have not completed our study of human proportions, when we have measured them according to merely rectilinear standards. The outlines of the body are almost invariably curved. This necessitates measurements according to a curvilinear standard. In most of the faces of the Greek statues, the curves made by the outlines of the top of the skull, the hair at the forehead, the eyebrows, eyes, nostrils, mouth, and chin, can be regularly described on either side of parallel horizontal lines drawn through them. See Fig. 45, page 86. The whole contour of the face, which, as viewed in front in Fig. 45, is oval, is sometimes represented as formed upon parts of the circumferences of three circles described from centres, one, as in this figure, at the middle of the forehead, one at the bridge of the nose, and one at the nostrils. If we suppose, as is usually done, that the three circles, one below the other, are diminished according to regular degrees or ratios of *gradation* (see chart on page 3, also note at the bottom of page 61), then, as is evident, they fulfil certain æsthetic requirements very literally. In a similar way, the contour of the head, as viewed from the side, is sometimes represented as formed upon parts of two circumferences, the centre of the larger of which is in the middle of the temple, and of the smaller in a straight line back of this and immediately above the ear. The form of the head, however, is so largely determined by the mental idiosyncrasies of individuals, that rules of this kind can have only a very limited fulfilment. Fig. 69, page 128, shows a different method of measurement. The face is related to an oval, and certain parts of it to radiating lines drawn from a point back of the ear. No such methods, however, are of invariable applicability. Perhaps their chief interest lies in the fact that they all suggest, in a general way, the existence of arrangements indicating proportion as a possibility.

What seems to be a more regular fulfilment of curvilinear requirements, the author has observed in the effects of the like circumferences drawn about, not the faces, but the forms in Figs. 31, page 57; 32, page 58; 35, page 70; 36, page 71; 73, page 137; and 74, page 139. These circumferences describe, of course, only very general outlines, in accordance with the principles unfolded in pages 68 to 72. But, even as applied to general outlines, the effects indicated are far too numerous, and too uniformly present, not to be seriously considered among the factors entering into the proportional result. Were the likeness in curvature thus suggested absent from any form, the eye would recognize the fact, and miss an impression of unity to such an extent as to get an impression of deformity. See page 71. We may accept these curves, therefore, especially when taken in connection with the facts of binocular vision to be explained in Chapter XVI. as a testimony to the æsthetic impression conveyed by putting like measurements with like. At the same time, it is true that, in all cases, when examined carefully, the outlines of the body, after conforming to these circumferences for a distance sufficient to establish a certain similarity of curvature, pass into other forms of curvature, either abruptly or gradually, and very often in exact fulfilment of the principle explained on pages 60 and 61;

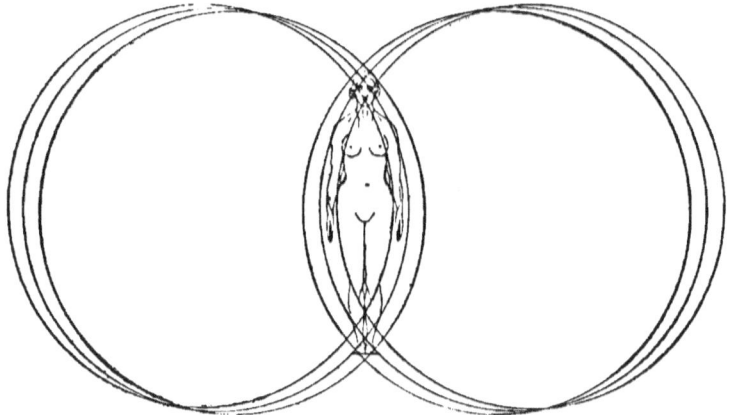

FIG. 72.—WOMAN'S FORM ENCLOSED BETWEEN CIRCLES.
See pages 59, 138, 290, 291, 295.

in such a way, therefore, that it can be said that there is an exact ratio between one part of the curve and each other part of it. Sometimes, too, as between the calf and the knee, the thigh and the waist, the forearm and the elbow, and the upper arm and the shoulder, there is a distinct likeness in the method characterizing all the changes in curvature. In fact, the whole outer contour of the leg from ankle to knee seems to be repeated with an increment between the knee and the hip, as well as also between the ankle and the hip, and the wrist and the shoulder. See Figs. 31, page 57; 32, page 58; and 73.

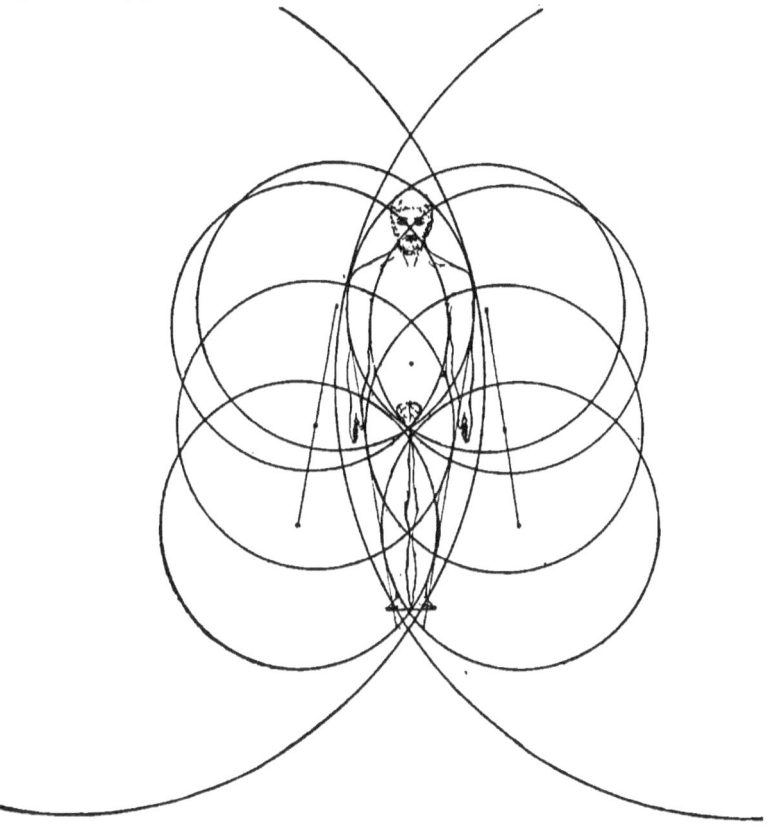

FIG. 73.—MAN'S FORM ENCLOSED BETWEEN CIRCLES.
See pages 15, 59, 72, 87, 135, 137, 138, 290, 291, 295.

Now, taking a more comprehensive view, we shall find that the form of both a man and a woman, as seen either from the front or the side, fits into a shape which may be termed elliptical because resembling that of an ellipse.

See Figs 72, page 136, and 73, page 137. As will be unfolded on page 280 of Chapter XVI. of this volume, treating of harmony of outline, there is an æsthetic reason for this elliptical shape aside from any requirements of proportion. Confining ourselves at present to only these latter, it will be noticed that a man's form, when he is facing us, requires a more broadened elliptical framework than a woman's. His form from the shoulders downward is wedge-shaped, the shoulders, as a rule, being about as much wider than the hips as these are than the width of the combined calves, and as these latter are than the width of the combined ankles. That is to say, the ratio of decrease in all these cases is about the same, thus manifesting proportion according to the method of *gradation*, already mentioned in the note on page 61, and in the chart on page 3. A representation of this wedge-shaped formation, as we usually see it, will be found in Fig. 31, page 57. A somewhat exaggerated illustration of the same is given in connection with Mr. Hay's conception of a typical man in Fig. 73, page 137. Notice in it the straight lines drawn diagonally downward between the outsides of the shoulders and the feet, as well as the other straight lines at either side of the body moving outward as they extend toward the feet, which latter lines connect the centres of the different inscribing circles.

A woman's form is perhaps more nearly describable in an exact ellipse (see Fig. 72, page 136), the shoulders being about the same width as the hips, and narrower than they are when combined with the width of the arms, and the relative difference between the width of the hips and of the combined calves being greater than in the case of a man. Compare Figs. 31, page 57, and 73, page 137, with Fig. 74, page 139.

As for other differences in human shapes, there is a reason for this one too, which is ascribable to significance. A larger size emphasizes the part of the form in which it appears. That which is of chief importance in a man is strength, and strength as required in labor. The seat of this kind of strength is in the shoulders that control the arms. Therefore, when the shoulders are broad the man

FIG. 74.—WOMAN'S FORM ENCLOSED IN LIKE CIRCLES.
See pages 15, 59, 72, 87, 135, 138, 290, 295.

appears to be made right. Moreover, the shoulders, being at the broadest part of the form, naturally attract our attention first. But, as will be shown on pages 277 to 280, the point on which the eyes are fixed is always horizontal to the widest part of the outside limits of distinct and easy vision. In order to conform to all the requirements of such vision, the part of the form below this point must taper downward. If we be looking chiefly at the shoulders, this wedge-like shape beneath them is that which best meets the requirements of ease of vision. On the contrary, that which is of chief importance in a woman is her sympathetic nature, and the seat of this is in the torso sufficiently below the shoulders to cause the same requirements of ease of vision to be best fulfilled when the wedge-like tapering begins lower down than in the case of the man, accompanied, too, by a tapering tendency in the direction of the head.

In all that has been said, reference has been made to only very general outlines. As applied to any but these, and, indeed, to some extent, even to them, it is impossible to find rules for guidance which, as used in particular cases, do not constantly need to be authenticated and modified by the facts that can be learned from studying models. All art is the representation of nature. The art that portrays human nature represents that which is, presumably, the highest embodiment of creative intelligence. A man who tries, after no matter how faithful a study of the human form in general, to create such a form *de novo*, is in danger of representing his own conceptions to the detriment both of nature and of that creative intelligence which gives human nature its highest significance. As indicated on page 89, a knowledge of proportion can do little more than enable an artist, in the presence of models, to select for portrayal features that are beautiful, and, where these are combined with such as are not, to avoid copying the latter, or, if he must regard them, then, as a result of observation and experience, to correct their defects. To do this last satisfactorily, however, or even to choose a model wisely, requires that an artist's judgment should be regulated by some correct general theory.

Such a theory may afford equal aid, too, when one is called upon to form practical or theoretical judgments with reference to mere posture. Notice how exactly most of the main lines in Fig. 35, page 70, correspond to the circumferences described about them. A little study of the forms in Figs. 43 to 47, pages 82 to 92, or in Figs. 49 to 59, pages 95 to 105, will reveal similar effects. Observe, too, the long simple curve between the right armpit and the right foot, also the similar but compound curve between the left hand and the left foot, in Fig. 75, page 142. There is no doubt that, when limbs are arranged so that their combined outlines suggest these like curves, the effect of beauty is enhanced on account largely of their influence in producing effects not only of harmony of outline, but of proportion. Indeed, it is while speaking of methods of securing these effects, that Vitruvius tells us that: " Applying the principles of Geometry," the Greeks " supposed the human figure with the arms and limbs extended to be first enclosed in a square or a circle, and then in a cube or sphere. Standing erect, with the arms extended at right angles, the height of the body from head to foot, and its breadth from finger end to finger end being the same, they inscribed it within a square [Fig. 63, page 122]; while with the arms extended obliquely but symmetrically, they drew the human figure with the hands and feet in the circumference of a circle whose centre was the navel [Fig. 62, page 121]. Every posture of action, as in walking, running, wrestling, boxing, was then mathematically studied, and the line of the centre of gravity was carefully marked; when the position of each limb and the breadth of each portion of the

142   *PROPORTION AND HARMONY.*

whole frame first conceived to be located in a circumscribed circle or square, and then in an enclosed cube or sphere, was measured with the greatest accuracy." Evidently, so far as the mind is influenced by the appearance of likeness in measurements, or in the outlines manifest-

FIG. 75.—FIGURE FROM NAUSICA. E. J. POYNTER.
See pages 59, 133, 141, 369.

ing them, it is essential to arrange forms in pictures and statues so that their general features shall reveal the effects of such measurements.

In fact, as applied to any of the products of the fine

arts, it seems inevitable that our general conclusion should conform to that already indicated, which is that proportion, while necessarily involving the use of such ratios as 1 : 2, 2 : 3, 3 : 4, 4 : 5, etc., is nevertheless, fundamentally considered, no more than an application to measurements, and, as connected with these, to spaces, of the methods of art already described in " The Genesis of Art-Form," and developed in the order in which they are arranged in the chart on page 3 of this volume.

CHAPTER IX.

PROPORTION IN ARCHITECTURE.

The Study of Proportion is still more Essential to the Architect than to the Painter or Sculptor—Ways in which a Building may be Given Expression and Character—The Essential Condition of Form is the Grouping of Factors that in Part are Alike—Architectural Likeness by Way of Congruity—of Repetition, Alternation, Consonance, Interchange, Gradation, etc.—All these Methods may be Applied to Measurements—Ratios of Measurements Recognizable when Expressed in Small Numbers—This Fact as Applied to an Exterior—To Interiors—Relative Measurements Need to be Apparent—Apparent Measurements Differ with Circumstances—Effects Produced by Apparent Subdivisions—Horizontal Subdivisions as Indicated by Outlines—Vertical Subdivisions—Horizontal as Related to Vertical Subdivisions—Influence of Subdivisions as Counteracting Real Dimensions by Apparent Ones.

ARCHITECTURE, like music, deals with forms that to only a limited extent can be said to result from an imitation of nature. In some regards, this fact gives the builder greater freedom for invention than is possible in painting and sculpture. He is not expected to accept forms as he finds them. Like the musician, who is at liberty to shorten and lengthen sounds so as to make them rhythmical, he is at liberty to shorten and lengthen shapes so as to make them proportional. But this fact places him, in some regards, under peculiar restraints. If the effects of the proportions produced by him must depend upon his own invention, it is particularly necessary for him to understand what the right proportions should be.

A painter not knowing this may succeed because he may be able to copy accurately the proportions of objects that form his models. But the architect, barring the instances, necessarily limited, in which he may exactly imitate the buildings of others, must design his own forms. In such circumstances, so far as beauty depends on proportion, if ignorant of its requirements, he will fail as certainly as a musician attempting to compose a march, without knowing how to produce rhythm. To show this fact, as well as the effects that proportion, in such cases, can add to a structure, and the places where it can be introduced, let us consider, for a moment, in accordance with the line of thought unfolded in full in Chapters XVII. to XIX. of " Painting, Sculpture, and Architecture as Representative Arts," some of the possible ways in which a building may be treated.

To begin with, it may be made to appear to be no more than a uniformly constructed blank wall. In this form, of course, it will be utterly expressionless. Altering it for the better, the blankness of the wall may be interrupted by lines where the bricks or stones composing it are joined. These will give it some expression, but not much. Then mouldings may be run along the base and top of the wall. These will reveal that there is a foundation below and an attempt at completion above. If sufficiently massive, they may impart to the structure as much expression as we find in the old-fashioned walls erected around ancient cities. See Fig. 9, page 36. But besides this, openings may be made in the wall for doors and windows, and a roof placed above the upper moulding. These will show it to be designed for the entrance of objects, and of light, and for shelter. Still again, to the tops and bottoms of the openings may be added elaborate caps and sills. These will emphasize the openings. In addition to these, between the windows or doors, mouldings may be carried horizontally around the building or in pilasters or buttresses perpendicularly up and down its sides. These will suggest arrangements designed for support,—possibly of floors dividing the building into different storeys, or of partitions dividing it into different rooms; and thus will tend to reveal the kind of building that it is. Finally, the outlines of the roof may be carried up into gables, turrets, domes, spires; and thus give additional representation, and so expression and character to the general effect. See Fig. 76, page 147; also what is said of certain representative features of this building on pages 349 and 352 of " Painting, Sculpture, and Architecture as Representative Arts."

Notice, however, that, even yet, all may not be done which is essential in order to make the form of the building, as a form, thoroughly satisfactory. As brought out in " The Genesis of Art-Form " and in this volume in the note at the bottom of page 61, the fundamental requirement of form as form is the putting together of factors which, notwithstanding some inevitable differences, are nevertheless partly alike. In its endeavor to group these features into *organic form*, the mind combines them in accordance with such methods as those termed in the chart on page 3, *unity, variety, complexity, order, confusion, counteraction, comparison, contrast, complement, principality, subordination*, and *balance*.

As influenced by the particular requirements of each product, the artistic tendency is first exercised through comparison by way of *congruity* (page 3). This causes parts that are to be alike to be selected so that they shall conform to the mental purpose of the building. In the degree

FIG. 76.—UNIVERSITY AT SYDNEY, AUSTRALIA.

See pages 146, 158, 163, 165, 175, 226.

in which they are to represent that which is heavy, strong, immovable, substantial, dignified, or near, congruity gives them all a tendency to be more or less large and bulky; in the degree in which they are to represent the opposite, it gives them an opposite tendency. In the degree in which they are to represent repose, congruity makes them characterized by horizontality; in the degree in which they are to represent aspiration, it makes them characterized by perpendicularity. In the degree in which they are to represent thoughtful contrivance, congruity makes them straight and rectangular; in the degree in which they are to represent more emotive effects, it makes them irregularly angular or curved. Notice these facts and others, as brought out in Chapters III. to VI. of " Painting, Sculpture, and Architecture as Representative Arts."

The general character of the outlines that are to be associated having been determined by the mental purpose, they are then put together according to such methods as are stated in the chart on page 3, and in the note at the bottom of page 61, prominent among which are *repetition*, *alternation*, *consonance*, *interchange*, *gradation*, and *transition*. As in the case of painting, so too we shall find here that all these methods may be applied to relative measurements as well as to relative shapes; and, therefore, to the production of effects of proportion. These relative measurements are usually estimated according to heights, lengths, or breadths considered in perspective, but sometimes also they are estimated according to the directions of curves or acuteness of angles. But it is well to notice that in these latter cases, it is wellnigh impossible to distinguish such effects as are attributable to the measurements, from such as are attributable to the outlines that are measured. For instance, when one says that the angles described by the coverings over the gable-windows, turrets, and different parts of the roof in Fig. 27, page 51, are not in proportion, he necessarily refers to appearances produced both by measurements and by shapes. In the mind of the observer, therefore, the two different classes of effects are often confounded.

In order to develop rightly the subject that is to be considered, let us try to start with a correct conception of what architectural proportion requires; and, for this purpose, let us recall what was said of it in Chapter IV., page 39. It was there stated that the measurements of certain parts of a building should appear to be related to one another according to certain ratios. But, in order to appear thus related, it was pointed out that the ratios should be such as to be easily recognized; and that, in order to fulfil this condition, they should be expressible in small numbers. For instance, if, in a window, or in a blank space inclosed by mouldings, or in the interior of a room, or in a whole façade, the height be to the breadth as $1:1$, $1:2$, $2:3$, $3:4$, etc., it is easy to recognize that the two are in proportion; but if they be to one another as $5:11$, or $9:14$, or $12:17$, etc., it is not easy to recognize this.

An illustration of what is meant, as well as of one or two other facts necessary to point out here, may be obtained by glancing at Fig. 77, page 150. This figure is all the more convenient for our purposes, because of its excess of ornamentation, justifiable to some extent, however, as said on page 348 of " Painting, Sculpture, and Architecture as Representative Arts," on the ground of its being one of the chief entrances to the palace of the Louvre. Notice that if we represent the width of each large window by 2, this will apparently be to the width of the space between the window and the nearest pillar as 2 : 1 ; to the width of the space occupied by the two pillars as 2 : 2 ; to the height of the window as 2 : 4 ; to the height of the whole storey in which each high window is situated as 2 : 5 ; to the height of the triangular pediment at the top as 2 : 3 ; and to the distance that the curved part of the roof extends above the pediment as 2 : 5. These relationships seem apparent to a first glance and to recognize them gives us a certain degree of satisfaction.

FIG. 77.—PAVILION OF RICHELIEU, PARIS.
See pages 42, 44, 149, 152, 154, 158, 160, 162, 163, 175.

The same principle is true as applied also to interiors. The proportions of some rooms are such that the moment that we enter them they give us satisfaction. Others do not. What the relationships of length, breadth, and height should be, in order to produce the former result, has sometimes been stated with great exactness. Vitruvius, for instance (see page 119), tells us that the length should be to the breadth as 5 : 3, or as 3 : 2 ; in very large halls, as 2 : 1, and sometimes as 5 : 7. As to their height, Peter Legh, in the " Music of the Eye " (see page 27), in commenting on Vitruvius, says : " If simple analogies are to be our guide in all the eurithms and all the symmetries, the best rule for height seems to make it equal to half the sum of the length and the breadth ; these would be lofty rooms, but lofty rooms are always handsome, and this system would always give us a good proportion, for when the proportion of length to breadth were as one to two, the height would be one and a half, that is to say, the breadth, height, and length would be respectively two, three, and four."

Whatever may be thought of these and other like statements, notice that, whether applied to exteriors or interiors, the important consideration is that there should be some apparent relationship between the length, height, and breadth. If we perceive that there is such a relationship, our minds are satisfied. If we fail to perceive it, they are confused; the effects are distracting and disquieting. As will presently be shown, the use, on exteriors, of window-caps, string-courses, cornices, pilasters, pillars, and also of some of these, as well as of color and of upholstery in interiors, may sometimes counteract a confusing tendency. But sometimes, too, it cannot; and when needing to suggest relationships that do not really exist, it can never do so except by apparently shortening or lengthening actual dimensions.

This last sentence will remind the reader of what was said in Chapter IV., and will be unfolded further in Chapter XIV., namely, that, as the principles of proportion have reference to appearances and to these alone, they cannot be fulfilled in a satisfactory way without regard to circumstances. A number of straight lines enclosed within a space, for instance, increase the apparent length of that space in the direction in which they point or incline. Any other spaces containing no such lines, yet intended to appear of equal length with it, ought really, therefore, to be a little longer. Again, if when we are looking at a building a projecting cornice hide part of a wall, window, pediment, or roof that is above the cornice, so that this upper part appears too short or too low to be in good proportion, then, as we shall find was the case in the Parthenon, it must be made longer or higher, no matter what its real measurement may be. The end to be attained is not factors with like or related measurements, but factors that appear to have these.

To illustrate this statement, by referring again to Fig. 77, page 150, as we look at this façade it appears to be—though it is not—constructed according to a ratio of breadth to height, if we include the rounded part above the pediment, of 2 : 4; or, if we do not include this, of 2 : 3. But the height is not relatively so great as these figures would indicate. It merely appears to be so ; and one reason for this is the cumulative effects of the perpendicular lines of the pillars. Similar effects will be noticed in Fig. 78, above. To many, this arch seems to be exactly as high as it is broad, but it is not. This is true, however, of the arch in Fig. 79, page 153, and of the temple in Fig. 80, page 153 ; but the pillars in both these latter make the height seem greater than the breadth.

FIG. 78.—ARCH OF SEPTIMIUS SEVERUS.
See pages 152, 163, 175.

There is another fact worth noticing in connection with the façade in Fig. 77, page 150. This fact is, that we judge the whole breadth to be related to the whole height as 1 : 2, or as 2 : 4, because of the effect produced upon the mind by the smaller spaces into which the whole is subdivided. The clear inference from this is that the mind judges of the proportions of a whole from the proportions of the parts composing it ; precisely, indeed, as it judges of rhythm as a whole from the separate effects of the measures as it hears them, one after the other. It is

ARCHITECTURAL PROPORTIONS. 153

needless to say that this is not the method usually attributed to judgments formed of proportion. Critics generally start, rather than end, by saying that the height of the Parthenon is to its breadth as 9 : 14. But it is a question whether the mind, however rapidly it works, does not draw its conclusions from a comprehensive glance, first, at details. Look, for instance, at the façade of the Cathedral of Cologne, Fig. 81, page 155. Considering each long window with the moulding under it to represent one storey, we may say that the height of the two towers,

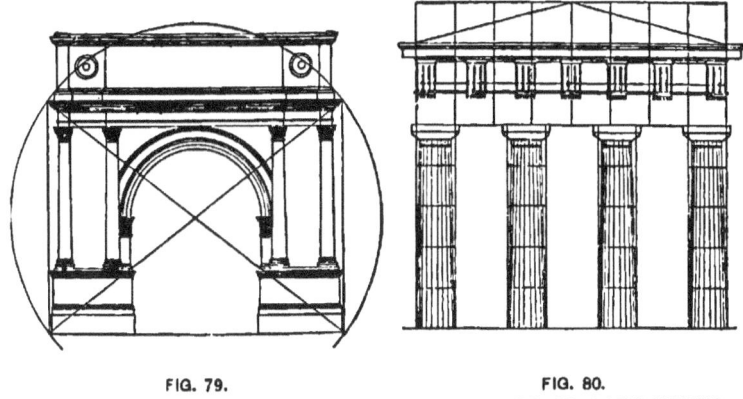

FIG. 79.
ARCH OF AUGUSTUS AT AOSTA.
See pages 152, 163.

FIG. 80.
TEMPLE OF THEMIS AT RHAMNUS.
See pages 152, 154, 163, 164, 168, 175.

exclusive of the finial at the extreme top of the spires, is equal to that of six storeys. As a fact, each storey is slightly less in height than the storey under it, an arrangement which, while not introducing sufficient difference to lessen the appearance of likeness in the dimensions, does increase the apparent altitude of the building, because, if a dimension, apparently meant to be the same, seems to be slightly less, it appears to be at a greater distance. So we may say that the height of this cathedral represents that of six storeys. The height of the nave—as seen between the towers—exclusive of a finial resembling that at the top of the spires, may be said to represent the height of two storeys and one half; though, as a fact—with no addition, it may be said, to the artistic effect of the building—it is slightly more than this. The reason why the nave has an upper one-half storey seems to be because its gable, to correspond in pitch—one cannot help saying that it might correspond still more closely in pitch—to the other angular outlines of the building, needs to be just half as high as a whole storey. Therefore, though we may say that the height of the nave is to the height of the towers as 5 : 12, it is not of this proportion, as a cause, that the mind thinks when looking at the building, but of the smaller as well as general arrangements of the building which make this proportion a result.

Now notice, once more, that arrangements such as have been indicated, especially in Fig. 77, page 150, illustrate what was said on page 43, of the effect produced upon the mind when determining ratios, by outlines dividing, according to some unit of measurement, the parts to be compared. Relative measurements may, of course, be indicated merely by the width of windows and doors. But it is evident that these measurements can be more clearly indicated, when emphasized by other vertical or horizontal indications of subdivision. In Willesden Church, Fig. 14, page 40, the width of the tower and of the church is the same, giving two equal divisions. In St. Stephen's, Caen, Fig. 11, page 37, the width of each tower and of the space between the two towers is the same, giving three equal divisions in width, as there are also in the temple in Fig. 80, page 153. In St. Sulpice, Paris, Fig. 82, page 156, con-

FIG. 81.—COLOGNE CATHEDRAL—FAÇADE.

See pages 42, 44, 153, 154, 156, 157, 160, 163, 165, 175, 180, 207, 226, 236, 237.

156   PROPORTION AND HARMONY.

cerning which, however, something more will be said presently, each tower is exactly half as wide as the space between the towers, giving four equal divisions; and in the temple of Theseus, Fig. 10, page 36, as also in the cathe-

FIG. 82.—ST. SULPICE, PARIS.
See pages 42, 43, 44, 154, 158, 160, 161, 166, 175.

dral at Cologne, Fig. 81, page 155, we can see five equal divisions. Notice, in the latter building, how artistically effects of *variety* and *balance* are introduced without interfering at all with this appearance of exact subdivision.

In the side divisions, one of the huge buttresses flanking the towers is joined with each of the comparatively narrow windows of the towers; but, in the central division, there are no large buttresses and the central window fills almost the entire width.

FIG. 83.—ST. SULPICE MODIFIED.
See page 161.

What is true of horizontal divisions is true, of course, of vertical ones. The six storeys in Cologne Cathedral have already been noticed. Similar divisions need hardly be pointed out in St. Sulpice, Fig. 82, page 156. In Chichester Cathedral, Fig. 15, page 41, the two bands dividing the spire into three equal parts of the same height as the square part of the tower above the roof, indicate, at once, the proportion of 3 : 1. In Fig. 76, page 147, there are many different ways in which the horizontal stringcourses, by dividing the spaces, reveal the fact of apparently like or related measurements. It is these that, by separating into two subdivisions the distance between the windows of the first and of the second storeys, cause this space to seem the same as the space also divided into two subdivisions, between the top of the second-storey windows and the top of the castellation above the eaves. It is these string-courses too that cause the large gable over the bay windows at the left to appear to add a third storey to the building of exactly the same height as each of the two storeys below it, and that cause the four storeys of the central tower, and the five storeys of its corner turrets, all to seem of the same height. On pages 349 and 352 of "Painting, Sculpture, and Architecture as Representative Arts," these string-courses, and other features of this exterior, are shown to be artistic because they represent the arrangements of storeys and rooms in the interior. Now they are shown to be so for a reason that has nothing to do with such representation. This is only one more of many illustrations of the fact that genuinely artistic effects usually accord equally with the requirements both of form and of significance.

Now let us observe in what complex ways (see page 15) these outlines, emphasizing the subdivisions, work together to indicate the ratios between horizontal and vertical measurements in façades as wholes. In Fig. 77, page 150, the square formed by all of the building that is under the

PROPORTION IN ARCHITECTURE. 159

string-course immediately above the windows in the second storey seems to be divided in height into two parts and in width into three parts. In each part, the width seems to be to the height as 2 : 3. The 2 of the three widths multi

FIG. 84.—ST. SULPICE MODIFIED.
See page 161.

plied by 3 give 6 parts for the whole square; and the 3 of the two heights multiplied by 2 also give 6 for the whole. This equality of results suggests another reason why this space below the third storey seems, as said on page 152, to be—although it is not—just as wide as it is high, *i. e.*, square. In Cologne Cathedral, Fig. 81, page 155, it was shown, on page 154, that the height of the nave appeared to be to the height of the towers as 5 : 12. On page 156 the width was shown to be apparently divided into 5 parts. Therefore the width, too, of the building appears to be to the height of the towers as 5 : 12 ; while to the height of the nave, it appears to be as 5 : 5, or as 1 : 1.

The inference drawn from the subdivisions is more accurate as applied to the Cathedral of Cologne than to the pavilion in Fig. 77, page 150, but in neither case can the mind escape from a mistaken impression. It cannot believe that the proportions are one thing, when the subdivisions suggest that they are another. A very convincing proof of this may be obtained from the façade of St. Sulpice, Paris, Fig. 82, page 156. Has any one ever looked at this church without finding himself involuntarily asking why it is that its proportions seem so unsatisfactory? And yet it is not because the measurements, as applied to the building as a whole, violate any of the principles of proportion. The extreme width of each tower is to the width of the space between the towers exactly as 1 : 2. Could any scheme of ratios be more simple? Why, then, does it not appear so? Why, but because of the five divisions made by the pillars in the space between the towers? How can the mind recognize that each tower's width is to the space as 1 : 2, or, what is the same thing, as 2 : 4, when it sees five instead of four divisions in this space? It cannot do so, or, at least, not without at first being confused. Were there a pediment above the cornice over the nave, the apex of this would divide the space there into two equal parts ; or were the central door of the nave made more prominent than the two doors each side of it, then the present unfortunate effect would be prevented. But if such changes cannot be made, the mind would be better satisfied, in that it would judge the proportions to be more correct, even on a supposition that they were 2 : 4, in case there were only four arches between the towers, as in Fig. 83, page 157; though, in fact, the proportions would be less correct. Or, if, instead of four arches, which are objectionable because allowing no central door, there were three arches, as in Fig. 84, page 159, with these again the mind would be satisfied, but for a different reason. A single glance at this Fig. 84 reveals the fact that neither of the towers is as wide as the central space between them, and yet is not twice as wide. The three arches, as well as the open space higher up between the towers, give an impression that each tower is to this space as 2 : 3, besides which, as the towers are much nearer together than in Fig. 82, page 156, the mind is more easily reconciled, according to the principle of *balance*, to an arrangement of the arches in the towers different from that shown in the space between them.

CHAPTER X.

PROPORTION IN ARCHITECTURE, CONTINUED.

The Mind Takes Satisfaction, not in Ratios, but in the Repetition of Measurement Indicated by them—This Form of Repetition Illustrated—Repetitions of Measurements and Shapes Go together—Illustration of an Absence of both Forms of Repetition—Alternation of Measurements—Consonance as Applied to Shapes—Interchange as Applied to Shapes—A Unique Illustration of it—Consonance and Interchange as Applied to Measurement—An Illustration of them and of Complication—Gradation of Shapes and Measurements—Complement and Balance of Shapes and Measurements—Proportion an Application to Measurements of the Art-Methods Mentioned on Page 3.

THE conclusion reached in the last chapter will serve to verify a statement made many times already, to the effect that the main reason why the mind takes satisfaction in seeing outlines related to one another as 1 : 2 or 2 : 3, etc., is because it recognizes that the first is another expression for 1 : 1 + 1, and that the second is another expression for 1 + 1 : 1 + 1 + 1. In other words, the mind does not take satisfaction in the ratio *per se*, but in perceiving the fulfilment of the art-method of *repetition* as applied to measurements. It is not too much to say that the main impression with reference to proportion conveyed by Fig. 77, page 150, is that of likeness in certain spaces occupied by the various openings as surrounded by pillars or mouldings.

Now observe the same fact as exemplified in the primitive manifestations of proportion illustrated in Figs. 6, page 33; 7, page 34; 8, page 35; and 9, page 36. Observe the fact

REPETITION IN ARCHITECTURAL PROPORTION. 163

as exemplified also in the artistic manifestations of the same characteristics in Figs. 10, page 36; 11, page 37; 12, page 38; 15, page 41; 30, page 55; 76, page 147; 77, page 150; and 81, page 155. Similar repetition is evident, too, in con-

FIG. 65.—AN AMERICAN CHURCH.
See pages 164, 166.

nection with just enough of that variety which the Greek knew so well how to introduce, in Fig. 80, page 153, as well as in the Roman arches in Figs. 78, page 152, and 79, page 153.

Most of these figures will recall and exemplify what was said on page 148, with reference to the artistic necessity of *repetition* in shape as well as in measurement. Here it is chiefly important to notice how inevitably the two kinds of repetition go together. Fig. 27, page 51, was used in order to illustrate how an absence of one kind of it involves an absence of the other. Notice the same fact now as illustrated in Fig. 85, page 163.

Not only do the horizontal caps of the upper windows in the apse fail to correspond to the arched caps in the same, but the distance between these upper caps and the roof fails to correspond to any other vertical distance in the apse. So, too, not only does the lower large arch of the large tower fail to correspond in shape to the other arches of the tower, but the distance from it to the twin arches under it, as well as to the horizontal sill of the large arched window over it, fails to correspond to any other vertical distance in the tower. The same is true, also, of the relative heights of different spaces in the small tower. How a man could construct a building supposing that the eye would not immediately recognize and resent these incongruities in the shapes and measurements is inexplicable. But one is forced to say that this is often done, and—what is worse—is done by those considered to be our foremost architects.

The *repetition* of measurements as influenced by the art-methods of *variety* or *alteration* (see chart on page 3) is wellnigh certain, as intimated on page 116, to pass into more or less *alternation* of measurements. For instance, the pillars in Figs. 10, page 36, and 80, page 153, alternate with the spaces between the pillars. In such cases, if all the pillars, as compared with one another and not with the spaces between them, are of like apparent dimensions, and also all the spaces, as compared with one another and not with the pillars, then it is not necessary that the ratio between the dimensions of the pillars and the dimension of the spaces should be easily recognized; in other words, it is not necessary that this ratio should be represented by a small number (see page 117). Whatever may be the ratio, the mind will take in at a glance the fact that one pillar is to the space next to it as a second pillar is to a second space.

Accordingly, while it may be desirable that the measurements of each set, whether of pillars or spaces, should sustain a certain relationship to the measurements of each other set, this is much less important than that the measurements of all the members of each set should seem to be alike. To illustrate what is meant, it is important in Fig. 15, page 41, that the two dark bands surrounding the spire should both seem of the same height as the ornamentation at the top of the square part of the tower, also that the larger spaces of the spire should seem of the same height as the square part of the tower between the roof and this ornamentation. But it is less important that the exact ratio between these bands and the larger spaces should be recognized. So in Fig. 76, page 147, it is important that the two subdivisions between the front windows of the first and second storeys should seem the same as the two subdivisions between the tops of the windows of the second storey and the top of the whole front wall. But it is less important that the exact ratio between the height of these spaces and the height of the windows, or, say, of the breadth of the windows, should be recognized. So again, in Cologne Cathedral, Fig. 81, page 155, it is important that the storeys, as they have been termed, should seem—though gradually diminished in order to increase the apparent height—of like height, and that the same should seem to be the case with the cornices or mouldings separating these storeys; but it is less important that the exact ratio between the height of the storeys and the height of the mouldings should be recognized. In all these cases, too, it is important, as intimated on page 164, that, while the alternating measurements seem alike, the intervening ones should seem sufficiently unlike the others not to confuse the mind by suggesting likeness where it is not intended to be suggested.

Consonance (see page 3) results from likeness or repetition in the general principles of construction, rather than —though it involves more or less of this—in the particular details of form. The choir of Ely Cathedral, for instance, Fig. 30, page 55, is consonant throughout. So are the towers of St. Stephen's, Caen, Fig. 11, page 37. So are the roofs and turrets in Fig. 28, page 53. But in Fig. 27, page 51, the different shapes of the gables, window-caps, and turrets of the roof are not consonant. Neither are the pediments over the third storeys in the towers in St. Sulpice, Fig. 82, page 157. The only thing that could excuse these pediments would be a pediment over the central nave. Of course, in Fig. 85, page 163, there are many features that are not consonant. The façade of the Grand Opera House, Paris, Fig. 86, page 167, would be more consonant if the lintels over the windows behind the colonnade of the second storey surmounted arches corresponding to the arched openings of the lower storey, as well as to the rounded roofs at either end of this colonnade.

To defer, for a moment, our consideration of *consonance* as applied to architectural measurements, let us notice that architectural *interchange* in form is a variation of consonance in accordance with which different sets of forms, all the members of each of which sets are alike,

ARCHITECTURAL INTERCHANGE. 167

are introduced into different parts of the building. Thus, in this Opera House, at Paris, Fig. 86, the round arches over the entrances of the lower storey, and the rounded outlines over the sides of the colonnade, and in the dome

FIG. 86.—OPERA HOUSE, PARIS.
See pages 15, 166, 167, 170, 175, 226.

seen against the upper pediment, interchange with the horizontal lines over the colonnade, as well as with the windows behind it, and the panels in the storey above the colonnade.

A unique attempt to produce effects of *interchange* may be noticed in the façade of St. Étienne du Mont,

Paris, Fig. 87, page 169. In connection with almost all the openings there is a combination of horizontal, angular, and curved effects. All three doors have horizontal lintels. But over the central one is first a curved cap, and above this a large angular pediment-shaped cap. Over the doors at the sides, however, are first angular caps and above them small curved caps. All the windows are either rectangular or curved; but those that are rectangular have curved forms inside of them. Above the large pediment over the central entrance is a rounded cap over a circular window, and above this a smaller rectangular blank window, enclosing a circular one, and above the whole is a sharply angular gable in front of the roof. Possibly if the large rounded cap over the central front round window had been lower down, *i. e.*, just above the central entrance, and if the pediment-shaped cap which is just over this entrance had been higher up, *i. e.*, above the round window, and if the gable in front of the roof had corresponded or very nearly corresponded in shape to this pediment-shaped cap, there might have been some suggestion of logic in the arrangement, inasmuch as there would have been a gradual increase of pitch in the forms from the lowest upward. (See "The Genesis of Art-Form," pp. 291–295). But the front, as it is, merely shows the method of *interchange* run mad.

As applied to measurements, *consonance* and *interchange*, respectively, are merely less regular forms of *repetition* and *alternation*. Every Greek temple (Figs. 10, page 36, and 80, page 153) manifests *alternation* in the measurements of pillars and spaces and also of triglyphs and spaces, or sometimes metopes, in the frieze (Fig. 3, page 12), but it also suggests *interchange*, there being a tendency toward the same height in the foundation, the entablature,

FIG. 87.—ST. ETIENNE DU MONT.
See pages 167, 168.

and the tympanum (Figs. 10, page 36, and 94, page 183), while the pillars are much higher than these, though usually sustaining to them, as we shall find, an apparent proportional relationship. In St. Stephen's, Caen (Fig. 11, page 37), all the storeys are of the same height except the lowest storey of all and the highest storey of the square part of the tower, the storey out of which the spires seem to spring. This lowest storey and the highest storey of the square part of the tower seem to agree in height.

The Opera House in Paris, Fig. 86, page 167, gives us some unusual illustrations of *interchange* as well as of *complexity* and, one might say, of *complication* in measurements. Its whole height seems easily divisible into four parts, the lowest division of which extends above the base of the pillars of the second storey as far as to the railing of its balcony. Looked at thus, the height from the lower arches to this railing is the same as that between the tops of the windows of the second storey and the bottom of the cornice above them; the same, too, as the rounded ornamental front above the pillars at either side of the building, and also the same as a clearly-defined space between the top of the cornice over the pillars and the bottom of the ornamental cornice above this. If, however, we take the second storey to be the most prominent in the building, and therefore consider the entire height of its pillars, which is evidently the representative intention, then between the arches below the pillars and the bases of the pillars we find a height exactly equal to that of the cornice above the pillars, and also of the ornamental cornice some distance above this, and, once more, of the rounded cornice over the dome seen just under the central pediment. Added to this, notice the rounded outlines over each end of the row of pillars on the second storey. By placing a finger over each of these rounded ends, one can recognize how much they assist the effect of the dome seen against the pediment in the centre by way of *balance;* and also how they serve to connect this dome-form and the rounded arches over the entrances of the lower floor by way of *interchange.* This front would have been more successful perhaps if these rounded pediments at either side of the second storey had been half domes corresponding to the part seen of the large dome of the building, or if the window-caps between the pillars of the colonnade on the second floor had suggested a correspondence in shape to the arrangements over the four pillars at either side of the colonnade. Nevertheless, as the building stands, it is an admirable example of successful proportions manifesting great *variety, complexity,* and even *complication* of design, and yet great apparent simplicity.

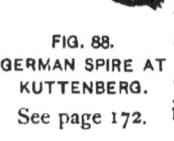

FIG. 88. GERMAN SPIRE AT KUTTENBERG. See page 172.

FIG. 89.—STEEPLE OF BOW CHURCH, LONDON. See page 172.

Gradation, as applied to forms, causes likeness in degrees of difference. As applied to measurements, of course, it would give likeness in degrees of these. Figs.

FIG. 90.—STREET AND BELFRY AT GHENT.
See page 172.

88 and 89, page 171, Fig. 90, and Fig. 91, page 173, all illustrate *gradation* both in forms and measurements. The regularity with which the diminution of size takes

ARCHITECTURAL BALANCE. 173

place in each could evidently not be produced except as a result of a regular ratio of diminution. Compare the tower in Fig. 91, with the unsatisfactory effect produced by a disregard of gradation in Fig. 92, page 174, and the connection between gradation in the form and gradation in the proportions will be at once apparent.

In the chart on page 3 of this volume, *complement* and *balance* are represented as art-methods of earlier development than the others that we have here considered. But this is true only as related to theoretical requirements. Practically, as used in art, these methods may be applied not at the beginning of production, but at its end, in order to complete the form. When thus used, it

FIG. 91.—TOWER OF BORIS KREMLIN MOSCOW.

See pages 172, 173.

174 PROPORTION AND HARMONY.

will be noticed that, in a sense, *balance* is merely *alternation* containing three factors, the first and third of which are alike, and the second, or middle one, different. In

FIG. 92.—DOME OF CHIAVAVALLE, IN ITALY
See page 173.

the human form, the trunk is the middle factor, and the arms and legs balance. So, in the primitive art-form in Fig. 6, page 33, there is a central part, and the equal

shelves arranged on either side of it balance. In Figs.
11, page 37; 12, page 38; 81, page 155; and 82, page 156;
the nave is central and the two towers balance. Even in
Figs. 10, page 36; 76, page 147; 77, page 150; 80, page
153; and 86, page 167, we can detect a central part distinguished, if not by a pediment or tower, at least by having
like spaces at each side. The balance suggested in Fig. 86
by the two round-arched coverings at each side of the
colonnade, corresponding with each other and—though
only in a much broader sense—with the dome seen resting against the upper pediment, has already been noticed.
Now in the arch in Fig. 78, page 152, observe the high
central opening and the two balancing openings at
each side of it. All the proportions of this arch, too, will
bear study. The perpendicular sides of the small openings are to those of the large central opening as 2 : 3. So,
too, is the horizontal distance between the pillars at each
side of the small openings and between the pillars at
each side of the large central opening. The height of the
space between the pillars at each side is divided horizontally into three equal parts, the lowest extending to the
tops of the large bases of the pillars, and the second to
the tops of the horizontal ornamentation above the small
arches. The distance from the top of the large central
arch to the top of the upper cornice is the same as that
between the pillars that are each side of the central arch;
and the height of the panel, exclusive of the cornice, extending across the entire top of the arch is the same as
the height of the inclosed space above each of the small
arches at the sides. As has been said before, the arch is
not square, though owing to the effect of the vertical lines
of the pillars it seems to be so. At the same time, the
breadth of the arch, as measured from the outside lines

of the outside pillars alone, is the same as its height. It is partly for this reason that though, when looked at in one way, it is not square, when looked at in another way it is square, and when looked at in any way it appears to be square.

From all that has been said in this chapter it is apparent that we can draw the same conclusion here as was drawn from our review of proportion as manifested in the human form, namely, that while it necessarily involves the use of such ratios as 1 : 2, 2 : 3, 3 : 4, 4 : 5, etc., it nevertheless, fundamentally considered, is no more than an application to measurements and, as connected with these, to spaces of the same methods of art which are indicated in the chart on page 3, and, as applied in all the arts, are described in a general way in "The Genesis of Art-Form."

CHAPTER XI.

PROPORTION IN GREEK ARCHITECTURE.

Greeks Pre-eminent in Architecture—The Secret of their Methods of Proportion Involves more than the Study of Measurements—The Mind is Conscious of Ratios in Proportion—It has Reasons for Using them—The Reasons of the Greeks may have been Different from what we Suppose—To Understand the Reasons we must Judge their Buildings as we do Other Art-Products, by their General Effects—And Draw our Conclusions from Many Specimens—The Authorities Consulted in the Measurements to be Quoted in this Book—The Greek Temple Composed of Different Sets of Factors, each Set Having the Same Measurements—To Show this we are to Start with Factors of Small Dimensions—Same Height in the Abacus and Corona of Horizontal and Raking Cornices, the Ovolo, Cyma Recta, etc.—Measurements of these Parts in Different Temples—Variations and Explanations—Like Proportions of all the Parts just Mentioned to the Height of the Capitals, and of both the Cornices and the Steps—Ratios of 1 : 2 Sustaining this Statement—Of 1 : 3—Of 2 : 3—Like Ratios of the Parts just Mentioned to the Height of the Architrave, Frieze, and Raking Cornice with Cymatium—Also to Upper Diameter of Shafts and Width of Metopes—Explanations—Ratios of 1 : 2—Of 1 : 3—Remarks—Like Ratios of the Parts just Mentioned to the Height of the Entablature, Tympanum, and Width of Upper Inter-Columnation—Confirmation—Insufficiency of Data with Reference to the Tympanum and Pediment—Like Ratios of the Height of Entablature and Pediment Spaces, Differently Divided, to the Height of Column-Space—The Different Methods of Dividing these Gave Opportunity for Originality Exercised in Conformity to Law.

WHEN speaking of the human figure it was said that of all artists who have ever studied its proportions the Greeks are acknowledged to have known most about them. The same is true with reference to architectural proportions. This subject of proportion in all its applications is supposed to have been mastered by them as by no other people; and almost all the works written upon it in modern times that are of value have been attempts to prove that the writer has at last discovered the clew to the methods of measurement exemplified in the masterpieces on the Acropolis, where, as Lloyd tells us in the appendix to Cockerill's "Temples of Ægina and Bassæ," page 68, "architectural elements combine with the harmonious flow of the poetry of Sophocles, and with a coherence and cogency that are truly Demosthenic," comparing "with some of the great works of classic music in which the genius of the composer has only to contend against his matchless command of the scientific resources of his art." It seems desirable, therefore, before leaving this subject, to find out whether, in any degree, the principles that have been unfolded are sufficient to account for the measurements underlying the proportions of the Greek temples, which so many admire, but apparently without knowing why they do so.

In order to accomplish our object, it is necessary to begin by recalling the line of thought in Chapter IV., and to recognize again that it is impossible to solve the secrets of the Greek proportions by studying accurately merely the measurements of their buildings. It is only in a very slight degree that we are made wiser for practical architectural work when we have learned that in the Parthenon the width of the column was to that of the whole breadth of the front as $5 : 81$, or that the "height was to the breadth as $9 : 14$."

As has been said, proportion is not the analogue of musical harmony. Therefore the mind cannot, as from harmony, experience the effects of ratios aside from being conscious that they exist. The analogue of proportion is rhythm; and in this, though one may do no counting, he knows that he could do it, if he chose, and with satisfactory results. He evidently could not know this if confronted with the effects of any such ratios as 5 : 81 or 9 : 14. Nor, even though the ratios be expressible in comparatively small numbers, can one be sure that by knowing merely these he can know all that is to be learned about proportion as it was developed by the Greeks. "I believe," says the Greek scholar, "in using the proportion 7 : 12 or 9 : 14 because the Greeks used it." This kind of an argument may do for a pedagogic Hellenist, but it will not do for a practical architect. If the Greeks used this, or any other proportion, they had a reason for doing it. If the architect of our day use it without knowing this reason, he will use it irrationally, and very likely erroneously. If, for instance, the breadth of a hall be to its length as 7 : 12, and it have an altar or columns or heavy doorways at one or both ends, it is possible that the proportions may look like 6 : 12. As has been shown to an extent, and will be shown more clearly in Chapters XIII. to XV., there were many of the dimensions which the modern Hellenist would follow slavishly, which the Greeks used on account not of what they were, but of what they appeared to be. Nor, even admitting that the proportions were used on account of what they were, is it certain that the parts of the buildings which modern students suppose these proportions to determine are the parts which the Greeks intended them to determine. When, for example, the height of a temple, pediment included, is to its breadth as 7 : 12, or 9 : 14, is this ratio the cause of these dimensions, or only an incidental and, therefore, almost accidental result of arrangements for which the cause is to be sought elsewhere,—for instance, in a desire to make the entablature and pediment appear of the same height, and both together to appear to sustain a certain ratio to the columnar space below them? See what is said of Cologne Cathedral on pages 153 to 155. In any view of the subject, it is surmisable, at least, that the consideration which modern students pay to an accidental result may overlook an essential cause, which alone can enable one to interpret the proportion rationally. Whatever benefit we may derive, therefore, and it may be much, from the accurate measurements of the buildings of the Greeks, we can never find out, in this way alone, those elements of proportion which they esteemed of most importance.

To understand what these elements were we must examine their buildings, as intimated on page 35, not near at hand, but from a distance. The same holds good in principle as applied to the processes through which we come to understand any works of art. If we wish to study Raphael, we do not start by trying to detect the way in which he put the paint upon his canvas. We sit before a finished work of his where we can gaze, unconscious of the paint, at what seems flesh and blood infused with thought and grace and beauty. We feel his composition in our souls before we touch it with our fingers. If we wish to study Shakspere, we do not start by testing how his lines will parse and scan. We read, or we hear read, an act or a scene. We listen to the music of his sentences. We heed the accents of the living men of his drama. We note the play of fancy that passes between them, their bursts of passion and the friction of their thoughts as they flame out so that heaven and hell both brighten to reveal their secrets. We move with ordinary men and women, but cast in an heroic mould. We live in history that was dead but has found a resurrection. We revel in the bliss of a new world that the poet's genius has created. These are facts that pedants never seem to realize. They teach the spelling-book and mathematics, and think that out of these the works of art develop. But works of art are germed in seed that drops down from above. Like Minerva from the brain of Jove, they spring to life full-armed; and soar through air before they tread the earth; and when, through using spelling-books and mathematics, men make the art-forms fit intelligence, these forms have no artistic value save to those who know enough to search beneath them for the principle that formed them, a principle manifested in results that cannot be perceptible except to larger and more comprehensive views in which the parts appear related to the wholes, and the wholes related to the parts. So, to judge of these Greek buildings, we must see them from a distance where such views are possible. Indeed, the very conception that the Greek had of proportion indicates as much. How could he study what he considered the *intermeasurement* between the parts, except from a point where all, or at least a majority of all, the parts were visible?

Again, in order to find what the Greeks considered desirable in architectural proportion, we should draw our conclusions from examining as many temples as we can. The results to be given here have been compiled from the measurements of almost every ancient Doric temple in existence, as these are variously indicated in Penrose's "Principles of Athenian Architecture," Cockerill's "Temples of Ægina and Bassæ," Stuart's "Antiquities of Athens," and the summaries made of the results of the labors of such men as Delagardetta, Ross, Shaubert,

Hansen, and Blouet, in Hittorf's "Architecture Antique de la Sicile." The figures to be used are the same as in these works. By consequence, as can easily be determined, they sometimes represent feet and decimals of feet, sometimes relative measurements of a given standard,

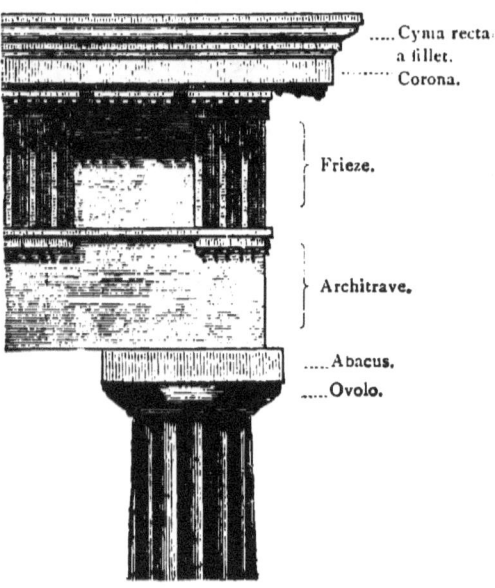

FIG. 93.—COLUMN AND ENTABLATURE OF TEMPLE OF ÆGINA.
See pages 183, 185, 187, 188, 191, 192, 203, 219.

and sometimes follow the French system. But as measurements of the same temple are always indicated according to the same system, and as it is necessary for us to observe merely the relationships between these, the results, as represented in the figures used in each of these works, will answer our purposes. The initial letters of the authorities already mentioned, P., C., S., and H., with

GREEK ARCHITECTURAL PROPORTIONS. 183

L. for Lloyd's appendix to the works of Penrose and Cockerill, will indicate sufficiently the sources of the measurements. It is to be understood, too that in many cases no measurements of the parts that we wish to compare are given, the measurers not deeming them of importance, or the temple being in ruins. Especially do we find lacking the measurements of the corona and the

FIG. 94.—GREEK DORIC TEMPLE OF ÆGINA.
See pages 42, 170, 183, 185–189, 191, 192, 196, 197, 204, 207, 224.

cyma recta of the cornices, both horizontal and raking (see Fig. 93, page 182, and Fig. 94), and of the cymatium, or pedimental moulding, over the raking cornice. This is unfortunate for several reasons, chiefly because, as we shall find, the dividing line between the space occupied by the entablature and the pediment was not infrequently below the upper mouldings of the cornice; and the cymatium needs to be included with the pediment before one can make out the latter's exact relationship to the rectangle of the entablature beneath. But it is hoped enough is known to justify the conclusions that will here be reached.

It seems strange that any who have undertaken to unravel the mysteries of Greek proportion should have failed to begin by recognizing the most apparent fact with reference to it. Yet, notwithstanding the rows of like columns and of like equal horizontal divisions in the entablatures, which stare every one in the face the moment that a Greek temple is seen, many have apparently failed to notice that the whole is composed of different sets of factors, all the members of each set of which are intended to appear to have the same measurements. Of course, if what has been said thus far in this discussion be true, each of these measurements represents what in rhythm would be a note or bar of the same length; and it was by combining these notes or bars with others in proportion to them, that the Greek built up his architectural rhythm. What though, as tested by plummet and line, some of these measurements that seem to be exactly alike do not prove to be so? There are reasons for this, which will be explained in Chapters XIII. to XV. At present, it is enough to recall that such discrepancies are in analogy with facts exemplified in all the arts. If slight enough to escape easy detection, differences in things supposed to be alike are always allowable. In musical rhythm, the first of three equal notes beginning a bar, owing to its accent, is allowed a longer time than the other two. In harmony produced by instruments tuned according to the present temperate scale, the chords used do not represent with absolute accuracy the partial tones composing their separate notes. In poetry, successive lines ending in words like *laud* and *God*, are accepted as substitutes for rhymes; and in painting, colors that fail, and yet just fail, to form perfect complements, are sometimes used for them. Why should it not be the same in architecture?

In examining these sets of measurements in the Greek temples, it will be convenient, as well as logical, to take up first the parts that are comparatively smaller, and then those that are larger. Of the smaller parts again, some, like those in many of the mouldings or fillets, are so apparently alike that even if their exact measurements could be ascertained, which is not the case, we should not need to consider them here. In mentioning other sets of members, in order to be able to refer to them readily when speaking of them later, they will be put into classes designated by Roman letters, thus, I., II., III., etc.

I. We shall start with small enough numbers, if we compare first (see Fig. 93, page 182) the *abacus*, *i. e.*, the square flat stone at the top of the capital of the column, with the *corona*, or flat stone forming the lowest projection of the horizontal cornice over the entablature, and also with the corresponding lowest projection of the *raking cornice* forming the angle over the *pediment*. (See Fig. 94, page 183.) These three were usually of the same apparent height, and the similar flatness and plainness of the three emphasize their likeness. They were usually also of proportions that make them seem of the same height as the *ovolo* (Fig. 93, page 182), *i. e.*, the rounded part of the column's capital immediately under the *abacus*, and also, at times, to seem of the same height as the united mouldings at the top of the *architrave* or of the *frieze*, as well as of the *cyma recta*, *i. e.*, the partly rounded moulding of both the horizontal cornice and of the raking cornice (Fig. 94, page 183) immediately over the corona of each. Here are three and, at times, more members of like height. Occasionally, exactly six of these, three that are flat and three adjoining them, respectively, that are curved, are of like height. Now for our proofs. In the temple of Ægina (Fig. 94, page 183), the height of the abacus (C., T. at Æg., pl. 7) is 7"650; corona of cornice, 7"666; that of the raking cornice is not given but is apparently the

FIG. 95.—RESTORATION OF THE WEST END OF THE ACROPOLIS, ATHENS.
See pages 186, 190, 210, 211, 216, 219, 252, 257.

same; ovolo of capital, not to the rings, but to the point where it swells out from the upper diameters of the column (estimated), 7"6; moulding over architrave, 7"3+. Temple of Phigaleia (C., pl. 6), abacus, 7"125; corona of cornice, 6"9; of raking cornice, apparently the same; ovolo, 7+ (estimated); mouldings over architrave, 6"975; over frieze, 6"660. Propylæa, the central building in Fig. 95, above (P., pl. 13), abacus, .96; corona of horizontal cornice, .882; of raking cornice, .751, but the latter has mouldings not included in this. Parthenon (Fig. 96, page 190) (P., sec. 2 and appendix), abacus, 1.149; corona of cornice over entablature, probably including, as it need not, the fillet, 1.302; of the raking cornice, 1.174. In the temples in Hittorf's summary, the dimensions of the corona are not given; but to one recalling what has been said, namely, that the abacus is usually of the same height as the ovolo, and half that of the cornice, it is evident that the following indicate the same apparent proportions as those already noticed:

	Abacus.	Whole Cap. to Rings below Ovolo.	Cornice.
Nemesis at Rhamnus	0.131	0.251	0.212
Themis at Rhamnus	0.158	0.308	0.310
At Sunium	0.196	0.376	0.390
Ceres at Eleusis	0.329	0.562	0.567
Neptune at Pæstum	0.432	0.882	0.797
The Theseum	0.199	0.396	0.346
Concord at Agrigentum	0.320	0.669	0.615
Juno Lucina at Agrigentum	0.445	1.013	1.034
R. at Selinus	0.508	1.063	1.031

In some other cases the ovolo, as measured, seems higher than the abacus; but this result is probably produced, as in the temple of Phigaleia, by the fact that the rings or fillets are some inches below the place where the ovolo swells out from the column, and therefore (see page 182) below where the effect begins that we wish to compare with the abacus. (See Figs. 93, page 182, and 94, page 183.) In other cases, the likeness in height between the abacus and the corona of the cornice is not indicated quite so distinctly. But we must remember that the entablature contained many mouldings or fillets, and of the measurements that we have some are made to include one of these and some another. There is no temple in Hittorf's summary that seems more out of the way than that of Phigaleia. Yet the detailed measurements of this, as made by Cockerill and quoted from him on page 186, sufficiently prove our ground. As given by Hittorf, they are as follows: abacus, 0.178; capital to below ovolo, 0.409; cornice, 0.284. All that we wish to show now is that the abacus and coronæ of the cornices were, as a rule, of the same *apparent* height, and that, usually, the same was true of the other members that have been mentioned; and it may be said that there is nothing in the known divisions of any temples that disproves this rule, although some furnish no evidence either for it or against it. However, if the reader wish to examine this subject for himself, the measurements given under the next heading (II.) will enable him to do so.

II. The height of each of the six members just considered bore a relationship expressible by low numbers— usually 1 : 2 or 1 : 3, and in a few cases of 2 : 3—to the height of each of three and sometimes of four other members, three of which were a combination of one flat and of one curved member. These were the whole horizontal cornice, the whole raking cornice (Figs. 93, page 182 and 94, page 183), the whole capital of the column, and sometimes the steps of the stylobate, *i. e.*, the foundation. (See Fig. 94, page 183, also Fig. 10, page 36.) As has been intimated before, the exact measurements of the capitals and cornices are sometimes difficult to determine. Both contain several mouldings separating them from other members, yet entering into the general effect; and the measurers have not considered these mouldings. Nevertheless, by bearing this fact in mind, their measurements may indicate ratios sufficiently exact for our purpose. The ratios indicating the relationship between the abacus or cornice and the steps, as also the whole foundation, would vary. In some temples, but not in all, the steps were for convenience, and would always be of a somewhat similar height. In a large temple they might be as high as the cornice; in a small one, they might be higher. What is of importance is that they always were made to sustain a certain relationship to something. It is well to observe, too, that, as they were nearer to the spectator than the members above the column, and also were seen on a level, and not at an elevation and therefore obliquely, as were the latter, we should expect, in accordance with Greek methods, that to appear of the same height as these members they would sometimes be given a little different height. It seems well to add that in few of the temples is the height of the steps or of the whole stylobate given.

In confirmation of what has been said the reader may begin by noticing the measurements of the temples in Hittorf's summary, mentioned in the third paragraph above. In every one of these temples the proportion between the abacus and cornice is 1 : 2. The same is true of the temple at Ægina (Fig. 94, page 183) (C., pl. 7), in which the abacus is 7″625, or, if we include a slight space between it and the entablature, 7″650; while the horizontal cornice, leaving out the 2″8-inch fillet at the top, which, if colored differently, as in Cockerill's plates, would look like a dividing line between cornice and pediment, measured 1′4″665. The raking cornice seems the same; so does the capital of the column including abacus and the ovolo to the point where it is no wider than the upper diameter of the column. And so, too, does the top step of the stylobate, which happens to be given in this temple, as 1′3″875. In the Theseum (Fig. 10, page 36), in which, as Hittorf's summary has shown, the cornice is twice the height of the abacus, we find, in a place (P., pl. 35) where the height of the latter is not given, that the cornice measures 1.090, while the two steps of the foundation that are mentioned measure, respectively, 1.190 and 1.129.

In other temples, the proportion between the parts that we are considering is 1 : 3. At Selinus, where this method, in imitation of the old temple T., seems to have been common, we find (H.) :

	Abacus.	Cap. of Column to Ring below Ovolo.	Cornice.
Temple T.	0.568	1.076	1.618
Temple S.	0.334	0.658	0.953
Temple D.	0.359	0.716	1.029
Temple C.	0.386	0.716	1.009
Minerva at Syracuse	0.445	1.013	1.407

There are other temples in which these proportions seem to have been intended to be 2 : 3. In that of Jupiter at Olympia (H.), the abacus measures 0.420; from the top of the same to the rings of the capital measures 1.020; while the cornice measures 0.680. In the temple of Phigaleia (C., pl. 6), the abacus measures 7″125, the corona 6″9, the cornice 9″73, and the middle step of the stylobate 9″883. In the Propylæa, the central temple in Fig. 95, page 186 (P., pl. 13), the corona of the cornice measures .882, the whole cornice 1.316. In the Parthenon (Fig. 96), the abacus measures 1.149, the whole cornice 1.951, and the upper step of the stylobate

FIG. 96.—THE PARTHENON.
See pages 15, 186, 190, 201, 211.

1.814. In the Temple of the Giants at Agrigentum, the abacus measures 0.853 and the cornice 1.374. We have left now only two temples to which we have not applied these principles. In that of Jupiter at Nemea, the abacus measures 0.260, the capital with the ovolo measures 0.475, and the cornice 0.339; but in this temple the architrave is given as 1.023, and the frieze, which, according to rule, should be nearly the same, as 1.140. By a slip of the pen in transcribing, or by the very natural mistake of including mouldings which should go with the cornice, this may have been made 1.140 instead of 1.040, which would make the cornice 0.439, and related to the abacus as 1 : 2. Some similar error may account for the measurements ascribed to the Temple of Diana at Eleusis. Here the abacus is 0.181, capital with ovolo 0.330, and cornice 0.263. If the latter were 0.363 we should have 1 : 2 again. But, admitting the recorded measurements to be correct, we can say at least that abacus to cornice in both these cases is as 2 : 3.

III. Again, the like height of each of the three members just considered, *i. e.*, of the two cornices and of the capitals, bore a relationship expressible in low numbers, usually 1 : 2, 1 : 3, or 2 : 3, to the like height of two other members, namely, the architrave and the frieze (see Fig. 93, page 182), and apparently also, in the smaller temples, to the combined height of the raking cornice and the cymatium, both together forming the angular top of the gable of the pediment (see Fig. 94, page 183). This latter statement, however, cannot be proved, as almost all the pediments are in ruins and restored only according to supposition.

But this is not all. These vertical dimensions are the same, as a rule, as the horizontal diameters of the columns just below their capitals, where, therefore, because nearer together, the eye could best compare the columns, architrave, and frieze. The horizontal dimensions of the metopes (see Fig. 3, page 12) of the frieze also frequently measured the same. In other cases, these metopes, as well as the triglyphs which separated them, seem intended to appear just as wide as the height of the cornice, rather than of the frieze (see Fig. 93, page 182).

In considering the measurements needed to sustain these statements, great difficulty is experienced, even with the drawings before us, in determining exactly what mouldings ought to go with the architrave, the frieze, the cornice, and the pediment—not as they are outlined in modern times, but as their builders meant them to be outlined. When, as in Ægina, there is reason to think that the upper mouldings of the cornice were painted precisely like the pediment, we infer that they were intended to enter into the effect of the pediment, and the same of its lower mouldings as related to the frieze. At other times, certain mouldings between all these members seem to have been intended to have the effect merely of dividing lines. If so, in calculating the proportions, the measurements of the architrave, frieze, and cornice should be considered so far only as they are between these lines. In the measurements that we have, these facts are ignored. However, notwithstanding all that can be said of the impossibility of obtaining exact data, it is remarkable how clear the proof is of a general intention to produce such like effects as have been mentioned.

To show the bearing of what has been said, according to C., pl. 7, in the temple of Ægina (Fig. 94, page 183) the cornice measures $1'7''465$, the architrave $2'9''$, the frieze $2'9''125$, and the upper diameter of the columns $2'5''25$. If from the cornice we take the upper moulding $2''8$, which clearly belongs to the pediment, the result is

GREEK ARCHITECTURAL PROPORTIONS. 193

1′4″665, just half of 2′9″330, with a ratio of 1 : 2. Apparently, too, the horizontal measurement of the upper column would look near enough 2′9″. But we can do better than this. Treating one moulding of 3″9 as a dividing line over the architrave, and another of 3″259 as a dividing line over the frieze, we can make these members, respectively, 2′5″10 and 2′5″866; and if at the same time we treat the two mouldings 2″8 and 2″ over the cornice in the same way, we can make that member 1′2″665, and twice of this is 2′5″330. Precisely the same methods are pursued in each case, and the proportions are almost exact. The bearing of this upon the measurements of Hittorf, in which these mouldings are not noticed, is that he represents the measurements of the temples thus: architrave 0.845, frieze 0.847, upper diameter of the column 0.733, metopes, 0 800, cornice 0.380, abacus 0.193. If the members thus represented accord with our conception so exactly, we have a right to conclude that the same would be found true of those concerning which we have nothing more to guide us than the following:

	Architrave.	Frieze.	Width of Column	Width of Metope.	Cornice.	Abacus.
Nemesis at Rhamnus	0.575	0.575	0.558	0.574	0.212	0.131
Themis at Rhamnus	0.584	0.586	0.594	0.582	0.210	0.154
Minerva at Sunium	0.834	0.825	0.793	0.740	0.390	0.196
Neptune at Pæstum	1.492	1.376	1.434	1.390	0.797	0.432
Small Temple at Pæstum	0 990	0.910	0.970	—	—	—
Theseum	0.835	0.826	0.778	0.774	0.346	0.199
At Segesta	1.447	1.447	1.560	1.326	0.691	0.375
Diana at Eleusis	0.642	0.615	0.628	0.590	0.363(?)	0.181
R. at Selinus	1.729	1.721	1.796	1.380	1.030	0.508
Concord at Agrigentum	1.106	1.106	1.099	0.932	0.615	0.316
Juno Lucina at Agrigentum	1.053	1.034	1.073	—	—	0.320
Esculapius at Syracuse	0.975	0.975	0.932	—	0.480	—
Minerva at Syracuse	1.488	1.407	1.520	—	—	0.445
Parthenon	1.348	1.347	1.467	1.304	0.622	0.346

In the latter building we have, to guide us, the measurements of Penrose (sec. 2, appendix, page 114). These give us the metopes all the way from 4.050 at the extreme side of the front to 4.375 in the middle of it, the architrave 4.425, and the frieze 4.417. In view of the indications of paint on the mouldings above the latter two in the temple of Ægina which gives us a right to surmise that they were intended to have the effect of wide dividing lines, we are warranted in concluding that each of these, *i. e.*, the architrave and frieze of the Parthenon, would seem about twice the height of the cornice, which is 1.951, and which differs very slightly from the height of the stylobate, namely, 1.814.

There are other temples in which the ratio between the cornice and architrave seems to be as 1 : 3. Lloyd says (C., appendix, p. 75) that in the temple of Phigaleia, "of the entablature proper, three sevenths was given to the architrave, three sevenths to the frieze, and one seventh to the cornice." Here are the figures (pl. 6): architrave 2′7″30, frieze 2′7″50, cornice 9″37, and the upper diameter of the columns—but they differ in size—3′0″8. Notice too that, in this temple, the middle step of the stylobate measured 9″883. This proportion, 1 : 3, seems to be found in the following (H.):

	Architrave.	Frieze.	Width Upper Col.	Width Metope.	Cornice.	Abacus.
Ceres at Eleusis	1.696	1.622	1.620	1.474	0.567	0.329
Jupiter at Nemea	1.023	1.142	1.060	1.137	0.339	0.260
Apollo at Delos	0.791	0.770	0.711	0.660	0.278	0.203
Jupiter at Olympia	1.670	1.700	1.696	1.650	0.680	0.420

In the remaining temples the proportions seem more like 2 : 3 or 3 : 4 :

	Architrave.	Frieze.	Width Upper Col.	Width Metope.	Cornice.	Abacus.
Corinth	1.440	1.440	1.323	1.167	1.061	0.327
S. at Selinus	1.516	1.492	1.248	1.250	0.953	0.334
T. " "	2.892	2.332	2.464	1.940	1.618	0.654
D. " "	1.484	1.482	1.149	1.209	1.029	0.359
C. " "	1.760	1.489	1.502	1.123	1.009	0.386
A. " "	1.106	1.054	1.058	0.902	0.635	0.275
Giants at Agrigentum	3.329	3.328	2.983	2.547	1.374	0.853

When we take into consideration the mouldings, which, if included or excluded, would slightly change these figures as originally recorded, and when also we make allowances for the mistakes that invariably arise in copying and re-copying figures, the uniformity of these results is remarkable. No one looking at them can doubt that the measurements were meant to produce the effect of putting like with like, or where not so with like multiples of like.

IV. Once more, the height of the architrave and of the frieze, and the width of the upper diameter of the columns, and of most of the metopes, bore a relationship, expressible by the low number 1 : 2, to the combined height of the architrave and frieze, that is, of the entablature without the cornice, and also to the height of the tympanum,[1] except where, as in the Parthenon, this was equal to the height of the whole entablature, and also to the apparent horizontal distance between the columns just under their capitals. As will be pointed out on page 263, the distance between the columns at the extreme sides of the front was less than between the others. But, as will also be pointed out, this less distance, in all cases, was intended to appear the same as the greater distance. The apparent distance between the columns just under their capitals

---

[1] By the tympanum is meant that part of the pediment which was between the horizontal and the raking cornice.

was generally the same as the height of the entablature without the cornice, and also as the height of the tympanum. There was undoubtedly an intended proportion also between the lower diameter of the columns and the lower space between the columns and the height of the stylobate or foundation, but the measurements are not sufficient to warrant a positive statement of what this generally was. Lloyd says (C., appendix, page 73) that in the Propylæa and Parthenon the height of the stylobate was to the space between the columns as 2 : 1, and to the diameter of the column as 3 : 2.

In confirmation of what has been said, it will be noticed that the dimensions of every architrave and frieze given under the last head show that, as each was intended to appear of the same height, both together would be to each alone as 2 : 1. The upper distances between the columns cannot be ascertained in a sufficient number of cases to furnish demonstrative proof; but all the carefully drawn elevations, like those of the west front of the Propylæa and of the Theseum (Fig. 10, page 36) in the plates of Penrose, and of the temples at Ægina (Fig. 94, page 183) and Bassæ and others in the plates of Cockerill, show that the effect produced is that of twice the upper diameter of the columns, and therefore of a measurement exactly equalling that of the combined architrave and frieze. That the latter two together were designed in most cases to have the same apparent height as the tympanum, is evident not only from these drawings, which are all intended to represent the measurements, but also to an extent from the measurements themselves. For instance, in C., pl. 4, the entablature of the temple at Ægina is given as 6'9"790, and the pediment as 7'3". But if we look at pl. 7, we find the architrave 2'9" and frieze 2'9"25, together 5'8"25, and if from 7'3", the height of the whole pediment, we take the height of the raking cornice and cymatium over it, the measurements of which are not given, but are apparently fully equal to that of the horizontal cornice with mouldings under it, which is represented to be 1'7"465, we get 5'5"535, which would very nearly represent the height of the tympanum. The measurements of the other temples will be found on page 221.

At best, however, the measurements that we have of the pediment and tympanum of all the temples examined are exceedingly unsatisfactory. In some cases it could not be otherwise. The temples are in ruins and the pediments are usually the first to disappear. Even where they remain, or enough of them to indicate what their angles were, the cymatium, or crowning moulding of the raking cornice, is usually gone, and without it their apparent heights cannot be properly estimated. Some temples, too, had what was called the *acroterium*, an ornament on the apex which increased its apparent height. (See Fig. 94, page 183.) But in addition to this, those who have made the measurements have themselves not been interested in the matter. Penrose has nothing in connection with any of his plates to indicate the measurements of the tympanum, raking cornice, or cymatium, although in his text he states what they were. In the case of the Parthenon, Cockerill ignores them altogether, and in the measurements collected by Hittorf it is not possible to make out whether the tympanum is meant or the whole pediment, or whether, if the latter, the measurement of the cymatium is also included. This is the more unfortunate inasmuch as the entire question concerning the Greek idea of proportion depends largely on the relative heights of these members of the front. How true this is, and what mistakes are made because this fact is not recognized, is evident from a book that lies before me now, "The Architecture of Marcus Vitruvius Pollio," translated by Joseph Gwilt. Its text is accompanied by plates. In six of these are representations of temples supposed to be constructed in the Greek style, and not one of them bears much more resemblance to the Greek style than a human being who could be a fit subject to be exhibited in a museum on account of his deformity, would bear to a man, and this largely because of the disproportionate size of the pediment. It is possible that the draftsman of these pictures supposed that the proportions of the Parthenon would justify his drawings, but he has altogether missed the meaning of that which, presumably, he desired to indicate. However, notwithstanding the lack of data and interest in these subjects, enough measurements have been made to sustain, though only in a general way, the principle that we are trying to establish. But before quoting the figures, let us state another fact that will be confirmed by them.

V. Not only was the apparent height of the entablature under the cornice or, at times, under only the corona of the cornice, equal to that of the tympanum, but the apparent height of this same part of the entablature, including sometimes the abacus, sometimes it and also the ovolo under it, and sometimes the whole capital of the column, was equal to the height of the whole pediment including the raking cornice and cymatium; and each of these heights bore to the height of the column-space beneath it a relationship expressible by low numbers, like 1 : 2, 1 : 3, or 2 : 3.

The variousness of result thus indicated is very important. It solves the riddle of the differences that we find in the measurements and proportional measurements of different temples. It shows us how the Greek artist could manifest originality, and yet continue to carry out the first principles of his art. The differences in these measurements are found not only in the heights of entablatures and pediments, but also still more of columns. How can this fact be reconciled with any fixed principle with reference to proportion? An endeavor to answer this question will be made in Chapter XII.

CHAPTER XII.

THE LARGER DIVISIONS OF THE FRONT OF THE DORIC TEMPLE.

The Column-Space and the Method of Principality—Proportion on the Flanks of Height of Columns to the Entablature—Variety of Exact Proportions on the Front might Arise from a Desire to Have Similar Apparent Proportions—Difficulty of Determining the Line of Separation between the Tympanum, Entablature, and Column-Spaces—Illustrated in the Temple at Ægina—How its Tympanum and Entablature each can be Made to be to Columns as 1 : 3—How Pediment and Entablature, Including Capital, each can be Made to be to Shaft as 1 : 2—How Rectangles of Front in Foundation, Columns, Entablature, Pediment, etc., Are all in Proportion—Triangle of both Tympanum and Pediment are in Proportion to Spaces under them—These Arrangements Illustrate the Complexity of Harmony, but are Analogous to those of Rhythm, not Pitch—Illustrated from Temple at Bassæ—Entablature, Pediment, and Columns—Proportions of the Rectangles Formed by the Front Spaces—Temples in which the Abacus is Treated as Part of the Entablature Space—Proportions of the Rectangles of the Front in Propylæa and the Theseum—The Parthenon at the Beginning of a Transition—Departure in it from Former Methods—How these, nevertheless, Conform to the Principles here Unfolded—Other Subordinate and Complementary Proportions—All Tending to Produce General Harmony of Effect.

WE have reached a place where we must consider the proportions, each to each, of the heights of the pediment, the entablature, and the columns, which together, with the less important stylobate, or foundation, made up the whole front of the Greek temple. Of these, the principal, or distinguishing, feature was undoubtedly the row of columns through which the worshipper entered. The law of principality, therefore, as unfolded in Chapter

V. of "The Genesis of Art-Form," would require the emphasizing of the vertical space given to these columns. We find that it was emphasized. In all cases it was made larger than that given to any other feature ; and in most cases larger than that given to all the other features combined. "It appears," says Lloyd (P., appendix, page 112), "that the greatest importance was attached to making the height of the column exceed the joint height of the other members, that is, stylobate, entablature, and pediment, by a single aliquot, . . . in other words, the height of the column may compare with the complementary height of the front as 7 : 6 or 6 : 5." The ratio applied in the Parthenon, he tells us, is 10 : 9 ; at Bassæ, 7 : 6 ; in the Theseum, 5 : 4. On the sides both of the Parthenon and Theseum, where, of course, there is no pediment, the ratio of the height of the column to that of the joint foundation and entablature, which latter is made higher by the ornament above the cornice called the cymatium, is 2 : 1, and at Bassæ there is a close approximation to this (C., appendix, page 72). The exact measurements are usually given by Lloyd, but there is no need of quoting them here.

They become important only as we advance a step farther. It has been said that the features attracting attention in the Greek temple are the columns, the entablature, the pediment inclosing the tympanum, and the foundation. The proportions of the columns, entablature, and foundation, as determined without reference to the tympanum, may be studied on the flanks, or sides, of the buildings, as well as on their fronts. Examining them on the flanks, we find that in the temple of Phigaleia (C., pl. 3) the columns (19' 5" 125) are to the height of the entablature (6' 5" 208) as 3 : 1. In the Parthenon (Fig.

96, page 190) the entablature is 10.794, which, added to the fillet of the cymatium above it, 0.299, gives us 11.093, and this, as we are told, is to 34.288, the height of the column, very nearly as 1 : 3 (P., appendix, page 14). One would naturally infer that if such simple proportions were used on the flanks, they would be used on the fronts; and it will be shown presently that this inference is justified. But although 1 : 3 is the very ratio employed by Lloyd when speaking of the flank effects of the Parthenon, he says (P., ap. page 112), "the ratios 1 : 3 and 2 : 5 are most extensively and importantly employed in the temple at Bassæ, but—referring evidently only to the front effects—are absolutely unknown in the Parthenon." Other reasons for doubting this statement, besides the one thus indicated, will be given hereafter.

Taken just as they are reported, many of the measurements of the fronts of temples do not indicate with exactness any proportional ratios. From what was said, however, on page 165, of an excusable absence of apparent ratios between sets of measurements, as well as on page 35 of judging architectural effects from a distance, one might take the ground that the measurements need not indicate proportions exactly, because approximate proportions are all that can be recognized from a distance. One might say, therefore, that these are all that are necessary. But he may do more than this. He may say that, owing to certain peculiarities of situation or of shape, these are all that are not misleading. Very often it is impossible for one form to be made to appear just the size of another, unless its real size is lessened or increased. Stripes, for instance, as said once before, tend to lengthen the effects of fabrics in the direction in which they run. A space filled with upright columns, therefore, naturally seems higher in proportion than one filled by an entablature, in which most of the lines are horizontal. This fact alone would justify the architect of the Parthenon and of the temples at Corinth and Nemea in making the columns a little shorter than would be necessary in order to make the actual ratios exactly 2 : 1, 3 : 1, or 4 : 1.

Now, however, we come to a still more important consideration. It is not at all certain that the line which we suppose to separate one feature, like a cornice or architrave, from another made proportional to it, is the line by which the Greek builder intended to indicate the boundary between the two. For instance, did the measurement for the rectangle of which the entablature is the chief feature, always begin above the capital of the column and end above the cornice? Undoubtedly it did sometimes, especially upon the flanks, where there was no necessity for any feature below the entablature proper to balance the raking cornice and cymatium that were above the pediment. But if anyone will glance along a colonnade, he will perceive that the bottom of the *abacus*—*i. e.*, the flat stone parallel to the entablature, forming the top member of the column's capital (see Fig. 93, page 182)—forms just as effective a dividing line for the eye as the bottom of the entablature proper.[1] The same might be affirmed, especially in connection with the Ionic and Corinthian orders (Figs. 97, page 204; 98, page 220), of the whole capital.[1] The fillet, moreover, which is at the top of the entablature's horizontal cornice and is carried all around the pediment, as well, too, as around the whole corona of the cornice (Fig. 93, page 182), may form an equally effective dividing line between the entablature and the pediment.

[1] Since writing this, the author has found a similar suggestion in Figs. 1, 2 and 3 of the " Theorie des Proportions " of P. Fauré.

There is no façade more suggestive of exact proportions than that of the temple of Ægina (Fig. 94, page 183), yet the apparent ratios on page 196 are as much astray when applied to it as to any other of the temples. Moreover, the ratios seem still more astray when we examine them more carefully (C., plate 4). We discover that the columns measure 17′ 2″ 8, the entablature 6′ 9″ 790, and the pediment 7′ 3″ 0. There are no indisputable ratios to be made out of these numbers, and yet, as was said, the proportions of the building, as one looks at it, seem unusually satisfactory. If the fault be not in the building, it must be in the way in which it has hitherto been supposed that the ratios were determined.

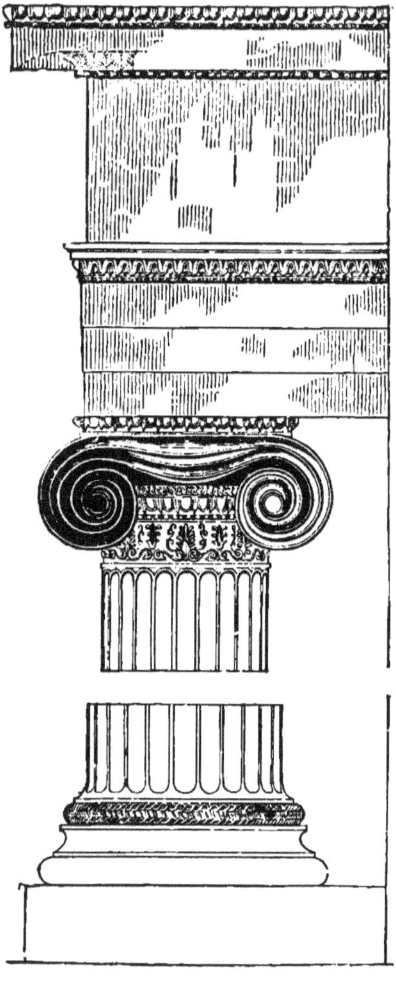

FIG. 97.
IONIC COLUMN AND ENTABLATURE.
See pages 203, 219, 220.

We ascertained on page 197 that the tympanum of this temple measured about 5′ 7″ 6. Under this tympanum came the cornice, the distinguishing feature of which was the flat corona, and this measured 7" 675. Under the corona came the architrave and frieze, the two together measuring 5' 6" 25, or, if we include a slight moulding under the corona, 5' 7" 875. Under these came the abacus measuring 7" 650, the same as the corona. Under the abacus came the rest of the column, measuring in all 17' 2" 8, or 16' 5" 150 without the abacus. One third of this latter number is 5' 5" 05. Recalling now that straight lines increase the apparent length in the direction in which they point, we see that here are three heights which are in proportion, viz. : tympanum to entablature-height without the corona of the cornice, as 1 : 1 ; each of these to the height of the columns, as 1 : 3 ; and both together to the height of the columns, as 2 : 3.

But this is not all. These three heights do not touch one another, but are separated by members having the effects of broad dividing lines. Some one may ask, Should not the proportions include the entire space exclusive of dividing lines ? We will let them do this. Take the height of the pediment, 7' 3" 0, and add to it that of the entablature, 6' 9" 790, and of the capital of the column including abacus 7"650, and ovolo 1'0"75 : result 16'1"190. Now take the capital from the column and we have left 15'4"400, enough shorter to make its upright lines seem to the horizontal above (page 202) as 1 : 1. Half of 16'1"190 is 8'0"595. We have found that the pediment measures 7'3". C., pl. 7, shows us that above the corona of the horizontal cornice there are several small mouldings measuring 2"8, 2"0, and 1"125 ; all together, 5"925. Adding this to 7'3" we get 7'8"925, within about two feet of the middle point of the space above the columns. If we look at the front again, especially where, as in some large illustrations, it is colored, we shall see that the effects of these mouldings above the horizontal cornice clearly belong to the pediment. The pediment, therefore, is to the height of the entablature-space as thus indicated as 1 : 1, and each to the column-height as 1 : 2.

Now if we look again we notice that the stylobate or basement of this temple measures 3'8"25. This is only a few inches less than one half of 7'7"200, or than one quarter of the height of the column. According to principles sometimes exemplified, this is what we should expect. The near and low members are made slightly smaller, so as to seem of the same size as the remote and elevated members. In this temple, the stylobate represents 1 (3'8"25), the columns below the ovolo, 4 (15'4"400), and the entablature-space and pediment each a little in excess of 2 (8'0"598), and both the latter together, a little in excess of 4 (16'1"190). Once more, the breadth of this temple is given as 45'1"9. This would make the proportions of the rectangle formed by the general outlines of the height and width of the stylobate about 1 : 12; of the portico below the capitals, 4 : 12; of the capitals with the entablature, and of the pediment, each 2 : 12; of the stylobate, portico, capitals, and entablature, all together, 7 : 12; of the same without the stylobate, 6 : 12; and of the whole height to the breadth 9 : 12, or 3 : 4. Besides this, inasmuch as the larger members measure, as a rule, just twice as much as the smaller members, it follows that these larger members are all in proportion to the smaller members. It has been shown already that while pediment entablature and capitals are to portico below as 1 : 2, tympanum and entablature without the cornice are to the same as 1 : 3. It could be shown also that the whole cornice, 1'7"465, and probably the raking cornice and cymatium, the measurements of which are not given, are intended to have the same effect of height as the capital of the column, 1′ 8″406. At any rate, the raking cornice and cymatium are perfectly balanced by the effect of the capitals of the columns in case we consider them to be treated like pendants of the entablature.

If at the top of the corona of the horizontal cornice where are situated the mouldings that have been mentioned, we could fold the angle of the pediment downward, its apex would be just on a line with the bases of the capitals. In fact, it is well to notice that above the rectangular entablature space we have two triangles, the smaller one of the tympanum, the lines of which are inside of the raking cornice (see Fig. 94, page 183), and the larger one of the pediment, which includes the former, and the lines of which are outside of the cymatium. Each of these appears to be of exactly the height of a rectangle under it. The first is of the height of the smaller rectangle formed by the architrave and frieze of the entablature; the second is of the height of the larger rectangle outlined above by the horizontal cornice, and below by the bases of the columns' capitals. Both the tympanum and whole pediment therefore appear to be exactly conformed to a rectangle under them. This arrangement, as will be noticed, corresponds to that complexity of effect already pointed out on page 156 in the cathedral at Cologne; on page 170, in the Grand Opera House at Paris; and on page 175, in the Arch of Septimius Severus. Indeed, all through the front of this Greek temple, as of these other buildings, there are these correspondences, which, on account of their blendings of almost countless effects, may be said, in a general way, to manifest the harmony of proportion. At the same time it needs to be emphasized again that this harmony results from putting like effects together according to the principles underlying not pitch but rhythm.

The proportions of the temple of Ægina have been used to illustrate these facts, simply because they are accessible, and, as will be shown presently, when we quote the more general measurements of Hittorf's summary, because they represent a type. Another temple of which we have measurements sufficient for our purpose is that of Phigaleia (the same as Bassæ). One who had not had experience of the intricacies of Greek proportion would be greatly pleased with his first examinations of this temple (C., pl. 3): columns 19′ 5″ 125, entablature 6′ 5″ 208. It seems evident at once that this means 3 : 1. There is another way, however, of interpreting the meaning of these measurements. The pediment-height is not given; but adding together the stylobate, 2′ 5″ 833, and the column and entablature as already given, we get 28′ 6″ 166; and as the whole height is given as 36′ 0″ 166, we infer that the pediment-height is 7′ 4″. Taking a hint from what we have learned from the temple of Ægina, let us take from the entablature (C., pl. 6) the mouldings above the corona of the horizontal cornice (2″ 75), and add them to the pediment. The result is 7′ 6″ 75+. Let us next, after taking this 2″75 from the entablature, add to it the abacus, 7″125, and the ovolo, 7″875, and the rest of the capital of the column, 4″750. The result is 8′2″ 208. Let us now take the combined height of the abacus, ovolo, and the rest of the capital from the full height of the column. The result is 17′5″375. Now look at the stylobate (C., pl. 3). It is 2′5″833. Take a very few inches from this and it will equal one seventh of 17′5″375; and take a still smaller amount, and it will equal one third of 7'6"75. Following the principle suggested in the case of the temple of Ægina, in accordance with which (page 202) the upright members are made slightly shorter than the horizontal ones, we have this result : height of foundation to that of the column-space excluding the capital is 1 : 7 ; height of the entablature-space including the column's capital, and also height of the pediment-space to the height of the column-space, each as 3 : 7 ; together as 6 : 7 ; the combined height of stylobate and column as far up as to the base of the capital to the whole height above this is as 8 : 6, or 4 : 3. Or, if we take the combined height of the stylobate and of the whole column (22'0"958, or if only to the abacus, 21'3"833) we get, as a result, to the combined height above it (in the one case, 13'9"208 ; in the other 14'6"333), the ratio very nearly of 3 : 2.

The breadth of this temple is given as 48' 2" 66. If we take the height of the stylobate for our standard, this will make the proportion of the rectangle of the stylobate —by which is meant the ratio of the height to the breadth— 1 : 18 ; of the column-space to capital, 7 : 18 ; of entablature-space above this and pediment 3 : 18, or 1 : 6, or together 6 : 18, or 1 : 3 ; and of the whole front 14 : 18, or 7 : 9. The actual proportions, however, are more like 3 : 4, which could be obtained by averaging the heights of the members. In the drawings, the tympanum of this temple seems intended to appear of the same height as the entablature below the corona of the horizontal cornice. Assuming this to be the case, adding together (C., pl. 6) architrave, 2' 8" 75, frieze, 2' 9" 083, and moulding under corona, 1" 660, we get 5'9"493. This is to the column below the 7"125 of the abacus, i. e., to 18'8", about as 3 : 10.

In the two temples that have been considered, the

whole height from the base of the column to the apex of the pediment seems to have been divided into equal parts at the bottom of the column's capital. The same, as we shall find presently, was true of the Parthenon. In other temples, this division seems to have been made at the bottom of the abacus of the capital. One of these is the Propylæa at Athens, the central temple in Fig. 95, page 186 (P., pl. 30). Here the pediment measures 9.747, the entablature 8.849, and the column 28.134. If we take the height of the abacus (P., pl. 31), .96, from the column, we have left 27.174. If we add this .96 to the entablature, we get 9.80, almost exactly the height of the pediment, and only a small fraction larger than one third of the height of the column, the proportions of which to the entablature and pediment therefore would appear to be 3 : 1. In this temple too, as in Ægina and Bassæ, the tympanum and the entablature below the corona of the cornice seem to be of exactly the same height. In the Theseum, too (Fig. 10, page 36), all these proportions seem to be determined as in the Propylæa, but (P., pl. 35) they are not indicated in sufficient detail to prove this.

Nor in either of these two temples are the measurements sufficient to indicate unmistakably the proportions of the rectangles formed by the spaces devoted to the columns, entablatures, and pediments. But if the breadth of the west front of the Propylæa be taken at about 72, as seems to be indicated, its entablature, as calculated with the abacus (see page 203), being a little over 9, and its columns 27.174, we have for the rectangle of entablature 1 : 8, of the columns, 3 : 8, and of both together, 4 : 8, or 1 : 2; and of the whole with the pediment 5 : 8. This figure 8 corresponds, as will be noticed, with the regularity of the effect produced in this temple by separating the columns of the front into two parts, three columns being on each side with a very wide intercolumn-space in the middle. See the middle temple in Fig. 95, page 186.

Of the Theseum (Fig. 10, page 36), the breadth is given as 45.011, the height of the front entablature with abacus as suggested on page 203, 6.2, and of the columns 18+; and the proportions of height to breadth are perhaps meant to appear in the entablature like 1 : 7, in the column-space like 3 : 7, and, in both together like 4 : 7, or, including the pediment, like 5 : 7.

It is ordinarily supposed that the Parthenon represents the highest point of perfection reached by Greek architecture. It does, and yet it was the beginning of a decline, just as we recognize to have been the case with the poetry of Milton and the music of Wagner, when we notice the effects that the works of each produced upon their followers and imitators. The Parthenon is the building which modern people have studied and imitated most in their efforts to understand and apply the Greek methods. They ought to have it impressed upon their minds that those who first began to study and imitate it were the ones who began that very process of degeneracy in art, the current of which it is now supposed by some that a return to Greek methods can stem.

The architect of the Parthenon (Fig. 96, page 190) had not ceased to be controlled by the principles which had been exemplified in the earlier Doric structures; but he suggested that such was the case, and others soon carried out his suggestions to their logical results. According to Lloyd (P., appendix, page 114), the height of the column in this building was 34.253, of the front entablature, 10.794, and of the pediment, 14.073. Here is great apparent irregularity. How in this case is like put with like? Can any simple ratio such as can be easily recognized apply to these figures? It can. The building is one of those examples which we often find in the highest art, in which exact regularity is produced through apparent irregularity.

In this case again, as in most of the others that have been mentioned, take the capital of the column which measures 2.833 and add it to the entablature. The result is 13.627, which from below to one looking upwards, especially when comparing a rectangle with a triangle pointed at its centre, would appear to be to the 14.073 of the pediment above as 1 : 1. This capital of the column, moreover, exactly balances the pediment's combined raking cornice (1.174), and cymatium (1.430), *i. e.* (2.604), which two as seen from below, owing to the projections of the cornice, would appear slightly higher than this. Here, too, as in the temple of Ægina, if at the edge of the horizontal cornice, the pediment were folded down over the entablature, its apex would be on a line with the bottoms of the columns' capitals. Taking the height of the capital now from the column, we have left 31.420, and adding the capital to pediment and entablature-space above this, we have 27.700. It is conceivable, considering the height of the pediment, that these numbers were intended to produce the effect of a ratio of 7 : 6. 27.254, twice the combined capital and entablature height with which the column-space below is immediately compared, would represent this ratio still more nearly. The height of the foundation is 6.050, just enough less than half of 13.627, the height of the entablature-space, to accord with the principle which we have found everywhere exemplified, that the near and low member is made slightly shorter than the remote and high one. The heights of the different members of the front may therefore be proportioned thus: that of the stylobate to that of the column-space excluding capital of column, 3 : 14; that of the capital of column with entablature, as also that of the pediment, to that of the column aside from capital, 3 : 7; and both the former together to both the latter as 6 : 7. These figures suggest what Lloyd (P., appendix, page 112) says with reference to the prevalence of certain ratios similar to these in the Parthenon,— for instance; that its height is to its length as 2 : 7, its height to its breadth as 9 : 14, and its length to its breadth as 4 : 9. See page 217.

The proportions that have been indicated in the front height of this building, however, are not all that it is important to notice. As in the case of the other temples that we have considered, it contained other subordinate or complementary proportions, intended to be blended with these, and thus to secure that complexity of effect already noticed as applied to other buildings (see pages 170 and 175), and which, as shown in Chapter XIII. of "Art in Theory," is an important constituent of harmony.

If instead of taking the whole capital from the column and adding it to the entablature, we take only the abacus 1.155, we have left for the column 33.098, for the entablature, 10.794 + 1.155, *i. e.*, 11.949 (P., sec. 2). But the pediment, 14.073, without the raking cornice, 1.174, and the cymatium, 1.430—in other words, the tympanum of the pediment measures 11.469. Thus calculated, the height of the front, excluding the corona of the pediment, gives us for the columns 3, for the entablature 1, for the tympanum 1. Even the stylobate, 6.050 is not so far from one half of 11.949, that it would not seem to blend harmoniously with the proportions thus suggested, giving us in all for the height of the stylobate 1, of columns 6, of entablature with abacus 2, and of tympanum 2. This would leave out of the calculation the raking cornice and cymatium of the pediment. But we have already shown another method of division in which they would be included. Let us now notice still another method (P., appendix, page 114). The height of the pediment was 14.073, of the entablature 10.794, of the abacus 1.155, making together 26.022, or without the cymatium (1.430), 24.592. If we divide the former of these last numbers by three we get 8.674; if the latter, we get 8.197. But the height of the column, 34.253, excluding the abacus, is 33.098. Dividing this by 4 we get 8.274. Taking into consideration what has been said before, that the upright lines of the columns always have the effect of increasing their apparent height, we can say that the proportion between the height of the column-space here and of the space above it, was meant to appear to be as 4 : 3. Indeed, if we exclude the cymatium, it was almost exactly this. Moreover, this space above the columns seems to have been divided into three parts by way of suggestion, the lower part being separated from the next higher by the chief continuity of line suggested by the figures in the metopes of the frieze, and the next from the very highest by that of the figures in the tympanum. At any rate, whether we concede the existence of these suggested divisions or not, there is no doubt about the main fact that the columns' height to the height above them would appear as 4 : 3.

CHAPTER XIII.

OTHER GREEK ARCHITECTURAL MEASUREMENTS AND GENERAL CONCLUSIONS.

Unusual Size of the Tympanum of the Parthenon—Reasons for this—Proportions of the Rectangles of the Front of the Parthenon—Same Principles Revealed in the Measurements of Other Temples—Exact Squares Formed by the Width and Height of Three Adjacent Columns in Many Temples—Proportion between the Diameters and Heights of Many Columns—Measurements from Twenty-three Doric Temples Verifying the hitherto Unverified Statements in Chapters X. and XI.—Why the Doric Temples are Chosen for Illustrations—After Experiment had Determined the Laws of Proportion, Art Imitated and Degenerated—Because Artists no longer Followed out the Natural and Instinctive Art Tendency, Founded upon Comparison—This Tendency Apparent in that which Originated the Gothic and Renaissance Styles—No Great Architecture without it—Possibilities of Architecture not Exhausted but must be Developed from the Principle of Comparison.

THE details of measurement in the case of the Parthenon have been explained so fully, in order to reveal how careful the Greek architects were to carry out the general principle underlying their methods of construction even when they differed in the applications of it to details. The difference between the Parthenon and the other temples that have been examined was in the size of the tympanum. In those, the height of this was equal to that of the entablature under the corona of the horizontal cornice; in the Parthenon, to that of the whole entablature together with the abacus. The important matter for us to observe is that, nevertheless, the tympanum and the pediment, also, were made just equal to the height of something, and in exact proportion to something else. More than this, too, there were so many parts of these members that could be compared to other parts, and so many different ways of making out the proportions intended, that, no matter what the observer's theory might be, he could have no doubt that in some way the general laws of proportion were fulfilled. This was the complexity of result at which the Greek architect seems to have chiefly aimed. And, in view of this fact, the Parthenon is particularly interesting, because, involving as it did a departure from ordinary methods, it would evidently be essential that in it this complexity should be especially suggested.

Why the tympanum of the Parthenon was made higher than usual may be accounted for in various ways. Possibly it was in order to accommodate the statuary to be placed in it. Possibly it was thought that if the raking cornice and cymatium were treated in the general scheme of the proportions as a border above and aside from the tympanum, while the latter was made to be of like size with the whole entablature, this arrangement, on account of its very unusualness, would give particular emphasis to the statues. Perhaps, however, it is more consonant with what we know of the Greek methods to suppose that this particular pediment was made higher in proportion in order that it might not appear lower than that of the ordinary temple. The Parthenon itself was high—it stood on a hill; it was impossible to look at it from any position without looking upward. (See the temple at the right in Fig. 95, page 186.) In these circumstances the heavy projecting cornice over the entablature would necessarily seem to increase the height of the entablature and at the same time, by hiding part of the tympanum, would seem to lessen the height of the pediment. Very likely, too, some of the outlines of the statues in the tympanum would augment the effect of lessening its apparent height. It may be that both in this temple and in others, in which we find the pediment as a whole higher than the entablature proper, the reason is the same. To one looking upward, the measure of the space given to the entablature extends from its base diagonally to the edge of its cornice, while that of the tympanum extends upward from this same edge and not from the actual bottom of the tympanum, which is always concealed. Recalling that the Greeks, as will be shown in the next chapter, always determined proportions, not by real measurements, but by apparent effects, we can recognize that this is exactly the way that they would treat entablature and pediment as contrasted with each other.

The proportions, each to each, of the rectangles formed by the width and height of the three spaces occupied, respectively, by the columns, the entablature, and the pediment of the Parthenon will, of course, seem to us to differ according to the places where we separate them. The breadth of this temple at its base was 101.341. Making allowance for the diminution of this breadth above the columns, the 27.700 between the apex of the pediment and the bottom of the columns' capitals, would be to the breadth about as 4 : 14, of which the height of the space given to the pediment and to the entablature, each respectively, would be as 2 : 14, or 1 : 7. The rest of the front down to the bottom of the stylobate would be as 5 : 14, both together 9 : 14. Or if we compare the rectangle enclosing the entablature including the abacus, 11.94, with that enclosing the columns under it, we find the height to the breadth of the first as 1 : 9, of the second as 3 : 9, or 1 : 3, and of both together as 4 : 9—the same numbers used by Lloyd (P., appendix, page 112) to represent the whole breadth and length of the building. If to this we add the rectangle inclosing the tympanum, aside from the pediment, the whole is as 5 : 9.

It may be well to notice here again, in passing, that Lloyd says (P., appendix, page 112), that the height of the Parthenon is to its length as 2 : 7, and that the same proportions hold good of the temple at Bassæ; that the height of the former temple is to its breadth as 9 : 14; that the same dimensions at Bassæ and in the Theseum and west front of the Propylæa are as 3 : 4, as also that the Parthenon has breadth and length as 4 : 9. It is essential, however, to bear in mind that the different ways of comparing the parts or wholes of heights or lengths or breadths, each of which ways reveals the appearance of some different but consistent system of measurement, are all of them merely the necessary and inevitable results of applying to each of the dimensions that are brought together the principle of making them, as often as feasible, appear to be alike, or to be divisible by like factors. Those who hitherto have dwelt upon these resulting ratios as though they were the main things to be considered, have done merely what so many others have done before them, namely, taken the effect for the cause. See page 152.

Before passing from these Greek temples, it is well, perhaps, to point out that often the front, as a whole, seems to have been constructed upon the principle of putting a like height with a like breadth, as, for instance, where three of the six columns with the two spaces between them constitute an exact square. This arrangement is emphasized in the west front of the Propylæa (see the middle temple in Fig. 95, page 186), by making the space between the two central columns unusually wide, thus suggesting at once the way in which the three columns on each side of it are grouped. "In the Parthenon," says Lloyd (P., appendix, page 112), "this symmetry is applied to three ordinary columns and the two intercolumns included, and the same appears to be the case at Sunium. . . . In the temple at Rhamnus, the dimension is taken from the outer edge of the angle column to the centre of the third from the angle; in the Theseum [Fig. 10, page 36], we have a like division, but involving only ordinary columns. I apprehend that the introduction of these equalities of heights with breadths was found to give repose to the effect of a long range of columns as a repetition of similar spaces and dimensions." This seems probable. As has been shown abundantly in this discussion, repetition, or rather measurements that gave the effect of repetition, were elements of artistic method which the Greeks seldom neglected.

They also made the breadth of the column—usually calculated from the abacus, which itself was equal to the lower diameter—sustain a certain proportion to its height. Lloyd (P., appendix, page 113) says that at Bassæ, in the Theseum, and in the outer columns of the Parthenon, the width of the abacus is to the height of the column as 1 : 5. Vitruvius tells us (" De Architectura," bk. iv., chap. i.) that the relations in a Doric column of the breadth (Fig. 93, page 182) of the base to the height represent the proportions of a man, *i.e.*, of the length of his foot to his whole height, viz., 1 : 6; the proportions of the Ionic column (Fig. 97, page 204) represent those of a woman, viz., 1 : 8, but later of a Chinese maiden, perhaps 1 : 9 and also 1 : 10.

Thomson says in his poem on Liberty :

> First unadorned
> And nobly plain the manly Doric rose;
> The Ionic then, with decent matron grace
> Her airy pillars heaved; luxuriant last
> The rich Corinthian spread her wanton wreath.

It yet remains for us to show how, by actual measurements, the statements under the headings IV., page 195, and V., page 198, can be verified, and made applicable to all the Doric temples of which we have records. Fortunately Hittorf repeats, according to his system, the measurements of the temples of Ægina and Bassæ, and in the Theseum and Parthenon. With what we have learned about these from the more detailed measurements of Penrose and Cockerill, it will be easy to recognize, and be logical to infer, that, in the other temples, like measurements exemplify like principles. See page 221.

FIG. 98.
CORINTHIAN CAPITAL OF PILLAR.
See pages 203, 220.

It is not necessary to pursue this subject further. There are many Ionic and other temples, gateways, and monuments, the drawings of which, in the superficial way in which they must be judged in the lack of exact measurements, reveal the application of the same principles. But it would not accord with the design of this essay to consider such forms of testimony here. Besides, it is unnecessary. Everyone admits that the Doric style, especially in the temples, represents Greek architecture in its

MEASUREMENTS OF GREEK TEMPLES.

	Column.	Pediment as Usually Measured.	Entablature as Usually Measured.	HEIGHTS. Architrave and Frieze.	Cap of Column.	Ped. and Ent. with Cap of Col.	Half of Latter.	Column without Cap.	Ped. or Lengthened Ent. to Shortened Col.	Whole Space above to Col. Space.
Ægina	5.285	1.940	2.072	1.690	0.629	4.641	2.320	4.656	1:2	1:1
Bassæ	5.943	1.680	1.891	1.600	0.543	4.114	2.057	5.405	3:7 or. 3:8 or. 1:3	6:7 3:4 or. 2:3
Parthenon	10.434	3.913	3.317	2.695	0.860	8.190	4.095	9.574	3:7 3:8 or. 1:3	6:7 3:4 or. 2:3
S. at Selinus	9.110	3.620	3.061	3.108	0.756	8.237	4.119	8.354	1:2	1:1
T. at Selinus	16.229	6.400	6.842	6.224	1.474	14.716	7.358	14.755	1:2	1:1
R. at Selinus	10.187	3.390	4.510	3.450	1.334	9.144	4.572	8.853	1:2	1:1
Concord at Agrigentum	6.713	2.057	2.827	2.112	0.668	5.552	2.776	6.045	1:2	1:1
Nemesis at Rhamnus	4.100	1.230	1.362	1.150	0.251	With Ovolo of Cap to Rings. 3.843	1.921	Without Ovolo and Abacus. 3.849	1:2	1:3
Themis at Rhamnus	4.200	0.910 (?)	1.380	1.170	0.308	2.598	1.299	3.892	1:2	1:3
Neptune at Pæstum	8.732	3.542	3.665	2.868	0.882	8.089	4.044	7.850	1:2	1:3
C. at Selinus	8.623	3.072	4.258	3.249	0.710	8.040	4.020	7.913	1:2	1:3
A. at Selinus	6.235	2.150	2.794	2.150	0.594	5.538	2.769	5.641	1:2	1:3
Theseum	5.709	1.771	1.977	1.671	0.199	With Abacus. 3.947	1.973	Without Abacus. 5.510	1:3	2:3
Ceres at Eleusis	10.934	3.644 [1]	3.885	3.318	0.329	8.962	4.481	10.372	1:3	2:3
Minerva at Sunium	6.140	1.700	2.049	1.659	0.195	3.995	1.997	5.054	1:3	2:3
Jupiter at Olympia	11.200	3.390	4.050	3.370	0.420	7.766	3.880	10.780	1:3	2:3
Jupiter at Nemea	10.360	2.630	2.502	2.163	0.266	5.392	2.696	10.100	1:4	1:2
Giants at Agrigentum	24.196	6.930	7.931	6.658	0.853	15.711	7.855	23.343	1:3	2:3
Diana at Eleusis	4.536	0.797 (?)	1.530	1.257	.....	With None of Col. 2.267	1.133	Whole Col. 4.536	1:3	1:2
Segesta	9.366	3.066	3.585	2.894	.....	6.651	3.325	9.366	1:3	2:3
D. at Selinus	7.512	3.840	4.092	2.966	.....	7.932	3.966	7.512	1:2	1:1
Apollo at Delos	5.200	.....	1.791	1.513	.....					
Small at Pæstum	5.400	.....	2.400	1.900	.....					

[1] 5.644 H., probably 3.644.

prime; and only in its prime is it important for us to study it. It must be borne in mind, too, that the object of our inquiries has been to ascertain the general principles in accordance with which the Greek builder worked, not his special applications of them. Nor are these principles necessarily invalidated merely because, in some temples, the ratios that have been mentioned do not seem to be indicated as unmistakably as is desirable. All that is necessary is that, as in the case of the Parthenon, there should be evidences of some scheme or schemes of ratios, indicative of like subdivisions.

Of the existence in all these temples of some such scheme, we may be certain. Every list of figures that we have found proves it. The Greek builder was careful to preserve the appearance of putting like dimensions with like. And this fact was probably the cause not the result of whatever proportions his buildings manifested. If, in time, laws like those mentioned by Vitruvius arose, it is more than likely that most of these in the forms in which they have been preserved, were after-thoughts, derived from what, at a period when architecture was no longer in its prime, was discovered by measuring the buildings of the fathers. Why it should ever have passed its prime and begun to decline is easy to perceive. When any form of art is young, men are never tired of going back to first principles and experimenting with their designs, not only in painting and sculpture but in architecture too, just as often as effects seem unsatisfactory. See what is said further upon this subject on page 300. After the earlier, creative periods of the art, however, men begin to think that the whole subject, and all its methods, have been mastered. They imagine that no more practical experiments are needed. They are first contented with what

FIG. 99.—PANTHEON, ROME.
See page 224.

has been achieved by their ancestors, and then they begin to have a traditional veneration for it. That which should stimulate them to thought, stirs them only to reverence, and, like many of the critics and architects of our own day, they come to teach in their schools, and to believe in their hearts, that to be a successful imitator is to embody the only praiseworthy artistic ideal. Undoubtedly this was the fate that, after a time, overtook the architects of Greece. They became imitators. Because their copies stood before them, they ceased to experiment. Because they did not need to conceive their own designs they ceased to think about them; and when they ceased to do this they necessarily ceased to cause them to develop, and began to cause them to deteriorate.

Before long, they began to regard as ends those methods which the great architects had used as means They reproduced the subordinate features in the older temples, but overlooked the principal ones. Finally all the measurements that they used grew discordant, and it was beyond the power of any rules like those of Vitruvius to make them otherwise. Columns, entablatures, and tympanums, bore a general resemblance to those upon the Acropolis, but contained not one element that, in the estimation of the merest tyro of the art, could entitle them to be considered architectural models. Compare the front of the temple in Ægina or of the Theseum, Figs. 10, page 36, and 94, page 183, with that of the Pantheon of Rome, Fig. 99, page 223, or of St. Paul's, Covent Garden, London, Fig. 100, page 225. Could any building be more completely caricatured than is each of the Greek ones by either the Roman or the English imitation?

What makes the difference between these buildings? Look at them. The Greek temples emphasize results, which the others do not, attained by putting like with like. All the best Greek buildings show similar effects, and why? Because the Greek lived near to nature. His buildings emphasized corresponding measurements for the same reason as the card houses of a child. The Greek carried out the instinctive promptings and prescriptions of the mind. It was in the endeavor to do this that he originated those scientific adjustments to accommodate actual proportions to optical requirements, which will be considered

FIG. 100.—ST. PAUL'S, COVENT GARDEN, LONDON.
See page 224.

in the following chapters. Only much later did this end absorb the whole interest of builders, as it has that of modern students who have examined their works, and thus divert attention from more important matters on account of which alone these optical requirements were at first studied. The result was on a par with that of the exclusive attention paid to the secondary details of poetic form in the time of Queen Anne, leading to the pompous prosaic jingle that during most of the last century passed in England for the only permissible poetic phraseology.

As has been pointed out, the proportions of the Parthenon are more intricate, and the recognition of them more difficult than in earlier buildings. So while it represents the highest achievement of Greek architecture, it also represents the beginning of its decline. Subsequently men came, more and more, to forget to have their designs manifest clearly the results of relative measurements. Gradually they became accustomed to see buildings in which such requirements were disregarded. But study will show that at the time of the Gothic and the Renaissance revivals, the manifestation in buildings of the principle of

FIG. 101.--OLD PICTURE OF ST. SOPHIA, CONSTANTINOPLE.
See page 226.

putting large numbers of like dimensions with like, again came to be considered necessary. See Figs. 11, page 37; 12, page 38; 76, page 147; 81, page 155; 86, page 167, and 101. It is considered so in all great architecture.

In case our own builders ignore this fact, we can expect but little from them. They may turn out of their planing mills or stone quarries, pillars that look like those of Greek temples, or arches that look like those of Gothic cathedrals; they may discard these older models altogether, and try as hard as savages to be original by bringing together discordant mixtures of shapes, sizes, styles, and colors, and doom to eternal infamy the names of Queens Anne and Elizabeth by calling their hotch-potch after them; but no great architecture or school of architecture can be produced in this way. Great architecture is founded upon principles that are in the constitution of nature and of mind, the applicability of which all men recognize. Nor can they be ignored or neglected in any product of art without lessening the force of its appeal to human interest.

As has been suggested, proportion, in its character, is not only simple but complex, and its effects cannot be produced on a large scale without the most careful and profound study. These effects, too, are still capable of further development. The forms of Greek, Gothic, Moorish, Romanesque or Renaissance art have no more exhausted the possibilities of architecture than analogous developments in poetry, painting, or music. In this land and age, we can, and should, have an architecture of our own, to meet the requirements of our climate, as the Greek may not; of our customs, as the Gothic may not; and of our artistic instincts, as the Queen Anne may not. Such an architecture can be thoroughly original, yet if, in trying to make it so, we neglect the principles according to which the minds that are to view it must judge of it, we cannot expect it to commend itself to general approval, even in our own times, and much less in coming times. Whatever may be the nature of his designs, the architect who deals with shapes must remember that shapes fill space just as sounds fill time, and that for the purposes of art the appearances of similarly related measurements in the one are as necessary as in the other. In short, he must never forget that which it has been found necessary to repeat so many times already, that the fundamental principle in art is to group sizes as well as shapes by putting together those that, if not in wholes, in parts at least can be made to seem alike.

CHAPTER XIV.

HARMONY OF OUTLINES: PERSPECTIVE.

Outlines and Colors, the Respective Analogues of Words and Tones—Form-Harmony is less Essential than Significant Representation, yet Important—In Poetry Harmony is Owing to Apparent Like Effects as in Alliteration, etc., and also to Subtle Effects Adapted to Ease of Auditory Action—Analogous Conditions in Arts of Outline : The Perspective and Circumspective—Perspective Relates all Objects to a Centre of the Field of Sight : Lines, Directed toward this Centre, Converge—Appearance of Horizontal Lines—Of Vertical Lines—Both Lines as Represented in Painting and Architecture—Optical Illusions in Triangles—In Horizontal with Crossing Vertical Lines—Exact Explanation of these Illusions not as Important as to Recognize that they Exist—Analogy Drawn from Effects of Color Remote and Near—Failure in our Time to Recognize the Fact as Applied in Architecture—A Building was once Judged by its General Effect as Seen from a Distance—Proof of this Furnished by Discoveries in Egypt and Greece by Pennethorne, Hofer, Schaubert, and Penrose—By Goodyear—His Special and General Contribution to the Subject—Some Measurements of Penrose—To be Interpreted as Related to Perspective, not to Proportion—Differences in Measurement Accord with this Interpretation—Greek Architects Experimented with their Products as Artists do in other Arts.

THE harmony of outline seems related to that of color precisely as the harmony of words is related to that of musical tones. In using words, as also outlines, the primary consideration is their significance, a requirement mainly psychological, depending upon the definiteness of the effect produced by a form as a whole. In using musical tones, as also colors, the primary consideration is harmony of effect, a requirement mainly physiological, produced by the methods of blending together the different factors of the form. But while this is true, it is also true that the harmonious arrangement of words and of contours, though secondary, is extremely important, just as is definiteness of significance in tones and tints. It is with the methods through which outlines may be made to conform to the physiological requirements of harmony, that we are to deal in this chapter.

In Chapters VII. to XII. of "Rhythm and Harmony in Poetry and Music" it was said that, in order to produce harmony, the tones of speech never have been, and never need be, selected and arranged as in musical scales or chords. Speech may use any tone that can be uttered, so long as it is appropriate for definite reference. Nevertheless, in artistic speech, as in poetry, the harmonic ratios that underlie musical pitch are often exactly though subtly reproduced. At the same time, the poet who reproduces them successfully, does not do so directly, *i. e.*, by thinking of the pitch of his tones while he is composing. He does so indirectly, *i. e.*, while thinking merely of accommodating the sounds to the physiological requirements of the ear; so that, as the tones pass, the one into the other, they shall produce a satisfactory, agreeable, and artistic effect; in other words, so that the transitions shall seem not sharp and abrupt, but smooth, euphonious, and natural. In order to attain this end, poets use such methods as in the repeated, or regularly recurring sounds in alliteration, assonance, and rhyme, or in the very easily coalescing sounds in phonetic syzygy and gradation,— all of which, as shown in Chapters VII. to XII. of "Rhythm and Harmony in Poetry and Music," are developments, in as true a sense as are the harmonics of music, of the principle of grouping complex wholes through putting together those that have like partial effects.

So in the arts of outline. What the artist successful in these thinks of, is the method of accommodating their appearance to the physiological requirements of the eye so that they shall have satisfactory, agreeable, and artistic effects. How can they be made to have these? How but by being made to pass into one another so as to require, in the whole eye or in different parts of the eye when regarding them, the least possible effort, or conflict between different tendencies of effort? Exactly what this means, will be understood when it is recalled that the eyes, in comparing together and uniting part after part of the field of sight, are almost constantly moving upward, downward, and sideward, as well as changing divergence, convergence, focus, axis, and lens. See Fig. 114, page 273. With these conditions, it is needless to argue that, as a rule, the least possible effort of this kind is required where outlines involve some form of *repetition*. When we are using a phrase like " Many men of many minds," though the unaccented syllables differ, the fact that the organs, being once arranged for the *m*-sound in the accented syllables, regularly, when these recur, return to this same position, makes the utterance easy. So the regular repetition in a building of like pillars or openings, as in windows or doors, makes it easy for the eye, as well as mind, to take in the whole; just as irregularity, or the absence of repetition—pillars, windows, doors, all of different shapes and sizes—causes a confused effect, and makes an appearance difficult for the eye to take in. Ease of ocular action, therefore, may be said to attend upon *repetition*. If so, it must attend, in some degree, upon partial repetition also, as in *balance, alternation, consonance*, and *interchange*, or any of the methods indicated in the chart on page 3. Exactly why this should be the case, is fully discussed in what is said of shapes and outlines in "The Genesis of Art-Form." In this place, it is necessary to consider only a more subtle phase of the subject. This has to do not with the mere repetition or recurrence of the same forms of lines, but with that which underlies such effects, and renders them important, namely, the repetition or recurrence of the same forms of ocular action. Chapters VI. to XII. of "Rhythm and Harmony in Poetry and Music" show that, as elements of harmony in poetic verse, we have to consider not only actual repetitions, as in the like sounds in alliteration, assonance, and rhyme, but also effects produced by combinations or successions of vowels, consonants, and syllables, when easily coalescing. In these effects, the associated sounds are not as nearly alike as in alliteration or assonance, but they are allied; and are arranged in such ways as to necessitate as little effort as is compatible with any change at all in the organs while uttering them, either actually, as when reading aloud; or imaginatively, as when reading to oneself. Of course, outlines can be arranged in ways corresponding to this. They are so arranged, for instance, when they are adjusted in such ways as to accommodate themselves to that which can be seen at a single glance from a single viewpoint, and therefore without any change, at least any conscious change (see page 271) in the axis, focus, or lens of the eye. This condition involves a fulfilment of what is termed the principle of *perspective ;* and it may be said to correspond to such verse-effects as are most nearly connected with actual repetition (see chart on page 3). Again, outlines, or those parts of them nearest to one another, may be said to be arranged according to the requirement just indicated, when they are adjusted in such ways that straight lines are made to pass into curves, or curves of one kind into those of another kind, by regular degrees of change. This method, as distinguished from the *perspective*, which means literally *looking through* a scene, one is tempted, coining a word or rather a new application of an old word, to call the *circumspective*, which means, literally, looking around—looking around the sides or extremities of an object, or at its surroundings. According to this method, though there may be conscious changes in axis, focus, or lens, as the eyes look from one line or part of a line to another, the changes are as slight as possible, and occur by regular degrees—in these regards evidently producing effects corresponding to those of verse which are most nearly connected with phonetic *gradation*. See chart on page 3, also Chapter XI. of "Rhythm and Harmony in Poetry and Music."

Of these two methods of producing harmony of outline, let us first consider—of course only so far as is necessary for our present purpose—the one concerning which the most is known, and can be said,—namely, *perspective*. Of this, the essential fact interpreting all its phenomena is that, owing to the effect of distance upon the eyes, all objects perceived by them are related to a centre of the field of vision, about which centre every line has a tendency to appear either to radiate or to form a circumference. Let us apply this fact first to lines—and here we need to consider only straight lines—extending in the same direction as the glance of the eye regarding them. These lines, though in nature they may be parallel, are never parallel in the image of which we are conscious on the retina, and which, as must always be borne in mind, is the model for imitation in art. They converge toward a vanishing-point as it is termed, where, in the extreme distance, they apparently meet. See the left upper corner of

Fig. 102, page 235. They converge thus, of course, because the spherical shape of the eye causes the lines or axes of vision as they extend outward to radiate, and thus to render visible, when far enough away, not only an object which is exactly in front of the eye, but also much that is on both sides of this object. (See Fig. 4, page 22, also Fig. 113, page 272). But, for this reason, anything held within a foot or two of the face may appear as wide as the whole field of sight appears at the horizon, a stick three feet long measuring as much when near, as does a reach of country three miles long when at a distance. But at this distance, an object three feet long would be indistinguishable, which is the same as to say that at this distance straight lines drawn from the two extremities of this object as held immediately in front of the eyes, would appear to meet.

Now let us apply what has been said of objects' being related by the eye to a centre of the field of vision, to lines—and here again we may confine consideration to straight lines—extending in a direction different from the glance of the eye, *i. e.*, to lines crossing the field of vision horizontally or vertically. It will be found that only when lines horizontal in nature—*i. e.*, parallel to the earth's level—are on an exact level with the eyes, are they necessarily horizontal in the image of which we are conscious on the retina; and only when lines vertical in nature—*i. e.*, perpendicular to the earth's level—are directly in front of us, are they necessarily vertical in this image. Horizontal lines, if above the level of the eye, will, at the place directly in front of us, curve upward in the image. The circumferences of the dotted circles—not of the inside undotted one—surrounding the man in Fig. 103, page 236, represent —though, for the purpose of illustration, in an exaggerated

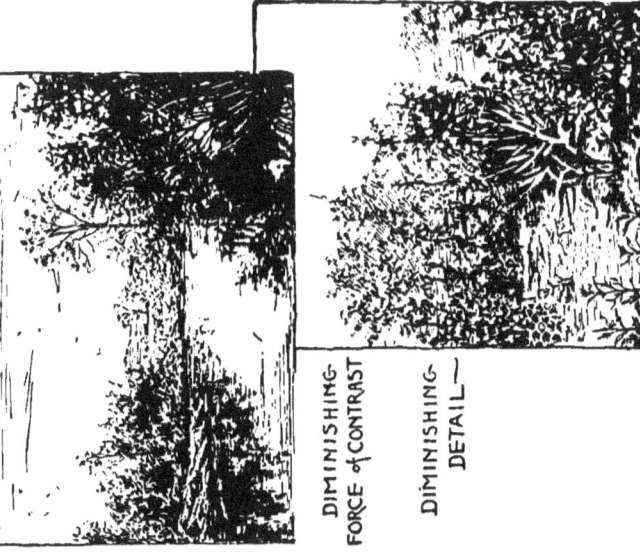

FIG. 102.—EFFECT OF DISTANCE ON MAGNITUDE, LIGHT, CONTRAST, AND DETAIL, BY J. W. STIMSON.

See pages 13, 47, 234, 237, 241, 329, 369, 412.

way—the direction of lines that appear to him to be horizontal. Evidently, in the degree in which he gazes upward, each of these lines above him will describe more and more of a curve. In Fig. 81, page 155, the summits

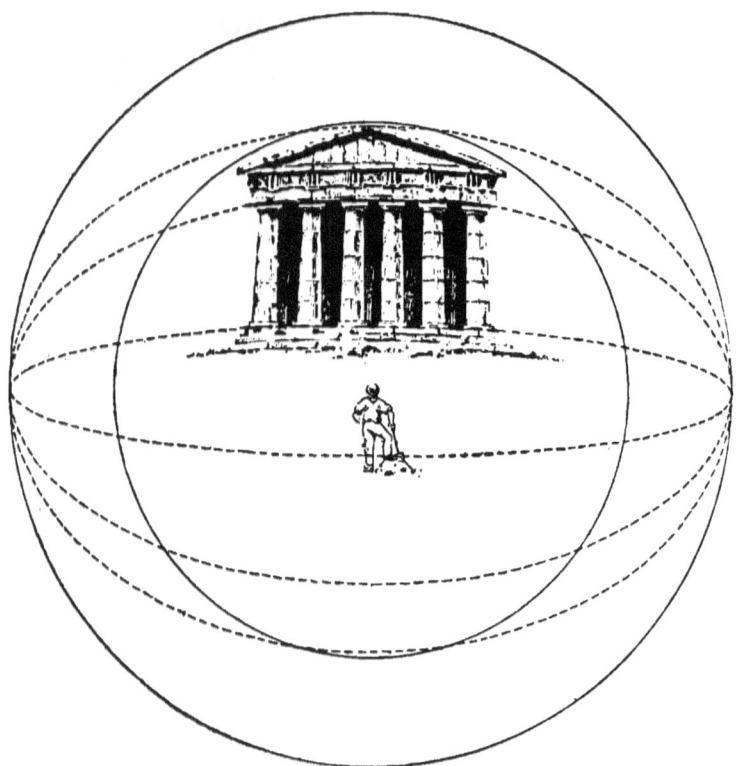

FIG. 103.—GREEK TEMPLE INSCRIBED IN CIRCLES REPRESENTING HORIZON LINES.
See pages 234, 237, 239, 251, 255, 257, 258.

of the two steeples are on a level. A line drawn from one to the other is that which represents the horizontal; but notice, if actually drawn between them, what a sharp curve it would necessitate.

The principle of perspective as applied to vertical lines is more complex. In one regard, however, it corresponds to that which is true of horizontal lines. If the railway tracks represented in the upper left drawing in Fig. 102, page 235, ran up a steep hill, or even a perpendicular hill, they would continue, as they do now, to approach one another. In other words, in extreme distance, two parallel vertical lines, the one to the right, and the other to the left of the perpendicular in front of us, incline toward each other. See this vertical effect, purposely exaggerated, in the sides of the temple in Fig. 103, page 236. Compare also the horizontal distance between the two towers in Fig. 81, page 155, at their bases, and at their summits; also the decided leaning toward the central perpendicular of the field of sight of the tower of St. Mark's which rises at the right of the reproduced photograph in Fig. 31, page 88, of "The Genesis of Art-Form." Undoubtedly, too, could we perceive straight lines drawn from the horizon to the zenith, those on each side of the perpendicular in front of us would seem to meet entirely, as well as to describe slight curves. So much with reference to the appearance of vertical lines, if at a distance and rising to extreme height. But it is important, in connection with them, to have attention directed to the fact that, if these lines are near, or rise but little above the horizontal level, their appearance is determined by an entirely different principle, which has an exactly opposite effect. The principle is derived from the fact of the rotation of the eyes. They rotate whenever the axes of the two eyes converge—*i. e.*, whenever in order to see distinctly and specifically, as distinguished from indistinctly and generally, the two eyes move away from each other—not toward each other, as some might suppose, forgetting that the lines of vision—*i. e.*, the axes—of the two eyes cross in passing outward (Le Conte's "Sight," p. 203). The eyes rotate thus, not only when moving apart to look fixedly at the scene in front, but when, moving in the same direction, both are glancing from side to side of this scene. But now, when the eyes rotate, what must be the effect? What but to cause each eye to roll not only sideward but also downward? And when this has been done what should we expect but—to describe the result more graphically than scientifically—that each eye should turn the vertical lines at one side of the field of sight slightly away from the perpendicular? As shown by a series of experiments in chapter i. of part ii. of Le Conte's "Sight," this is exactly what does happen ; in the resultant image on the retina formed by the combined action of both eyes (see what is said of binocular vision in Chapter XVI.), the vertical lines, as they rise at the sides of the field of sight, seem, immediately above the horizontal level, to incline slightly away from the perpendicular in front of us. Nevertheless, at a comparatively short distance above this level, in accordance with the effect of the altogether different principle determined by *distance* or *perspective* which has already been pointed out, these same vertical lines seem to incline toward the perpendicular. It will be noticed, however, that, as applied to the horizontal lines above the level of the eyes, though less to those below it, this rotary action does not change, but, if anything, augments the effect of the upward curve described in the last paragraph.

The fact just mentioned with reference to the side vertical lines, as well as the very slight effect which, when very near, is exerted upon them by the principle of *perspective*, justifies painters in not inclining toward the perpendicular, at the centre of the field of sight, trees or other objects, if of no great comparative height, even when rising at the extreme sides of their pictures. Moreover, the subtle curves, not only in the vertical lines but even in some of the horizontals, are comparatively so slight that in painting they need not often be given consideration. But in architecture, where the products fill a large space in the field of view, it is a question whether the conditions of nature just indicated can be disregarded without artistic detriment. Consider, for instance, the uses of the horizontal line. In nature, from which we get our conception of this, it represents a level every part of which is equally distant from the centre of a globe. Such a line is never really straight. It is really curved; and if a horizontal line be far enough away from us to be seen for a long distance, which mainly happens, of course, when it is above us, then, as when we are looking at a level range of high mountains, we can recognize the curve so distinctly that a painter, wholly aside from the reasons already given, owing merely to its unmistakable appearance, would reproduce it in his picture. But if so, why should it not be correspondingly reproduced—not wholly, but according to the laws of perspective—in the supposed horizontal part of a wide building, standing above but comparatively near us, and immediately in front of the curved horizon? It may be supposed that, if such a curve were introduced, this part of the building would not appear horizontal. But this is a mistake. It is the only thing that can make it appear so. If the curve be not introduced, that which should appear horizontal, will appear, at the point which is nearest us, to sag downward. See Fig. 103, page 236, also—to be explained farther on—Fig. 108, page 247.

There is another principle, too, involved here. It is

this,—that the horizontal line at the exact height at which the eyes, when turned upward, are directed, represents to them, for the time being, the absolute horizontal level, and all other straight horizontal lines supposed to be parallel to the first, will, at a point perpendicular to that at which the eye is directed, appear to curve downward from the line if they are below this horizontal level, or to curve upward if above it. Notice the lines, all of them perfectly straight, in the upper triangle in Fig. 104, this page. When the eyes are directed toward this triangle as a whole, they are, of course, directed toward its mathematical centre; and the lower base line, of course, is below this centre. Observe, as a result, how this line appears to sag, or curve downward, at its middle point. Now observe also the second drawing in Fig. 104. In this the lower line of the triangle is made to curve slightly upward at its middle point. As a result, this line no longer appears to sag, but to be perfectly straight. In the lower drawing of this Fig. 104, the effect of an apparent curve in a really straight line is brought out still more decidedly. In this drawing two similar triangular figures are placed together, but the shorter sides of each triangle are emphasized by being

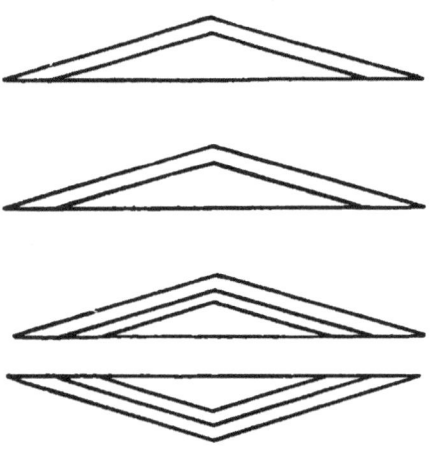

FIG. 104.—OPTICAL ILLUSIONS CAUSED BY LINES ARRANGED AS IN PEDIMENTS.
See pages 240, 241, 242, 250, 254, 256.

tripled. This emphasis, according to a well-known mental law, renders it impossible for the mind, when comparing the two triangles, to confine attention to the single line forming the longer side of the triangle. The central point of attention, when looking at each triangle, is drawn toward its mathematical centre, and the two triangles are compared together as wholes. The effect produced by each triangle therefore is the same as that produced by the single triangle at the top of this Fig. 104. In both triangles, the long line seems to curve away from the angle opposite it, and the two long lines,—one of the one triangle and the other of the other,—though placed in a po-

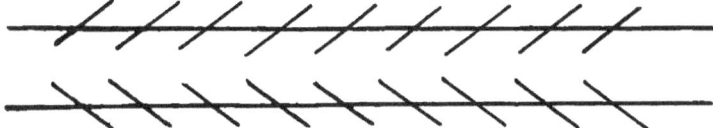

FIG. 105.—OPTICAL ILLUSIONS WITH TWO PARALLEL HORIZONTAL LINES.
See page 241.

sition where they are exactly parallel, do not seem to be so.

When one looks first at Fig. 105, and observes that the two horizontal lines, which are really parallel, seem at the left to move away from each other, he may suppose this to be because the ends of the cross lines at that extremity are farther apart. But he may prolong these lines, and bring them quite near together, without entirely changing the illusive effect. The truth seems to be that, in accordance with the principle of perspective which draws attention in the direction of converging vertical lines, as may be observed in the upper left drawing of Fig. 102, page 235, the vertically directed lines crossing the upper horizontal line draw attention upward, and, because these lines never become perpendicular, draw it also toward the extreme right; whereas the vertically directed lines, crossing the lower horizontal line, draw attention downward, and toward the extreme right. A single cross line might not have had this effect, but the emphasis imparted by the repetition of the lines, forces it upon the mind. The result is that both horizontal lines—the one appearing to the eye as it would if the centre of the field of sight were above the right, and the other as it would if this centre were below the right—are made to seem to bend away from one another. That is to say, what the eye compares, is not merely the two lines, but the way in

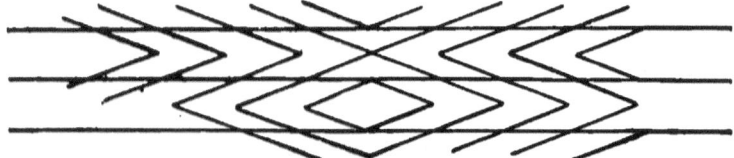

106.—OPTICAL ILLUSIONS WITH THREE PARALLEL HORIZONTAL LINES.
See pages 242, 243.

which each line appears related to a central point, the exact position of which central point is determined by the resultant effects of each horizontal line together with the vertically directed lines crossing it. The effect is evidently the same in principle as that of the apparent bending away from each other of the two longer lines of the two triangles in the lower drawing in Fig. 104, page 240. The same conditions, differently presented, may explain the apparent curves in the really horizontal lines in Fig. 106, above. If we place a series of small upright pegs in a flat rubber band, and then curve the band downward at either side, all the pegs will incline outward from a common centre. The lines above the upper horizontal line in Fig. 106 give us an exaggerated representation of this arrangement; and, on account of the emphasis given by their repetition, they force the eye to consider the horizontal line as related to some imaginary centre below it, above which centre, therefore, the line seems to curve upward. The same is true of the lower horizontal line also, the lines crossing which have exactly the same direction; while the opposite is true of the middle horizontal line, the lines crossing which are directed in such a way as to suggest a centre of attention above the line. The apparent curving of this line therefore is away from this centre, and accordingly downward.

These illusions are explained somewhat differently here than in Thiersch's "Optische Täuschungen," from which the drawings were borrowed for an article by Prof. Goodyear in the "Architectural Record." Indeed, in some cases the effects are owing to several different causes, or to combinations of them. But the exact method of explaining the illusions is less important, for our present purpose, than is a recognition of the fact that they exist, and, in connection with this, of the particular influence which they exert upon particular combinations of outlines.

One not acquainted with the methods of reproducing in color the effects of nature, might suppose that it would be necessary merely to go into the fields, and examine near at hand the colors, appearing, say, on a rose or a bush, match them exactly with his pigments, and then use, on his canvas, these pigments thus determined. But every one of experience knows that much more is necessary; and this for the simple reason that colors, when blended and seen from a distance under the influence of light and shade, are very different in appearance than when seen near at hand. A certain fresco in Paris, when examined closely, shows the flesh of a human figure to be painted in green. Owing to the influence of surrounding colors, no other color, at a distance, could be made to have the effect of flesh. Contours are impressed upon the retina in connection with the same processes as those that impress colors upon it. These latter indeed frequently seem to compose the whole image, outlines being merely effects produced where one color changes to another. Why should it not be recognized that to imitate the appearance of outlines necessitates the reproduction of general effects, in the same sense that it does to imitate colors? But is this recognized? Undoubtedly—in painting and sculpture; but not, in our times, in architecture. Yet it is as rational for a man to suppose that he can produce satisfactory effects of outline through causing a building to measure just as many inches across the top as across the bottom, or through causing a cornice to be exactly straight, or causing columns to be exactly the same distance apart, as it would be for him to suppose that he could produce satisfactory effects of color by exactly matching with his pigments the apparent hues of a rose or a bush, when examined close at hand.

The failure in our times to recognize this fact is all the more remarkable in view of the undoubted recognition of it, as will presently be shown, not only by the Greeks, but also by the Egyptians before them and by the Romans after them. Subsequently, the fact seems to have been completely ignored, and though, within the last half century, attention has again been directed to it, its full import has not yet been apprehended. Measurements designed to cause a building to appear in perspective as it does appear, *i. e.*, with outlines or spaces wide, high, straight, parallel, or of even sizes, are still confounded

245   FIG. 107.—DRAWING OF MAISON CARRÉE, NIMES, SHOWING CORNICE CURVE : JOHN W. McKECHNIE.
See pages 246, 249, 250, 251, 252, 255, 258.

with measurements designed to cause the parts of the building, when appearing as they do, to seem to be in proportion.

To avoid the confusion of thought resulting from confounding these two different aims it seems necessary, as intimated on page 180, to notice, first of all, that, whether with or without reference to what we now term proportion, there was a time in history when a building was looked upon as presenting an appearance which, as in the case of every other work of art, was to be judged by its general effect. This is produced upon a spectator when examining it, as one does a painting or a statue, from a certain definite eye-point, as it is technically called, where one can see the interrelations of all its members and form an estimate of the composition as a whole. In other words, these buildings were erected with primary reference to the appearances that they would present when seen from a certain definite distant position.

The proofs of this fact are abundant. In 1832, Mr. John Pennethorne, an English architect, accidentally, as it were, noticed that the architraves surmounting the four square sides of the second court of the Egyptian temple of Medinet Habou at Thebes were so constructed as to lean forward at a middle point between their ends, thus causing their apparently straight lines as they passed from corner to corner to describe a slight curve, or entasis as it is technically termed. Notice the effect, exactly corresponding to this, in the line at the side of the roof of the Maison Carrée, as represented in Fig. 107, page 245, and Fig. 108, page 247. Returning to England, he reread the passages from the Latin writer Vitruvius, partly quoted on pages 256 and 258, passages which, strange to say, had been familiar to scholars for years, with-

FIG. 108.—PHOTOGRAPHIC EFFECT OF CORNICE CURVE IN THE MAISON CARRÉE.

See pages 239, 246, 249, 250, 251, 255, 258.

out suggesting the feasibility of making any attempt to verify their statements. Determining to do this himself, he went to Athens in 1837, made measurements, and discovered the existence of certain curves in the buildings there. About the same time, two Germans also, Hofer and Schaubert, did the same, and published an account of their discoveries in the "Wiener Bauzeitung." These discoveries, however, did little more than prove that the curves existed. Not till the publication of the "Principles of Athenian Architecture," detailing the results of the more searching and minute measurements of the English architect, F. C. Penrose, was it made plain that the curves were not accidental but, probably, every one of them intentional. Indeed, they were found to characterize almost all the apparently straight lines. In connection with this fact he discovered, too, many unexpected and evidently intentional variations of measurement of other kinds.

With reference to the latter, as Prof. Wm. Henry Goodyear says in an article on "The Greek Horizontal Curves," in "The Architectural Record" for the quarter ending June 30, 1895, "although we can occasionally trace some scheme in the variations by comparing two halves of one end or one side of the building, instances of two adjacent measurements being equal are almost absolutely unknown." As compared each with each, the sizes of columns, of their capitals, of the spaces between them, and of the various ornaments in the entablatures over them are seldom the same. Nevertheless, notwithstanding these curves and irregularities, Stuart and Revett, who had measured the whole Parthenon in 1756, and Lord Elgin and Cockerell and Donaldson, who had subsequently tried to make a most careful study of it, had failed to notice anything beyond the swelling and leaning of the columns. Penrose tells us that he was months in Athens before he could detect with his eye even which way a given column was leaning; and with all his investigations in which he did not depend upon his eyes, he still left many very important facts undiscovered. Prof. Goodyear, in the article just mentioned, gives an account of his own measurements of the Maison Carrée in Nimes and of the Egyptian temples at Karnak, Luxor, and Edfou, and he says that in all of these he has found an outward curve of the entablature, as represented in Fig. 107, page 245, and Fig. 108, page 247. Yet these buildings had been inspected for years by tourists and artists, intent on making every discovery possible with reference to their modes of construction. Could anything afford more convincing proof that these curves and other irregularities were designed to produce just what they do produce—*i. e.*, effects of regularity—in conjunction, at times, as intimated on page 260, with those of augmented width, height, dignity, or symmetry?

One special contribution of Prof. Goodyear to the general subject lies in his discovery that the same form of curve previously noticed by Mr. Pennethorne in the temple of Medinet Habou is found not only in the Egyptian temples at Karnak, Luxor, and Edfou, but also in the temple at Nimes. As the curve thus applied is not found in any of the temples at Athens; and as Nimes was founded by Alexandrine Greeks from Egypt, this fact, in his opinion, points to a direct Egyptian influence.

As related to our present line of thought, it will be recognized that the supposition that all these buildings were constructed with primary reference to producing a certain apparent effect when viewed from some point or points at a distance, is the only one that can furnish the same reason, and a sufficient one, for all the different methods of producing these effects,—methods as different, for instance, as that in the forward curve of the entablature represented in Fig. 107, page 245, and Fig. 108, page 247, and as in the upward curve of the entablature represented in Fig. 103, page 236, or of the stylobate as in Fig. 109, page 251. Moreover, such a supposition is the only one that can give the same reason, and a sufficient one, for the application of the same method in order to produce the same effects, yet with almost infinite differences in measurements, in different temples. Here are some of these measurements as reported by Penrose.

Buildings.	Actual length of the front or flank measured.	Actual rise above a straight line joining the extremities.	Proportional rise corresponding to a length of 100 feet.
Jupiter Olympus, stylobate, flank	354.2	.25 nearly	.07
Theseum, stylobate, front	45.	.063	.140
flank	102.2	.101	.097
Parthenon, sub-basement, front	104.2	.150	.145
flank	221.	.233	.105
stylobate, front	101.3	.228	$.225 = \frac{3}{2}.145$ } very nearly
flank	228.1	.355	$.156 = \frac{3}{2}.105$ }
entablature from east front	100.2	$.171 = \frac{3}{4}.228$	.171
do. on flank restored	227.	.307	.135
Propylæa, entablature from east portico	68.1	.119	.175

As will be noticed, all of the measurements differ, and in all regards. The same is true, too, of the comparative measurements of other parts of the same and of other temples. This fact has caused no end of perplexity. It has done so mainly, however, because, as said on pages

29, and 30, the measurements have been thought to represent certain mathematical ratios supposed to be essential to results of proportion. But, as has been also said, they probably have nothing to do with proportion, *per se*, but merely with producing the appearances to which, after being made to appear as they do, the principles of proportion apply. The best clue to the interpretation of these irregularities seems to be afforded by the methods of introducing perspective into painting. (See the quotation from Vitruvius on page 252.) It is not considered necessary in this latter art to apply the laws of perspective with mathematical exactness. Each

FIG. 109.—PHOTOGRAPHIC EFFECT OF CURVED STYLOBATE AND COLUMN OF THE PARTHENON.
See pages 250, 255, 258, 260.

draftsman, in arranging his outlines, feels at liberty to stand off from his drawing, and, as a result of repeated examinations and experiments, to use his own ingenuity. Indeed, even if these laws were applied with mathematical exactness, the required measurements would differ with every foot by which a man stood nearer to his product, or farther from it. Precisely so in architecture. A single glance at Figs. 103, page 236, 107, page 245, or 108, page 247, will show that, in order to produce any given general effect, every measurement in a building would have to be changed with every change in the point of view. Let the man in Fig. 107, page 245, step a few feet farther away from the building, and in order to preserve the same effect, not only would the curve in the cornice have to be lessened, but the columns at either end of the colonnade would have to be brought nearer together. Let a temple placed upon the brow of a hill be intended to produce a certain effect upon those ascending it, and its pediment would have to be higher than if it were intended to produce the same effect upon those on a level with it; or, as Vitruvius says, very unequivocally, in book iii., chapter iii., "To preserve a sensible proportion of parts, if in high situations or of colossal dimensions, we must modify them accordingly, so that they may appear of the size intended." No wonder, therefore, that the Parthenon which crowned the Acropolis (Fig. 95, page 186), was given a relatively higher pediment than the Theseum (Fig. 10, page 36) which stood on a level with the plain surrounding it.

In addition to these facts, suggested by the methods of applying the laws of perspective in painting, let us recall now that, in a sense not true of our own architects, those of ancient times pursued in other regards the same methods as did their fellow-artists in the other arts. The Parthenon was not sketched in its completed form upon paper, and then let out to some contractor to be erected in so many months. It took, as some say, ten years, and, as others say, sixteen years to complete it; and most of the marble in it—each column, for instance, with its capital—is said to have been shaped after being lifted to its place. We know that some of the Gothic cathedrals were almost entirely pulled down and rebuilt, because their appearance was not satisfactory. Why should it not have been the same with the Greek temples? In the age in which they were constructed other artists believed—why should not the architect?—that a man should study upon a product, if he intended to have it remain a model for all the future. It is natural to suppose that the structural arrangements intended to counteract optical defects, or to produce optical illusions, were largely the results of the individual experiments of individual builders. If they were not so, why were they invariably different in different buildings? But if they were so, and if, therefore, it be justifiable to compare the methods of arranging the outlines of these buildings to the methods of arranging outlines according to the laws of perspective in painting, then why is not the general principle which these ancient architects endeavored to fulfil of more practical importance than any particular manner in which, in any particular case, they fulfilled it? More than this, why might not the architects of our own time, by applying, each for himself, as a result of his individual experiments, the same general principle, produce approximately successful results? But these they certainly cannot produce (for reasons stated on page 26) until they get out of their heads the conception that the measurements in the ancient buildings are merely representative—in some mysterious way not possible to fathom—of ratios related to one another as are those of pitch in music. As applied to this case, at least, we have an illustration of how utterly destructive of true practice in art is a false theory.

CHAPTER XV.

HARMONY OF OUTLINES: PERSPECTIVE AS DETERMINING ENTASIS AND IRREGULARITY IN GREEK ARCHITECTURE.

Upward Curves in apparently Horizontal Architectural Lines Ascribed to Effects of Pediment—To the Formation of the Eye—An Explanation of Vitruvius—Ascribed to a Desire to Increase Apparent Size—To a Desire to Represent Relationship to other Lines—Forward Leaning of apparently Perpendicular Lines—Inward Leaning and Tapering of the Columns—Designed Physically to Meet Requirements of the Eye and Artistically to Suggest Height—The Same is True of the Outward and Inward Curving of the Column's Sides—Laws of Vitruvius with Reference to Columns—Differences in the Measurements of Different Greek Columns—Difference between the Greek and Roman use of Principles—Columns and Spaces at the Corners of Colonnades—Sizes of Columns as Determined by their Positions in Exteriors and Interiors—General Conclusion.

THE references made in the last few pages to the curves and irregularities discovered in the Greek temples naturally suggest an examination of some of these in detail, as well as of some of the reasons that have been, or that may be, assigned for them. Penrose tells us in his "Principles of Athenian Architecture," chapter 15, page 104, that the upward curve in the entablature was "to obviate a disagreeable effect produced by the contrast of the horizontal with the inclined lines of a flat pediment, causing the former to be deflected from the angles." This, as will be noticed, is exactly the effect, rather illusive than "disagreeable," produced by the straight lines in the upper drawing in Fig. 104, page 240, for which effect a reason is given on page 240, and which effect is corrected in the middle drawing of the same figure by means of a slight upward curve in the lower horizontal line. We may therefore conclude that Penrose was right in assigning this as the cause of the slight upward curve in the entablature when under a pediment. At the same time, the reason given by him may not have been the sole one. His own words seem to show that it was not. His argument is that the curved entablature is not found on the sides, but only in the fronts—where alone the pediment is visible—of certain temples, noticeably those at Pæstum and Corinth, and of the Propylæa. But this argument would have had more force, had not he himself—subsequently, probably— discovered (see page 250) many other temples in which the entablature at the side is curved. Indeed, Prof. Goodyear, in the article already quoted on page 248, says that, according to Jacob Buckhart, the very temple at Pæstum mentioned by Penrose, has a side entablature leaning forward, like the one in Figs. 107, page 245, and 108, page 247. Moreover, though what Penrose says may explain the upward curve in the entablature it would not explain the curve in the stylobate, *i. e.*, the lower platform just under the columns. (See Fig. 109, page 251.)

The truth seems to be that the reason given by Penrose, though correct so far as it goes, is not the only reason, nor does it get down to all the principles underlying the subject. As shown on page 234, when explaining Fig. 103, page 236, if, from a little distance, we look at a horizontal line before us, and extending to both sides of us, in the degree in which this line is long its central point in front of us will seem to curve away from us, the inclination of the curve being upward, in case our eyes be directed to what is below the line, and downward, in case they be directed to what is above it. As shown, too, on page 240, when explaining Fig. 104, the eyes, when looking at a triangular pediment, are directed toward its mathematical centre. This is above the entablature, the horizontal level of which, being below, might seem to sag downward unless, like the lower line in the second drawing in Fig. 104, it really curved upward. So again, when looking at a temple, the eyes are instinctively directed toward some level above the stylobate, and its horizontal too might seem to sag downward, if it did not curve slightly upward. It is said that this appearance of sagging downward is very marked in the celebrated Walhalla, near Regensburg, Bavaria, erected by Von Klenze under the auspices of Ludwig I., in imitation of the Parthenon, but at a date previous to that at which in modern times the existence of these curves had become known.

Now if, with these plain deductions from commonsense, we turn to book ii., chapter iii., of the "De Architectura" of the Roman writer Vitruvius, we shall find that this conception of what ought to be done accords exactly with his statement of what was done by the ancient builders. The stylobate, or lower platform, he says "ought not to be constructed upon the horizontal level, but should rise gradually from the ends towards the centre so as to have there a small addition. . . . If the line of the stylobate were perfectly horizontal, it would appear like the bed of a channel."

But before we leave the consideration of these horizontal lines, another thing needs to be said. If a long line seem to curve upward naturally at the centre, a line not so long, by being made to curve upward artificially, may be made, for this reason, to seem to be long. Therefore, if one wish to increase the apparent length or width of a building, especially if it stand a little above the spectator, as did the Parthenon on the Acropolis at Athens (see Fig. 95, page 186), he can accomplish his object by causing the horizontal lines to curve upward slightly more than lines of the same length would naturally seem to curve. We may conclude, therefore, that while one object of the Greeks in using these horizontal curves was to meet the natural requirements of the eye, and produce the effects of nature, another object was, in accordance with the requirements of art as well as of the eye, to enhance and emphasize the effects of nature. (See page 258.)

Any outlines that are used in any way have to be considered not only in themselves, but in their relations to other lines. As we shall find presently, the perpendicular side lines of the columns of these temples approached one another as they extended upward. This being so, to one for whom the centre of the field of view would, according to what was said on page 241, be drawn toward the pediment, the downward lines formed by the outer edges of, at least, the side columns would be liable to have the effects of immense spokes in a wheel, of which the horizontal lines of the platform beneath would seem to form a circumference, while the slightly shorter horizontal lines of the entablature would seem to form a slightly shorter curve corresponding to this circumference. Not to make too much of this suggestion, might it not have been partly to correct this optical illusion, that, in both platform and entablature, the centres of the long horizontal lines were made to curve upward? (See Fig. 103, page 236.) And might it not have been partly to correct the same illusion, as well as to fulfil the requirements in the case of very high horizontal lines, as explained on page 236, that the degree of curvature was greatest where, as in the Parthenon, the columns were relatively longest?

Before we leave this subject of the horizontal lines, it will be interesting, in view of the discoveries of the forward inclinations of the entablature represented in Fig. 107, page 245, and Fig. 108, page 247, to note a corresponding arrangement mentioned by Vitruvius, book ii., chapter iii. "All the members," he says, "placed above the capital of the columns, as the architrave, frieze, cornice, tympanum, etc., ought to be inclined forward each the twelfth part of its height; since, if a person looking at the face of an edifice conceives that two lines separate from the eye, one of which touches the bottom, the other the top, of the object of vision, it is certain that that which touches the top is longer; and the farther up one line extends, the more it makes the upper part appear to tip backward; so that if the members which form the face of the upper portion are made to lean forward the whole appears to be perfectly upright and plumb."

Now let us turn to the columns. First of all, it has been found that they incline slightly inward toward the temple's walls. (Figs. 103, page 236, and 109, page 251.) Evidently this was for the purpose, partly, of increasing the appearance of stability in the structure as a whole by causing it to seem to rest upon an exceptionally broad foundation; and, partly (see page 259), of increasing the appearance of height by causing the ascending lines to seem to be brought nearer together than, according to the laws of perspective, they naturally would be at no more than their actual elevation (see Fig. 103, page 236). In connection with this inward inclination of the columns, causing the whole building (see the measurements of the Parthenon, on page 250) to be narrower at its eaves than at its base, each of the columns also was narrower at the top than at the base. To such an extent was this the case, that, notwithstanding the fact that they leaned slightly toward the wall of the building, their inner outline would have appeared to lean away from this wall, had not this appearance been obviated by making the caps of the antæ or pilasters in these walls bend slightly outward.

It need hardly be said that these arrangements must have been for the same general purpose as the curves in the platform and entablature. They were designed, first, to meet the natural requirements of the eye; and, second, to do this in such a way as to give artistic emphasis to the members, and to increase their suggestions of length, height, parallelism, regularity, symmetry, or of other æsthetic effects. To notice only the diminution of the column toward its capital,—in nature, the trunks of trees, in accordance with the principle explained on page 237, decrease in diameter according to the degree of their height. Even if they did not do this, to one looking at them from below, their higher diameters, according to the principle explained on page 234, would seem to be decreased. For this reason an ascending column as broad at its top as at its base has a tendency to appear to reverse this principle; and, according to the laws of association, may seem actually to be broadest at the top. Moreover, it may appear to be shorter also than its real height, for, if it were tall, one would expect it to appear relatively diminished. Besides this, the capital of a column, if distinctly broader than its base, may cause the whole to look top-heavy. But to have the capital seem no broader than the base, the shaft immediately below the capital must be narrower.

The Greek columns not only diminished in diameter toward their tops, but each of their sides, as they ascended, described a slight hyperbolic curve, which began by bending outward a little from the base. (See Fig. 109, page 251.) It is noteworthy that this arrangement corresponds exactly to the requirements of the appearances of ascending vertical lines as brought out in recent experiments and explained on pp. 237, 238. When looking at a column, an ideal line rising exactly in the middle of it represents, of course, the perpendicular in front of us; and the foundation on which the column rests represents the horizontal level. On page 238, it was said that vertical lines to the right and left of the perpendicular appear to incline outward for a little distance above the horizontal level, and then to incline inward; and, on the same page, it was said that such lines, like horizontal lines, undoubtedly describe a slight curve. Such being the conditions, the shape given by the Greeks to their columns both prevented their sides from appearing to sag inward where they should not have done so, and, according to the principle already mentioned several times, augmented their apparent height. As in the case of the horizontal lines, too, there were probably other reasons for these arrangements. If the columns in the Greek temples had begun from their very bases to be diminished in size, their side lines, as compared with those of one another, or of the perpendicular walls of the building or of the entrances, to say nothing of the lines of the erect figures of men standing on the platform, would, for this reason, have seemed to incline inward altogether too rapidly. At their bases, therefore, they began by inclining slightly outward. Possibly too, as the platform on which the columns rested was slightly curved, it was felt that they must be correspondingly curved, if they were to appear to correspond exactly to it. But whatever may have been the reasons of which the Greeks were conscious, it is evident that they were all connected in some way with an endeavor to meet the natural requirements of the eye, and, at the same time, to give artistic emphasis to the members, and increase their suggestions of length, height, parallelism, regularity, symmetry, or of other artistic effects.

Vitruvius, as usual with him, gives very inflexible rules to regulate the dimensions of these columns. "The diminution of the shaft," he says, in book iii., chapter ii., "in its taper from the top to the bottom, is to be thus regulated. If the height of the shaft be fifteen feet, the upper diameter should be five sixths of the lower; if the shaft be from fifteen to twenty feet high, the upper should be eleven thirteenths of the lower; if thirty feet high, the proportion should be thirteen fifteenths; if from thirty to forty feet high, the diminution should be one seventh; if from forty to fifty, the decrease should be one eighth. To the eyes the diameter of the column diminishes as its height increases; hence to preserve the same apparent proportion of the diameters it becomes necessary to decrease those of the upper portion of the shaft. The eye alone is the judge of beauty; and where a false impression is made upon it through the natural defects of vision, we must correct the apparent want of harmony in the whole by instituting particular proportions in particular parts." This last remark conforms in principle to that which undoubtedly was the object sought by the Greeks. But the same cannot be affirmed of what is said in this passage of the particular methods through which they sought to attain this object.

In the proportions supposed to determine the curvature of the Greek column the same difference appears as in those supposed to determine that of the horizontal line. Here are figures given by Penrose in "The Principles of Athenian Architecture," chapter iv., page 44.

	Entasis (or swelling) in terms of length of shaft.	Ditto in terms of lower diameter.	Ditto in terms of semi-diminution.
Erechtheum	$\dfrac{1}{1080}$	$\dfrac{1}{134}$	$\dfrac{1}{9}$
Theseum	$\dfrac{1}{708}$	$\dfrac{1}{140}$	$\dfrac{1}{16}$
Parthenon	$\dfrac{1}{552}$	$\dfrac{1}{110}$	$\dfrac{1}{12}$
Propylæa, small order .	$\dfrac{1}{500}$	$\dfrac{1}{100}$	$\dfrac{1}{11}$
ditto, large order .	$\dfrac{1}{400}$	$\dfrac{1}{80}$	$\dfrac{1}{9}$
Jupiter Olympus . . .	$\dfrac{1}{382}$	$\dfrac{1}{56}$	$\dfrac{1}{4}$

One or two other statements of Vitruvius with reference to these columns may be of interest. But while reading them it is important to bear in mind that their significance lies not in the figures given but in the general principle which they exemplify. The figures are Roman, the principle is Greek. Greek architecture was original, and apparently, for reasons already indicated, what might be termed individual and independent. Roman architecture was imitative, and, as these quotations from Vitruvius show, traditional and mechanical. The principles that the Greeks sought to carry out in a spirit of freedom, the

Romans sought to carry out in servility to the letter; and it is as true in art as in religion that "the letter killeth."

"At the angles," or corners of the temples, Vitruvius tells us, in book iii., chapter ii., "the columns should have their diameters enlarged by a fiftieth part, because, being from their situation more immediately contrasted with the light, they appear smaller than the others." Modern measurements have shown that in the Greek temples these corner columns are not only larger than those associated with them, but that the space between them and the column nearest them is less than between other columns of the series to which they belong. In the Parthenon, according to Penrose, the spaces next to the corner columns are only six feet and a fraction, whereas between the other columns they are eight feet and a fraction. This arrangement, too, like that of the larger size of the side corner columns, was undoubtedly designed largely to counteract the effects of the light. Behind the space between these outer columns there was no masonry, whereas behind the space between all the other columns was the solid wall of the temple; and, as is well known, the space between two pillars appears less where it is filled in with material of the same composition, than where it is not.

The Greeks probably had, too, another reason for the same device. The divisions indicated in each horizontal line in each rectangle in Fig. 18, page 44, are all of exactly the same length. Yet it is impossible to look at them without suspecting that the divisions nearest the ends of the lines are the longest. This is the same as to say that to cause these end divisions to appear of exactly the same length as the others, they should be made shorter. The reason why this is so is owing, of course, to the roundness of the eye. When we look at the middle of a horizontal line there is actually more eye-surface covered by the divisions at the sides than there is by the divisions seen directly in front, which latter divisions are opposite that part of the eye which is most nearly flat.

Once more, Vitruvius tells us, in book ii., chapter iv, that "If the width of a temple be more than one half its length, the proportion should be apparently restored thus: Columns should be placed within and opposed to those between the antæ. These should be of corresponding height; but their diameters should be less in the following proportions: if the columns in front be eight times their diameter in height, the inner ones should be nine diameters; if the exterior be nine or ten diameters in height, the interior should preserve a proportionate augmentation. The difference in the bulk of the columns will not be apparent because they will not be seen contrasted with the light. If, notwithstanding, they should appear too slender, the number of flutings should be increased. Thus, if the columns in front have twenty-four flutes the inner ones may have twenty-eight or even thirty-two; so that what is in fact taken from the bulk may be restored by the additional number of flutings. This optical deception arises from the idea of greater magnitude which is impressed by the transit of the visual rays over a greater surface. For if the peripheries of two circles of equal diameter, one of which is fluted and the other not, be measured by a line which is made to be in contact with every point of the peripheries, the length of the line will not be the same in both cases; because in one it has been made to touch every point in the concave surfaces of the flutings in the intervals between the fillets. Since this deception therefore may be accomplished, it is allowable to make columns which are in confined situations and little exposed to the light less massive than the others, because their want of bulk may be rendered imperceptible by augmenting the number of flutings as circumstances may require."

But enough has now been said to verify the statement that the ancient architects in order to fulfil both visual and æsthetic, both physiological and psychical, requirements erected their buildings with primary reference to their general effects when seen from some definite point or points at a distance. In connection with this it has been shown also that these architects differed materially with reference to the particular methods through which to secure these effects, arriving at their conclusions, probably, as a result of many individual experiences and experiments.

Since the printing of the first edition of this book, Professor W. H. Goodyear has discovered that the methods attributed in this discussion to only the ancient Greeks, the Egyptians, and the Romans, were used also by the early Gothic architects. He himself has measured eighty-five of their churches in Italy which have floors rising between the front door and the chancel, sometimes, three feet, while, often, the successive key-stones of the arches between the nave and the aisles descend in the same direction,—evidently to increase the effect of distance according to the laws of perspective. To what extent the same methods are exemplified in the Gothic churches of northern Europe, has not yet been determined.

CHAPTER XVI.

HARMONY OF OUTLINE: BINOCULAR VISION.

Curvature—The Field of Vision for Both Eyes not the Same—The Horopter which Both Eyes See—At Either Side of the Horopter Something Else Seen by but One Eye: Its Influence on the Recognition of Relief in Form—·This Fact as Developed in Stereoscopy—Other Illustrations—Perception of Relief at the Sides of an Object through Unconscious though Constant Movement of the Eyes—As a Result of no Movement—Seeing the Sides of an Object Important to Gaining a Conception of its Form—Shape of the Eyes' Field of Sight, for Each Eye and for Both Eyes—The Horizontal Shape Seen with the Least Effort is Rounded Backward—The Perpendicular Shape is Elliptical—Convergence of Axis, and a Lack of it as Applied to Near and Distant and to Many and Few Details—Practical Experiments Evincing Ease of Perception of All Outlines in an Elliptical Shape—To Perceive Outlines of this Shape, no Conscious Movement of the Eye's Lens is Necessary—Therefore they Realize the Condition Required by Visual Rest, Enjoyment, Beauty—This Fact may Explain the Use of the Ellipse in Art—The Ellipse in General—In Vases, Leaves, Birds, Animals, Fishes—Human Form—Its Like Curves are Accommodated to the Least Expenditure of Visual Effort—The General Method through which, when the Eye's Axis changes, it can Look from One to Another Line with the Least Visual Effort.

THUS far we have been considering the connection between the principle of perspective and the representation of straight lines, or, if of curves, of these so far only as they may be necessary in the art-product in order to enhance the natural or artistic effects of straight lines. We have now to consider the representation of lines that are actually curved in nature. In doing this, we shall come upon certain facts which, though intimately connected with the requirements of both perspective and proportion, have not hitherto, so far as the author is aware, been recognized.

What is to be said of these curves, may best be introduced, perhaps, by observing that when we examine carefully an object or scene, we seem to have a distinct perception of one point of it, as we may say; and, in connection with this, to have a less distinct perception of a small space, surrounding this point, as well as a decidedly dim perception of a much larger space surrounding the small space. This larger space, *i. e.*, the space the most dimly perceived of all, represents the whole field of sight; and we would better begin here by noticing that it is not for both eyes absolutely the same. If, while concentrating our gaze upon an object, we close in succession first one eye and then the other, we find that in closing our right eye we have removed from the sphere of vision something that seemed indistinctly visible at its right, and in closing our left eye we have removed something that seemed indistinctly visible at its left. This shows—to quote from Dr. M. Foster's "Text-Book of Physiology," sec. ii., on Binocular Vision—that "when we use both eyes a large part of the visual field of each eye overlaps that of the other; but that, nevertheless, at the same time, a certain part of each visual field does not so overlap any part of the other. If the right hand be held up above the right shoulder and brought a little forward, it soon becomes distinctly visible to the right eye; it enters into the field of sight of the right eye. But if the right eye be closed, the right hand kept in this former position is not visible to the left eye; it is outside the field of sight of that eye; it has to be brought much further forward before it comes into the field of sight of the left eye." While this is true, however,—while the field of sight is not for both eyes absolutely the same, it has to be acknowledged that, when we are closely concentrating attention upon any object or scene, that which is visible to only one eye exerts but little influence. When, looking intently forward, we bring a hand at one side of us in sight of only one eye, though we are conscious that something is there the vision conveys only a vague impression of what this something really is. We can hardly be said, in any full sense, to observe it.

Let us turn, therefore, from that which is noticed by only one eye to that which is noticed by both eyes, because it occupies the point where the visual axes of both eyes converge. (See A and B in Fig. 113, page 272.) This is the point which is technically termed the *horopter*. With reference to the character or shape of this, physicists have not yet come to any agreement. Joseph Le Conte tells us in his work on " Sight " that Aguilonius, the inventor of the term, believed it to be a plane; Claparède, a surface; Prévost and Müller, the circumference of a circle, and Helmholtz, to be sometimes a circle, but to vary according to the position of the point of sight. That this horopter exists, however, which is all that we need to know here, is universally admitted.

But now the question comes whether any part of the field of sight between the horopter and the exceedingly dim outside limits of this field which were mentioned in a former paragraph, exerts a distinct visual effect which must be considered in calculating the general influence of outlines. In other words, is any effect, essential at times to that of form, produced in the region immediately surrounding the horopter, of which, of course, we have a less distinct perception than of it ? In order to determine this, let us begin by holding in front of the eyes, the forefinger of one hand, represented either by *a* or by *a'* in Fig. 110, and then immediately in front of this finger, the forefinger of the other hand, represented either by *b* or by *b'*. As we do so, we shall find the effect indicated in Fig. 110, and if we hold the fingers near enough to our eyes and concentrate our gaze upon the farther finger of the two, represented by A in Fig. 111, we shall see

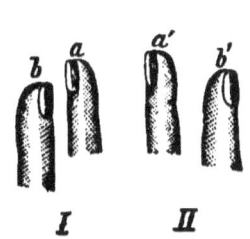

FIG. 110.—FINGER BEHIND ANOTHER AS SEEN BY ONE EYE.
By left eye (I)
By right eye (II)
See page 269.

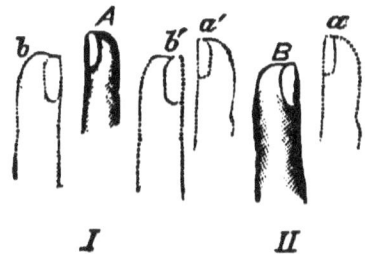

FIG. 111.—FINGER BEHIND ANOTHER AS SEEN WITH BOTH EYES.
When looking at back finger (I)
Or at front finger (II)
See pages 269, 278, 279, 280.

the finger in front of it dimly doubled as in *b* and *b'*; and that, if we concentrate our gaze upon the finger nearer to the eyes, represented by B in Fig. 111, we shall see the farther finger dimly doubled, as in *a* and *a'*. In other words, we shall find that, while we are looking at one finger with both eyes, which finger therefore is at the horopter, where the visual lines or axes of both eyes cross, each eye for itself sees the other finger also, but, as this is not in the place where the visual lines or axes of both eyes cross, each eye sees it in a different place. Notice, too, that the farther from the finger seen single we remove the apparently doubled finger, the farther apart do its two dim representatives seem to be. Again, if we stand a very thin book in such a way as to have its back directly in front of our two eyes looking at it conjointly, and then, without changing our position, close the right eye and look at it with the left eye, we shall distinctly see the left side of the cover. Then again, if we close the left eye, and look at it with the right eye, we shall just as distinctly see the right side of the cover. If now, opening both eyes, we once more look at its back, we shall not see either side as distinctly as before; but we shall have a perfectly clear impression of an effect produced by both sides,—an effect enabling us, as it were, to look around the corners of the back, and recognize its form. Or if we cannot do this in every sense, we can obtain at least an impression that the book as a whole stands out in relief from whatever is behind it. If now, once more, we look straight at the back of the book with only one eye, we shall perceive that such a view of it very much lessens this last impression—that of being able to look around the corners and recognize the form in relief.

This is the fact with reference to binocular vision which is applied, as probably most of us know, in stereoscopy. In preparing stereoscopic views, two photographs, taken from different positions, a few feet apart, are made of the same object, or scene. Then they are placed together side by side on a card, in front of two glasses through which they are intended to be seen, the photograph taken at the right being in front of the right eye, and that taken at the left being in front of the left eye. As thus arranged, each photograph is supposed to represent the object of view as it is seen in nature by one of the eyes regarding it, but not by the other eye. Any one familiar with the effects of the stereoscope, knows how much more natural and satisfactory views so doubled are than are those of a single photograph. Especially is this the case with representations of statues, or of any objects the impressions conveyed by which depend upon the appearance of thickness of form, particularly of that kind of thickness which, for full effect, needs to convey the impression of being rounded at the sides. See Fig. 112, page 272, as explained on the same page.

Not only the stereoscope, but other things with which all are familiar can be explained only upon the hypothesis that each eye has a different field of view. If we look at a comparatively large object, like a typewriter, near at hand, first with a single eye, and then with both eyes, we shall find ourselves, at a certain distance, consciously shifting the glances, or, as a physicist would say, the axis of the single eye first to one side of the object, and then to the other, because only thus can we make out its exact shape. But, at the same distance, both eyes looking together can perceive the shape without any change or, at least, any conscious change of axis.

This word *conscious*, just used, introduces a question which, as will be recognized presently, has an important bearing upon æsthetic effects as related to this particular subject. The question is whether the eyes, when directing attention away from a single point in an object to the whole object, including its two side contours, do this by a single act which focusses attention on a more distant background in front of which the two contours are clearly perceptible; or do so by many successive acts, which focus attention first on the single point and then on one and the other of the contours, and, finally, as a result of successive examinations, draw a general inference with reference to the form as a whole. To determine how the eyes act in these cases, two drawings represented in Fig. 112, are given by Le Conte in his "Sight." By placing a sheet of paper between the two eyes, in such a way as to exclude a view of the right drawing from the left eye, and of the left drawing from the right eye, and then looking at the two drawings, at a certain distance the two will be found to be blended into one; and, in this one, we shall apparently be looking, not at lines described on a flat surface, but at what resembles a wire net standing on end, the smaller end of which, represented by the smaller circles, seems nearer us, and the larger end, represented by the larger circles, seems farther from us.

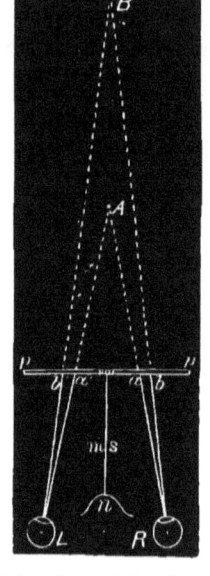

FIG. 113.—PARTS OF OBJECT, AS SEEN WITH NEAR AND DISTANT BACKGROUND.

p, p, object; *A, B*, backgrounds: *L* and *R*, eyes; *n*, nose.

See pages 234, 268, 273, 280.

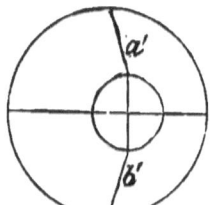 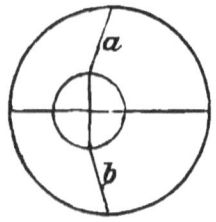

FIG. 112.—SAME OBJECT SEEN DIFFERENTLY BY EACH EYE. NEAR AND DISTANT BACKGROUND.

See pages 271, 272, 274, 280.

The explanation of this effect is, that to see both circles equally well from the same distance, the eyes, in taking in all sides of the larger circle, must adjust themselves to a more remote background, for which reason the larger circle seems more remote from us than the smaller circle. The same effect is illustrated in a different way in Fig. 113, page 272. In this, a and a' represent the two side contours of the object seen with the eyes when adjusted to a background at A; and b and b' represent the two side contours of the object seen with the eyes when adjusted to a background at B. L and R represent the left and right eyes, n the nose, and ms the paper placed between the eyes. Fig. 114, will show what is meant by the eyes being adjusted to take in one rather than another background, a in this

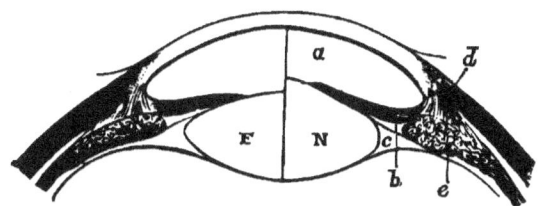

FIG. 114.—LENS OF EYE ADJUSTED TO NEAR (N) AND DISTANT (F) OBJECTS.
a, aqueous humor ; d, ciliary muscle.
See pages 231, 273, 323.

figure representing the aqueous humor, F the crystalline lens made flatter, and thus adjusted to take in a more distant background ; N the same made more rounded in order to take in a nearer background ; and d the ciliary muscle which does the work. It will be perceived that the adjusting of the eye to one background or the other requires the exertion of considerable muscular energy. The question before us now, the æsthetic bearing of which will be brought out presently, is with reference to the degree or quality of the effort expended by the eyes in perceiving outlines, first at the one and then at the other background. According to Le Conte, in his "Sight" (Binocular Vision, chapter iv.), the answer to this question, as given by Brücke, Brewster, and Prévost, is as follows: "In regarding a solid object or a natural scene, or two stereoscopic pictures in a stereoscope, the eyes are in incessant *unconscious* motion, and the observer, by alternating greater and less convergence of the axes, combines successively the different parts of the two pictures, as seen by the two eyes, and thus by running the point of sight back and forth, reaches *by trial* a distinct perception of binocular perspective or binocular relief." This explanation supposes that the eye does not take in the whole form at once, but as a result of incessant action. Notice, nevertheless, that it is acknowledged that, of this action, the mind is *unconscious*. On page 271 it was said that in trying to make out the shape of a typewriter with one eye we are constantly conscious of shifting attention from one side of the machine to the other. It is something to have it acknowledged that when, with both eyes, we look at both front and sides of an object, both sides of which can be seen only as the eyes' lenses are adjusted to take in a comparatively distant background, we are *unconscious* of this action.

But does this action take place? Wheatstone's theory, as stated by Le Conte (Binocular Vision, chapter iv.), is that "in viewing a solid object or a scene, two slightly dissimilar images are formed in the two eyes, as already explained; but the mind completely unites or fuses them into one." Notice again what is said on page 272 of Fig. 112. Le Conte says also that "the instantaneous perception of binocular relief is demonstrated by the now celebrated experiment of Dove. If a natural object or a scene or two stereoscopic pictures be viewed by the light of an electric spark or a succession of electric sparks, the perspective is perfect, even though the duration of such a spark is only $\frac{1}{24000}$ of a second of time. It is inconceivable that there should be any change of optic convergence, any running of the point of sight back and forth, in the space of $\frac{1}{24000}$ of a second. Evidently, therefore, binocular perspective may be perceived without such change of convergence. This point is certainly one of capital importance. The instantaneous perception of relief is fatal to Dr. Brücke's theory in its pure unmodified form." Then, after mentioning his own experiments confirming Dove's discoveries, Le Conte gives his own theory thus: "All objects or points of objects either beyond or nearer than the point of sight are doubled. . . . In case of double images each eye, as it were, 'knows its own image,' although such knowledge does not emerge into distinct consciousness. Thus I conclude that the mind perceives relief *instantly*, but not *immediately*; for it does so by means of double images, as just explained. This is all that is absolutely necessary for the perception of relief; but it is probable—nay, it is certain—that the relief is made clearer "—*i. e.*, may be made clearer—" by a ranging of the point of sight back and forth, and a successive combination of the different parts of the object or scene or picture as maintained by Brücke."

Now let us apply the same principle not to relief merely but, in connection with it, to the method of perceiving in connection with the front, the two series of outlines describing the two sides of an object as it stands fronting us; and, in carrying out our purpose, let us recall the experiment with the book mentioned on page 270. As we stand the book up with its back exactly facing us, we see more of both its side covers while looking at it with two eyes than we do while looking with one eye; but we do not see as much of either side cover as we do while looking at it with one eye. Now whether we explain the effect, when using both eyes, by saying that it results from the incessantly alternating action first of one eye, and then of the other; or from a synchronous unchanging action of both eyes together, we are obliged to infer that the general effect is not a combination of the two different perceptive actions of the eyes. If it were, we should with both eyes see both sides of the cover as plainly as, with one eye, we see one side of it. As we experience the effect, it is a resultant. A resultant of two forces never corresponds to either the one, or the other, or to both in their entirety. It represents each as modified by the other.

Now we are prepared to retrace our steps somewhat, and consider the bearing of what has been said upon the particular subject of which this chapter was to treat, namely, curvature. Let us begin by trying to determine, so far as we can, the exact shape of the field of sight. As applied to each eye singly, Dr. M. Foster, in his "Text-Book of Physiology," says "The dimensions of the field of sight for one eye will, even in the same individual, vary with the width of the pupil and other dioptric arrangements of the eye; individual variations are also considerable; but the ordinary dimensions may be stated as subtending an angle of about 145° in the horizontal and about 100° in the vertical meridian. . . . The outline of the field is an irregular one, and stretches farther toward the temporal side," *i. e.*, the side nearest the temple. (See Fig. 115, page 278.) And why this should be so, most of us can recognize upon closing one eye, and trying to look forward with the other. We shall usually detect the presence of the nose, which, of course, is the same as to say that it limits the field of vision of the eye on that side on which it appears. In the same way, too, it is evident that, in certain cases, the eyelids and lashes have an influence. But, though the whole field of vision may have irregular outlines, extending just as the field of each eye does somewhat farther in a horizontal than in a vertical direction, notice that the pupil of the eye is itself circular, and that objects which can be seen with exactly the same degree of clearness are generally seen at very nearly the same distance from the pupil's centre. If, for instance, there were an exactly similar nose exactly similarly situated on each side of the eye, no one doubts that, to one looking straight forward, both noses would produce an exactly similar impression of their presence. The mere fact that there happens to be no nose on the temple-side of the eye, while widening the actual outline of the field of vision on this side, does not change the principle that the same degree of clearness in outline will generally be found in every direction at the same distance from the point on which the eye's centre is fixed.

The bearing of this upon the subject before us is that it is approximately appropriate to represent, not the whole field of vision but that smaller field of comparatively distinct vision mentioned on page 267, a field immediately surrounding x and x in Fig. 115, page 278, by a circle. Nor, even if it be insisted that this should be a circle elongated horizontally, will anything that is to be said here be found to be inconsistent with such a conception of it. But though the field of distinct sight for one of the eyes be circular, it does not follow that this is true of the field for both eyes when looking together. If we compare Fig. 115, page 278, with Fig. 116, page 278, we shall perceive that this field for both eyes is appropriately represented neither by the single circle at the left of Fig.

116, nor by the two separated circles at the right of this figure; but rather by the space enclosed between the two circumferences of the circles where they overlap, as in the second and third drawings of this figure.

Of these drawings, notice now that the first from the left represents the more clearly of the two the result that would follow, were we to describe about each x in Fig. 115 a circle the circumference of which would pass exactly through the other x. This being so, let us ask what shape in an object would best enable the eyes to see all its outlines in a single unchanged glance or, at least,—to recall what was said on page 274,—in a single unconsciously changed glance, or with the least visual effort. In answering this question, let us divide it, and make it apply, first, to a shape considered horizontally, *i. e.*, from

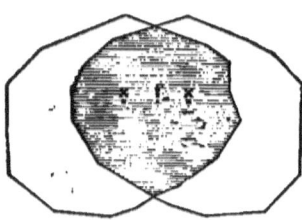

FIG. 115.—FIELD OF VIEW OF BOTH EYES AND OF EACH EYE.
From Foster's "Anatomy."
See pages 276, 277, 278, 279.

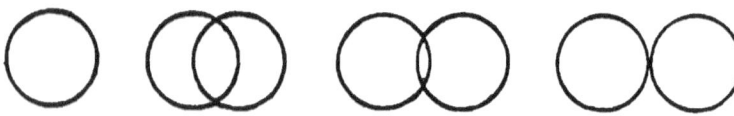

FIG. 116.—CIRCLES ILLUSTRATING FIELD OF DISTINCT VISION FOR BOTH EYES TOGETHER.
See pages 277, 280, 288.

side to side when facing us. We may gain a clue to the right answer from Fig. 111, page 269. Suppose that we be looking with both eyes at an object, the middle front of which is in a place corresponding to that represented by B in Fig. 111; and its two sides in places corresponding to those represented by *a* and *d* in the same figure. In this case, the B would evidently be seen at the point represented by f in Fig. 115: and the *a* and *d* at the points represented by x and x in Fig. 115; and, if so, the natural effect produced by binocular vision as represented by *a* and *d* in Fig. 111, would reinforce the effect produced by the two sides as seen at x and x in Fig. 115. In fact, the effect represented by *a* and *d* in Fig. 111, when the fingers are placed as explained on page 269, is no longer perceived when, at the same distance, we are looking at the front (B) of an object, the sides of which are in the places respectively represented by *a*, and *d*. Now, in addition to what has been said, it needs to be observed here, if we are to complete the answer to this part of our question, that, in order to accommodate itself to the natural rounding of the eye, the outline of the object between B and *a* or *d*, as represented in Fig. 111, or—what is the same— between that which is seen at f and at x and x, as represented in Fig. 115, would not be a straight line, as if there were a sharp angle at the middle of the front, as at B in Fig. 111, or as seen at f in Fig. 115; but this outline would be a line turning toward the backgrounds at *a* and *d*, or as seen at x and x, by regular degrees. In other words, the shape would be that produced by a curved line, which is the same as to say that the object considered horizontally, *i. e.*, from side to side, would be rounded from its middle front backward.

Now let us take up the second part of our question, and ask what shape in an object when considered perpendicularly, *i. e.*, from top to bottom, would best enable the eyes to see all its outlines at a single unchanged or, at least, unconsciously changed glance. Recalling what was said on page 278, namely, that the field of distinct vision for both eyes together would be appropriately represented by the space enclosed between the intersecting circles in the second and third drawings in Fig. 116,—is it not evident that some shape fitting into this space would best fulfil the requirement for which we are in search? The space has the shape termed by botanists elliptic lanceolate, —an ellipse pointed; and of all outlines wholly curved, those of an upright ellipse fit into it most nearly.

The explanation for the formation of this shape between the two circles is, as indicated on page 278, that, at distances farther off than the object, or than the part of the object at which both eyes are looking, there are places upon which attention is not concentrated, and in these places the respective fields of distinct vision for the two eyes cross in such ways that each eye sees a different circle. But it must not be supposed that this condition accompanies the perception of objects or of parts of objects at merely different distances, as in the cases of the two fingers in Fig. 111. It accompanies the perception of objects at the same distance when attention is more or less concentrated upon a larger or a smaller part of them. When we see a man, we may concentrate our attention upon some ornament that he wears—a buckle or a button —to such an extent as not to see clearly anything else. Or we may consciously relax from the effort at concentration, which means that, by changing the form of the lens, we may re-adjust the focus of each eye, or let it adjust itself, so as to take in a more distant background; and then, at the same time, without noticing particularly this background, we may notice that which stands in front of it, and thus see clearly the man's whole form. (See Figs. 112, page 272, and 113, page 272.) Of course, when this is done, it is some space like that enclosed by both circles in the second drawing in Fig. 116, page 278, that represents, at a point nearer than the background, the limits of the sphere of distinct vision for both eyes. To apply this to the illustration used on page 270, supposing the back of a book to be exactly in this enclosed space, the right eye, when the left was shut, would see its right covers extending outside this space toward the outer circumference of the right intersecting circle; and the left eye, when the right was shut, would see the left cover extending toward the outer circumference of the left circle. But both eyes, when looking together, would see clearly nothing outside the enclosed space.

As already intimated, it follows that, if what has been said be true, the whole of a form facing us can be recognized with ease, *i. e.*, in a single glance, or, at least, a single conscious glance (see page 271), in the degree in which it is conformed to vertical elliptic-lanceolate outlines. Indeed, this fact, thus theoretically unfolded, can be confirmed by practical experiments. If we describe at the nearest point at which it is possible to perceive all its outlines, an ellipse longer vertically than horizontally, and about it a circle of the same diameter as the vertical length of the ellipse, there will be not a few who will find it slightly more easy at a single glance, or without consciously changing the axis of the eye, to perceive all the outlines of the former than of the latter. If we describe about the circle and ellipse a square of the same diameter as the circle, no one can see all its outlines without consciously changing the axis of the eye, as when glancing from corner to corner; and if we describe about the square a rectangle of the same vertical but twice the horizontal dimensions, we cannot see all its outlines without changing the axis still more consciously.

We have found now that the difference between inspecting carefully some particular ornament, as a button or a buckle on a man's form, and taking in a general view of his form as a whole, is the difference between conscious convergence of axis or concentration of sight and no consciousness of it. We have found also that the method through which the two eyes, acting conjointly, recognize the effects of binocular vision is, according to Brücke, Brewster, and Prévost, an incessant but unconscious movement or change of axis; and, according to Wheatstone and Dove and, to an extent, of Le Conte, not necessarily any movement or change of axis at all; and we have found that in the degree in which the contour of a form is elliptical or even circular, rather than square or rectangular, it can be recognized without ocular movement, or, at least, conscious ocular movement.

In the use of the eyes, the difference between movement and no movement, or, if the other theory be adopted, between *conscious* movement and *no conscious* movement, is the difference between activity, work, or effort, and rest, play, or enjoyment. Notice now that this is the same difference as, in Chapters VII. and VIII. of "Art in Theory," is said to distinguish that which is done with a utilitarian aim and an æsthetic. But if a form of outline naturally fitting into the shape of an upright elliptical figure, be the one which requires, to recognize it, the least visual activity work or effort, or—what is the same thing—which is consistent with the most rest play or enjoyment; then this form of outline must be the one most conformed to the physiological requirements of the eye. In other words—and this explains why the term is used in this work—it is the form most in *harmony* with these requirements; therefore the most agreeable, the most pleasurable, the most " fitted to be perceived," which is

SHAPES PERCEIVED WITH LEAST EFFORT. 283

the exact etymological meaning of the word *æsthetic*. But this fact furnishes the best possible justification for calling the curve,—particularly, as we shall notice presently, the one found in the ellipse,—the line of beauty.

What has been thus found to be true with reference to the elliptical contour, renders significant many other facts —indeed, whole classes of facts with which few of us can fail to be familar. Recall, for instance, the extensive use in art of this elliptical shape. If we go into the shops where they sell implements for drawing, whatever else they may not keep, assortments of models for different sizes of ellipses are sure to meet our eyes. The one orna-

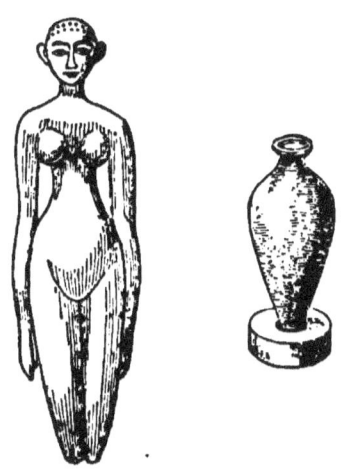

FIG. 117.—EGYPTIAN DOLL AND VASE.
See pages 284, 295.

FIG. 118.—PRIZE VASES FOR ATHENIAN GAMES.
See pages 284, 295.

mental object, avowedly not modelled after an appearance in nature, which the arts of all lands and races have united

284   PROPORTION AND HARMONY.

in producing, is the vase; and this is almost invariably conformed to vertical elliptic-lanceolate outlines. See Figs. 117, page 283, and 118, page 283. Again, in architecture, the form that general usage has shown to be the most satisfactory is one which, whether we consider it as exemplified in the cupola or the dome, is like that described within

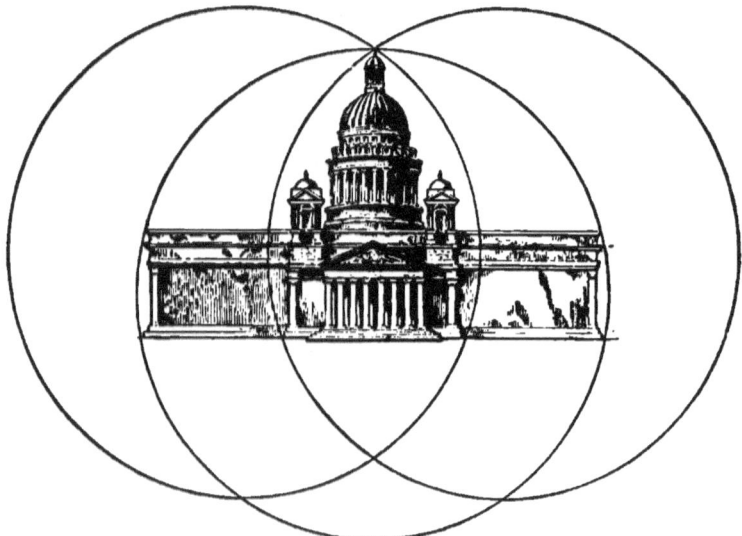

FIG. 119.—BUILDING ENCLOSED BY CIRCLES.
See page 284.

the space enclosed between circles in the centre of Fig. 119, and even if the building be wide, the form preferred for this is one containing at least a central part which, as in Fig. 119, it is possible to enclose in such a space. Of course, there are other reasons for the arrangement of the dome, shaped as it is, in the centre of such a building—reasons founded on the fulfilment of such principles as *unity*, *principality*, and *balance*, as explained in Chapters II. to

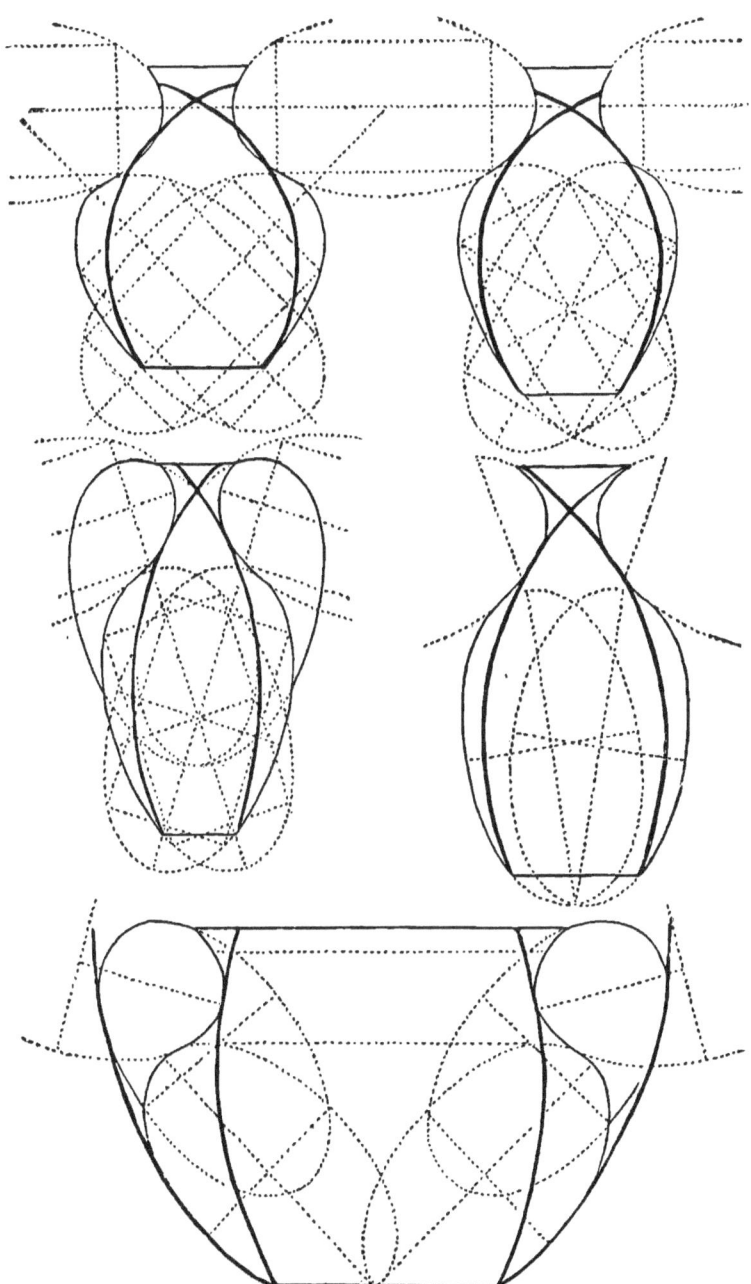

FIG. 120.—VASES OUTLINED BY ELLIPSES AND CIRCLES.
See pages 68, 286, 287, 295.

V. of "The Genesis of Art-Form." But these principles do not explain the particular shape of the contour as a whole, as does the reason attributing it to ease of action on the part of the eye when looking at it as a whole.

In art, as in everything, there may be more than one reason for an effect. D. R. Hay, in his interesting work entitled "Ornamental Geometric Diaper Designs accompanied by an Attempt to Develop and Elaborate the true Principles of Ornamental Design as applied to the Decorative Arts," says of the ellipse, that it "possesses that essential constituent of beauty, variety. . . . Its outline being formed by two radii, one of which is continually decreasing while the other is increasing, it imperceptibly varies from an oblate to an acute curve." This statement will be recognized to be almost identical with the one in Chapter XVII. of " The Genesis of Art-Form," and made on page 61 of this book with reference to the effects of the kinds of curves which Ruskin declares to be the most beautiful in nature. In accordance with the principle which he is unfolding Mr. Hay, in his work just mentioned, goes on to say that "the ellipse the proportions of which arise out of the harmonic divisions of the circle . . . . is entitled to be termed the primary of its class or, in distinction to all other forms, *the* ellipse." By this ellipse he means one exactly described about a rectangle twice as long as it is wide, a rectangle, therefore, whose length is to its breadth, or to the length of a square as 2 : 1. Such an ellipse is described by many of the lines in Fig. 120, page 285. That this ellipse, as well as others based upon exact multiples of the circle, fulfils, in a peculiar sense, the requirements of the art-methods indicated on page 3, and of beauty as determined by these, as well as of proportion, as unfolded in Chapters II. to VIII., is evident; and the conclusions with reference to the desirability of its use in geometric designs are sound. Notice the graceful and yet greatly varied curves through which, when placed together as in Fig. 121, the outlines of such ellipses pass into one another.

But Mr. Hay's conclusions hardly explain the origin of the ellipse as a whole; or why innumerable forms in nature, like those of vases, trees, and men, are not consid-

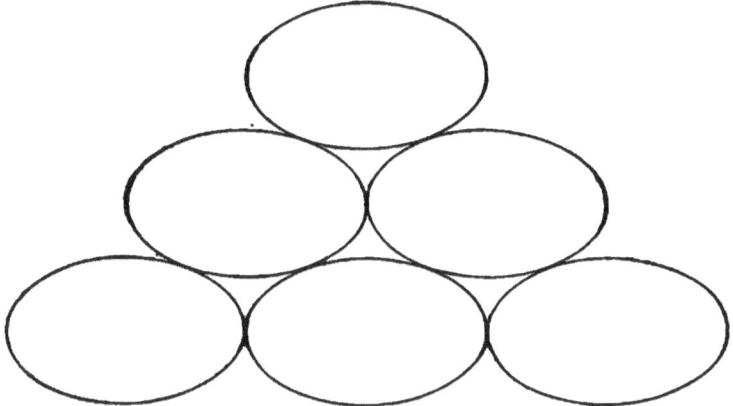

FIG. 121.—CURVED LINES AS OUTLINED BY ELLIPSES.
See page 287.

ered less beautiful than others even though their outlines are not conformed even proportionately to the ratios of that ellipse which he declares to be the most beautiful. For instance, Fig. 120, page 285, was drawn by him to show the influence of this ellipse upon the forms of vases. The dotted lines indicate these ellipses, and the finer continuous lines the vases described by him. To the same figures the heavier continuous lines have been added by the author of the present volume to show the shapes representative of vases whose sides conform exactly to parts of intersecting circumferences drawn as exemplified in Fig. 116, page 278. There will probably be little doubt in the minds of any examining the figures, that these heavier lines, fully as well as the lighter continuous lines drawn by Mr. Hay, represent the forms which usage in all countries has shown to be most generally considered satisfactory. To what extent the contours of leaves and bushes conform to this elliptical-lanceolate shape will be found illustrated sufficiently in Fig. 39, page 78. But a very interesting exemplification of how the same shape may be supposed to be seen in the forms of animals, birds, and fishes may be noticed in Fig. 122, page 289. It is copied in Mr. Hay's volume, already mentioned, from Sir William Jardine's " Naturalist Library," the birds representing the cuckoo and the blackbird; and the fishes representing the salmon and the turbot. It will be noticed that the outlines of many of these are so placed in nature that the elliptical spaces to which their shapes are here shown to conform have their longest dimensions horizontal rather than vertical; and that, so far as this is the case, these shapes do not exactly fulfil the principle illustrated in Fig. 116, page 278. But may we not, without making too much of a mere suggestion, suppose this lack of correspondence to give significance to the fact that, when examining such forms closely, men instinctively turn their heads first to one side and then to the other, where, whatever may be their real, not to say conscious reason for the movement, it is a fact that the elliptical space will appear to be in the same upright position as it is when between the overlapping circumferences in Fig. 116, on page 278? Besides this, is it not true that, when one has come to recognize an æsthetically satisfactory effect in an ellipse prolonged vertically, there is a tendency, according

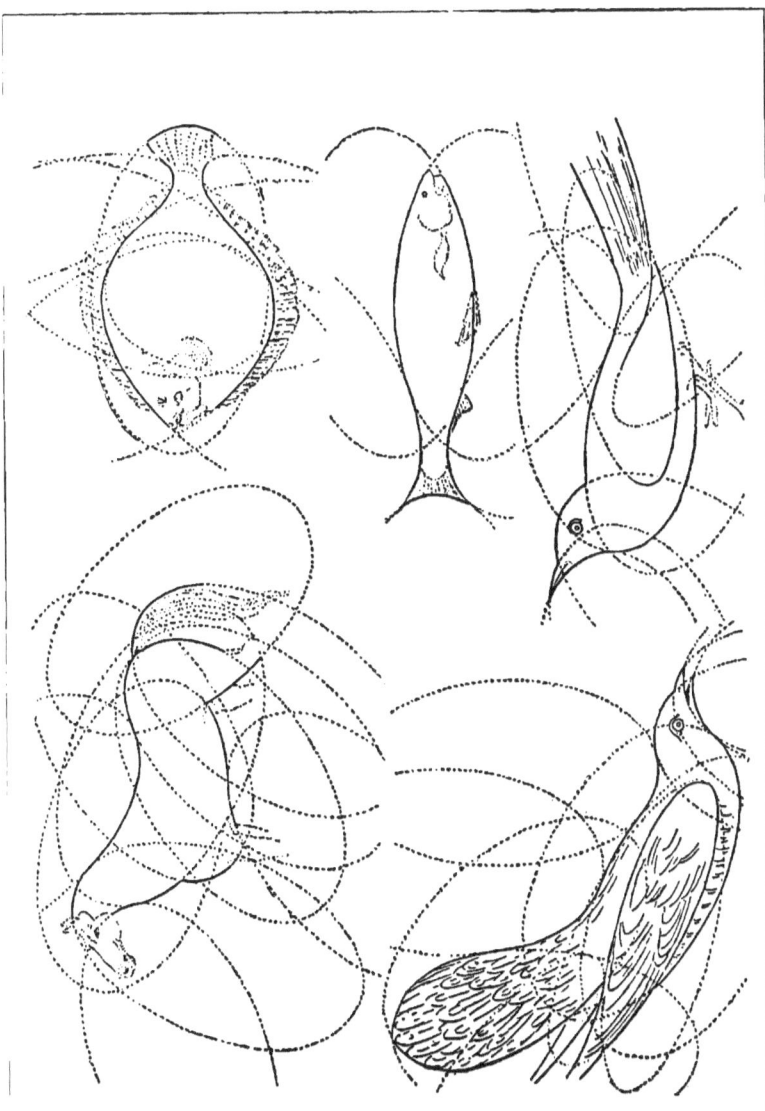

FIG. 122.—BEASTS, FISHES, AND BIRDS AS OUTLINED BY ELLIPSES.
See pages 78, 288, 295.

to the laws of association, for him to recognize the same effect, even when suggested by an ellipse prolonged horizontally? Take, for instance, the form of a man's limb—not when standing but when sitting down; and in such a position that one can see only a small part of him. We certainly should not admire this part, in case it were comparatively small, and we knew that, when he stood up, he would prove to be, as a whole, comparatively large. This shows that the standard by which we judge is one in which the limbs are in their normal standing posture; and, when they are not so, that we form our inferences of them by way mainly of association.

This reference to the human figure reminds us that in it alone do we find the form which is supposedly the most perfect in nature, the form therefore which we should expect to find the most perfectly adjusted to this elliptical requirement. In order to show that it is so, as a fact, and, at the same time, to show this in such a way as to prevent any one's imagining that the fact might not be true of drawings not prepared by the author, none of those to which the principle is applied in this book have been prepared by him. All are copied from contours drawn by others in accordance with what they suppose to represent perfect proportions. Figs. 72, page 136, and 73, page 137, show how the form as a whole fits into an elliptic-lanceolate shape. Figs. 31, page 57, 36, page 71, 73, page 137, and 74, page 139, show how different outlines of the same form fit into spaces formed between circumferences of the same dimensions; and Figs. 32, page 58, and 35, page 70, show how the same is true as applied not only to the shape of the body when the limbs are held together, but when it is assuming positions in which, as in action, they are more or less separated.

It will be noticed that most of the circles drawn about each body are of the same size. This size, in Fig. 72, page 136, as also, in one instance, in Fig. 73, page 137, is determined by the height of the enclosed space needed in order to take in the whole form; and in all the other figures by the height needed in order to take in certain parts of the form. One reason why the circles drawn about the same forms are of the same size, is connected with the requirements of proportion, as indicated on page 71. Another reason is connected with the requirements of ease in the act of perception, in accordance with the principle mentioned on page 282. Circles of the same size represent the same general convergence of the eyes' axes; and the wider enclosed space formed by the intersecting of two such circles may be supposed to include the narrower space. In other words, if in such a case, one can see both side contours of a form inscribable in the wider enclosed space, he can also, without changing the axes, see both contours of a form inscribable in the narrower space. Or if the latter form necessitates, at times, a different convergence, when this takes place by shifting attention from one contour inscribable in a wider to another inscribable in a narrower space, and so on by regularly graded degrees, as in passing the eye downward from the shoulders to the shins of the form in Fig. 31, page 57, or Fig. 73, page 137, this condition may be supposed to represent the least possible expenditure of visual effort. In fact the tapering of the whole form, as in these two figures, and of some of the limbs, very accurately fulfils the requirements of ease of vision as mentioned on page 237. According to these requirements, the parallel vertical lines below the horizontal level of the eyes at the point in the perpendicular at which we are looking have a tendency to approach one another. This is one explanation of the satisfactory effect produced by the tapering downward of the whole form, as well as of the arms and legs and different sections of these, in all cases in which they are seen in their normal upright position.

It was noticed on page 61, that besides like circles, like curves of a more varied and intricate character can be drawn about the forms, causing, though with differing widths and lengths, the same general effects in the outlines of the arms from shoulders to elbows, as also of the same from elbows to wrists; and of the legs from hips to knees, as also of the same from knees to ankles; as well, too, as of a larger part of the form both from hips to heels and from shoulders to heels. In connection with this, the presence was pointed out of a similar curve in the arm just below the elbow, in the thigh just below the hip, and in the calf just below the knee—a reason for the æsthetic effects of which curve was suggested in accordance with the principles of proportion. Here it may be interesting to consider, as an additional explanation, that this same curve may be supposed to describe exactly a direction according with the most gradual changes in the lenses of the eyes, when they are looking from one to another part of the form. Fig. 123, page 293, will crudely suggest why this is so; and, in suggesting it, will also suggest a principle necessarily more or less applicable whenever the eyes in glancing up or down the contour of a form are obliged, for the reason mentioned on page 280, to adjust outlines to backgrounds at different distances. Let the circle A B represent the general field of vision of both eyes when looking at some point on a straight line supposed to be drawn between *a* and *b*. If then attention be directed first upon *a*, and from it passed upward to *b*, and, while this is being done, the circle representing the field of vision of one eye be gradually pulled apart from the circle representing the field of vision of the other eye (which would represent what is done when the eyes are adjusting their lenses to a more distant background) then, instead of the one circle A B, we should have the

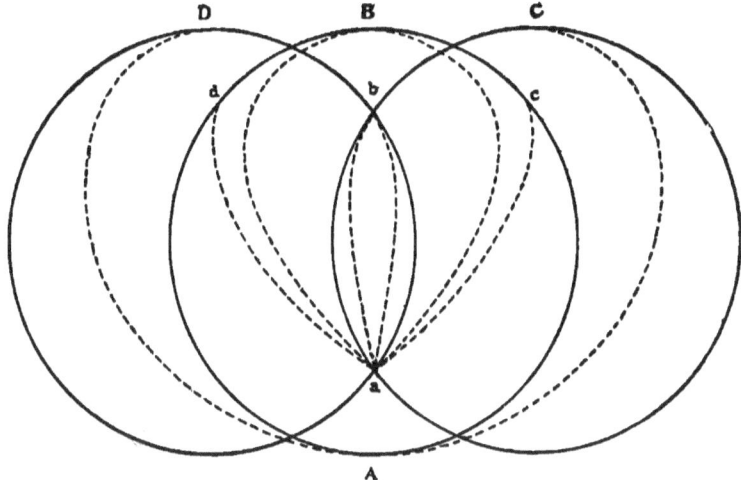

FIG. 123.—OUTLINES OF CURVES AS DETERMINED BY CHANGES IN BACKGROUNDS.
See pages 292, 293, 294, 295.

two circles under C and D, and instead of the one straight line between *a* and *b*, we should have, as representing the appearance which the eyes could perceive with the least change of focus, and therefore with the least effort, the contour indicated by the dotted lines between *a* and *b*. Or suppose, when the general field of vision of the two eyes may be represented by A B, and they be looking in a general way at the figure indicated by the undotted lines between *a* and *b*, that attention be directed upon *a* and passed upward along the sides of this figure to *b*, and, while this is going on, that the circle A B be gradually pulled apart so as to form the two circles under C and D, then the figure now represented in the one circle A B by the undotted lines between *a* and *b* would in the two circles under C and D be perceived with the least effort when assuming the form represented by the dotted lines between *a* and *c* and *a* and *d*. Or, if we suppose that, in exactly the same time, the eyes glance from *a* toward *c* or *d*, but finally to rest on B, then the figure represented by the dotted lines between *a* and B, would be perceived with the least effort. Once more, if we suppose attention to be directed upon A and started around either side of the circumference toward B; then, while the one circle A B is being gradually extended into the two under C and D, it will be the outlines indicated by the dotted lines between A C and A D, that the eyes will perceive with the least effort. The courses of the dotted lines in this Fig. 123, are determined by measuring the whole height and the whole breadth of the space to be covered, and passing the dotted lines through the points representing, say one eighth of the height, and also representing at the same time one eighth of the breadth and after that one fourth of each, and so on. In other words, the distances of the dotted lines from the undotted ones is always graded according to an exact ratio of measurement between the height and the breadth. The dotted lines, therefore, represent results the same in principle as those of proportion. It will be noticed, moreover, that in all cases these lines resemble more or less closely those represented in Figs. 33, page 60, and 34, page 61. They therefore suggest, in addition to what was said on page 61, why such curves should be characteristic of grace in visible movements, or in fixed lines which the eye, through its own movements, has to trace from one part of a figure to another. It will be noticed, too, that, somewhere between the different gradations of contours between dotted *a*—*b* and *a*—B we can find contours to represent all the forms most readily suggested by the configurations of arms, legs, hips, or the whole framework of the human body as indicated in Figs. 31, page 57; 32, page 58; 35, page 70; 36, page 71; 37, page 72; 45, page 86; 72, page 136; 73, page 137; and 74, page 139, to say nothing of Figs. 117, page 283; 118, page 283; 120, page 285, and 122, page 289. But enough. The applications of Fig. 123, page 293, would be made to conform more to all cases if the circles under C and D were also represented as being elevated and enlarged at the same time as being pulled apart; and if, in addition to considering effects due to adjusting the lens of the eye, horizontally, those were considered which are due to its convex shape, as well as to the rotary action of the whole eye while moving. But the object of this discussion has been merely to unfold a general principle. It is evident that none of these considerations would change this principle, however much they might extend its scope, or, by conflicting conditions, modify its applications. Besides this, the subject itself is a large one, and in the present state of knowledge concerning it, any thorough treatment of it would demand, if not a mathematical genius, at least a man with less to do, and with less interest in other directions than the author of this volume. He must be content with these few suggestions, and leave to others whatever possibility there may be of developing from them anything like a complete system of geometric æsthetics.

CHAPTER XVII.

ARTISTIC COLORING AS INFLUENCED BY SCIENTIFIC METHODS.

Imitative and Decorative Use of Color—The Two Connected—Scientific Study of Color Important—Art can Advance beyond the Discoveries of Science—Yet in Every Age is Helped by Them—Artistic Invention as Related to Scientific Investigation of Effects of Color—Illustrated from History of Greek Painting—Roman—Christian—Italian—Spanish and Dutch—English—French—German—Modern—Need of Learning from Experience and Experiment.

THERE are two methods of using color, one having to do with imitating it so as to represent it as we find it in certain agreeable or beautiful appearances of nature; the other with applying or arranging it, irrespective of anything but the general principles in accordance with which it appears to be agreeable or beautiful. As painting gives us pictures of the forms of nature, and architecture does not, it is natural to suppose that the first of these methods is, or should be, used mainly in the former art, and the second mainly in the latter, *i. e.*, in the decoration of the interiors or exteriors of buildings. This natural supposition it would be well if some of our modern painters would ponder. When they imagine that they can use color merely "for its own sake" they are on ground almost, though not quite, as dangerous—owing to the far more subtle requirements of color when used in any circumstances whatever—as are poets who imagine that they can use rhyme, or any other element of sound, merely "for its own sake." The primary object of both painting and poetry is to represent certain effects that are, or that may be supposed to be, in nature; and the moment that this primary object is forgotten the artist or author has crossed the boundaries of his own art, and must compete with the decorators or musicians, in circumstances where imitative limitations by which they are not hampered will materially interfere with his success.

It must not be supposed, however, that the painter, while subordinating his arrangements of color to effects of nature, has no more to do than to imitate these, even though our conception of imitation include its greatest breadth and dignity of meaning. In Chapter IV. of "Art in Theory," it was argued that the aim of high art is never mere imitation; and the truth of the statement is nowhere exemplified more clearly than when applied to the use of color. Merely because blue in the natural spectrum stands between green and purple, is no proof, as we shall find by-and-by, that a blue object should be represented in a painting as standing next to one that is green or violet. In the natural spectrum, as in a natural scene, bounded by only the horizon, there are other counteracting, balancing, or complementary influences of color, which may render an effect entirely different from that which alone is possible where a few colors are introduced into the narrow framework of a picture. Besides this, the mere association of certain hues in nature does not make the arrangement beautiful; and, if not, art has no business to reproduce it. For both reasons, it must always be borne in mind that art deals with selected colors, just as poetry and music deal with selected tones; and harmony in all these arts, though discovered from a study of principles in nature, is distinctively a human invention. The same general principles of harmony, too, apply, as has been said, though with a different aim, in both painting and decoration. Therefore it will not be necessary to separate the two departments in our discussion, a few references, here and there, to the differences between them being sufficient.

What has been said of the necessity of harmony in color, will serve to obviate the impression, if, indeed, it exist in any mind, that the scientific study of the subject is not essential to the painter. It is true that he can depend for his copy upon nature to an extent which is not true of the decorator. But nature is a very broad term. What is in it, cannot be thoroughly perceived without a good deal more than mere superficial observation. In view of the few great colorists that the world has known, it is certainly no idle question whether more attention to the underlying principles of the subject would not have made others more successful.

Not, of course, that one would wish to intimate that the arts, in certain cases, are not able to advance without the aid of science. As a fact they often anticipate the discoveries of this by many centuries, the intuitions of great artists being a better guide to achievement than the inferences of the logicians. As A. J. Symington has shown in the second volume of his work on "The Beautiful in Nature, Art and Life," a Crystal Palace was built by Chaucer's imagination in his "House of Fame," years before commercial enterprise and engineering skill had devised the one at Sydenham.

> "But as I slept, me mette I was
> Withyn a temple ymade of glas;
> In whiche there were moo ymages
> Of golde standynge in sondry stages,

> And moo ryche tabernacles
> And with perrie moo pynacles
> And moo curiouse portraytures,
> And queynt maner of figures,
> Of golde werke, than I ever sawgh," etc.

"In this," says Mr. Symington, "we have mention of the assembling together of all nations in a wondrous temple made of glass, containing works of industry and treasures of art; with details of its sculpture, and portrait galleries, its rich carvings and jewellery, the indescribable variety of its splendors within, and the glorious, far-stretching landscape without. We have even 'a noble Queen' seated on the dais and awarding honors to worthy competitors, the whole affording another striking illustration .... that the germs of all inventions or discoveries, like the tulip in the bulb, already exist in the mind of man as possibilities, frequently finding expression ages before they are realized."

Notwithstanding his occasional prescience, however, the artist, like every one else, is "the heir of all the ages." The principles taught him and exemplified in the products around him, have been gradually learned by patient thought, investigation, and experience continued through centuries. And there is still more to be learned. Indeed, with reference to the very subject with which we are now dealing, in no age have more discoveries been made than in our own. And the artist of to-day whose name will live longest will probably be he who is the most nearly able to make as good use of what is known now, as Leonardo and Titian made of what was known in their times, contributing as they did from their very limited resources what has proved to be of lasting value not only to the art of the subject but also to its science.

In the history of the use of pigments especially, has the connection been very intimate between the study of the subject as a science, and the development of it as an art. With scarcely an exception, the greatest painters seem to have attained to fame almost as much on account of their discoveries as of their productions, the inspiration to investigation having apparently proved the surest stimulus to invention. At least, it can be said that the two tendencies have gone hand in hand; and undoubtedly the frequent temporary decline of painting, as of every art, immediately after great achievements, has been attributable in part to the supposition of men of genius that all its secrets had been discovered,—a supposition which has caused them to turn from it to pursuits like philosophy, science, or politics, which seemed at the time to promise a more certain reward for original effort.

The briefest review of the history of painting—excluding modern whose rank is not yet determined—will reveal the connection just indicated. The pictures of the Greeks have perished, but from what we read of them there seems to be little doubt that, after the century preceding that of Pericles in which the unshaded colors of the Egyptian style were imitated in the historical paintings of Aglaophon, and his son Aristophon, as, later, in the wall-decorations of Damophilus and Gorgasus at Rome, the art began to be studied scientifically. Pliny tells us that the painters Micon and Polygnotus improved the materials used in pigments; that, in the same age, Panænus, a nephew of Pheidias, invented a new vehicle for fresco. Apollodorus, in the age that followed, is said by Plutarch to have been the "first of men to discover the mixture of pigments and the gradations of shade." Eupompus, his contemporary, as well as Pamphilus in the next generation, is called a scientific teacher as well as a painter. Euphranor, although he had as rivals Zeuxis, the great master of still life, and Parrhasius, who "first gave symmetry" and "liveliness of expression" to figures, and "won the palm in terminating lines," surpassed both, we are told, in his coloring. The body of his Theseus was not "rose color," it is said, "but real flesh." Finally, when we come to the culminating age of Greek painting, that of Alexander the Great, we read that although Protogenes excelled in ideality, Nicomachus in facility, Nicias in shading and projecting figures from a background, and Pausias in foreshortening and encaustic painting, Apelles surpassed them all, not merely on account of his accuracy in drawing and his judgment in securing the best expressions, but on account of his skill in using colors. He brought out and softened them with a thin coating of black pigment that no one could succeed in imitating. "He painted," wrote Pliny, "what could not be painted, sheet lightning, chain lightning and heat lightning."[1]

After Apelles, we read of a few Greeks or Romans like Pyreicus and Fabius (B.C. 300) and, near the beginning of the Christian era, of Fabullus, Dorotheus, Pinus, and Turpilius, and later of Artemidorus (A.D. 100), Aristodemus (A.D. 150), Hermogenes (A.D. 250), and Hilarius (A.D. 365), but of no new discoveries, and, for this reason apparently, of no great artists. The paintings after this period, up to that of the Renaissance, were chiefly, so far as concerned the use of color, of the decorative kind, designed to set off the architecture of a church, or to increase the impressiveness of an altar. Their backgrounds were

[1] See Pliny's "Nat. Hist.," xxxiii., 13, 56; xxxiv., 8, 19; xxxv., 6, 25; 8, 34; 9, 36; 11; 12, 45; also Plutarch's "In Gloria Athen.," 2.

usually gilded, and the drapery of their figures was composed of full colors, red, blue, or yellow, and little varied, while different parts of the hands and faces, which were sadly out of proportion, were indicated by black lines, such as caricaturists of our own time would use for a similar purpose.

At last, between the thirteenth and fifteenth centuries, Cimabue, Giotto, Orcagna, Lippi, Masaccio, Perugino and others, among whom Gentile, merely because, as the predecessor, some suppose him to be the founder of the Venetian school of colorists, ranks well, prepared the way in Italy for the advent of Leonardo da Vinci. The latter applied himself to the task of representing with literal truth just what he saw in nature, and succeeded in drawing figures and drapery that looked like those of life. In the treatment of his coloring there was a gradation, too, that had not been seen in the works of his predecessors, notwithstanding much excellence that they had exhibited, especially in the way of flesh tints. Immediately after Leonardo, came three painters deemed by some the greatest that have ever lived, Michael Angelo, excelling in his knowledge of anatomy, and in the grasp and grandeur of his designs, Raphael in the expressive grace and beauty of his forms and faces, and the dramatic character of his compositions, and Titian in his use of color. These three lived at a time when they could, as they did, make original contributions to their art; though it is true that only the latter made them distinctively in the sphere which we are now considering. Titian was, in the strictest sense of the term, a great *painter;* though his works were also characterized by force and refinement of draftsmanship. Among other things he developed the effects of contrast between the light and dark hues. He did this, however, in a more limited way and with a less intelligent use of the difference between the cold and warm colors than was developed subsequently by the painters of the Netherlands. He taught that shadows are not merely darker shades of the colors casting them, but are different from them, and above all that effective composition must have breadth, yet softened by gradation, *i. e.*, must have massings in large quantities of light and shade, yet passing into one another by degrees, as illustrated in Chapters XIII. and XVII. of "The Genesis of Art-Form." (See also Fig. 129, page 359.) With the greatest of the Venetians we are accustomed to associate the other prominent painters of his school, namely, his predecessors, Bellini and Giorgione, and his successors, the two Palmas, Tintoretto, and Paul Veronese. While Titian was still living, Correggio of Parma, born A.D. 1494, had gone beyond him in his development of the possibilities of light and shade, or of chiaroscuro, as it is called, involving a thorough study of gradation as applied to color. For this reason, as well as because of the idealized beauty of the faces in his pictures, he ranks very high. After these men, we have in Italy, beginning half a century later, the eclectic painters of religious subjects, the three Caracci, Domenichino, Guido, and Carlo Dolci, who, acknowledging themselves to be imitators, strove to combine the excellencies of their predecessors; and the naturalists, Caravaggio, born A.D. 1569, who turned from religious to secular subjects, and Salvator Rosa, born A.D. 1615, who excelled in landscapes.

In Spain, Velasquez, born A.D. 1599, was the first to perceive and attempt such atmospheric color-effects as are mentioned on page 307. He is credited, too, with using his brush with as much delicacy, force, and precision as others did the pencil; while De Cespedes, born A.D. 1538, and Murillo, born A.D. 1615, celebrated for finished coloring and sweet grace of style, reproduced the effects in chiaroscuro of Correggio. But few would say that the latter's imitators rank quite as high as he, and this, apparently, because they did not add essentially to his discoveries.

Among the Dutch painters, the two Van Eycks, who, about A.D. 1390, started the Flemish school, invented oil-painting, and designed landscapes, as well as large religious compositions, in which there was a sincere and, for that time, an original endeavor to represent the effects of nature. Though producing nothing which, in these days, would be considered excellent, they are still highly esteemed, as is also their most eminent follower, Hans Memling, born about A.D. 1430. The Flemish painter Rubens, born A.D. 1577, was the legitimate and foremost successor of the great Italians, especially of the Venetians, whose works he studied in their native cities. He applied, as had not been done before, their gorgeous coloring and their harmony of light and shade to every variety of subject, landscape, animal and human, religious, historical, and secular. His followers developed, beyond anything that had been done by the Italians, the contrasts, to be presently explained, between the warm and cold colors, using broken or, what is the same thing, pale colors extensively, almost exclusively, and making much of slight variations in them. The foremost among these followers were Van Dyck, born A.D. 1599, a painter of a style similar to that of Rubens, with less force and more sweetness; Teniers, the originator of the very successful Belgian school of genre painting; and Rembrandt, born A.D. 1607, who, notwithstanding the inferiority of some of his subjects taken from real life, is a Flemish Correggio, with a development beyond the

Italian which all of his school manifest. Many of his excellencies, too, are shared by his contemporaries and successors, men like Franz Hals, Bol, Douw, and Maas; Ruysdael, celebrated for his landscapes; Wouvermanns, for his hunting scenes; and Van der Velde, for his marine views.

English painting, like everything else springing from that country, has managed to manifest the characteristics of the English people. Their enjoyment of domestic life has led, from the time of Hogarth, born A.D. 1697, to that of Wilkie and others of our own century, to a line of original painters of domestic fiction; their pride of ancestry to portrait and historical painters, like Reynolds, Gainsborough, Opie, Lawrence, Raeburn, Romney, and Etty; and their delight in country scenery to landscape painters like Constable and Turner. The fame of the last of these once promised to surpass that of all the others. To some extent these others were imitators. He certainly was not one, either in his mode of coloring or of blending literalness with ideality. It is the school of water-colors, however, founded by Sandby and others about A.D. 1750 and still flourishing, which has given to England its chief reputation among foreign artists; because by this school it is felt that the country has made its chief original contribution to the progress of the art.

In France, Poussin, born A.D. 1594, united the results of the Italian and Flemish schools. Claude Lorraine, born A.D. 1600, developed an original way of producing atmospheric effects in landscapes,—hence his reputation. His method consisted in increasing by delicate gradations the strength of the light in the centre of a hazy background where the sun was usually represented; and against the background, apparently at an infinite distance from it, the trees and buildings of the foreground were made to stand out as if in a silhouette. From the time of Claude to the middle of the present century, notwithstanding the great reputation at one time attained by Lesueur, born A.D. 1617, with his religious subjects, by Joseph Vernet, born A.D. 1714, with his landscapes, by Greuze, born A.D. 1725, with his genre pictures, by the "classical" David, by the "eclectic" Delaroche, both of the period following the Revolution, as well as by Gros, born A D. 1771, and by Horace Vernet, born A.D. 1789, with their historical paintings, perhaps it can be said with truth that no one has secured more permanent renown than the "romantic" Delacroix; and that this has been largely secured because of the thorough study that he is known to have made of the subject of color.

In Germany,—previous to the time of Claude,—Dürer, Cranach, and Holbein, the latter much the ablest of the three, who all flourished in the fifteenth century, had produced works which rank with the best of those of Italy before the time of Leonardo. Many years later, Raphael Mengs, born A.D. 1728, a special friend of the great art critic, Winckelmann, became head of the Academy of Florence. Overbeck, born A.D. 1789, tried to produce sacred pictures like the great Italians, and had no little indirect influence in inclining towards a similar object the pre-Raphaelite movement in England. Cornelius, born A.D. 1783, together with Schadow, restored historic fresco, and inspired much that was popular in the Academies of Dusseldorf and Munich, in both of which Cornelius taught. Subsequently Lessing and Bendemann applied the methods of Overbeck and Cornelius to non-Romish subjects, and Kaulbach, who died A.D. 1874, left behind him a well earned reputation for the force and grasp of his drawing and composition. None of these, however, were masters of the art of coloring, much less discoverers of anything new with reference to it. And it is significant, therefore, that, as compared with successors who are better colorists, the reputation of all of them is declining.

Within the last half-century, the art of painting, according to some of our foremost authorities, has been almost revolutionized; and here again we have to attribute the result to a change in the methods of producing effects in color. The older painters, as a rule, mixed their hues before placing them on the canvas, and put them there exactly as they wished to have them appear when seen from a distance. Velasquez introduced another method which, of late, modern painters have been developing. According to it, colors are placed on the canvas so that, tho not mixed, they shall, when seen from a distance, mix in the eye. This is the way in which the color-effects of nature are usually produced; and the method, in many cases, renders the art-product much more satisfactory, suggesting that the elements entering into a scene, like those of leaves and grasses, are separated from one another, and thus conveying impressions of transparency and atmosphere, which were impossible according to the older method. As in the case of every "good thing," however, this method is often carried too far. Certain absurd extremes of impressionism are developments that never would have had existence but for what is true in it; and the same may be said of the equally absurd conception that a smooth surface, as in the human countenance, requires no different treatment from that which would be afforded the rough surface of a flower-bed. At the same time, the general effect of having colors mix in the eye, with the attendant impressions conveyed of transparency of atmosphere, and of infinity in gradations seems to be accepted as a crucial test of excellence in modern painting. It is safe to say that the Fontainebleau-Barbizon and the Spanish-Roman schools, which have been chiefly instrumental in introducing these new methods, have changed the whole character of much of the contemporary art in other countries, and of all of that in our own. The former school has led to results mainly in the deeper tones of color, such as we find in the works of Rousseau, Corot, Troyon, Diaz, and Millet, and the latter to those largely in the higher tones, such as we find in the works of Fortuny, Zamaçois, Boldini, Rico, and Villegas. As a master of composition, Gérôme has no equal, and he as well as Cabanel, Bouguereau, and Baudry, surpass those just mentioned in effects of draftsmanship. But notwithstanding this, it is the others of whom we hear most, and who have had the most imitators. Thus, at present, as in the past, the fact which this brief review of the history of painting was designed to illustrate, is shown to be true, namely, that the rank of the artist depends very largely indeed upon the advance that he has made in developing the possibilities of color.

This advance is connected, too, with a study of scientific principles. There are infinite diversities of shades and tints in colors, and these often influence and entirely neutralize one another when brought together in pigments. No matter, therefore, how much taste or observation an artist may have in the abstract, these cannot always guide him to successful execution. He needs the largest aid that can be afforded by the experience and experiments of others. This fact will appear more clear, as, taking it for granted, we go on to consider the subject as it will be unfolded in the following chapters.

CHAPTER XVIII.

EFFECTS OF COLOR AS DISCOVERED BY SCIENTIFIC EXPERIMENTS.

Newton's Discovery of the Colors of the Spectrum—They are Contained only in White Light—The Diversity and Brilliancy of the Spectrum's Colors Dependent on the Amount and Intensity of the Light—Brightness and White Making all Colors Pale; Darkness and Black Making them the Opposite—Names of the Chief Colors—The Terms: Hues, Full, High, Dark, Light, Pale, Broken, Shades, Tints, Tone, Local, Positive, Neutral, Warm, Cold, Primary, Secondary—Colors Transmit and Reflect Rays of Like Color with Themselves—Practical Bearing of this upon the Kind of Light with which Objects are Illumined, Lamps, Sun, etc.—Shows why Colors are Most Vivid when Illumined by Light of their Own Color—Why White Objects Reflect the Color Illuming them—What are the Actual Colors of Nature—Of Foliage—Of Water —Of the Atmosphere—Of Objects in External Nature in Light or Shade, when the Sun is on the Horizon—Especially at a Distance— When the Sun is in the Zenith—Colors of the Same Objects in Cloudy Weather; the Terms Cold and Warm—Effects of Light and Shade within Doors—Cold and Warm Colors in the Representation of Distance—These Effects Dependent on the Degrees of Light—Difference of Opinion with Reference to Certain Deductions Made from Acknowledged Facts of Aërial Perspective—The Apparent Truth with Reference to the Subject.

IT is now more than two centuries since Newton, analyzing the rays of the sun, detected that all the different colors, except perhaps extreme purple, are contained in light. Most of us know how to reproduce his analysis. By means of a mirror, the sun's rays are reflected in a small band through a narrow opening in a window-shade, or blind, and sent into an otherwise darkened room. See

Fig. 124. When they enter this room they are made to pass through a glass prism the edges of which are placed as in this figure. The prism turns the band of rays aside from its direction, and, at the same time, separates it into an infinitely large number of bands of rays which are colored, and each of which, after leaving the prism, continues in a straight line. If these bands fall on a white wall or screen, each produces a different color,

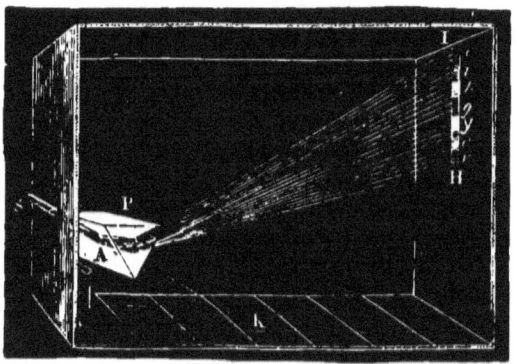

FIG. 124.—BREAKING UP A RAY OF WHITE LIGHT.
See page 310.

and all together a series of colors in which we recognize all that are in the rainbow. Nearest where the white would have fallen, if the prism had not intervened, we find red, and next to this the other colors in this order: orange, yellow, green, blue, indigo, and violet. This series of colors is called the Spectrum.

If now, in the white on which we see the spectrum, we make another narrow opening parallel to the one made first, and back of this receive into another darkened room, and send through another prism, a ray, red or green or blue as the case may be, we get, as a result, no further analysis of the light. The red or green or blue ray, after passing through the second prism still remains red or green or blue. The conclusion is inevitable that it is only compound light, which, when analyzed, can be separated into the different colors.

But let us experiment further with the results of our analysis. If, by bringing our curtains near the prism, we reduce the size of the spectrum, we see only a few of the more prominent colors,—red, green, blue, and violet perhaps. If we increase its size we find orange and yellow between the red and green, and, in these as well as in all the colors, we notice an incalculable number of distinct varieties. If we reduce the amount or brightness of the light passing through the prism, the colors, one after another, become more and more dull and disappear. Yellow and orange and turquoise blue go first, leaving a brownish red, green, and violet; then the red and violet go, and last of all we lose sight of the dull green. On the contrary, if we increase the amount or brightness of the light analyzed, all the colors become more brilliant and diversified.

If again, turning from the spectrum, we test the effects of different degrees of light on colored pigments, we find that in a darkened room, a colored surface, say of blue, appears to be dark blue, but as we gradually increase the light it becomes first full blue, then light blue, then pale blue, then, in light of great intensity, loses its blueness almost entirely, becoming very nearly white. So, too, if in place of different degrees of light, we use black or white pigments, mixing them with colored pigments, we find the colors becoming respectively darker or lighter. To make a practical application of these facts before we leave them, they show us why landscapes representing bright sunshine require brilliant and diversified tints and shades of all kinds, whereas those representing twilight and moonlight, which are only diminished sunlight, require an absence of all brilliant colors and often of anything like even a decided red, yellow, or blue.

From what has been said, it will be seen that the different kinds and degrees of colors that can be produced by the action of light or with pigments are practically infinite. At the same time, just as musicians have found it convenient to select a few from thousands of possible notes and name them A, B, C, D, etc., so physicists have agreed upon designating certain colors by the following names which, with the definitions of some other terms, may as well be given here. The names of the colors are taken from Von Bezold's "Theory of Color." They are Red (Carmine, Vermilion), Orange, Yellow, Yellowish-green, Green, Bluish-green, Turquoise-blue, Ultramarine, and Violet (Bluish-violet, Purplish-violet, and Purple).

These different kinds of colors are termed *hues*. When hues are in the state in which they appear in the spectrum, they are called *full* or *high* colors. If darker than in the spectrum, the colors are termed *dark*, if lighter, *light*; if very much lighter, *pale* or, what means the same thing, *broken*. When full colors are made darker, their different degrees of darkness are termed *shades*. When they are made lighter their different degrees of lightness are termed *tints*. The degree of coloring or of dark or light in a shade or tint determines the *tone*, as when we speak of a golden and gay, or a gray and sombre tone. Paintings, however, are not generally said to be distinguished by tone except when pervaded throughout by a similarity of tone. *Local* color is a term given by artists to what appears to them to be the *inherent* hue of an object aside from any influence upon it of sunlight, moonlight, shade, reflection, or refraction. However, while these terms, *local* and *inherent*, are thus used, it must be borne in mind that, according to physics, the colors perceived in objects do not pertain to them aside from effects produced in connection with them by the vibratory action of the ether waves. Some bodies have such a molecular constitution that they absorb certain quantities or kinds of these waves, and reject others. A black object absorbs nearly all of them; a white reflects nearly all; and a gray absorbs some and reflects others. These three differ not in the kinds of waves that they absorb or reflect, but in their *quantities*. Objects that have what we term *color* differ in the ways in which they act toward different *kinds* of waves, rejecting or reflecting back upon the ether in unequal proportions certain partial constituents of the waves, which they cannot receive because these do not accord with their own natural rate of oscillation or with any multiple of it.

In a *positive* color the tint or shade of a single hue is prominent; in a *neutral* color, there is so much of a mixture that there is no predominating hue. The *warm* colors, so called for reasons to be given hereafter, are the reds, browns, oranges, yellows, and associated colors; the *cold* are the greens, blues, grays, violets, and associated colors. *Primary* is a term formerly applied to red, yellow, and blue because they were supposed to be primitives from which the *secondary* colors, orange, green, and violet, were derived, orange by mixing red and yellow, green by mixing yellow and blue, and violet by mixing blue and red. For reasons to be given by-and-by, however, these distinctions between primary and secondary are not now considered tenable.

Now let us return to the spectrum on the curtain. If

we take a piece of colored glass—say red flashed glass colored with protoxide of copper—and hold it before the opening made for the light in the window, so as to allow only red rays to enter the room and pass through the prism; or if we hold the red glass between the prism and the spectrum; or if we hold the red glass to our eyes and look through it at the spectrum;—in all these cases we find that all the rays passing through the red glass, either between the sunlight and the spectrum, or between the spectrum and our eyes, is red, or, owing to a slight imperfection in all colored glass, orange, which is nearly related to red. We notice, too, that the red and orange are situated in the spectrum on the screen just where they were when the other colors were visible, which other colors are now obliterated. We may continue in the line of these experiments by painting screens in many different colors and sending white light through the prism on to them. In such cases we shall find invariably that the spectrum which would have been produced on a white screen is represented by only certain colors allied to those in which the screen is painted, which colors appear in the same relative places on the painted screen in which they would have appeared on the white screen. Those who have read thus far this series of volumes, or even the first part of the present volume, will be interested in noticing how this natural tendency of color to transmit or reflect rays that are like its own accords with the artistic tendency in the direction of unity, and of grouping like with like, from which, as shown by the chart on page 3, all the methods of art composition are developed.

Now let us notice the bearings of the facts just stated upon the effects and therefore upon the methods of representing *light and shade*. We may begin by observing that we see, from what has been said, why it is that colored objects appear black, if illumined only by a color which they do not possess. Little blue and violet are present in the light of lamps and candles. Therefore, in the nighttime, while red and yellow colors in dresses, paintings, and decorations can generally be seen with their full effects, blue, if allied to green, appears like green, and if allied to violet, like black; and violet, if allied to blue, like gray, and if allied to red, like reddish-brown. Some years ago, an "Academy of Music" in one of our principal cities was refitted and papered in blue. The effect, on the opening night, was so gloomy and disagreeable that, before a second performance, the entire interior was re-papered in a warmer color. In cases where it is desirable to know by daylight how decorations or paintings will appear by candle-light, a reasonably trustworthy opinion of this may be gained by looking at them through an orange- or yellow-tinted glass.[1]

The facts that we are considering show us again why colored objects appear most vivid when illumined by light of their own color. The reason is that, under such conditions, they transmit or reflect all the light illumining them, none of which is lost. In this way, all colors act like

[1] The following tables will be of interest here. They are the results of experiments published by Prof. O. N. Rood, in his "Modern Chromatics," chap. xi., pp. 152–154.

YELLOW LIGHT falling on paper painted with

Carmine gave............Red-orange.	Blue-green gave.........Yellow-green (whitish).
Vermilion ....Bright orange-red.	Cyan-blue..............Yellow-green.
Orange ....Bright orange-yellow.	Prussian-blue..........Bright green.
Chrome-yellow..........Bright yellow.	Ultramarine-blue.......White.
Gamboge...............Bright yellow.	Violet.................Pale reddish tint.
Yellowish-green ....Yellow.	Purple-violet..........Orange (whitish).
Green..................Bright yellow-green.	Purple ....Orange.
	Black ....Yellow.

white toward light of their own color. Red figures on a white ground, for instance, disappear in red light. For the same reason, colors are always more dark, when inside of a fold of drapery, or of a niche, or in the corner of a room, especially where there is gilding.

The same facts explain, too, why white objects reflect often the color illumining them. A white wall, for instance, appears white by daylight, and red by firelight. Of course the reason of this is that white contains all the colors, and

RED LIGHT falling on paper painted with

Carmine gave............Red.	Blue-green gave.........Nearly white.
Vermilion...............Bright red.	Cyan-blue..............Gray.
Orange................Red-orange and scarlet.	Prussian-blue...........Red-purple or blue-violet.
Chrome-yellow ....Orange.	Violet ....Red-purple.
Gamboge...............Orange.	Purple-violet ....Red-purple.
Yellowish-green ....Yellow and orange.	Purple ....Purple-red or red.
Green.................Yellow and orange (whitish).	Black ....Dark red.

GREEN LIGHT falling on paper painted with

Carmine gave...........Dull yellow.	Prusssian-blue gave.....Blue-green, cyan-blue.
Vermilion..............Dull yellow or greenish-yellow.	Ultramarine-blue.......Cyan-blue, blue.
Orange................Yellow and greenish-yellow.	Violet.................Cyan-blue, blue, violet-blue (all whitish).
Chrome-yellow.........Yellowish-green.	
Gamboge..............Yellowish-green.	Purple-violet...........Pale blue-green, pale blue.
Yellowish-green.........Yellowish-green.	
Green.................Bright green.	Purple.................Greenish-gray, gray, reddish-gray.
Blue-green ....Green.	
Cyan-blue.............Blue-green.	Black ....Dark green.

BLUE LIGHT falling on paper painted with

Carmine gave ....Purple.	Blue-green gave........Cyan-blue, blue.
Vermilion.............Red-purple.	Cyan-blue.............Blue.
Orange................Whitish-purple.	Prussian-blue..........Blue.
Chrome-yellow.........Yellowish-gray, greenish-gray.	Ultramarine-blue.......Blue.
Gamboge..............Yellowish-gray, greenish-gray.	Violet.................Ultramarine, violet-blue.
	Purple-violet...........Blue-violet.
Yellowish-green.........Blue-gray.	Purple ....Violet-blue, purple-violet.
Green..................Blue-green, cyan-blue.	Black ....Dark blue.

so is prepared in each case to give back the color that it receives.

Once more, these same facts show us how to find out what the colors of objects actually are. The results of using colored glasses in connection with spectrums, as explained on page 314, and of sending white light through a prism upon a colored screen, must follow if applied to an object of any color. If so, the use of colored glasses and spectrums must enable us to detect everywhere in the appearances of nature, the presence of color which otherwise we might not see. The connection is apparent between a knowledge of the discoveries thus made, and the successful representation of many of the appearances both of *texture* and of *life*. Especially is it important to notice what has been found out in this way with reference to the colors actually visible in the foliage, water, and atmosphere about us, as perceived under different conditions of light and shade, by day and by night.

With reference to the first of these, namely, foliage, it has been observed that a spectrum, which, when thrown upon green pigment, shows only a green color, if thrown upon the green of foliage shows tints both of red and yellow. Or if the trees be examined through a red glass, it has been observed that in the degree in which the glass transmits only the red rays the leaves are red, although the blue sky above them, as also green fabrics and pigments about them, appear black. The conclusion is inevitable that the coloring matter of foliage, which is called chlorophyl, contains, besides green, other and warmer colors. Of course, for one who knows this, the suggestion of the tints of red and yellow, in the green about him, will greatly augment his interest in natural scenery. Nor does it require more than a slight degree of effort to enable him actually to perceive these. In coloring, as in everything, men come to see what they try to see. What but persistence in scrutinizing and criticising their neighbors' attire makes the color-sense in women so much stronger than in men? As shown in Chapters XII. to XIV. of "Art in Theory," beauty, even as recognized by the senses, depends largely upon effects produced upon the mind. The truth underlying such injunctions as "Seek ye first the kingdom," "The kingdom is within you," and "Except a man be born from above he cannot see the kingdom," is of universal applicability. Those who strive to enter into the realm of coloring will find capabilities within themselves which, if properly used, will introduce into their field of vision an infinite variety of tints and shades which, so far as concerns the effect upon the senses, transcend in beauty those which the ordinary man perceives, in a degree akin to that in which the new earth pictured in the Apocalypse transcends the old earth of ordinary experience. It is only the man, too, who is able to perceive these colors in nature, by whom they can be fully recognized as representing truth when they are placed upon the canvas of the painter. Yet here they are essential. That indescribable effect of vitality which characterizes the grasses and grains of some landscapes is owing largely to the presence in them of these red and yellow tints. It is these that make of the dead green a "living green," just as surely as the same tints, were they used, would give to the picture of a corpse the glow and warmth of life.

Experiment has found also that water has a color of its own, which is blue. But, besides this, it may transmit the color of whatever material happens to be beneath it, and may reflect from its surface the color of a blue or of a gray sky, or of anything that happens to be above it. Direct rays, too, falling upon it from the sun, or moon, or any like source of light, are polarized.

The atmosphere, which probably contains water in the form of minute bubbles, has a whitish-blue tint when the light falls upon it as it falls upon the horizon at noon or on the space intervening between us and distant mountains. But the same atmosphere has a reddish and yellowish tint when the light is transmitted through it like the rays of the sun or moon if near the horizon.

Returning now, more particularly, to *light and shade*, which, in every case, are necessarily modified by the particular colors of the object which transmits or reflects them, we may notice, first, how what has been said with reference to the coloring of foliage explains the great differences between the trees of a landscape when illumined and when in shadow, as well as the differences in color in both their illumined and their shaded parts if lighted by a sun near the horizon, or by one near the zenith. In the morning or evening the direct rays coming from the sun to the object and from the object to the eye make a long passage through the atmosphere, and this, because the light is thus transmitted through it, has, as has been said, a reddish or yellowish tint. Possibly, too, the fact that this atmosphere lies close against the warm colors of the ground may influence its own color to some extent. At any rate, the sunlight at this time gives to foliage and other objects the red and yellow tints that are in the medium through which it passes. Objects in shadow, however, that are not lighted up by these direct rays of the sun are illumined mainly by the reflected blue and gray light of the sky. They therefore show cold tints.

This principle, as will be noticed, though applying to

some extent to all objects at sunrise and sunset, applies especially to those at a distance, the rays from which must make a long passage through the lower atmosphere. Therefore it is exemplified particularly in the colors of mountains and clouds on the horizon. The white snows of Mt. Blanc at sunrise are often as ruddy with reflected light on one side of the horizon as are the clouds immediately above the sun on the other. The green leaves of midsummer upon a mountainside are sometimes tinged at sunset with a color as brilliant as was ever seen in the full glory of autumn.

So much with reference to objects illumined or in shadow, when the sun is near the horizon. As this approaches the zenith, however, these conditions are reversed, and so are the colors. Then the light of the sun is reinforced on every side by the reflected cold colors of the sky. For this reason objects in sunshine at this time show bluish and cold tints; while those in shadow show the opposite, either by way of contrast, or because all the light illumining them is reflected from the warm colors of the ground.

In cloudy weather, the sun is obscured, and the light that we have is reflected from the cold blue or gray tints of the clouds. Nor are there any decided shadows on the earth. Accordingly, as we look off over it, all the tints partake of the character of those in the sky. Cloudy days are usually cold. It is for this reason, probably, that the tints and shades usually prevailing then are termed *cold;* whereas the yellows and reds which we associate with sunlight and firelight are termed *warm*.

Within doors, all direct illumining usually comes from the blue light of the sky. Therefore cold tints are seen wherever there is superficial reflection on the face or hair or drapery. For this reason, warm colors in interiors produce more agreeable effects than their opposites, not only because they light up better at night, as shown on page 315, but because they counteract the effects of the cold tints that appear by day.

There is one other important application of the distinction made a moment ago between the warm and cold colors. It arises in connection with the representation of distance or of aërial perspective. As stated in Chapter XVI. of "Painting, Sculpture, and Architecture as Representative Arts," the general principle underlying this is that, as objects recede in the distance, they grow more dull in color, and, in the extreme distance, change their color, passing from one containing more light into one containing less light, bright red, for instance, passing into darker red; orange into red-orange; and yellow into yellowish-orange; green into bluish-green; and blue into darker blue, and bluish-purple. In Prof. O. N. Rood's "Modern Chromatics," chap. xvi., p. 274, will be found the following table of small intervals, showing the influence upon the colors mentioned of a greater and lesser degree of luminosity.

TABLE OF SMALL INTERVALS.

Lighter.	Darker.	Lighter.	Darker.
Orange-red	Red.	Green	Cyan-blue.
Orange	Orange-red.	Cyan-blue	Blue.
Orange-yellow	Orange.	Blue	Ultramarine-blue.
Yellow	Orange-yellow.	Purple	Violet.
Greenish-yellow	Yellowish-green.	Red	Purple.
Yellowish-green	Green.		

These changes in colors take place in the distance because less light falls upon the objects there, and more atmosphere. In the degree in which less light falls upon them, we have found (see page 311) that bright colors, especially the warm reds, oranges, and yellows—and the same thing is true also of blues—disappear. We have found, too, that in certain cases in the degree in which more atmosphere intervenes between us and these objects, as, for instance, when we are looking at mountains and trees under a sun high in the heavens, they exhibit blue, gray, or violet tints.

The statements made with reference to this subject thus far, few will dispute. Though some otherwise good artists like Cabanel, Bouguereau, and Gérôme, seem at times to ignore the truth that they contain, the great majority of modern painters, men like Daubigny, Troyon, Lepine, Jules Breton, Millet, Corot, Lerolle, Frère, Israels, Decamps, Fromentin, De Nittis, and Inness, exemplify it. There is much difference of opinion, however, with reference to some of the deductions that are drawn from the acknowledged principles of "aërial perspective." It seems to follow from the facts instanced in the last paragraph, that if we see very bright warm colors associated with cold ones, we naturally judge that the warm are the nearer us. The correctness of this inference seems to be confirmed by an argument to the effect that the warm colors, being formed by waves of greater length than the cold, are more exciting to the optic nerve and therefore attract more of its attention. To this, a subjective consideration is added, by Von Bezold in his "Theory of Color." He says that the warm colors, especially red, are at the least refrangible end of the spectrum. The rays producing red, therefore, pass through the prism and onward very nearly in a straight line, whereas the opposite is the case with those producing cold colors. By consequence, we cannot at the same time see clearly the colors at both ends of the spectrum. We must place them at different distances, or vary the accommodation of the eye. If they are at the same distance, in looking first at red, say, and then at blue, we necessarily lessen the curvature of the lens by means of a muscle in the eye. (See Fig. 114, page 273.) That is to say, we do the same that we should do did blue belong to a more remote object. What more natural, then, than that it should appear to be more remote? Such facts show the basis and explanation of the theory that in painting, other things being equal, the warm colors cause objects depicted through the use of them to seem to be in the foreground, while the cold colors cause them to seem to be in the background. Painters tell us that it is therefore important in pictures of the silhouette style to use a warm color on a cold ground, and not the opposite. Decorators, too, recognize that warm colors used on walls and ceilings make rooms seem smaller or more cozy, while cold colors make them seem larger. A gentleman with whom the author is acquainted, in approaching in his company a row of houses all of which were colored gray except one, which was yellow, asked why the yellow house was not built back on a line with the others. He could not believe that it did not project in front of them. Ruskin, indeed, in his "Elements of Drawing," declares that this idea with reference to the effects of the warm and cold colors is erroneous, that it is their quality (as depth, delicacy, etc.) which expresses distance, not their tint; while, on the other hand, Von Bezold in his "Theory of Color" says that when the brightness of the colors is not approximately equal, the bright colors advance and the dark retire. But there is nothing irreconcilable in these statements, nor between them and what has been said here, or was said in Chapter XVI. of " Painting, Sculpture, and Architecture as Representative Arts." As a rule, warm colors appear where there is the most light, as in brilliant sunshine; and, whatever colors appear, the nearer they are, the greater usually is the light illumining them. Both principles undoubtedly have an influence in effects of aërial perspective. But besides this, it must be borne in mind that effects of color cannot entirely overbalance those of outline. A warm hue on a distant cloud in a representation of sunset, would not necessarily seem nearer than a gray hue on a cloud quite near us. In Titian's "Scourging of Christ" a soldier shown by the drawing to be in the extreme foreground does not, because he wears gray armor, seem farther off than the Christ who is clothed in red, yet, by the drawing, is shown to be a little back of the foreground. But the soldier, on account of the color of his armor, is not the foremost object thrust upon attention, and it was undoubtedly to prevent his appearing to be this that the painter represented him in gray.

CHAPTER XIX.

BASIS OF COLOR-HARMONY.

The Tendency in Natural Color for Like to Go with Like in Analogy with the Same Tendency in Natural Language—Differences of Opinion Regarding the Essential Requirements of Color-Harmony—Some Truth in All these Opinions, but only so far as Certain Principles are Fulfilled—Those of Unity, Variety, Complexity, Order, Confusion, Counteraction, Grouping—Like with Like in the Colors of Nature, is the Basis for the Same Arrangement by Way of Comparison and Contrast—Colors Called the Contrasting or Complementary Colors not All that really Contrast—The Complementary Colors—What they are as Determined by Dividing the Rays of Light—As formerly Determined by Mixing Pigments—Proof of the Erroneousness of the Latter Method—Von Bezold's Color Chart—As One Complementary Becomes Brighter, the Other Becomes Darker—Wide Differences in the Complementaries of Different Shades of Green.

IT was shown in Chapter XVIII. that objects in nature having what the artist, but not the physicist, terms *inherent* or *local* colors, acquire, when arranged together, as in a landscape, shades and tints from one another; and this tendency is sometimes exemplified so emphatically that in certain cases almost every appearance seems subordinated to the influence of one dominating hue. This natural tendency of color seems to prepare it, at least, to accord, as already intimated, with the artistic tendency in the direction of *unity* and of grouping like with like from which, as shown in the chart on page 3, all the methods of art-composition are developed. In Chapter VII. of " Rhythm and Harmony in Poetry and

Music" it was shown that a similar tendency in the use of natural language underlies many of its artistic developments. Each syllable has its inherent or local sound, and yet, when used with other syllables, as exemplified in the cries of street-venders, and in popular maxims and mottoes, an instinctive physical prompting connected with ease in utterance causes men to choose and arrange words so that like sounds shall go with like; and it is this fact with reference to natural expression that finally leads to the use of such methods as alliteration, assonance, rhyme, phonetic syzygy, and gradation, characterizing poetic harmony. So the fact just mentioned in connection with color—a fact which even an artist who did not know it would exemplify when giving merely natural expression to his desire to imitate nature—leads, when artistically developed, to many of the most important effects characterizing color-harmony.

With reference to the essential requirements of this harmony, there have been many different opinions. Some of the early Italians based it upon the presence of what were formerly termed the three primary colors, namely, red, yellow, and blue, or else of the three secondary colors, namely, orange, green, and purple; and in every painting, irrespective of its subject, they thought it imperative to introduce all three of one of these sets. Since then, others have supposed harmony to depend upon a combination of two complementary colors, which two, according to opinions formerly held, were either red and green, yellow and purple, or blue and orange. (See page 332.) In addition, moreover, to the question of the colors themselves, it has been discussed whether either the three, or the two thus deemed to be essential, should be distributed in approximately equal or unequal quantities.

Again, with a slight modification of the preceding theories, harmony has been based upon a greater proportionment of warm than cold colors; and finally it has been claimed that it consists mainly in arranging like colors together, varied mainly by minute gradations (see page 409) and producing thus the effect which is sometimes, by way of distinction, termed *tone*. (See page 355.)

Of course there must be some truth underneath each of these theories, or it would find fewer advocates. If so, there ought to be some general principle equally applicable to them all. But what this principle is, does not appear upon the surface. Possibly, however, it may be made to appear, in case we can look deep enough into the subject. In trying to do this, as the subject is the artistic harmony of color, there is no better course to pursue than to go back and trace from their beginnings the successive art-methods through which, as indicated in the chart on page 3, harmony has been developed. In carrying out this plan, notice, first, the relationship between the conditions of colors as they appear in nature and the possibility, in depicting them, of securing the general effect of *unity* by carrying out the fundamental art-principle of putting like with like. Whatever is copied from nature manifests, as a rule, much likeness of hue. Even when the foliage is not all green, or the sky all blue, or the rocks all brown, or the birds or beasts which one finds in the same group all of one shade, the very light with which they are illumined has a tendency to develop, as we found on pages 314 to 317, a sameness in them.

At the same time, the natural forms which furnish the painter with his subjects are never absolutely uniform in color, and although some peculiar condition of scene, as on a desert or a sea; or of light, as in a storm or at sun set, may give an objective *unity* of appearance, and, very likely, for reasons that physiology has not yet fully discovered, a subjective *unity* of effect upon the retina (see page 347), this *unity* must include much *variety*, and, therefore *complexity* both of inherent hues and of these as modified by the never failing influence of light and shade and distance. Owing to these facts, it is evident that the artist cannot, in many cases, secure the *unity* of effect which he desires without very consciously availing himself of his possibilities by selecting for presentation objects of such hues, and arranging them with reference to their color-influence upon one another in such an *order*, as to avoid *confusion*, or, as one would say, to *counteract* this by means of the *grouping*. See page 3.

The fundamental method of putting like with like and thus securing effects of unity through order, is, as we have found, *comparison*. But comparison, as we have also found (see page 3), can never apply to all the appearances brought together in an art-form. Some of these must *contrast*. Contrast, as an art-method, has the effect of emphasizing one form or color—whichever it may be—by placing it in juxtaposition to some contrary form or color. Thus the differences between the two are made to seem greater than they really are. The impressiveness of the tragedy in Shakespeare's plays is often much enhanced by being presented side by side with comedy. (See Chapter II. of "The Genesis of Art-Form.") Perfectly harmonic chords in music often seem much sweeter by being made suddenly to follow an abrupt transition through a series of unresolved sevenths. (See Chapter XV. of "Rhythm and Harmony in Poetry and Music.") So in painting, two colors in juxtaposition have their peculiarities particularly emphasized. An object slightly darker than a surface upon which it is placed appears to be very much darker than it, or, if slightly lighter, very much lighter. This is a principle that applies to crayon as well as to color. See the upper right picture in Fig. 102, page 235. There is a *contrast* between mere light and shade; and the term used in the general way thus indicated may apply to the juxtaposition of any colors that are not the same.

But in painting the term has come to have a specific meaning,—a meaning more appropriately expressed, however, by another word, which is used interchangeably with it, *complementary*. Certain colors, when brought together, have the effect of greatly enhancing one another's brilliancy. Because they differ, they are called contrasting colors; because they differ in a particularly effective way, they are called *the* contrasting colors. But experiments conducted according to various methods, some of which will soon be described, have proved that, while these colors *contrast*, there is a sense in which they are fitted to go together, in fact are allied, and thus manifest the influence of *contrast* as *counteracted* by that of *comparison*. They do this, moreover, in accordance with a law which is exemplified in every department of art, whenever *comparison* and *contrast* are both present and yet are joined by way of *complement*. See page 3, also Chapter III. of "The Genesis of Art-Form."

In order to recognize how these colors popularly called the *contrasting* ones are in a true and scientific sense *complementary*, let us go back to an examination of the results of experiments with the spectrum. On page 310, it was shown that white light, *i. e.*, ordinary sunlight, produces, when analyzed, all the different colors; from which fact it was said that the conclusion is drawn that the different colors combined produce white light. Many experiments have served to confirm this conclusion. If, for instance, by means of an apparatus made for the purpose, the prism causing a spectrum be made to revolve rapidly, a white round image will take the place of the spectrum on

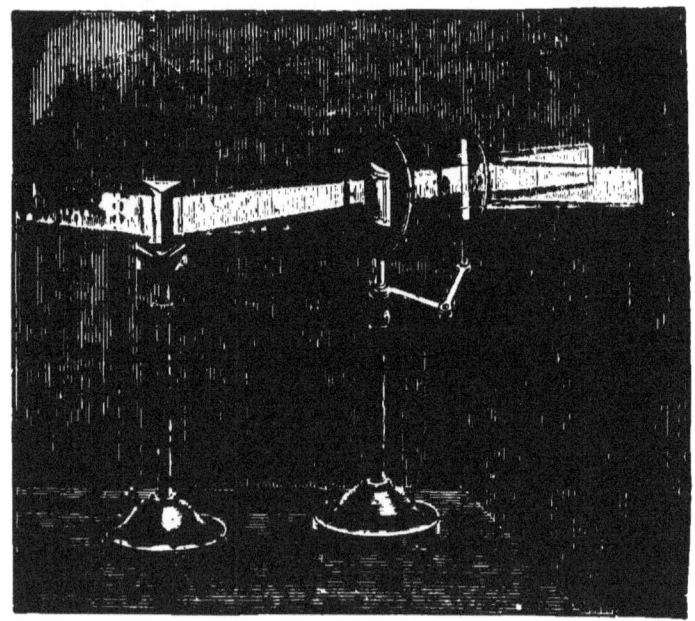

FIG. 125.—FORMATION OF COMPLEMENTARY COLORS.
See page 331.

the wall. If a color top, on a disk of which all the colors are represented, be spun rapidly, a grayish-white appears where the colors are. But if all the colors together make white, it follows that the absence from white light of any of its constituent elements must produce a color. This logical inference has been confirmed by the following among other experiments. Between the prism and the spectrum cast by it, according to the explanations given on page 310, a lens bounded by cylindrical surfaces is introduced. See Fig. 125, page 330, and C in Fig. 126. This lens is so constructed that it reunites the prismatic bundle of rays into a single band, *i. e.*, it restores these rays to the same condition in which they were before they reached the prism from the slit in the window. This cylindrical lens now gathers the rays together, and casts upon the wall, where the spectrum was before, merely a small white image of the slit in the window, giving thus a proof,

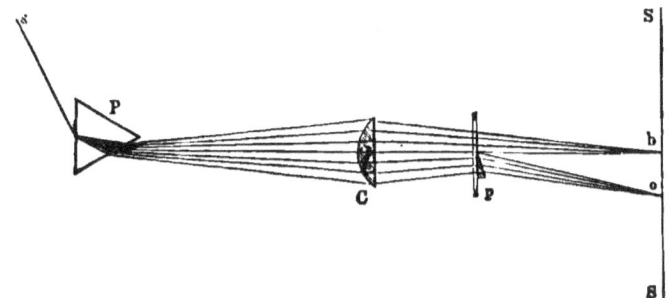

FIG. 126.—FORMATION OF COMPLEMENTARY COLORS.
See page 331.

in addition to the others just noticed, that all the colors together make white. If now between the cylindrical lens and the wall a part of the light be shut off by means of a screen, a colored image instantly appears upon the wall. If, for shutting off this part of the light, one use, cemented to a plate of glass, a prism finer than a knife-blade, and showing therefore no sensible dispersion of colors, although its power of refraction remains, it will divide the rays into two bands which will form two images on the wall, each of which will be colored. See Fig. 125, page 330, and S—S in Fig. 126.

In such cases the colors depend upon where the rays are divided. Beginning with the rays that produced the red end of the spectrum and moving the dividing prism gradually toward the rays that produced its violet end, it is found that

if one color be red	the other is bluish-green;
" " " " orange	" " " turquoise-blue;
" " " " yellow	" " " ultramarine-blue
" " " " yellowish-green	" " " violet;
" " " " green	" " " purple.

These then are the two colors which together make white, termed for this reason the *complementary* colors.

They are not, as some will notice, the colors which in former times were supposed to make white. Those were derived from experiments with pigments in the following way. It was found that red, yellow, and blue paint when mixed together made white or rather a whitish-gray. It was supposed therefore that if two colors were to be used they also, in order to represent white, should be compounded of these three primitive colors as they were called. Artists therefore took as their complementary colors

red and green, which latter they had found could be formed by mixing yellow and blue;
yellow and purple, " " " " " " " " " " blue and red;
blue and orange, " " " " " " " " " " red and yellow.

The German physicist, Helmholtz, revealed very clearly the erroneousness of this supposition, showing that the results are different when pigments are mixed and when the colors themselves are mixed. It was noticed that while a combination of blue and yellow pigments makes green, a blue veil spread over a yellow ground, and seen from a distance, where both colors blend, makes gray. So vermilion and ultramarine mixed on the palette produce a reddish-brown, but vermilion lines on a blue ground seen from a distance produce purple. Experiments with pigments, too, showed in the spectrum of Prussian blue, a deficiency of light at the red end, and in that of gamboge (yellow) a like deficiency at the violet end. Both spectrums, however, did contain green. So, according to the principle that colors transmit or reflect rays of like color with themselves (see page 314), the result of mixing the two was to obtain green, a result which had to do with the particular ingredients and colors of these particular pigments, but not with colors in the abstract. It did not warrant a general rule to the effect that blue and yellow make green. Similar tests with other pigments have revealed that nothing can be known certainly of the colors produced by mixing them until a mixture has actually been made. On the contrary, if colors be mixed as is done when by their effects on the eye two are made to seem like one, either because a fabric of one color is placed over another of a different color, or because lines of one color are painted over another color, or because the colors of two spectrums are made to intersect, or because two colors are made to revolve in the color top,—in all these cases the result has been found to be determined by a fixed law. In accordance with this law, the colors making white have been found to be not those formerly supposed to be complementary, but the others that have just been mentioned.

Von Bezold's "Theory of Color" contains the chart in Fig. 127, page 334. In this chart the colors are so arranged that those complementing each other are always at two ends of a diameter drawn exactly through the circle's centre. It is one of many charts of the kind; but is much more simple in construction than are most of them and, therefore, is much more easy to understand and apply.

334   PROPORTION AND HARMONY.

Let us consider some facts which this chart illustrates. It shows us that of two complementary colors, one—say yellow—is usually brighter than the other—say ultramarine. As intimated on page 311, all the colors can become darker or lighter without changing their hue; but it is suggested by this chart that if a color becomes darker, its com-

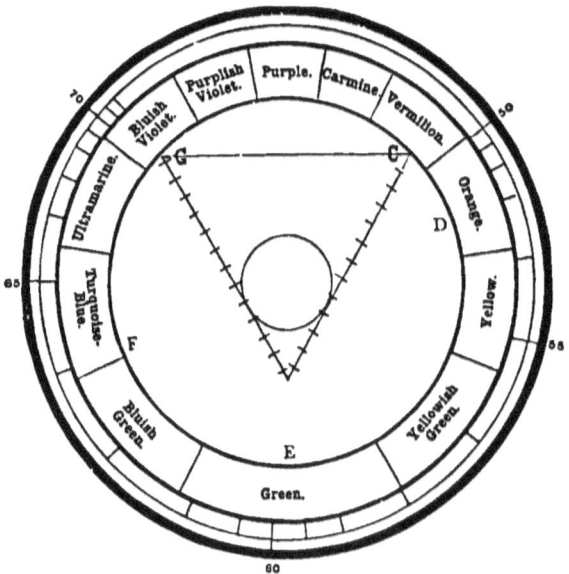

FIG. 127.—VON BEZOLD'S COLOR-CHART.
See pages 333-336, 390-393, 398, 403, 414.

plementary, in order that the two together may still continue to make white, must become correspondingly lighter. This suggestion is confirmed by an experiment with a color top; two equal parts of the disk of this, which, when they revolve together, form white or gray, continue to do the same if we put a piece of black over part of the red and also a piece of white of equal size with the black over part of the green. Accordingly if when using pigments black be mixed with one complementary color, the balance between the two can be preserved by mixing white with the other. It needs to be borne in mind, too, that white and black pigments used by themselves have effects analogous to those of color, the white being necessarily many degrees darker than white light, and the black many degrees lighter than absolute darkness.

Another fact that needs to be noticed is that, inasmuch as every shade and tint of every color, and not only so, but every mixture of the shades and tints of different colors, has its own peculiar complementary shade or tint or mixture, the possible number of complementary pairs of color-effects is practically infinite. But it must not be supposed that, because complementary, all of these pairs are agreeable or beautiful. An ugly mixed color may have an ugly mixed complementary. The two together may fulfil certain laws of harmony, as may, so far as concerns effects of pitch, the notes of a cymbal and a kettledrum. But neither the colors in the one case, nor the sounds in the other, fulfil all the laws of harmony. Each of the factors constituting each pair is inharmoniously mixed. Two color-effects used together, therefore, even when complementary, are not necessarily beautiful, except when they are pure, or are the tints or shades of pure colors; that is, of pure hues mixed with only pure brightness or pure darkness.

The chart reveals, too, that between violet, purple, and red there are differences in degree by no means matched by the differences between their complementaries, yellowish-green and bluish-green. This fact makes the difficulty of using green with its proper contrasts very great; and this difficulty becomes still greater in view of the position of green on the dividing line between the warm and cold colors, concerning the entirely different uses of which in sunshine and shadow mention was made on page 320. We see one reason, therefore, why a decisive test of a good landscape painter is the way in which he manages his greens, as well too, perhaps, as why decorators in all times have made but a limited use of them.

CHAPTER XX.

PHYSICAL AND PHYSIOLOGICAL CORRESPONDENCES BETWEEN HARMONY IN MUSIC AND PAINTING.

Study of Color-Effects in the Eye itself—Not as far Advanced as the Study of Sound-Effects in the Ear; Facts Known with Reference to the Effects of Amplitude and Rate of Sound-Waves—Of their Form—Compound Waves—Determining Quality—Partial Tones—Their Influence upon Harmony, Simultaneous and Successive—Correlation of Rhythm and Harmony ; the Latter's Physiological Effect—Foster's Explanation—Correspondences between Vibratory Effects in the Ear and in the Eye—Differences between them—Inferences from the Minuteness of Color-Waves—Two Main Questions Involved in the Discussion of Color-Harmony.

EXPERIMENTS made with color as it appears in the external world have naturally been supplemented, as knowledge has progressed, by endeavors to ascertain the influence exerted upon it in the eye itself; and before we can go on intelligently to develop the relations to color-harmony of the facts brought out in the preceding chapter, we must consider this latter subject. As was said on page 307, too, what has been learned concerning it has of late years almost revolutionized the practical methods of painting, the aim of the modern, as distinguished from the older artist, being to use pigments with reference to the way in which they shall mix, as is said, in the act of perception in the eye. No further proof is needed to show the practical bearing upon art of conceptions that may be held with reference to the subject that is to be discussed in the present chapter.

It is well to notice, also, that the study of color has not yet advanced as far as that of sound. The main reason for this, perhaps, is the fact that it is more easy to come to conclusions concerning vibrations, say, of 32 *per second*, which are in the region of those considered necessary to the least multiplied force causing a musical tone, than concerning the 458,000,000,000,000 *per second*, which are in the region of those considered necessary to the least multiplied force causing a hue. The same reason, too, makes it natural and sensible for us here, while studying the effects of color, to take suggestions from the course generally pursued by others when tracing out analogous facts with reference to sounds. As we turn to do this, it will be noticed that, in the case of sounds as well as of colors, the earliest experiments were confined to conditions supposed to be manifested in the external world. It was through comparing the sounds of cords of different lengths that the Pythagorean system, based upon ratios determining the relations between harmonic tones, was first developed. Only of late years has it been conceived that there is a physiological principle deeper than that of these ratios, of which they are a result, not a cause. Exactly what this principle is, has not yet been indisputably determined. But three facts with reference to the subject are generally acknowledged (see Chapter XIV. of " Rhythm and Harmony in Poetry and Music "): First, that degrees of loudness are determined by the relative amplitude of vibrations. A string of a certain texture and length will produce a loud sound in the degree in which it is struck violently, and, therefore, caused to cover a greater space with its vibrations. The second fact is, that degrees of pitch are determined by the relative time of vibrations. A string shortened in length, and therefore vibrating more rapidly, will produce a higher tone. It was from this fact that, by very simple experiments, the law was discovered that harmonic tones are related to one another according to certain definite ratios.

After physicists had proved that degrees of loudness in sound are determined by the amplitude of vibrations, and degrees of pitch by the time of vibrations, they felt that nothing was left to determine the quality of sounds except the forms of vibrations. It was easy, too, for them to imagine that these should differ in form. For instance, when a bow is drawn across the strings of a violin, it may fall upon them, giving them an up-and-down motion; it may move over them, giving them a motion from side to side; it may turn them, giving them a twisting motion; it may bound over them, giving them a jarring motion; or it may do all these together; besides which, wherever it touches the strings it may check the movements caused by vibrations of their entire length, and cause smaller waves between the points where they are played upon by the bow and where they are attached to the violin. According to a similar mode of reasoning, it was natural to suppose that the waves of sound produced by a wind instrument, a trumpet, or a human throat, for instance, deviated as they are from a straight course by a number of curves and angles, must necessarily be more or less compound as they emerge from the instruments; and, being so, must differ in form for different kinds of instruments. Considerations of this sort caused investigations to be made into the forms of vibrations; and by means of very ingenious expedients,—by magnifying, for example, the vibrations of a cord or pipe, and making them visible, through using an intense ray of light to throw an image of them upon a canvas in a darkened room,—the forms assumed by the vibrations caused by many of the ordinary musical instruments have been accurately ascertained. These forms have been resolved, according to well-known mathematical principles, into their constituent elements. For instance, if the form of vibration be as in the first of these examples, it may be resolved into the forms that are in the second.

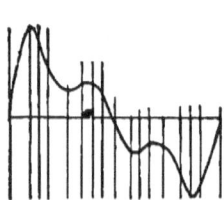 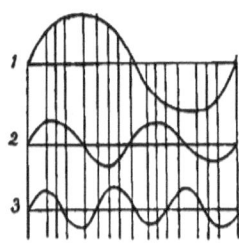

In short, investigations of this character have shown that musical sounds may result, and usually do result, not from simple but from compound forms of vibrations; that is to say, in connection with the main waves there are other waves. All of these are not invariably present, but when present they are related to the main wave—*i. e.*, in tones that make music as distinguished from noise—as 2 : 1, 3 : 1, 4 : 1, 5 : 1, 6 : 1, 7 : 1, 8 : 1, 9 : 1, and even in some cases as 10 : 1. In other words, these smaller accompanying waves vibrate two, three, and four times, and so on up to ten times, while the main wave is vibrating once. But this is not all. The sounds of these compound vibrations have been analyzed. By means of instruments like Helmholtz's resonators, which are small brass boxes or globes each made of such a size as to respond sympathetically to a certain pitch, it has been found that each form of vibration represented in a note produces a separate pitch of its own. When, therefore, a tone is sounded on a violin, we hear in it not only the pitch caused by the vibrations of the whole length of the string, but also in connection with it a number of other partial tones, as all the constituents of any one note are called, each of which has its own pitch, produced by vibrations of one half, one third, one fourth, etc., of the length of the string.

The difference in the number, the combination, and the relative loudness of these partial tones in a musical sound is what determines its quality or timbre. In instruments like kettle-drums, cymbals, or bells, one side is almost invariably thicker than the other. For this reason, the main vibrations are not uniform, and, of course, the partial tones cannot be so. Such instruments, accordingly, are less musical than noisy, and are used on only exceptional occasions. But in ordinary musical sounds the partial tones, if present at all,—they differ as produced by different instruments,—are indicated in the notation below. Notice that the prime tone is counted as the first partial tone; also that the second, fourth, and eighth partials are the same as the prime tone with exception of being in higher octaves.

The notes that are used ( ), in the degree in

which they are long, indicate tones which the reader needs most to notice; and the marks after the letters indicate the relative distance of a tone from the octave of the tone which is the standard of pitch. C′, F′, or G′, for instance, are one octave below C, F, or G, and these are one octave below c, f, or g, and two octaves below c′, f′, or g′.

In "Rhythm and Harmony in Poetry and Music" it was shown that tones—though they may be in different octaves—which are related to one another in pitch as are the *partial* tones *nearest the fundamental bass*, form the musical chords—as do, in the first measure on page 341, C, g, and e, with the addition also, if we include the chord of the seventh, of *b flat*. But because *b flat* is distant from the fundamental bass, the chord containing it is sometimes wrongly called a discord. It was shown, too, that these same partial tones in connection with the partial tones of G and F which are nearly related to C, form the notes of the musical scale. See the music on page 343. When we speak of musical harmony, we sometimes refer to the effect of a single chord whose notes are sounded simultaneously. But we also refer to the effects of many different chords when they are sounded successively. In other words, harmony in music consists not only in using harmonic chords, but in passing from one chord to another; and the principles of harmony, as determined by this latter requirement, necessitate using chords in succession that contain (as they almost invariably do) some prime tone, or else some partial tone, that is the same. See pages 213–217 of "Rhythm and Harmony in Poetry and Music." Therefore, whether applied to simultaneous or to successive chords, the system of musical harmony, as it has developed, is merely a pro-

cess of putting together, according to the methods in
the chart on page 3, vibrations that are alike or are
related, in that they are multiples or subdivisions of some
single standard of measurement. The following, for
instance, represents the usual method of harmonizing
the notes of the musical scale. In every chord it will

be noticed that at least one prime tone is repeated from
the chord preceding it. The fact that the same method
is really fulfilled even when it is only a partial tone that
is repeated, is that which justifies the occasional abrupt
transitions with which we are all familiar. Of course, the
partial tone used in such cases must be very near the
fundamental bass—*i. e.*, between the first and the fifth—
or the ear will not detect between the successive chords
any harmonic relationship whatever.

The reader will not fail to notice that the effects of
harmony as thus described are, in important regards,
analogous to those of rhythm, and yet of a rhythm so
finely grained that it is impossible that the mind should be
conscious of its constituent elements. In rhythm the
beats determining the measures necessitate the use of factors—*i. e.*, notes—that go into one another or into some
third factor a certain equal number of times: in harmony
the vibrations determining the different degrees of pitch
do the same. It is sometimes said that, as the mind consciously counts the beats in determining rhythm, so, in
some subtle way, it unconsciously counts the vibrations

in determining harmony. But is it necessary to suppose this? When influenced by tones that seem consonant we are certainly not conscious of counting. Are we conscious of doing it even when influenced by the effects of rhythm? Are we conscious of anything except of certain accentuations of tone that are equally subdivided into other accentuations—all of which, in some way, are so related that they exactly fit, the smaller into the larger and all into the largest? And if we need not count the accents in rhythm, why should we do it in harmony? Why need we do more than experience certain throbs or thrills of sound equally subdivided into other thrills, all of which are so related that they exactly fit, the smaller into the larger and all into the largest? As a result of experiencing these, every part of the auditory organism, under any influence of sound, is under the same influence,—as much so as is every part of a still pool when we have thrown a single stone into it, infinitely varied as may be the sizes of different waves that in remote places circle into ripples. The result, inasmuch as all the sound-waves represent a single impulse, is an unimpeded, free, regularly recurrent vibratory glow of the whole auditory apparatus. But if, on the contrary, the effect resemble that upon the waters of a pool when more than one stone is thrown into it, *i. e.*, if the sound-waves do not coalesce, if the smaller do not fit into the larger, and all together into the largest, then nothing ensues but a broken, impeded, constrained, irregular series of jolts or jars. The difference in the ear between the sensation of harmony and of a lack of it, is the physical difference between thrilling or glowing and jolting or jarring. Notice, too, that this illustration applies to notes when sounding not only, as in one chord, simultaneously, but, as in different chords, successively. Two things related to the same thing cannot fail, in some way, to be related to each other; and two chords, each containing sets of vibrations for which there is a common multiple, and both containing one set of vibrations (*i. e.*, one tone) which is the same, must both be entirely composed of vibrations for which there is some common multiple. This common multiple, moreover, for the vibrations of a first and second chord may be different from that of the vibrations of the second and third chord. It is possible, therefore, for a series of chords, each in part repeating the same tones as the last sounded, and in part introducing new tones, to change, very soon, the whole character of the general vibratory effect; and yet if this be done with sufficient gradualness, the auditory apparatus will experience no jolt or jar, while, at the same time, it will be conscious of constant progress and so of relief from anything resembling monotony.

That the illustrations just used to represent the effects experienced in the ear have a scientific justification may be shown by a quotation from Foster's " Text-Book of Physiology," § 850. " A complex sound," he says, " consisting of vibrations of more than one period, travels, as we have said, not as a group of discrete waves, each corresponding to a vibration of a particular period, but as a complex wave in which the simple waves are compounded into one; and the vibrations of the tympanic membrane (*i. e.*, the external ear-drum), followed by the vibrations of the perilymph (*i. e.*, the fluid behind the drum through which the vibrations pass), have the same composite character. When, for instance, a note is sung, or sounded on a musical instrument, the air in the external auditory passage is not the subject of one set of waves corresponding to the fundamental tone, and of other sets corresponding to the several partial tones, but vibrates in the pattern of one composite wave. The tympanic membrane executes one complex vibration, and a corresponding vibration excites the auditory epithelium (*i. e.*, the nerve-cells). And this holds good not for a single sound only, but for a mixture of sounds. We can, in a clumsy way, take a graphic record of the vibrations of a dead tympanic membrane by attaching a marker to the stapes ; could we take an adequate record of the movements of the living tympanum of one of the audience at a concert, we should obtain a curve, a phonogram, which, though a single curve only, would be, on the one hand, a record of the multitudinous vibrations of the concert, and, on the other hand, a picture of the actual blows with which the perilymph (*i. e.*, the fluid behind the ear-drum) had struck the auditory epithelium." Foster then goes on to say, as indicated by the fact that we can often detect the different instruments at play in an orchestra, by the minute organs at the ends of the auditory nerve, that it is probable that, after reaching these, " the complex vibration is analyzed again into its constituent simple vibrations, that the vibrations start afresh, so to speak, in the auditory epithelium, marshalled in the same array as that in which they started from the sounding instruments, as if the auditory epithelium itself constituted the band playing the music." It is interesting, too, to recall, in this connection, that investigations made with the microscope upon the nerve-fibres and cells of living beings, in the lower orders of life, have proved that the sensations of touch, at least, when communicated through the nerves, pass through them in the forms of waves. As the auditory, like the optic, nerve is merely a bundle of nerve-fibres, each of which, apparently, is connected with a separate termination, we can apprehend the reasonableness of Foster's conclusion. Exactly what is each particular function of each of these minute terminating fibres, however, has not yet been definitely determined ; the formerly accepted theory that each of Corti's rods, of which there are several thousand in the ear, is fitted to respond sympathetically to a particular pitch having been abandoned, largely because such rods are not discoverable in the ears of birds.

With reference to color, certain deductions, in all regards analogous to those made with reference to sounds, are now acknowledged to be justified. It is acknowledged that intensity of vibrations must determine the degrees of the brightness of the color, that rate or time of vibrations must determine its hue, and that form or shape of vibrations must determine its composition or mixture. From those deductions it would seem to follow—though it cannot be said to be generally acknowledged—that only such forms of vibrations can harmonize as can coalesce in the retina. In Chapter XIX. we found that all colors result from subdivisions of a ray of white light, also that white light can always be exactly subdivided into any two of the colors called complementary. From this the conclusion seems to be warranted, that both for the vibrations causing white light and also for those causing each of any two complementary colors so far as they are thus produced, there must be some common multiple. Therefore, when the three are put together, all their different vibrations, like all the notes of a measure in rhythm, can go some exact number of times into this common multiple. In other words, harmony would result, as in the case of music, from putting together vibrations that are alike, or are related, in that they are multiples or subdivisions of some single standard of measurement, or, as expressed in

"The Genesis of Art-Form," by putting together complex wholes that have like partial effects. Once more the hypothesis seems to be warranted that, just as in the ear, when different sounds, as the scraping of the bow, the twanging of the string, and the resonance of the body of a violin, are blended into a single mixed effect, it is impossible to analzye and separate the different elements, so there are certain blendings of colors that the eye cannot analyze. The mixed effects appeal to the senses as a simple, single effect. When, however, the differences between the constituent elements become slightly greater, as in the case of chords, especially as produced upon different instruments, or as in the case of a general impression of one color produced by a checkered or a plaided texture, the result is, at once, recognized to be complex, and the factors of its composition can be more easily determined.

Notice, however, that there are certain differences between distinguishing the elements in sounds and in sights. When separating the notes even of a single chord, we do this mainly in the order of time, *i.e.*, by successively directing attention first to the one note and then—of course by a very rapid change—to the other. We recognize first that this is C, and then that that is G, and so on. On the contrary, we distinguish colors mainly in the order of space, by perceiving and examining them as we compare one with another that adjoins it. This distinction between the actions of the ear and of the eye becomes still more marked when we consider the phase of harmony in color which is analogous to that produced in music not by simultaneous but by successive tones. That which in sight is analogous to this latter is the movement which the eye itself makes in examining first one part of a scene and then a different part of it.

Sound-waves are comparatively large. The quotation from Foster on page 345, suggests that we can conceive of each successive set of complex waves as agitating every part of the ear-drum. When the sound represented by this complex wave is succeeded by a different sound represented by a different complex wave, the first, according to the laws of music, is made harmonious to the second by having both contain a number of like kinds of vibrations, producing a like partial tone. As this fact was expressed in "Rhythm and Harmony in Poetry and Music," the complex wholes, *i. e.*, in this case the chords which are put together, have " like partial effects." Color-waves are exceedingly small. This we might infer, if from nothing else, from the fact that it is necessary to have, at every minutest point on the retina upon which the external scene is impressed, an exact representation of some part of the scene, and that the color of this part may differ greatly from that of the part beside it. These color-waves, indeed, are so small that, notwithstanding an existing theory to the contrary, it must seem to many impossible to conceive that any one set of them (*i. e.*, any one color), however complex in form, can influence more than a very minute part of the retina, unless, of course, accompanied by many other sets exactly like themselves. What is meant by suggesting that these waves may influence a minute part of the retina, will be understood when it is added that, according to Le Conte in his "Sight," there are in the centre of the retina, in a space not larger than one tenth of an inch square, no less than a million cones. (Compare Fig. 128, page 350, with Figs. 130, page 380, and 131, page 381.) As is known, too, all these are so connected with their surroundings, as Foster says, by a " basket-work " or "sponge-work," that they are apparently capable of vibratory motion. If their minute vibrations as affected by movements in the ether, may be supposed to influence the whole retina in any degree, how can they do so except as one set of waves may be supposed to influence the whole surface of a sea? On the same sea there may be breezes causing waves differing, as these vibrations do, in intensity, in rate, and in shape. But, in case these differences were far apart, and produced by very gradual changes from one form to another, there might be, to an eye capable of perceiving the whole surface at once, no appearance whatever of inharmonious action. It needs to be added, however, that, within the narrow limits of a picture, it is impossible for any colors to be very widely separated, and, not only so, but that, even if they could be, the eye, in shifting attention from one point to another while examining them, would constantly be bringing them into still closer proximity, in fact necessitating often the perception of all the colors on the canvas by exactly the same part of the retina.

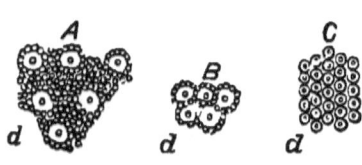

FIG. 128.—CONES AND RODS IN DIFFERENT PARTS OF THE RETINA.
A, usual surface; *B*, raised margin of central yellow spot; *C*, surface of central spot.

See pages 349, 350, 381.

These latter conditions, taken in connection with those mentioned on page 349, will show us that, in considering the harmony of color, there are two main questions to be discussed: first, the selection and arrangement of colors with reference to their general effects in a painting considered as a whole, corresponding to the selection in music of a key-note, involving that of the particular scale and chords that go with it; and, second, the selection and arrangement of colors with reference to their special effects when placed side by side, together with the ways of sufficiently separating and yet connecting them in cases in which placing them side by side would produce discord. This phase of harmony corresponds to what in music is termed modulation or transition from one key to another. The first of these questions will naturally be discussed while considering the methods in the chart on page 3 preceding *consonance*, and the second while considering *consonance* and the methods following it.

CHAPTER XXI.

GENERAL EFFECTS OF COLOR IN PAINTINGS CONSIDERED AS WHOLES.

Artistic Harmony not Imitated from Nature—Field-Theory with Reference to the Method of Securing it—Physiological Objection to it—Psychological—Principality, Subordination; Tone—Harmony, whether Due to Similarity, as in Tone, or to Variety, an Exemplification of Similar Physiological Requirements—Analogy from Music and the Key-Note—Balance and Organic Form—Their Effects both Psychical and Physiological—Congruity as Representing Conceptions and Conditions—Incongruity, Comprehensiveness, Central-Point, Setting, and Parallelism—Symmetry—Repetition—Alteration, Alternation—Massing, Breadth, or Chiaroscuro—Its Relation to Principality and Balance—And Other Methods—Interspersion, Complication, and Continuity.

AS suggested on page 297, it must always be borne in mind that harmony in art is not necessarily produced by copying nature. In this, all possible colors are found side by side; and many of their combinations are not beautiful. Of course in the narrower compass of a painting, where all may be seen in a single act of vision, they may appear still less so. The colors in paintings are selected colors. The question before us is, How shall they be selected in order to secure harmonious effects?

The facts discovered with reference to the complementary colors, as described in Chapter XIX., have led to the natural supposition that the eye takes pleasure in seeing these two together; and as, in all cases, the two have been discovered to make white, it has been supposed that a theory of color-harmony could be based on this fact.

Any two colors and, therefore, any three or more colors making white have been supposed to be sufficient to cause harmony. Moreover, in order to cause this, it has even been supposed by some that it is necessary to have them introduced into a painting in just such proportions as to make white. This was the conclusion reached by the English physicist Field, in what is termed the Field-theory. For instance, because he found that when, mixed in proportions of 8, 5, and 3, blue, red, and yellow make white, he argued that the quantities of these colors used in the same composition should represent these proportions. A law of this kind, however, though it might be applied to decoration, would evidently interfere with one of the first requisites of the art of painting, namely, that it should represent nature. In how many landscapes can we find the blue of the sky, or the green of the foliage, or the bluish-gray of a lowery day exactly mingled in these quantities with the warmer and lighter yellows, reds, or browns? Or, if now and then a landscape of this kind could be found, think how greatly a rule so exact would interfere with the freedom of the artist!

On the face of it, therefore, this theory does not seem tenable; and this fact ought to be accepted as an indication that, with all the truth that there is at the basis of the Field-theory, it does not contain the whole nor the fundamental truth. What this is may be inferred from what was said in Chapter XX. If we may suppose that a color associated with its complementary produces in the eye an agreeable effect because for the vibrations causing both colors as well as white light, or light in general, there is a common multiple; then we may also suppose that these colors influence, at the same time, the organs of the same retina without producing any sensation of jolting or jarring.

They all seem to be variations of the same *unity* in that they are partial effects of the same single impulse or set of impulses, resulting in a free, unconstrained vibratory thrill or glow. The quantity of color, therefore, makes no difference with the harmony of the effect. All that is necessary is that the form of vibration causing the one color, be it much or little, should exactly coalesce with the form of vibration causing the other color.

This is the same principle, explained physiologically, that those who perceive the insufficiency of the Field-theory usually explain psychologically. They say that the slightest spot of crimson against the green of a forest, or of yellow against the blue of the sky, is all that is needed in order to bring out the brilliancy of the complementary coloring; and they point, as an illustration of this, to effects like those in Jules Breton's picture entitled "Brittany Washerwomen," at one time in the Metropolitan Museum of New York, where a very little red in the bodice of the central woman is enough to put fire and brightness into the pervading greenish-blue tints of the whole. What is thus said of such arrangements of color is true. But when it is added that these effects are owing to merely a suggestion given to the mind, one must demur. Those who say it have forgotten a very important principle in æsthetics. This is, that psychological effects (see "Art in Theory," Chapter XII.) must harmonize with physiological, and, as the latter come first in the order of time, especially when, as in the present instance, the effects have to do primarily with form, it is not logical either to overlook them or to fail to consider them first.

What has been said of the influence in a painting of very slight quantities of complementary coloring will suggest a transition from the art-methods of *comparison, con-*

trast, and *complement*, which we have been considering in Chapters XIX. and XX., to *principality*. (See the chart on page 3.) Of course this method applied to our present subject would involve the main use of one color, to which other colors would be kept *subordinate*. To those acquainted with the terminology of painting, the mention of this effect recalls that which is ordinarily treated under the designation of *tone*. *Tone* is a term often used as if it meant merely a predominating or sometimes exclusive employment of one color varied only by the tints and shades resulting from the effects of different degrees of light. Thus, in a scene representing moonlight or twilight, or even a storm, especially if at sea, there would necessarily be one pervading color, in some cases banishing almost the suggestion of other colors; and such a picture would be said to be particularly characterized by *tone*. The same effect can also be produced merely by arrangement. For instance, in the painting by Carl Marr in the New York Museum entitled " Gossip," almost every prominent object—the window-curtain, the tablecloth, the apron of one of the principal figures, the bodice of another, the floor, etc.—is depicted in white. On the other hand, in Fortuny's " Spanish Lady," hanging near it, almost every article of clothing is depicted in black; while in Granet's " Monks in an Oratory," a little farther on, the color of the monks' robes, as well as of the walls and woodwork, is all brown. Such paintings are said to be characterized by *tone*, and, as this quality is usually understood, it is difficult to perceive why it does not fulfil a different law of harmony from that which is fulfilled through a use of great variety in coloring. Indeed, it is often represented that it does; as if the theory that harmony of coloring is produced by uniformity of coloring were antagonistic to the theory that it is produced by variety.

But, by taking into consideration the physiological requirements of coloring, suggested in Chapter XX., an identical law can be perceived to be operative in both cases. As shown on page 347, differences in tints and shades of the same hue, while they involve differences in the intensity of the sight-waves, do not necessarily involve differences in their rates or shapes of vibration. Therefore uniformity of coloring is fitted to cause all the vibrations of the same retina to coalesce, *i. e.*, to cause all to be exact subdivisions of some common multiple. Again, the same is true when an effect of principality in coloring is produced by the use of one predominating color with its various tints and shades, enlivened, as in the case of Jules Breton's "Brittany Washerwomen," mentioned on page 354, by an occasional introduction of some tint or shade of its complementary color. The same is true even where both complementary colors are used in almost equal proportions. In fact, the same may be true of paintings characterized by the very greatest variety, —variety so great that principality, while exerting a very powerful influence, can be discerned only as a result of much study.

To recognize how the same physiological principle, fulfilled in what is termed tone, is really exemplified in all cases, let us go back again to the analogy suggested by the relations of notes in musical harmony. It will be shown on page 397 that the colors of the spectrum represent differences corresponding to only those of a single octave in sound; but, at the same time, owing to the minuteness of the color-waves and to the innumerable changes produced by different degrees of light and of shade and of mixture with other colors, the possibilities of variety in the case of color are much greater than in the case of sound. It has already been shown that, if the forms of vibration produced by all the adjoining colors are to continue exact subdivisions of one common multiple, every change in one color, especially in the degree of the prominence of this color, as, for instance, when it is an atmospheric tint like the yellow of a sunset or the gray of a twilight, necessitates a change in every other color that is to be used near it. This is merely what is necessary physiologically if the eye would experience the harmonious effect of a thrill or glow, and not the inharmonious effect of a series of jolts and jars.

The connection between this principle and that exemplified in musical harmony is as follows: If we are composing in the scale of C natural, we use C for *do*, D for *re*, E for *me*, etc., and, for the major chord, C, E, and G. But if we make the slightest change in our *do*, passing, for instance, into the scale of D, then we use D for *do*, E for *re*, F sharp for *me*, etc., and, for the major chord, D, F sharp, and A, these three notes in the scale of D representing exactly the same relationships between ratios of vibrations that C, E, and G do in the scale of C natural. There is a sense in which it may be said that analogous changes are made in color-harmony. The only difference is that in music the number of vibrations causing tones is comparatively few, and men have been able to calculate them, to construct scales from them, and with well-nigh mathematical accuracy to relate them according to certain ratios. But in color the vibrations are so numerous, and the variations caused by them so beyond calculation, that the result is difficult to attain. Yet both cases illustrate apparently the same principle. When, in painting, we change one color, especially in the degree in which it is a prominent color, we change the *key* of the composition, and all the colors need to be *keyed* or *toned* into harmony with this. Inasmuch, therefore, as the same physiological conditions underlie the effect, whether there be uniformity or variety of color, the same word *tone* with equal appropriateness might be, though it is not, applied in all cases.

What has been said will explain sufficiently the relationship to effects of harmony of *principality* and its necessary accompaniment, *subordination*. The next method in the chart on page 3 is *balance*. This is the method that leads, in music or poetry, sometimes to repetition, and sometimes to alternation on upward, or downward, or long or short movements in phrases, lines, or rhymes; and that leads, in painting, sculpture, or architecture, to likeness in whole or part on opposite sides, as in eyes, ears, arms, or wings of living creatures or buildings. As brought out at length in Chapters III. to V. of "The Genesis of Art-Form," *balance* is necessary in order to convey, in connection with *principality* and *subordination*, the impression of *organic form*, the next method mentioned in the chart on page 3. The same must be true, of course, as applied to the arrangements of color. We gain an impression of *unity* or *organism* of form in a composition, considered as a whole, in the degree in which, through a use of light and shade or hue, the sides are balanced, as we say. Thus, in Rubens's well known "Descent from the Cross," Fig. 129, page 359, a white sheet, the whitest object in the picture, is placed behind the form of the Christ; but on both sides of this the light is reflected from surrounding faces or forms, and is so disposed that all of it that is on one side is carefully balanced by that which is on the other

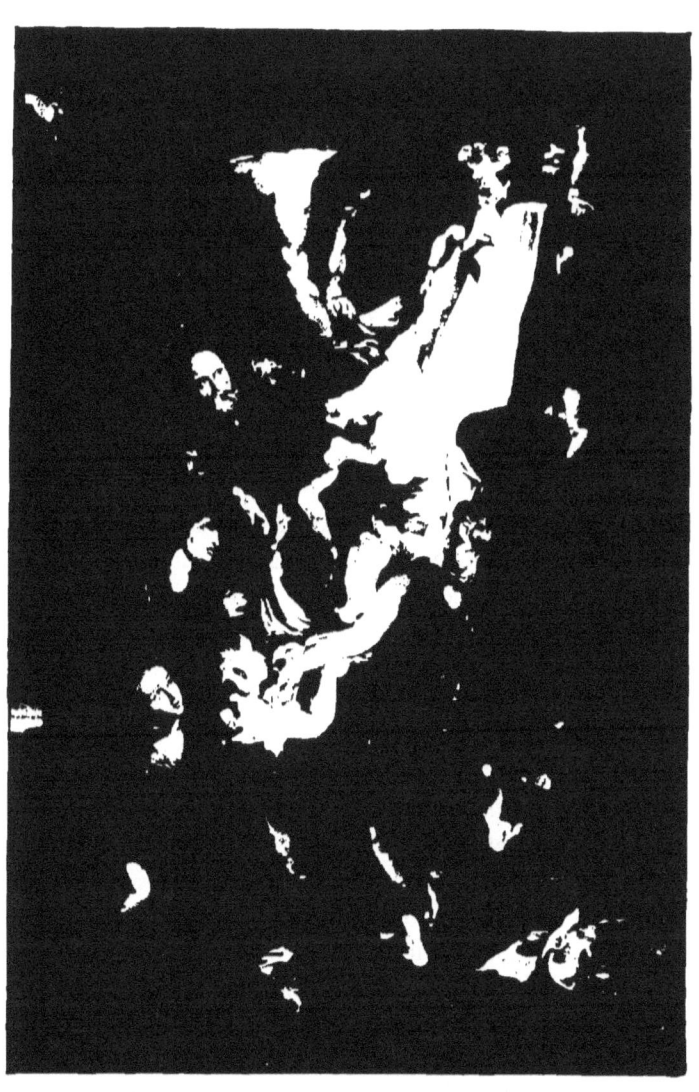

FIG. 129.—"THE DESCENT FROM THE CROSS," BY RUBENS.
See pages 59, 303, 358, 363, 365, 367, 369.

side, a dish and parchment at the lower right corner being especially prominent, as balancing the light from the shoulders of a man at the upper left corner.

The impressions of *balance* and of *organic form*, as thus produced, point toward a psychical rather than a physiological explanation. It is the mind, not the visual apparatus, that is satisfied by such a use of color. And yet we might mistake, did we suppose that from these effects physiological influences were wholly absent. It is impossible for the eyes to look at a picture without almost constantly shifting the gaze from one side of it to the other side. If, while doing so, they perceive exactly the same color on both sides, they will notice this color particularly. While doing so, moreover, the retina will experience no perceptible difference or change in the character of its vibrations, and, therefore, as explained on page 350, it will experience nothing interfering with the requirement of harmony. This physiological fact will explain why, in order to convey an impression of balance, equal quantities of color on both sides of a picture are not necessary. Things that harmonize with a third thing, harmonize with one another. A little color on one side, harmonizing with its surroundings, will harmonize with a great deal of this same color on the opposite side. In accordance with this principle, in one of Paul Veronese's pictures—he painted more than one—of the "Marriage at Cana," a small black dog on one side is said to *balance* a large mass of black upon the other side; and in Jules Breton's "Brittany Washerwomen," mentioned on page 354, a little blue in certain of the women's skirts *balances* a much larger amount of blue in a sea on the opposite side of the picture. The same fact explains, too, why a color on one side is often represented as *balancing* (though this is not an exact use of the term; see the chart on page 3) on the other side not the same color but its complementary. It is said to *balance*, of course, because the vibrations occasioning a color harmonize with those occasioning its complementary, as well as with those occasioning its own color. In a like way, one can explain the effect of an arrangement in Henri Lerolle's "Organ Recital" in the Metropolitan Museum, New York, whereby all the darker tones are in the shade at the left lower side of the picture, and all the bright tones are in the light at the right upper side ; the two classes of tones in this case being about evenly divided.

The general impression produced by *balance* enters largely as we shall find presently, into the effects, which are all, in fact, developments of it, termed *parallelism, alternation, symmetry*, and *continuity*. But before considering these, following the order of the art-methods, as indicated in the chart on page 3, let us take up for a moment that phase of comparison which is termed *congruity*. This is the principle which causes all factors, including color, to be selected not so much because they are alike in form, as because they represent like conceptions or conditions. See Chapter XI. of " Painting, Sculpture, and Architecture as Representative Arts." The degree of importance that should be attached to the representation of like conceptions in the forms that are grouped together, is difficult for some to recognize. Yet if, as was said on page 344, the difference between the effects of harmony and of discord be the difference between experiencing in the nerves an unimpeded, free, regularly recurrent vibratory thrill or glow, and experiencing an impeded, constrained, irregularly recurrent series of shocks or jars, then an application of the simplest physiological principles ought to show us that the artistic effects of which we have spoken can be produced in part by the representation of like conceptions. It is universally admitted that the nerves, merely as nerves, may be affected from the thought-side as well as from the sense-side. Whatever, therefore, owing to *incongruity* between thought and form or between different thoughts as represented by different forms, shocks one's conceptions or, as we say, one's sense of the proprieties, may so contribute to the general nervous result that, even though he may find the combinations of color thoroughly pleasing, it is physiologically impossible that he should experience the effects of beauty in its totality. On this subject the reader may consult Chapter XIII. of "Art and Theory."

A moment's thought will reveal, too, that having the colors represent like conceptions or conditions is often the most effective way in which to have them represent likeness in hue. According to the principles unfolded on page 314, gaslight, firelight, twilight, moonlight, cloud-light, and even sunlight, at certain times of the day, develop their own colors so far as they are found in surrounding objects, and cause these colors to be reflected from all other objects in the degree in which their surfaces are of a glossy kind of white, or, to use an unscientific term, are glass-like. If a painter wish, therefore, to have his work as a whole convey a general impression of cheerfulness or of gloom, the most effective way in which he can make it do this is to make it fulfil the method of *comparison* by way of *congruity*.

The modifications of *congruity* under the influence of *variety* and *complexity* causing the effects of *incongruity* and *comprehensiveness*, it is not necessary to explain. Everybody knows that the mere fact that a painting is a picture of some actual scene, often necessitates the introduction of *incongruous* hues, and that these can only be harmonized by the addition of other hues complementing or connecting them, and thus causing more or less *comprehensiveness* of effect. See what is said on page 364 of K. G. Hellquist's " Sonnänvater and Knut Entering Stockholm." A few words, too, will express all that is necessary with reference to the influence upon colors of the art-methods in the chart on page 3 termed *central-point* (or *radiation*), *setting*, and *parallelism*. Recalling that all these are methods of producing effects of *unity* in a composition considered as a whole, it will be noticed that *radiation*, though usually associated in our minds with the idea of very distinct outlines, does not necessarily involve these. For instance, in Fig. 38, page 75, as also in Fig. 129, page 359, there is a very decided effect of centring and, by consequence, of *unity* as produced by it, but, in Fig. 129, it is by the colors rather than by the lines that the effect is brought out.

Setting, as applied to color, is mainly an arrangement within a framework of *organic form*, when characterized by *central-point* or *parallelism*, or both, whereby, in accordance with the laws of *consonance*, to be considered presently, the degree of light illumining an object, or the peculiarity of hue characterizing it, causes its outlines to appear not only distinct and different but æsthetically effective. *Parallelism*, like *radiation*, is usually associated with the conception of lines; but in all cases these may be merely suggested by the colors, as when, for instance, we see a blue lake with a ridge of mountains behind them, and a blue sky perhaps above the mountains; or a river or ledge of rocks separating a line of green foliage in the foreground from a line of green forest a little farther back. Nor is the effect of parallelism through the use of complementary colors uncommon. How often we see a stretch of blue sky above a like stretch of yellow sand, or *vice versa*, ruddy or golden layers of sunset clouds lying above the greenish or bluish tints of grass or waves beneath them.

Symmetry involves the principle of *balance* applied to arrangements not on two sides, but on every side of a common centre. There is an illustration of this effect in the "Thusnelda at the Triumph of Germanicus," by Karl Piloty in the Metropolitan Museum. In this picture, with sufficient variety not to obtrude itself so as to seem unnatural, the color, whether light or dark, that is above or below or in one corner, is almost invariably balanced by a mass of the same color in very nearly the same position below or above or in the opposite corner. A more unusual illustration of this kind of arrangement, the influence of which, because not connected with much *massing* of light or shade, tends principally to a general picturesqueness of effect, is afforded in a painting that hangs near this in the same gallery, *i. e.*, K. G. Hellquist's "Sonnänvater and Knut Entering Stockholm." Here the legs of three of the figures, one in the middle and one on each side, are clad in the same shade of brown. A clown's coat on one side, a horse's tail on the other, and the legs of a figure in the centre are all in the same shade of yellow. A woman's cap on one side, a man's coat on the other, and a woman's dress far above these, all show the same shade of blue; while a bright red cap on one side balances a bright red cap on the other, and the same is true of a dark red cap as related to a dark red cape.

Repetition of form involves, in some regards, the most easy, because the most elementary way of putting like with like according to the art-method of *comparison*. Notice the outlines, in Figs. 38, page 75, and 129, page 359. But the same fact is also true as applied to colors. This is one reason why pictures characterized by *tone*, as its meaning is limited on page 355, are apt to be more satisfactory than those characterized by great diversity of coloring. These latter, notwithstanding the success of some brilliant colorists like Fortuny, Zamaçois, Rico, and others of the Spanish-Roman school, are usually avoided by wise artists. As Van Dyke says in his " How to Judge of a Picture ": " Beware of bright pictures, for they are generally bad. . . . Look at the grays and browns; the low-toned and half-tinted pictures—look at them, not once only, but several times, for there is likely to be something in them that you do not see at first glance." It must not be thought, however, that these latter pictures, though involving fewer difficulties in the way of securing unity of color-effect, do not involve other great difficulties. In cases where the color is almost absolutely the same throughout, it is no easy matter to represent different degrees of light and shade. Nor must it be supposed that pictures without diversity of coloring can always be made true to nature. In full sunshine, or in full light of any kind, in which the shadows are deep and the colors are brilliant, they are almost necessarily greatly varied. Even then, however, whether an artist take sunset in a land robed in the full glories of autumn foliage, or firelight in a room papered and upholstered in red, or a scene less harmoniously toned by nature, it is evident that, in spite of great brilliancy of coloring, he can produce unity of effect through *repetition*. At the same time, we are more accustomed to repetition when the colors are not bright; and, therefore, it seems more natural when the impression conveyed is that of weirdness and mystery, as indicated by twilight or moonlight, or of gloom or ruin, as indicated by a lowery or stormy atmosphere, which gives everything in cloud and earth a tinge of gray.

Alteration, the next method in the chart on page 3, is merely a phase of *variety* in connection with *repetition*, and *alternation* a phase of *balance* by means of *contrast*. Piloty's "Thusnelda at the Triumph of Germanicus," and Hellquist's "Sonnänvater and Knut Entering Stockholm," mentioned on page 364, furnish illustrations of both of these as well as of symmetry.

Next to alternation, and closely connected with both principality and central-point, is *massing*. This word, as applied to the use of crayon or pigments—and by some it is applied to these almost exclusively—refers to those effects of light and shade in connection with color whereby bright features are put with bright, and dark with dark. As a result of such arrangements, a *breadth* of distance seems to separate the objects in light from those in shade, and a corresponding *breadth* of view seems to be afforded him who sees them; hence the term *breadth* is sometimes used interchangeably with *massing*. In securing this effect the artist does not arbitrarily make objects bright or dim in order to have them correspond to the bright or dim parts of the picture in which he wishes to place them. He exercises ingenuity in arranging his materials so as to bring into the right relations objects that in nature are bright or dim, or that can be made so in nature by the presence or absence of an illuminating agent. Besides this, too, he arranges the light so as to fall where it will prove most effective. In Titian's "Entombment," it is made to illumine a figure in the foreground, notwithstanding the fact that the sun is represented as setting in the background. The painter produces the effect by supposing the sun's rays to be reflected from a cloud in advance of the field of vision. Notice also the way in which the light is massed in Rubens's " Descent from the Cross " (Fig. 129, page 359).

It is not to be supposed, however, that in any given picture there may not be more than one place where there is light and one place where there are shadows, although in the paintings of Correggio and Rembrandt, who developed most fully the possibilities of light and shade, or of *chiaroscuro*, as it is called, this plan was usually followed. According to Reynolds (Note xxxix. on " The Art of Painting"), there may be three masses of light, one of which, however, he would make more prominent than the other two, thus causing all three together to fulfil the methods both of *principality* and of *balance*. Titian, in order to impress the fact that every picture representing the effects of the atmosphere must indicate not only the general influence of the light and shade on all the objects depicted considered together, but on each specific object considered by itself, is said to have pointed to a bunch of grapes, and shown how the bunch considered as a whole has a light and a dark side, and also how each grape considered by itself has a light and a dark side. The effects resulting from each of these conditions render the representation of both difficult. Nor can they be represented at all except in the degree in which the general effect, which is the one connected with *massing*, is treated as the more important of the two.

From what has been said, it is evident that the effect of *breadth*, as thus produced, is identical with that of the accumulation of repeated characteristics which results from *massing* in poetry and music. The artistic end in view, too, is the same. By it, the *unity, comparison, principality, congruity, central-point*, as well as *repetition* of the product are all brought out more clearly. "Pictures," says S. P. Long in his "Art, Its Laws, and the Reasons for Them," essay vi.—" Pictures possessing breadth of the general light and dark or shade are not only very effective, but they likewise give great repose to the eye; whereas, where the lights and darks are in small portions, and much divided, the eye is disturbed and the mind rendered uneasy, especially if one is anxious to understand every object in a composition, as it is painful to the ear, if we are anxious to hear what is said in company, where many are talking at the same time. Hence . . . the reason why portraits make a more pleasing picture when but few objects are introduced into the composition than when the person is covered with frills and ruffles, and the background stuffed like a 'curiosity shop.' Such an arrangement cuts up the lights and darks and destroys the breadth "—a statement applicable, as will be noticed, not only to *massing* but also to *interspersion*, its opposite, according to the chart on page 3. Concerning the same subject Ruskin says in his "Elements of Drawing," letter iii.: "Such compositions possess higher sublimity than those which are more mingled in their elements. They tell a special tale and summon a definite state of feeling. We have not in each gray color set against sombre, and sharp forms against sharp, and low passages against low; but we have the bright picture with its single ray of relief; the stern picture with only one tender group of lines; the soft and calm picture with only one rock angle at its flank, and so on."

When there is no *massing* of color, and the lights and darks are mingled indiscriminately, there is little *unity*.

Instead of it we have that phase of *variety* termed, in "The Genesis of Art-Form," *interspersion*. When, in spite of apparent *interspersion*, there is *massing*, methodically distributed too, but apparently *alternating* in different places, as where the light falls through branches of trees or lattice-work, we have the picturesque equivalent in color of artistic *complication*. Notice again what is said on page 364 of Hellquist's "Sonnänvater and Knut Entering Stockholm." Once more, when, notwithstanding this form of *alternation*, we have, as in a sunset sky, or in views of rivers, seas, mountains, forests, similar coloring not merely continuous but, if interrupted, caught up and continued, so as to convey an unmistakable unity of impression, as if all the other colors were set into its flexible framework, then, though *continuity* as well as *complication* are words borrowed from the relationships of lines, we may say that we have examples of the effects in coloring of both of these methods. See the general lines, though in these illustrations necessarily indicated only by light and shade, in Figs. 38, page 75; 75, page 142; 102, page 235; and 129, page 359.

CHAPTER XXII.

SPECIAL EFFECTS OF COLORS WHEN PLACED SIDE BY SIDE.

Consonance—Importance of this Subject—Colors Placed Side by Side Produce Subjective Effects in the Eye—Successive Contrast or After-Image of Complementary Colors Following Colors Suddenly Obscured—A Similar Phenomenon among Sounds—Explanation of Differences between the Phenomena—Ordinary Explanation of the After-Images—Simultaneous Contrasts as in Shadows—Suggested Insufficiency of Reasons Ordinarily Given for Successive and Simultaneous Contrast—Suggestions with Reference to the Perception of Color—Nothing in the Organism to Throw Doubt upon these Suggestions—The Principle Involved Explains the Main Difference between Successive and Simultaneous Contrast—Colors Impart about them Tints of their Complementaries—These Effects on Light and Shade or on Light and Dark Neutral Surfaces as Produced by Warm and Cold Colors—By Different Tints and Shades—Same Effects as Produced on Colored Surfaces—Three Ways of Using Contrast to Relieve Objects from their Background.

CONSONANCE, the next art-method in the chart on page 3, is the element causing factors to be put together by way of *comparison* because they are alike in formative principles. How the theory is tenable that colors may differ and yet result from forms of vibrations having a common multiple, and all therefore coalescing and producing in the eye the sensation of an absolutely free, unimpeded, regularly recurrent vibratory thrill or glow, is suggested in Chapter XX. It is a further development of this suggestion to which attention will be directed in the present chapter.

On page 351, it was said that the art-methods which, in

the chart on page 3, precede *consonance*, and which we have now considered, determine the selection and arrangement of colors with reference, mainly, to their general effects in a painting considered as a whole; whereas *consonance* and the methods following it have to do mainly with the special effects of the colors when placed side by side. It may be said now, that, of all the methods, these latter are the most important because the most fundamental. In music, it is absolutely essential that all the tones sounded simultaneously as in chords, or in immediate succession, should fulfil certain physical and physiological requirements. If they do not, all the other art-methods, however scrupulously applied, cannot secure harmony. That the same is true with reference to the colors used side by side or one after another in the order of space is a fact which, even if not confirmed by our own observation, the investigations of science would have placed beyond dispute.

It was mentioned on page 332 that lines of vermilion drawn on an ultramarine ground, in other words, that vermilion and ultramarine in juxtaposition, produce in the eye the effect of purple. All colors placed side by side give rise to similar subjective effects. Under conditions favorable to such results, they may increase and diminish each other's brightness, change each other's hues, and even cause new colors in places where there are none.

The best way in which to come to recognize the full bearing of this fact, is to begin by studying, for a little, the phenomena respectively termed consecutive and simultaneous contrast. With the first of these we may become acquainted thus: If, after looking steadily for a few seconds at a white wafer on a black ground, we turn our eyes to a white or gray ground, with nothing on it, we often seem to see, nevertheless, a black after-image, as it is called, of the same shape as the wafer. If we look in the same way at a bluish-green wafer, and then turn our eyes to the gray ground, we often find on it an after-image of red, *i. e.*, of the color which complements the bluish-green. So, if we try other colors, as a rule we find their complementary colors in the after-images. If, when we turn our eyes away from the wafer, the surface at which we look be of the same color as the wafer, the complementary color in the after-image is pale and faint; if the surface be of the color complementary to that of the wafer, the complementary after-image is more brilliant than its own color which forms the background. If the surface be of any other color, the complementary color of the after-image blends with it and produces a new mixed color. In this way the after-image of the bluish-green wafer would be red on a white surface, faint red on a bluish-green, brilliant red on a red, violet (*i. e.*, mixed with blue) on a blue, orange (*i. e.*, red mixed with yellow) on a yellow, and so on.

Before attempting an explanation of this phenomenon, it is well to notice a correspondence between it and an effect produced in connection with musical tones. If we hold down the key of a piano, which if struck would sound g,—and the same would be true were we to hold down keys sounding one or two other of the lower partial tones of C′, as indicated in the music on page 341, —and then strike violently the key of the lower bass C′, lifting our finger instantly so as to cause the hammer to press against the string and check its sound, we shall in most cases hear a sound, but it will be that of the string the key of which we are holding down, and which therefore we have left free to vibrate. In other words, we produce one sound and, when its tone is checked, we hear not it but another with which it is in harmony, as is said. What is it that produces this other sound? Evidently the string left free to vibrate, because its tone is the only sound that we hear. But what has caused this string to vibrate? A sound-wave, of course. But a sound-wave—as proved by experiments with tuning-forks which produce no partial tones, and therefore never respond except to waves produced by a tone of their own pitch,—causes no string to vibrate except a string keyed to respond to a form of wave that exists in its own form. Therefore it is argued that the sound-wave caused by the string struck must have been compounded; and have contained, as one of its constituent elements, a sound-wave fitted to influence sympathetically the string sounding. This is the theory now universally adopted, especially as it is found that only certain strings will sound thus, and that these are invariably strings producing tones that are in harmony with the tone of the string struck. But notice, now, that that which causes the vibrations of the string that sounds, is not the string itself, which is only a means, but the sound-wave. Why, then, could not the wave without other strings cause other sounds? It certainly could. Faint accompanying tones, and even after-tones, are sometimes clearly distinguishable in the main tones of certain instruments, like violins and bugles. They are usually heard ringing very distinctly after the main tones of church bells and low-pitched steam whistles, while, as shown on page 225 of "Rhythm and Harmony in Poetry and Music," bass notes are sometimes heard in connection with chords containing two notes, both comparatively high. Now, in such cases, what are we to consider the results,—as always objective? No; as sometimes subjective, in just as true a sense as in the case of the after-image produced in the eye according to the method described in the last paragraph. This much for those who claim, as some do, that the phenomena of sound are objective, and those of color subjective, and therefore cannot be treated as analogous.

It is true that in the case of sounds we may hear not merely one harmonic over-tone or under-tone, but sometimes others, while we can never see more than one complementary color. But the limitation in the realm of sight has a cause. The numbers of vibrations in musical tones are doubled six or seven times in order to produce the six or seven octaves or scales ordinarily used; whereas the numbers of the vibrations causing the colors are never doubled,—for one reason, probably, because, owing to their minute dimensions, trillions of them being produced in a single second, all variations needed in them can be produced without their being doubled.

There is nothing, therefore, among the colors to correspond to different octaves. All possible hues can be represented within the limits of a single octave. It is true that the terms *high* and *low* are often applied, respectively, to bright and dull shades or tints of the same hue; and this fact is often supposed to warrant an analogy between *high* and *low* scales in music. But the analogy is justified only in the sense in which the key of C sharp, because this note is half a tone higher than C natural, is higher than the key of C natural. Between red and orange there is not, as between C and D in music, a single interval, like C sharp, that can be used, but trillions of intervals, any one of which may be chosen, as one might say, for the keytone of a different color-scale. While, therefore, there is an analogy between high tones and high colors, we must not suppose that it involves the existence among the colors of any such relationships as exist in music between scales a full octave apart. With this in mind, notice the music on page 341. It represents notes that are caused by vibrations respectively two, three, four, five, six, seven, eight, nine, and ten times as rapid as those causing the lower C, F, or G, immediately below them. These are the notes among which alone can be found, owing to the law mentioned on page 340, the after-tones which we are now considering. But notice that in the lowest octave in which any note except C appears, there is only one note, G or g. This, therefore, is the partial tone, whose relation to the prime tone most fitly represents the nearest relationship that can exist between harmonic colors. Such being the case, it is worth observing that the ratio between the vibrations causing a C and a G, when both are in the same octave, is, so far as can be made out, very nearly if not exactly the same as the ratio between the vibrations causing any given color and causing the color most nearly corresponding to that which, when produced in the spectrum, is termed its complementary. For the proof of this, see page 401.

It is not usually argued that these apparent correspondences result from any actual correspondence between the actions of the organs of sight and of hearing. The explanation for after-images that is most often considered satisfactory, is that certain of the possibilities of energy, or certain organs in the eye, which alone are sensitive to the color of the wafer held before it, as indicated on page 371, have become fatigued by looking at this, and have thus been made insensible to the general effects of the light, whereas all the other possibilities or organs, meantime, have been rested. Accordingly, when the eye turns where white light takes the place of the color of the wafer, all the other ingredients of this light affect it before that one which has been seen in the wafer. All these other ingredients, as we know, produce the color complementary to that of the wafer. Therefore when we look away from the wafer's color, we see its complementary.

As we shall find presently, this theory probably contains a glimmer of truth. But that much more is needed in order to make it a satisfactory explanation, will appear when, from successive contrast, as it is termed, we turn to consider simultaneous contrast. What is meant by this will be gathered from the following. Charles Blanc, in his "Grammar of Painting and Engraving," tells us that Eugène Delacroix, occupied one day in painting yellow drapery, tried in vain to give it the desired brilliancy, and said to himself, "How did Rubens and Veronese find such brilliant and beautiful yellows?" He resolved to go to the Louvre, and ordered a carriage. It was in 1830. At that time in Paris there were many cabs painted canary-color. One of these was brought to him. About to step into it, he stopped short, observing to his surprise that the yellow of the carriage produced violet in the shadows. He dismissed the coachman, entered his studio full of emotion, and applied at once the law that he had just discovered, which is, that the shadow cast by an object of a certain hue is always slightly tinged with the *complement* of that hue,—a phenomenon that becomes apparent when the light of the sun is not too strong, and our eyes, as Goethe says, who, as Eckermann tells us in his "Conversations," made a similar discovery, "rest upon a fitting background to bring out the complementary."

Such being the fact with reference to simultaneous contrast, to what can we attribute it? Is it conceivable that it is owing to any such cause as that which has just been said to be accepted as an explanation of successive contrast? Is it probable that the parts of the retina surrounding those on which the colored image is impressed could become fatigued because of the latter's proximity, and rest from fatigue by producing the complementary color? Hardly. Yet it is certainly philosophical to attribute both simultaneous and successive contrast to the same cause—is it not? And it is also philosophical to attribute both of them to a cause similar to that occasioning similarly subjective effects in the ear. Moreover, we know what causes these effects in the ear. It is the intensity, rates, and shapes of certain sound-waves. Why are not the subjective effects in the eye caused by the same characteristics in sight-waves? When the question is thus asked, probably every one who knows anything about the subject will be ready to answer, "It would seem so." But if he can give this answer, why should he not seek to explain the phenomena of successive and simultaneous contrasts by going back to that which is thus acknowledged to seem probable?

One reason, perhaps, is that an exceedingly important distinction has been overlooked. It is this,—that the organs or parts of the organs that vibrate in the eye in sympathetic response to the waves of what we may term *light in general*, as in the atmosphere, are much more susceptible to slight excitation, *i. e.*, they are more readily started and kept in a vibratory condition, than are the organs or parts of organs that respond sympathetically to the waves of light in particular, as in what is termed *local color*. This is shown by the fact, among others, that we perceive light at dawn, long before we can make out either outlines or the shades and tints that indicate them.

See also what is said on page 381. Now in connection with the fact just mentioned, which apparently must have some cause in the organism, let us consider another. It is the fact that when color is seen in an object, it is because the particles of this object have some effect corresponding to that produced by the dividing of the rays of light, through the use of the fine prism mentioned on page 331. But if such be the case, two colors are then produced, at least potentially. One is seen by the eye. What becomes of the other color?—or of the other part of the potentiality which was in the light before this other color was taken from it? Or, to state the question in terms of physics, if the sight-wave fitted to start in the eye vibrations[1] giving a sensation of *light in general*, be divided, and changed in form so as to give a sensation of color, must not the rest of the wave also be changed in form? It cannot be answered that the whole of the wave causing light in general passes into the form of the particular color-wave. If it did, we should have a condition strangely overlooked by physicists but that in this case would be inevitable,—namely, we should not be able to distinguish moonlight from a gray wall extending everywhere in front of us, or a pitch-dark night from a black wall. As things are, however, we see at every part of an object, not only *light in general* but *light in particular*,— *i. e.*, its own color. When looking at the object, therefore, the eye's organism must always be influenced by two forms of waves,—those giving rise to the sensation of *light in general*, as in atmosphere with its various direct and reflected rays, and those giving rise to the sensation of the

---

[1] The reader will observe that waves which are external to the eye are one thing, and that vibrations within the eye which are occasioned by the waves are another thing.

color perceived. But from the forms of the atmospheric waves, in this case, the wave-forms of the color have been taken. What have been left behind?—The wave-forms of the complementary color. Inasmuch as we see the color in the object before us, the eye undoubtedly is under the *direct* influence of these waves alone. They exert a strong and positive effect, causing strong and positive vibrations in the parts of the eye fitted to respond to their excitation. But what of the other wave-forms? At best their influence is *indirect*. They are weak and negative, almost entirely suppressed where the color-waves are operating, and, at a slight distance from the place where they start, they must pass like lesser waves at the edge of a whirlpool into the forms of the *general light-waves* of the surrounding atmosphere. This would cause the perception of a slight complementary color for a slight distance on every side of the place in which there was a distinct perception of the main color; and would account, therefore, for simultaneous contrast. Now remove the object causing the color, what would happen? The color-waves would cease to excite vibrations in what, on page 377, were said to be the parts of the organs susceptible to only comparatively great excitation, and these organs would therefore cease to vibrate. But how about the other organs, or parts of the organs,—those fitted to vibrate to the sensations of *light in general?* Would they cease to do this?—Not as long as there was any light visible. But what would be the form of their vibrations immediately after the object occasioning the color-waves ceased to exert an influence?—What but the form of the vibrations caused by the waves of light immediately surrounding—and not only so but accompanying—the color-waves, while these were direct, positive, and strong? What was this form? It was the form giving a sensation of light in general when, from that light, had been taken the wave-form giving the sensation of a particular local color. Therefore, it was the wave-form producing the complementary of this local color. This wave-form of the complementary had been operating all the time. But the strong, positive color-wave had kept it from exerting any influence except by way of conveying an impression of light in general, or atmosphere, and, while doing this, of producing, in places near the local color, the effects of simultaneous contrast. As soon, however, as the color-wave has ceased to exert an influence, this wave of *light in general*, which now contains the potentiality of the complementary color, keeps the more susceptible vibratory organism oscillating on till after a little it has assumed its usual condition representative of all the colors.

As confirming this conception, let us notice that the suggestions that have been made are not inconsistent

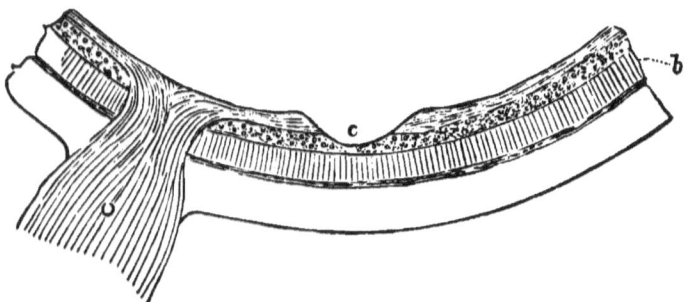

FIG. 130.—SECTION OF RETINA.
O, optic nerve; *b*, bacillary layer; *c*, central spot.
See pages 349, 380, 383.

with what we know of the formation of the organs of the eye. Fig. 130, represents the back part of the retina, and *b* the bacillary layer containing the rods and

PERCEPTION OF COLOR BY THE EYE. 381

cones, as they are called. Where the optic nerve enters the retina at O, the eye is blind. This seems to prove that the bacillary layer is necessary to sight. But this layer contains the rods and cones, as represented in Fig. 131. These are said in Foster's "Physiology" to be transparent, refractive, doubly refractive, and very sensitive to light, changing in size in different degrees of it. Possibly they may act in some way analogously to prisms. But however they may act, Fig. 131 shows that the rods because smaller should be more sensitive to slight vibratory effects than the cones; and Fig. 128, page 350, shows that the central spot, which sees outlines and colors the most distinctly, contains only cones. Are the rods, therefore, affected, according to what was said on page 379, by light in general, and the cones by local color? Again, each rod and cone possesses two entirely separated limbs, the larger of which is nearer the main body of the nerves than the smaller. If a wave of white light affect each limb similarly,

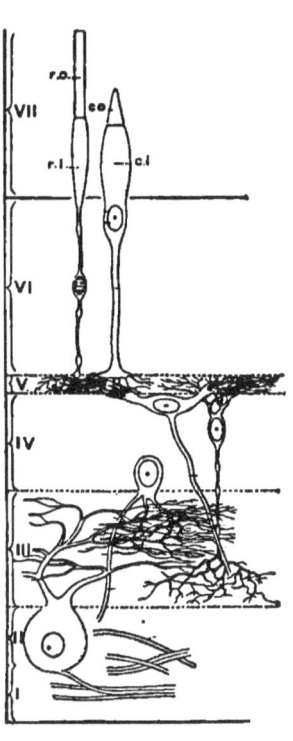

FIG. 131.—STRUCTURE OF RETINA.

c, cone; r, rod; i, inside; o, outside. I, II, etc., different layers as arranged from the front where light enters to the back.

See pages 349, 381, 383.

this wave divided and changed in form, as when color is produced, must affect each differently. In this case is the larger cone-limb affected by the local color-wave, and the smaller, with reflecting rods near it, by the twin complementary color-wave? All around the rods and cones, and inside the former, a purplish-blue liquid is constantly advancing and receding. It has been supposed that the sole purpose of this is to record different degrees of light and shade. But, while recording these, it may do very much more. Most of us must have noticed, when the power is turned from an electric light, that the one platinum wire vibrating at different rates produces all the warm colors,—white-yellow, yellow, orange, and red; and it is a fact easily shown that these colors respectively, when shining through blue glass, produce all the cold colors, —blue, green, olive-green, and purple. The attributing of articulative sounds to different rates and forms of vibrations when affecting the same ossicles in the ear suggested to Professor Bell that apparatus for converting the vibrations in an electric wire into sounds which made the telephone a success. Why is it not reasonable to suppose that the same rods or cones, when vibrating differently, shaded or not by blue, can produce all the colors, so that the mind can see them as well as the outlines in the picture impressed upon the retina. Another thought: vibrations of particles of matter against one another or the air usually generate heat. Heat thus generated usually generates chemical action. Different rates of vibration—and this is why, as has been proved, it is true of different colors—generate different degrees of heat and of chemical action. Chemical action, so scientists tell us, manifested in the pulling down and building up of tissue, is the method through which the nerves communicate sensations. What then? The author is aware that he has suggested an explanation of the way in which sound-waves or sight-waves may affect the organs of the ear or eye, and through them the nerves and the mind back of them, which is not in the books. But can any explanation be found in them as plausible, or as free from objections, as is this one? Certainly it is not any explanation ascribing the recognition of any pitch or color to a separate organ fitted to respond sympathetically to it and to it alone. So far, at least, as concerns the organism, as represented in Figs. 130 and 131, there is no reason to suppose otherwise than that all the rods and cones may be equally fitted to respond to the waves of light of any color, and yet with different degrees of susceptibility, some —possibly the rods—representing only atmospheric light and color, and some—possibly the cones—that color which appears to be local.

The explanation thus suggested not only refers to a similar cause the subjective effects both in the ear and the eye, and, in the latter, both successive and simultaneous contrast, but it seems to explain also the most important difference between the effects of successive and of simultaneous contrast. This is that the time of the continuance and the brilliancy of a color in successive contrast depend upon the length and strength of the vibratory condition preceding it, whereas, in simultaneous contrast, such effects depend neither upon the length of time during which one looks at a color, nor even upon its comparative fulness. This difference is exactly what, according to our hypothesis, we should expect. According to it, the continuance and character of the oscillations occasioning successive contrast will, of course, be determined by the quantity and quality of their previous excitation. On the contrary, the complementary color produced in simultaneous contrast depends upon the presence by its side of the local color, and it is neither increased nor lessened in intensity by its continued presence. Moreover, in every place where this complementary hue can become visible, there is already some other shade or tint with which its hue must blend, and doing so, according to the laws of color, it must always produce a mixed, and therefore never, save in very exceptional cases, a brilliant effect.

Even if the explanations of these phenomena thus suggested may do nothing toward rendering them and their bearings upon the subject before us more intelligible, they may, at least, serve to emphasize certain facts which, as facts, are indisputable. The most important of these is that all colors have the effect of imparting the tints of their complementaries to any surface adjoining their own. In such cases, if the surface have no color, they give it colors; if it have their complementary color, they make this more brilliant; if it have some other color yet not their own, they cause this and their complementary to blend and produce a mixed color different from either.

In the production of these complementary tints most important influences are traceable to degrees of light and shade. Experiments with the color-top show that when disks are so arranged that a single color is both on the circumference and in the centre, while a narrow circular band of white and black is between them,—that in this case, during the revolution of the top, this circular band appears to be not gray (*i. e.*, white and black) but of a color complementary to that on either side of it. This is as we should expect. But it has been found also that, in such an arrangement, the warm colors produce the brightest complementaries when there is more black than white in this circular band, and that the cold colors do the same when there is more white than black in it. The reason is evident. The warm colors are brighter than their complementaries and the cold colors darker. By consequence, the most favorable conditions for producing a complementary are present when the warm colors are brighter and the cold darker than the gray which is beside them. As each different color, too, represents a different degree of dark or light of course the gray, which is to receive the contrast, must represent a corresponding degree of light or dark. It is important to notice, besides this, that the cold colors, because they have warm or bright complementaries, invariably produce stronger contrasts on neutral hues than do the warm colors, for which reason it is often less difficult to obtain quiet, unobtrusive effects through using the warm. Now let us consider the influence of these near colors on a neutral ground as produced by different shades and tints. If, in trying the experiment with the color-top just mentioned, we take full colors and look at them in bright sunlight, we hardly perceive any complementary color at all cast on the gray. In the darkened corner of a room, however, where the colors appear no longer full but dark, the contrasting color is often very vivid. Again, if instead of full colors we take broken colors, *i. e.*, colors mixed with much white, the complementaries appear vivid even in sunlight. Accordingly, we see that the conditions most favorable for producing contrasts on a neutral ground are realized when we use dark colors, or broken. The explanation, more psychological than physical, which is ordinarily given for these facts, as stated by Von Bezold, is that "the eye is most sensitive to the contrasting colors in those cases in which, on account of the darkness or paleness of the colors, it is left in uncertainty as to the hue of the ground, that is to say, the hue of the inducing color actually present." A better explanation seems obtainable by recalling the fact that a complementary is always produced by the rays representing the difference between a full color and white light. A color is dark because it contains comparatively little light, and pale or broken because, in connection with much light, it contains comparatively little color. In these circumstances the complementary, because it contains either more light or more color than the hue producing it, appears brighter than it would otherwise,—a statement which accords with the facts already noticed (see page 334), that dark colors have light complementaries, which they produce best on light-colored surfaces; while light colors have dark complementaries, which they produce best on dark surfaces. In connection with this, it is well to notice that a black surface receives a complementary color only in the degree in which it contains some gloss or light, which is an additional reason for supposing that the presence or absence of light is that which determines the strength of the contrast.

Now let us examine the effects of complementary colors not on neutral but on colored surfaces. Here we notice that when two of these surfaces are placed in juxtaposition, each appears as if some of the complementary of the other had been mixed with it. Of course, the laws applying to the blending of colors with neutral gray apply here ; and to refer once more to the subject that we have just left, a confirmation of the view presented in the last paragraph may be found in the fact that invariably very light broken colors are those that impart their complementaries most strongly.[1] For this reason, such colors are peculiarly adapted for brilliant effects ; and we find them used for this purpose almost exclusively by the great colorists of Venice and the Netherlands.

[1] The following, from Professor Rood's " Modern Chromatics," chapter

Before leaving this subject it may be of interest to notice three prominent ways of using contrasts in order to relieve objects from their backgrounds. They are taken from Von Bezold's "Theory of Color."

I. The object may be a silhouette, light against a dark ground, or dark against a bright ground. In both cases usually, and in the latter case almost necessarily, the warm color should be in the foreground.

II. The light parts of the object may be lighter than the ground and the dark parts darker. Applied to coloring, this is best exemplified where neutral tints are given to the ground, while near objects are made warmer than the ground in their warm parts, and colder in their cold parts.

III. The bright side of the object may be placed on a

xv., p. 245, indicates the changes produced upon each other by the more important colors when thus brought together.

CHANGES DUE TO CONTRAST IN PAIRS OF COLORS.

Red............becomes more purplish.	Orange............becomes more yellowish.
and	and
Orange.......... " " yellowish.	Violet............ " " bluish.
Red............. " " purplish.	Yellow........... " " orange-yellow.
and	and
Yellow........... " " greenish.	Green........... " " bluish-green.
Red............ " " brilliant.	Yellow........... " " orange-yellow.
and	and
Blue-green...... " " brilliant.	Cyan-blue....... " " blue.
Red............ " " orange-red.	Yellow........... " " brilliant.
and	and
Blue............. " " greenish.	Ultramarine-blue. " " brilliant.
Red............ " " orange-red.	Green........... " " yellowish-green.
and	and
Violet........... " " bluish.	Blue............ " " purplish.
Orange........., " " red-orange.	Green........... " " yellowish-green.
and	and
Yellow........... " " greenish-yellow.	Violet........... " " purplish.
Orange.......... " " red-orange.	Greenish-yellow. " " brilliant.
and	and
Green........... " " bluish-green.	Violet............ " " brilliant.
Orange.......... " " brilliant.	Blue............ " " greenish.
and	and
Cyan-blue....... " " brilliant.	Violet........... " " purplish.

dark ground, and its shaded side on a light ground; *i. e.*, the warm side of an object may be placed against a cold ground, and the cold side against a warm ground. This was the usual method of the painters of the Netherlands, and is adopted very generally by the best painters of our own times.

CHAPTER XXIII.

COLOR-SCALES.

Object of this Chapter—Colors can be Used together that Differ either Slightly or Greatly—Theory that Two, Three, or More can be Used together if they Make White—Theory Based on Construction of Color-Scales : Von Bezold's of Twelve Colors—Rood's Summary of Combinations of Colors Founded on Experience—Combinations Determined as in Musical Harmony by Ratios between the Numbers of Vibrations a Second Causing the Colors—All the Colors can Represent only the Ratios Possible to a Single Scale—Compensating Possibility of Variety in Each Color—Correspondences Need to be Found only between the Ratios Underlying the Harmonic Notes and the Harmonic Colors—The Ratio Expressive of the Two Chief Harmonics of Music aside from that of the Octave, which has no Analogue in Color—The Same Ratio as Applied to Color—The Tonic and Dominant Harmonize all the Notes of the Scale as the Two Complementaries Contain all the Colors of the Spectrum—The Tonic and Dominant Represent the Same Ratios as the Complementaries – Reasons for Apparent Exceptions—Ratios Expressive of the Three Harmonics in the Major Triad of Music—Same Ratios Applied to Triads of Colors—Recapitulation—A Fourth Color would Naturally Correspond to the Seventh in Music, a Result Approximating that Reached by Von Bezold—The Reason why Notes and Colors thus Related Satisfy the Senses—Similarity of Method in Determining Consonance either in Sound or Color.

WHAT has been said of the complementary colors will aid us in deciding what other colors are fitted to go together. For reasons already given, the principles underlying this subject apply more absolutely to decoration than to pictures, but, just as arrangements of sound in verse are satisfactory in the degree in which they fulfil such laws of harmony as apply to music, so arrangements of colors in pictures are satisfactory in the degree in which they fulfil such laws of harmony as apply to decoration. Although the painter of pictures does not use color merely for its own sake, he ought nevertheless to use it in such a way as to cause it, for its own sake, to be a source of interest and pleasure.

Glancing back at the scale of colors indicated in Von Bezold's chart, Fig. 127, page 334, the first thought that suggests itself is that slight differences in color can go together in case they be no greater than we are accustomed to see produced by different degrees of light upon different parts of the same fabric, and which result in no more than different tints or shades of the same hue. In this case, as stated on page 347, though the color-waves differ in intensity and extent, they do not necessarily differ in rate or shape. This is not true, however, when we come to colors between which there are not slight but decided differences, colors separated by what Von Bezold in his chart (page 334) would term a whole interval. Suppose that two of these be in juxtaposition. Each, as we know, casts its complementary on the other. But this complementary is on the opposite side of the chart, separated as far as any color can be from that on which it is cast. The result is that when the two, the complementary and the color that receives it, are mixed, the change is as great as can possibly be produced by a mixture of this kind. For instance, if red and violet be side by side, bluish-green mixes with the violet, tending to give it a bluish cast, and green mixes with the red, tending to give it a yellowish cast. The two colors, therefore, when placed together, appear to differ more than they really do. This suggests a law applicable universally to the arrangement of colors, viz., that when in juxtaposition, those which differ the least, change each other's peculiar hues the most; and sometimes dim them greatly. The reverse is also true, namely, that colors which differ the most, change each other's peculiar hues the least. On the contrary, they often reinforce them and render them more brilliant. This is so because the colors that differ the most, in the sense of being the farthest apart on the chart of colors, are those that are complementary, like red and bluish-green, for instance.

Having found out which colors, when adjoining, have the worst effects upon one another, and which the best effects, we are prepared to understand other principles that have come to be accepted with reference to the general subject. For arriving at these principles, several different methods are worthy of consideration, the results of which, however, are not essentially different, and all of which appear to contain elements of truth. To begin where we left off, it seems to be a logical deduction, from what has been said, that any colors can be placed together which together make white. These may be included in three classes: I. Any two which together make white, *i.e.*, the complementary colors; as red and bluish-green, orange and turquoise-blue, yellow and ultramarine, yellowish-green and violet, and green and purple. II. Any two which, mixed with one another's complementaries, can make white; as red and turquoise-blue, for instance, because the red imparts a bluish-green tint to the turquoise-blue, and the turquoise-blue an orange tint to the red. Undoubtedly, some of the most effective combinations or pairs of colors, not complementary, may be accounted for according to this rule. The two are harmonious because, especially when one of the colors is very bright, like vermilion, orange, or yellow, it is possible for the two, when in combination, to fulfil the principle causing us to use complementaries even better than would complementaries themselves. It is this fact, probably, that accounts for the satisfaction taken in the combinations of the colors brought together by the application of the first rule of Von Bezold, given below, the colors to which it applies being the same as those to which the rule now being considered applies, and very nearly the same as the colors formerly supposed to be complementary. But before we pass to Von Bezold's rules, we must add the following to the two principles already mentioned: III. Any three (and sometimes any number of) colors can go together which together or mixed with one another's complementaries can make white. This rule applies to the old-fashioned primaries, red, yellow, and blue, and to the secondaries, orange, green, and purple; in short, it reaches a result practically the same as that following the application of Von Bezold's second rule, which will be given in a moment.

Von Bezold, in determining what colors should be placed together, drops altogether the Field theory that those should be used which together make white. In lieu of this, he divides all the colors into twelve and arranges them on a scale (see Fig. 127, page 334) intended to represent much what the scale of twelve half-tones represents in music. This scale is drawn up, as he says (chapter iii., page 114), on the principle of having it show "how the color-chart would look if the lines of division were so arranged that the apparent difference in the hue of the color between each two compartments would remain the same upon the whole of the circumference." His first rule, a suggestion with reference to which has been made above, is that any two colors can be placed together which are separated in this scale by six intervals, *i. e.*, beginning with purple,

Purple and Green.
Carmine and Bluish-green.
Vermilion and Turquoise-blue.

Orange and Ultramarine.
Yellow and Bluish-violet.
Yellowish-green and Purplish-violet.

Experience has shown, he says, that these form even better combinations than do the complementary colors. His second rule, to which reference is also made on page 392, is that any three colors can go together which are separated by four intervals, *i. e.*,

Purple, Yellow, and Turquoise-blue.
Carmine, Yellowish-green, and Ultramarine.
Vermilion, Green, and Bluish-violet.
Orange, Bluish-green, and Purplish-violet.

His third rule, applying to four colors, is not what might be expected, viz., to take those separated on the chart by three intervals. This, he says, would bring into proximity colors too nearly connected on the chart; and it would also produce the effect of two pairs without indicating a design to do so. Instead of this, he advises marking the effect strongly by taking two pairs,—as, for example, purple and green, carmine and turquoise-blue,—one in each of which is near one in the other, and then arranging all the colors so that the near colors shall not meet.

In this connection, the reader will be pleased to have brought to his attention the exceedingly interesting and suggestive summary with reference to certain combinations of colors given in chapter xvii. of Rood's "Modern Chromatics." The reasons for the agreeableness or the opposite of many of these combinations, he says, "cannot be solved by the methods of the laboratory, or by the aid of a strictly logical process," but, nevertheless, what is said of them seems to accord in the main with practical experience. The tables are in the note below.[1]

The third method of arriving at the principles underlying the joining of colors is advocated by those who hold that as in music the ratios between the numbers of vibra-

---

[1] SPECTRAL RED (a red between carmine and vermilion) with *blue* gives its best combination—with *green* gives a strong but rather hard combination—with *yellow* gives an inferior combination—with *red lead* gives a bad combination—with *violet* gives a bad combination. If *gold* be substituted for the yellow pigment, the combination becomes excellent. *Red* and *yellow* also make a better combination when the red inclines to purple and the yellow to greenish-yellow. The combination *red* and *yellow* is also improved by darkening the yellow or both colors ; this causes the yellow to appear like a soft *olive-green*. The combination *red* and *green* is also improved by darkening both colors, or the green alone.

VERMILION with *blue* gives an excellent combination—also with *cyan-blue*—with *green* gives an inferior combination—also with *yellow*—with *violet* it gives a bad combination. *Vermilion* and *gold* furnish an excellent combination. The combination *vermilion* and *yellow* is improved somewhat by darkening the yellow ; if it is considerably darkened, it tells as a soft *olive-green*. *Vermilion* and *green* are better when the green or both colors are much darkened.

RED LEAD with *blue* gives an excellent combination—also with *cyan-blue* —with *blue-green* gives a strong but disagreeable combination—with *yellowish-green* gives a tolerably good combination—with *yellow* gives quite a good combination—also with *orange*. The combination *red lead* and *bluish-green* is improved by darkening the green or both the colors (R.). *Red lead* gives a better combination with a *yellow* having a corresponding intensity or saturation ; if the yellow is too bright the effect is inferior. The combination *red lead* and *yellow* is much better than *red* and *orange*.

ORANGE with *cyan-blue* gives a good and strong combination—also with *ultramarine*—with *green* gives a good combination—with *violet* gives a moderately good combination.

ORANGE-YELLOW with *ultramarine* gives its best combination—with *cyan-blue* gives not quite so good a combination—with *violet* gives a good combination—also with *purple*—with *purple-red* gives an inferior combination —with *spectral red* gives an inferior combination—with *sea-green* gives a bad combination.

YELLOW with *violet* gives its best combinations—with *purple-red* gives good

tions per second producing the different notes determine
which should go together, so, in painting, the ratios between the numbers of vibrations per second producing
the different colors should determine this. As a rule,
combinations—also with *purple*—with *spectral red* gives inferior combinations—with *blue*, inferior to orange-yellow and blue—with *blue-green* gives
one of the worst possible combinations—with *green* gives bad combinations.
The combination *yellow* and *spectral red* is improved by darkening the
yellow. *Blue-green* and *yellow*, both much darkened, give a better combination. According to Chevreul, *yellow* gives with *green* a good and lively
combination; to this the author cannot agree, although it is true that the
effect is improved by darkening the yellow considerably. *Chrome-yellow*
and *emerald-green* give combinations that are not bad when both the colors
are very much darkened.

GREENISH-YELLOW with *violet* gives its best combinations—with *purple*
gives good combinations—also with *purplish-red*—with *vermilion* gives
strong but hard combinations—with *spectral red* gives strong but hard combinations—with *red lead* gives tolerably good combinations—with *orange-yellow* gives bad combinations—also with *cyan-blue*—with *ultramarine* gives
a somewhat better combination. The combination *greenish-yellow* and
orange-yellow is improved by darkening the latter color, which then appears
brownish. *Greenish-yellow* and *cyan-blue* make a better combination when
the blue is darkened.

GRASS-GREEN with *violet* gives good but difficult combinations—also with
purple-violet—with *rose* gives combinations of doubtful value—also with
carmine—also with *pink*—also with *blue*. The value of the last four combinations is a disputed matter. The combination *green* and *carmine* is improved by darkening both colors considerably (R.). The combination
green and *blue* becomes better as the green inclines to yellow and the blue to
violet. The combination *green* and *violet*, according to Chevreul, is better
when the paler hues of these colors are employed.

EMERALD-GREEN with *violet* gives strong but hard combinations—also
with *purple*—also with *red*—also with *orange*—with *yellow* gives bad combinations. All these combinations are very difficult to handle. *Emerald-green* and *yellow*, when both are much darkened, furnish somewhat better
combinations.

SEA-GREEN with *vermilion* gives good combinations—also with *red lead*
—also with *violet*—with *purple-violet* gives tolerably good combinations—
with *purple-red* gives, simply as pairs, poor combinations—with *carmine*
gives, simply as pairs, poor combinations—with *blue* gives bad combinations

physicists have had little respect for any advocate of this
theory, because he has usually started out with the
hypothesis that there is some absolute and necessary connection between the seven colors of the spectrum and the

—also with *yellow*. The surface of the *green* should be much larger than
that of the *vermilion* or *red lead*.

CYAN-BLUE with *chrome-yellow* gives moderate combinations—with *Naples
yellow* gives good combinations—also with *straw-yellow*—also with *carmine*
(light tones)—with *violet* gives poor combinations—also with *purple-violet*—
with *ultramarine* gives good combinations (small interval). The combinations of *cyan-blue* with *violet* and *purple-violet* are not good except in fine
materials and light tones.

ULTRAMARINE with *carmine* gives poorer combinations than cyan-blue—
with *purple-red* gives poorer combinations than cyan-blue—with *purple* gives,
simply as pairs, poor combinations.

VIOLET with *purple* gives poor combinations if extended beyond the small
interval—with *carmine* gives poor combinations.

The triads that have been most extensively used are: I. *Spectral red,
yellow, blue*. II. *Purple-red, yellow, cyan-blue*. III. *Orange, green,
violet*. IV. *Orange, green, purple-violet*. V. *Carmine, yellow, and green*
was, according to Brücke, a triad very much used during the Middle Ages,
though to us the combination is apt to appear somewhat hard and unrefined.
Here we have two warm colors (see page 327), but contrast is twice sacrificed;
that is, slightly in the case of the carmine and yellow, and more with the
yellow and green. VI. *Orange-yellow, violet*, and *bluish-green* is an example of a combination which is poor not from defect of contrast, but because
it contains two cold colors, one of them being the coldest in the chromatic
circle. VII. *Vermilion, green*, and *violet-blue* is a triad which has been
extensively used in some of the Italian schools. At first sight we have here
apparently two cold colors; but as the green was olive-green, the combination really amounts to—VIII. *Vermilion, dark greenish-yellow*, and *violet-
blue*, and corresponds in principle with those given above.

In the employment of any of these triads in painting or in ornament, the
artist can of course vary the hue of the three colors through the small interval
without destroying the definite character of the chromatic composition; and
even small quantities of foreign colors can also be added. When, however,
they begin to assume importance in the combination, they destroy its peculiar
character. White or gray can be introduced, and one of these is often used
with a happy effect, particularly in the triads *orange, green, violet; purple-
red, yellow, cyan-blue*.—Abbreviated from Rood's "Modern Chromatics."

seven notes of the musical scale. As was shown, however, in Chapter XIV. of " Rhythm and Harmony in Poetry and Music," these seven notes happen to be used merely as a matter of convenience. There have been scales extensively used of four and six notes, and possibly our own might be improved by the addition of two more. As it is, it contains not seven but twelve distinct intervals. There is a principle, however, underlying the formation of all musical scales, as well as of all melody and harmony, which depends upon the relative numbers of vibrations. One cannot refrain from feeling, therefore, that it is logical to suppose that this same principle should be exemplified in that which causes colors to harmonize.

It does not allay this feeling, to remind one that between, say, the 400 trillions of vibrations causing extreme red and the 750 causing extreme violet, the sum total of vibrations does not correspond to those of a single octave. It does correspond to the musical scale, so far as this can be produced without doubling one of its notes. It corresponds to all the intervals between *do* and *si* inclusive. If an upper *do* were represented, then, to make everything consistent, an upper *re, mi*, etc., should be represented. Otherwise one of the colors—that corresponding to *do*—would have double the value of each of the others. As it is, we have in the colors all the range of intervals corresponding to those of a single octave without encroaching upon a second. The possibility, however, of producing variations in a single color is much greater than that of doing the same in a single sound. Indeed, when we consider the innumerable shades and tints not merely of one color but of all other colors in connection with which this one may produce mixed effects, we are forced to recognize that the range both of single colors and of those that are exactly complementary to these is practically infinite, and thus far more than sufficient to make up for the absence in the color-scale of more than one octave.

So much for the theory; now for the facts confirming it. Let us take the ratios of the numbers of vibrations producing the sounds, not of all the scale, but of those that harmonize, and apply these ratios to the numbers of vibrations producing the different colors, and notice what colors they cause to go together. As the numbers of vibrations producing the colors are exceedingly great, and the difficulty in the spectrum of determining just where one color leaves off and another begins is also great, we must content ourselves with approximate measurements, but even with these we can attain our object. Let Von Bezold, too, who is opposed to this theory, confirm it by the numbers representing tens of trillions of vibrations which he has indicated for the colors placed in his chart (Fig. 127, page 334), and by the lines indicating single degrees of these with which he has divided the next to the outer circle.

In any given musical scale—aside from the notes that are an octave apart, represented by the ratio 1 : 2, and with which there is nothing in color, as has been said, to correspond—the notes most nearly related—to take them as represented in the scale of C'—are C, c, and g. This may be recognized by a single glance at the partial tones, as indicated in the music on page 341. In that, the numbers 1, 2, 3, 4, etc., will be observed just at the left of the notes respectively marked by the letters C', C, g, and c. The numbers represent, in another way, the same as those used by Pythagoras, when he divided a string into two, three, four, etc., parts, and found the note produced by each part to be in harmony with that produced by the whole string and by each other part. The numbers represent also that $C' : C :: 1 : 2$, that $C' : g :: 1 : 3$, and $C' : c :: 1 : 4$, as well as that $C : g :: 2 : 3$ and $g : c :: 3 : 4$. Our object now is to find the relationships of two notes contained within the limits of the same octave that can represent the relationships between the particular C or c and the g that we wish to use. Shall we take $C : g :: 2 : 3$, or $g : c :: 3 : 4$? In which of the two formulæ are both factors most nearly related in the same way to the fundamental base C'? Is it not in $g : c :: 3 : 4$? In this, g is the third note from C'; and c, though the fourth note, is the third c from C'; and g is related to the whole lower octave C'–C precisely as c is. Is not this ratio of $3 : 4$, therefore, the one best fitted to represent the ratio between the complementary colors? Here, as in other places, a reference to music may assist us. The most important chords in harmonizing the notes of any scale are undoubtedly those the bases of which are the tonic (*i. e.*, C in the scale of C) and the dominant (*i. e.*, G in the scale of C). Moreover, according to the conventionalities of music, when we come to a final cadence, the order of the succession of the fundamental bass notes which causes the cadence to be satisfactory to the ear, is from the dominant (g) to the tonic (c) above it and not to the C below it; *i. e.*, to c, representing $g : c$, or the ratio $3 : 4$, and not to C, representing $C : g$, or the ratio $2 : 3$. Next to the chords of the tonic and the dominant, the most important chord, in fact the only one that is important, as will be seen by a glance at the music on page 343, is that of the sub-dominant (*i. e.*, of F in the scale of C). But the second bar of the music on page 341 will show that C is related to F exactly as G is related to C, C being the dominant when

F is the tonic, just as G is the dominant when C is the tonic. Here again, then, we have as the basis of harmony in this chord of the sub-dominant, the ratios either of 2 : 3 or of 3 : 4. But the importance of the sub-dominant, as every one acquainted with modulation in music knows (see Chapter XV. of " Rhythm and Harmony in Poetry and Music "), is owing to the fact that it may be the tonic of a key whose dominant is the same note as the tonic of itself when the subdominant. We may say, therefore, that here, too, for the same reasons as were advanced above, the important ratio is 3 : 4, though, of course, considered merely as a factor of a scale in which the relation of the dominant to the tonic were represented by 3 : 4, the relation of the sub-dominant to the tonic would be represented by 2 : 3. In the earliest music only two of these chords—either the dominant with the tonic, or the subdominant with the tonic—were used in order to harmonize all the notes of their more limited musical scales, and even now it is possible, though not customary, to harmonize thus all the notes of our scale ; because the tones of the tonic and the dominant, as also of the tonic and (excepting the pitch for b or *si*) the sub-dominant, taken together represent all the notes of the scale, being composed of partial tones that contain them all. See the music on page 341. In the same way the complementary colors represent all the colors, because, taken together, they are compounded of them all. See page 331. Once more, the chords of the tonic and the dominant, or of the tonic and the subdominant, though related, appear, when alternating in succession, to be sharply contrasted. In fact, they are the chief sources from which, in perfect consistency with *unity*, all those modulations are developed which insure musical *variety*. (See " Rhythm and Harmony in Poetry and Music," Chapter XV.) Similarly, complementary colors, while related, are also contrasting colors.

Having said all this, it is now to be added that there is good reason to believe that the relation between the vibrations of complementary colors may be expressed by the same ratio as that between those of the dominant and the tonic above it, namely, 3 : 4. This good reason is that, although the slightest change in a hue makes an apparently great change in the numbers of its vibrations, yet notwithstanding this fact the calculations that have been made for the hues supposed to represent the colors that are exactly complementary, very nearly represent the exact ratio for which we are looking. It may be asked why we should content ourselves with this result—why we should not examine the complementary colors produced from light as explained on page 331, and expect to find them representing this ratio not very nearly but exactly. One answer is that, where waves are so minute as are those of color, it is hardly conceivable that the narrowest prism should divide the rays in such a manner as not to cut off entirely some of the light, and, therefore, as not to change the number of the vibrations causing each of the two colors produced. This is one reason why it seems necessary to content ourselves with approximate measurements. Wherever, in the list on page 402, the numbers of vibrations, according to Von Bezold's scale, do not approximate those used which indicate the ratio of 3 : 4, there is an interrogation mark. There should be considered in this calculation, too, the vibrations, omitted by Von Bezold, causing extreme red, numbering between 472 and 392 trillions, and those causing extreme violet, numbering between 727 and 773 trillions.[1] Here, among the vibra-

---

[1] It may be interesting to compare with these figures those given by Sir

tions causing colors, are those that would represent the ratio 3 : 4 : See Fig. 127, page 334.

	Number of Trillions of Vibrations.	Ratios.
Carmine-red	472	3 : 4
Bluish-green	630	
Vermilion	480	"
Turquoise-blue	640	
Orange or Vermilion	491	"
Turquoise-blue	655	
Orange (?)	500	"
Ultramarine (?)	666	
Yellow (?)	540	"
Bluish-violet (?)	720	
Yellowish-green	560	"
Violet	746	
Green	580	"
Purple	773	

It will be noticed that, with great accuracy for numbers so enormous, the ratio 3 : 4 in almost every case Thomas Young. They are as follows; and it will be found that in both columns the ratios representing the complementary colors approximate 3 : 4 :

	Breadth of Wave.	Vibrations per Second.
Extreme red	0000.266	458,000,000,000,000
Red	0000.256	477,000,000,000,000
Orange	0000.240	506,000,000,000,000
Yellow	0000.227	535,000,000,000,000
Green	0000.211	577,000,000,000,000
Blue	0000.196	622,000,000,000,000
Indigo	0000.185	658,000,000,000,000
Violet	0000.174	699,000,000,000,000
Extreme violet	0000.167	727,000,000,000,000

In one of the latest books on this subject, "Studies in Spectrum Analysis," by J. N. Lockyer, the number of vibrations causing extreme red light is given as 392,000,000,000,000; and causing extreme purple as 757,000,000,000,000.

expresses the relationship between complementaries. Where it does not, the boundary lines between the colors, as between yellow and orange, for instance, are exceedingly difficult to find on the spectrum, and we may be justified in doubting the computations from which the ratios have been derived. According to any view of the subject, it is remarkable how the conclusions drawn from these ratios coincide with those reached by Von Bezold, through an entirely different method. In its way, too, it confirms the trustworthiness of that scale.

Let us now consider the chords in music, that are formed by combinations of three notes. As shown on pages 217 and 225 of "Rhythm and Harmony," the most perfect chord of this kind is the major triad, represented by C, E, and G of the scale, or by *do*, *mi*, and *sol* of the solfeggio. The ratios between these notes are as follows:

do   mi   sol   ⎱ In these
1         $\frac{5}{4}$ $\frac{3}{2}$ ⎰ do is to mi as 4 : 5 and to sol as 2 : 3.

Let us apply these ratios to the colors. As a result, we get the very triads of colors which we have already obtained in two other ways. The numbers used indicate tens of trillions, with fractions below these either not considered or averaged. 45 for extreme red is taken from the computation of Young given in the note on page 401 ; 52 for orange-yellow is formed by taking an average between orange (50, as given on page 402) and yellow (54); and 60 for green not only corresponds exactly with Von Bezold's chart (Fig. 127, page 334), but is a result of an average between green (58, as indicated on page 402) and bluish-green (63).

Extreme red, 45.   Yellow-green, 56.   Ultramarine, 67.
Orange, 50.   Bluish-green, 63.   Purplish-violet, 75.
Orange-yellow (?), 52.   Turquoise-blue, 65.   Purple, 78.
Vermilion, 48.   Green, 60.   Bluish-violet, 72.

PROPORTION AND HARMONY.

To sum up the results obtained by comparing the numbers of vibrations per second of the sounds producing the musical chord with the numbers producing the colors that harmonize, we find that, although there is nothing representing the proportion 1:2, there are combinations corresponding to 2:3, 3:4, and 4:5. To understand the following, recall from page 400 that, in any scale, lower do (1) is to fa precisely as sol is to higher do ($\frac{1}{2}$), $i.\ c.$, as 3:4.

COLORS.	SOUNDS.			
Pairs (complementary)	do 1		fa $\frac{3}{4}$ ($\frac{4}{3}$)	
Triads (making white)	do 1	mi $\frac{4}{5}$ ($\frac{5}{4}$)		sol $\frac{2}{3}$ ($\frac{3}{2}$)

If now we wish to add a fourth color, and desire, in so doing, to follow out the analogy of music, we must use a color corresponding to the seventh si, and thus in the scale of colors very near the do. This would cause a selection of four colors, only two of which would affect one another so as to need to be separated in the way indicated by Von Bezold. See page 393.

One objection of this writer, as well as of others, to allowing the numbers of the vibrations producing the colors to have weight in determining which shall harmonize, is that these vibrations are too minute for the eye to recognize the difference between the numbers. Those who say this confuse the perception of an effect, which only is necessary in the eye, with the perception of its cause. As pointed out on page 344, the eye does not need to recognize the cause. When the forms of vibrations in adjoining organs of the retina coalesce, as they do when 2 vibratory movements of one organ occupy the same time as 3 of another, or 3 of one as 4 of another, or 4 of one as 5 of another, then the optic nerves experience a pleasurable thrill or glow, and this is all of which they need to be conscious.

Nor is there anything to gainsay the supposition that the forms of vibrations in adjoining parts of the retina may coalesce even when they are not related to one another as they are when producing the complementary colors. We may ascribe all that we know with reference to these colors, including both successive and simultaneous contrast (see pages 371 to 377) to physical organs so constituted that, when external waves of light are divided according to a ratio of 3 : 4, each of two parts into which these organs are correspondingly divided is affected in a peculiar way. But this fact—if it be a fact—need not make less plausible the supposition that, when the divisions of the external color-waves are related not only as 3 : 4 but also as 2 : 3 or 4 : 5, they may cause the vibrations of both these parts taken together to coalesce with those of other adjoining organs, and thus fulfil other conditions tending to render complete the analogies between the color-waves and the sound-waves as well as between the physiological effects which they respectively produce in the eye and the ear.

CHAPTER XXIV.

ADDITIONAL ART-METHODS CAUSING COLOR-HARMONY.

Dissonance and Interchange—Criticism by Sir Joshua Reynolds—Gradation —Suggested by Nature—Physiological Explanation of—Abruptness— Transition and Progress.

A FEW paragraphs more will contain everything not yet considered that needs to be said with reference to the influence upon harmony of the art-methods mentioned in the chart on page 3. In painting, as in music, *dissonance* is the occasionally necessary use, when representing the *variety* that is found in nature, of discordant coloring; and *interchange* aided by *gradation* harmonizes it. Notice what Von Bezold says, on page 393, of the arrangement of inharmonious colors by separating them. In Chapter XV., page 214, of "Rhythm and Harmony in Poetry and Music" the influence of interchange is shown upon the effects of musical chords and keys that otherwise would be inharmonious. Its influence in painting is similar. Various colors in one part of a picture, that correspond to colors in another part, whatever discordant colors may intervene, if these be not side by side, may make the whole harmonious through *interchange*. This effect, like that of *balance* which it closely resembles, is usually considered psychological. But it is not wholly so. Like balance, too, it may be explained physiologically on the ground that, although the vibrations in the retina may not absolutely coalesce, those that do not coalesce are, in the first place, separated so that the optic nerve is as little conscious of the fact as is possible, and, in the second place, are distributed so that in different places the differences between forms of vibrations are the same, producing a general effect of likeness in methods of contrariety which compensates in the same way in which *balance* always does, for a likeness in more essential regards.

Just how it does this is well brought out in the following criticism on the "Bacchus and Ariadne" of Titian. The criticism is attributed to Sir Joshua Reynolds; though the writer does not recall seeing it in any of his works. But it corresponds with something to the same effect which may be found in his " Eighth Discourse," and is worth repeating aside from its source. " If we supposed two bits of color omitted, namely, the red scarf of Ariadne in the upper and colder portion of the picture, and a blue drapery on the shoulders of a nymph in the lower and warmer portion, it would leave the composition divided into two masses of color, the one hot and the other cold ; the warm portion comprehending the reds, yellows, and browns of the foreground, and the cold portion comprehending the blues, grays, and greens of the sky and trees; and this, as in the rainbow with the green omitted, would be productive of great breadth, but it would be destructive of union and consequently of harmony, for it would leave the cold and warm colors as entirely unconnected as though they were separate designs on one canvas. To correct this, and restore the union, Titian has carried up the warm tints of the foreground into the sky or cold portion of the picture by means of the red scarf on the shoulders of Ariadne, and brought down the cold tints of the sky into the foreground by the blue mantle on the shoulders of the nymph in the lower or warmer portion of the picture;

and thus, by dividing the painting into masses of warm and cold colors, has preserved the greatest breadth by the opposition of warm and cold colors; has increased their splendor by exchanging those of one side for those of another, as just stated; has produced union and harmony; and, at the same time, preserved that variety so characteristic of nature's coloring. Nor is this all; for by a faithful imitation of those reflections which one object throws off upon another in its immediate neighborhood, and by that balance of light and dark colors which gives poise and symmetry, and by that tone produced by passing a thin transparent color over the entire surface (a process called glazing), assimilating and softening down the most opposite tints to

" ' Tones so just, in such gradations thrown,
Adopting Nature claims the work her own,'

he has combined in one design all those excellent qualities upon which depends perfection in this part of art."

As *interchange* separates the same colors, *gradation*, which is the next method in the chart on page 3, blends different colors, making them pass into one another by imperceptible degrees. For reasons that will be apparent without explanation, this method is almost necessarily attendant upon all effects of *principality*, in which the main color needs to be connected with the *subordinate* colors; as well as of *central-point* or *radiation*, in which the bright colors are connected with the dull ones, and of *massing*, in which cumulated colors of one kind are connected with surrounding colors of other kinds.

The necessity for *gradation* is suggested by nature. Owing to the operation of light and shade and of variety in outline, distance, and texture, there is hardly a square inch in the field of vision in which the colors appear to be absolutely the same. To quote from Rood's "Modern Chromatics": "One of the most important characteristics of color in nature is the endless, almost infinite, gradations which always accompany it. It is impossible to escape from the delicate changes which the color of all natural objects undergoes owing to the way the light strikes them, without taking all the precautions necessary for an experiment in a physical laboratory. Even if the surface employed be white and flat, still some portions of it are sure to be more highly illuminated than others, and hence to appear a little more yellowish or less grayish; and besides this source of change, it is receiving colored light from all colored objects near it, and reflecting it variously from its different portions. If a painter represent a sheet of paper in a picture by a uniform white or gray patch, it will seem quite wrong, and cannot be made to look right till it is covered by delicate gradations of light and shade and color. We are in the habit of thinking of a sheet of paper as being quite uniform in tint, and yet instantly reject as insufficient such a representation of it. In this matter, our unconscious education is enormously in advance of our conscious. . . . Ruskin, speaking of gradation of color, says: 'It does not matter how small the touch of color may be, though not larger than the smallest pin's head, if one part of it is not darker than the rest, it is a bad touch. . . . What the difference is in mere beauty between a graduated and ungraduated color may be seen easily by laying an even tint of rose-color on paper and putting a rose-leaf beside it. The victorious beauty of the rose, as compared with other flowers, depends wholly on the delicacy and quantity of its color gradations.' All the great colorists have been deeply permeated by a sentiment of this kind, and their works, when viewed from the intended distance, are tremulous with changing tints—with tints that literally seem to change under the eye, so that it is often impossible for the copyist to say exactly what they are, his mixtures never seeming to be quite right, alter them as he will."

In addition to the principles underlying the use of *gradation* derived, as thus indicated, from the presence of it in nature, there is evidently another derived from physiological conditions. This principle is that changes from one form of color to another should usually be made along the line of least resistance, and therefore with the greatest gradualness. Recall the application of this principle to curvature on page 292. To a certain extent *gradation* may give expression to the same physiological conditions as those underlying *repetition* and *consonance*. The play of light and shade upon colors does not necessarily change their hues, and, if not, it does not change the form—only the force—of their vibrations, and all of them, if already coalescing, can continue to do so. It is with a recognition of how largely gradation is influenced by effects of light and shade, that it is said to be imperative that a dark shade of a darker color should always be put with a light shade of a lighter color, and not the reverse. Light carmine, we are told, should not be put with dark vermilion, but dark carmine should be put with light vermilion. Except where there is a combination of blue and violet, which latter is darker though warmer than blue, or orange and yellow, which latter is brighter though colder than orange, this principle requires that the warmer of two adjacent colors should always be the brighter. In cases where, as in these, the hue as well as the degree of light is changed, the eye may not find the change even to an inharmonious color disagreeable, if it takes place through imperceptible degrees. Our senses have become so accustomed to differences of this kind in nature that they expect them, as it were, in art. Besides, in painting, things that are very nearly allied often seem to be alike, just as is the case with the slight variations from exact requirements allowable to rhythm, rhyme, and the notes and chords of the temperate scale now used in music. See pages 202 to 206 of "Rhythm and Harmony in Poetry and Music." Physiologically, the explanation of gradation seems to be that, even though all the parts of the retina do not vibrate to exactly the same general impulse, the eye does not experience a disagreeable sensation in case the vibrations of the parts that are near together differ in very slight degrees. In music, graduated differences of effect take place in time, as when the movement passes from one key to another. In painting, there is no reason why they should not take place in space, and, if they do, though the vibrations in one part of the retina may not coalesce with those in another part, the eye, for reasons indicated on page 350, may be hardly conscious of the difference. At the same time, as a whole scene is usually visible to a single glance, or to many glances constantly moving from one to another part of the scene, it is doubtful whether, in case the changes are from one decided hue to another, the best effects of harmony can be secured by gradation without the aid of such arrangements of color as have been described under the heads of *balance, symmetry*, and *interchange*.

Notwithstanding the constant application in art of the principle of *gradation*, there are occasional places in which one color needs to be sharply contrasted with another, and this necessitates the effect termed *abruptness*.

It is interesting to notice, too, that while *gradation* tends to a violation of the law of *consonance*, *abruptness* tends to its fulfilment, inasmuch as the greatest *contrasts* are really occasioned by the proximity of the complementary colors. *Abruptness* is always present, for instance, when an object in bright light is placed, as is frequently the case, against its own shadow. See Fig. 102, page 235. In Rembrandt's " Woman Accused by the Pharisees," the woman accused is robed in white and in the centre of the chief light. Her accuser stands at her side clothed in black. Of course, we have here, necessarily, the greatest possible *contrast* and *abruptness.* But evidently this does not interfere either with the most exact fulfilment of the principles of *complement* and *consonance* or with the most delicate kind of *gradation* used as a principal and general method.

Gradation and *abruptness* together, as they cause one color to seem to change and to pass into another, produce the effects of *transition* and *progress.* With these, which need merely to be mentioned, we reach the last of the methods of composition in the chart on page 3. It is the combined result of the application of all of these methods that produces the general effect termed harmony.

CHAPTER XXV.

THE FOREGOING PRINCIPLES AS APPLIED TO DECORATIVE PAINTING.

Differences between the Use of Color in Pictorial and Decorative Art—Differences between Classes of Forms to which Colors are Applied and Classes of Like Colors that are Applied to Like Forms—Monochromatic and Polychromatic Decoration—Color on the Exteriors of Buildings—Possibility of New Styles of Architecture in our Age—Modern Development of Mineral Resources and Facilities of Transportation and their Influence on the Shapes of Buildings—But Especially on their Sizes and their Colors as Produced both by Pigments and by the Materials Used—Errors to be Avoided in Attempting Originality, but Possibility of Success.

THE most of what has been said with reference to the harmony of color applies equally to pictures and to painting as used in architecture. For this reason, as intimated at the beginning of this discussion, to separate the two, when treating of the subject, would involve an unnecessary waste of time. But an additional chapter seems to be in place here, applicable—though necessarily in only a very general and superficial way—to decoration. Decorative differs from pictorial art, primarily, in the motive. In a picture, color is used in order to reproduce an appearance of nature. In decoration it is used for its own sake. While in the former, therefore, all possible shades and tints may be introduced, so long as, in some way, they can be harmonized; in the latter, those only ought to be introduced that in every way must of necessity harmonize. Connected with this difference in motive, is the same difference that was noticed on page 175 of " Rhythm and Harmony in Poetry and Music" between sounds in speech and in music. In the one, every possible degree of pitch may be used ; in the other, only certain degrees separated from one another by decided intervals. Of course, the method of gradation is exemplified both in pictures and decoration ; but in decoration the colors used are, as a rule, separated from one another by more decided intervals, such as are indicated in the color-chart on page 334; and they are more apt to be full hues, than light or dark modifications of these, such as are generally found in painting. These hues are placed, sometimes, side by side ; but they produce better effects when separated by black, white, gold, or silver lines, which lessen the influence of the adjoining colors on one another. Moreover, while painting deals largely with the greens, light blues, and grays predominating in the world about us, decoration shows a large use of the reds, oranges, yellows, and dark blues, as if one design of it were to produce contrasts to the colors seen in nature. Again, as imitation of form or outline in decoration is often of little importance, almost the entire effect depending upon the selection and arrangement of colors, it is still more necessary than in painting that these should be grouped so as to fulfil strictly scientific principles.

Another important fact recognized in decorative art is a difference between certain classes of forms. The chief of such classes are mouldings and surfaces ; and of these again there are sub-classes. Mouldings may be straight, angular, or circular ; and surfaces may be large or small, and shaped in many different ways. It is a rule in decoration that, in the same composition, like classes of forms should exhibit like classes of colors. In order to aid in securing this end, the colors are classed as follows: first, black, white, gold, and silver; second, the full colors; third, the dark colors; and fourth, the light colors.

Besides this, decorations are either monochromatic or polychromatic. In the former, different shades and tints of a single hue are used, separated at times, however, by black, white, gold, or silver. In the latter, all the hues are used, but, as a rule, only the full hues; and in case a darker or lighter effect is desired, black or white figures or lines are placed over the color. This method, which probably arose at a time when men were ignorant of other ways of producing different shades and tints, is now thought by some to be the only way in such kind of work of producing effects of unity.

There is no place in a treatise like this for extensive mention of the various modes of applying color in the painting and furnishing of buildings. There is, however, one important consideration that forces itself into the direct line of our thought, and that is the use which may be made of color upon the exteriors of buildings.

It is often urged that, in our age and country, no new style of architecture can be originated. With reference to this, something has been said already on page 95 of "Art in Theory," on pages 206 and 293 of "The Genesis of Art-Form," on pages 330 and 406 of "Painting, Sculpture, and Architecture as Representative Arts," and on page 227 of the present volume. It may be said here that probably we can find no other ways of bridging openings made for doors and windows than those which have been in vogue for centuries, and which have already determined the chief characteristics of the Greek, Romanesque, and Gothic styles, namely, the horizontal lintel, the round arch, and the pointed arch, and that probably also the necessity of securing correspondence in architecture must continue to cause all other outlines in our buildings to resemble these. Yet, while this is true, it must also be true that in every period in which there is progress, progress is possible in art.

Our own age has made an advance upon all preceding ones in two regards which should have, and already have had, some influence upon our architecture. These are the development of our mineral resources and of the facilities of transportation. The one has converted iron, together with various combinations and modifications of it, into a building material, and the other has lined our streets with structures of stone and brick exhibiting every variety of color. One can scarcely believe otherwise than that if one half of the thought expended on the Parthenon were expended upon incorporating the suggestions and possibilities derived from these two facts, we might originate an architectural style of our own which would become as classic and deserve to be as much admired as that of the Greeks. Iron used for the walls of buildings is inartistic. It looks like an imitation of stone produced by wood and paint, while it is standing; and it cracks, curls, melts, and ceases to stand as soon as a fire of any magnitude begins to heat it. But, used for roofs, it is more in place, and, where so used, the most economical and convenient shape that can be chosen for it is often the most beautiful. A correspondence between its arching forms and like forms in the stone- or brick-work underneath it, might give rise to a style equally novel and attractive.

See what is said on page 330 of "Painting, Sculpture, and Architecture as Representative Arts," with reference to methods of letting iron be seen in ceilings. Besides this, iron can span immense spaces, and this fact renders the columns characterizing the Gothic and, to some extent, the Greek structures as much out of the way architecturally in some of our modern buildings, as, with our modern uses, they are in the way optically. Large interiors, however, containing few or no columns, necessitate very artistic treatment of the wall-spaces. Otherwise, everything seems too airy and cold. Arrangements of mouldings and spaces can do something toward preventing such effects, but careful attention to the requirements of decorative art can do more. Nor in such cases should efforts be confined merely to painting. Decorative color, to be permanent, should be resident in the material used; and here, in treating both exterior and interior walls, architects might avail themselves of our modern facilities for transportation. Pictures have been made of mosaics, but few great buildings have been constructed on the principle of using differently colored bricks and stones and harmonizing them according to the principles of decorative painting.

Probably an architect who should undertake to erect such a building would be considered audacious; and, unless the materials and colors were judiciously chosen—not too brilliant or diversified—and were arranged in strict fulfilment of the principle that like classes of forms should be characterized by like classes of substances and hues, and were grouped in masses large enough to give dignity to the effect—probably the result would prove this opinion to be correct. Yet a great genius might produce something with a beauty as unique and successful as was the earliest Gothic church in its day, and surpassing the beauty of most of our buildings as much as the frescoed interiors of the present New York merchants' houses surpass the whitewashed walls of their Knickerbocker ancestors. Color is certainly an element of beauty. Why should it not be recognized as such in architecture? Even the Greeks acknowledged the fact. It is known now that the marble of the Parthenon, unsurpassed as it is in its capabilities for receiving polish, was painted. But the painting has perished. Used on exteriors, it always does perish. Can no imperishable colors be used thus? They can. In a country where brick and stone of all possible compositions and colors can be collected from all quarters at comparatively slight expense, one can imagine churches, halls, streets, entire cities, wholly different in hue and general appearance from any that have ever existed, built of material destined to remain unchanged as long as the pyramids, and, for a longer time, to continue to be models.

CHAPTER XXVI.

RECAPITULATION OF RESULTS REACHED IN THESE VOLUMES ON COMPARATIVE ÆSTHETICS.

Introductory Statement—Examination of Facts and Opinions in "Art in Theory"—Method Adopted in Volumes Following it—In "The Representative Significance of Form"—Art Developed from Natural Forms of Expression—The Methods of their Development—Elements of Representation in Arts of Sound, as Analyzed in "Poetry as a Representative Art" and in "Music as a Representative Art"—As Combined, according to the Same Essays, in Poems and Musical Compositions Considered as Wholes—Elements of Representation, as Analyzed in "Painting, Sculpture, and Architecture as Representative Arts"—As Combined, according to the Same Volume, in Paintings, Statues, and Buildings Considered as Wholes—Form in General as Treated in "The Genesis of Art-Form"—Form in Particular as Treated in "Rhythm and Harmony in Poetry and Music," and in "Proportion and Harmony of Line and Color in Painting, Sculpture, and Architecture"—This Series of Volumes Traces All Art-Developments, whether of Significance or Form, to a Single Principle—This Done with a Practical as well as Philosophic Aim—The Acknowledgment of No Standards Leads either to Imitation or Eccentricity in Production and in Critical Judgment—The Possibility of Finding Standards—These Need not Interfere with Originality—Necessity for the Study and Knowledge of Standards in our own Age and Country—Unavoidable Limitations in a Philosophic and Technical Treatment of the Kind Attempted in these Volumes.

ONE more of this series of volumes upon Comparative Æsthetics remains to be published. But, according to the order in which they will ultimately be arranged, this is the concluding volume. It seems appropriate, therefore, before closing it, to give a brief summary of the results that have been attained, together with sufficient references to the methods of attaining them to render what is said intelligible.

In the introductory volume, "Art in Theory," an attempt was made to derive a true conception of the requirements of art from a study of certain facts and opinions concerning it acknowledged by all, or held by writers of authority. Guided by these criteria, nature was first distinguished from art, and then the lower arts from the higher. It was found that an essential characteristic of these latter is what is known as form, but in their cases a form producing always two apparently different effects, one derived from an imitation of external phenomena, and the other from a communication of thoughts and emotions. The first effect, tending to emphasize the form in itself, was said to be mainly, though by no means exclusively, characteristic of classic art, and the second effect, tending to emphasize the significance in the form, was said to be mainly characteristic of romantic art. It was also argued that the emphasizing of either of these tendencies, if carried so far as to involve a neglect of the other of them, is fatal to artistic excellence. In indicating, then, the conception of artistic aims best tending to preserve the equilibrium between the two tendencies, it was pointed out that art neither imitates nor communicates in the most practically effective ways. Because aiming to do both, its chief aim cannot be to do either the one or the other. Art represents natural phenomena, as one may say, as a means of representing thoughts and emotions. Or, to express this differently, art emphasizes representation, developing and elaborating the factors of it in nature, and the possibilities of it in the mind. But in doing this, art is using the same means and continuing the same modes of expression as those that are attributed by men to the creative and divine intelligence. The impulse to art, therefore, may be considered creative and divine. But as it neither imitates nor communicates in the most usefully effective way, we must trace it less to the useful than to the non-useful, and so to what in elementary phases is called the play-impulse. This play-impulse, even in dogs and kittens, to say nothing of apes, tends to the imitation of that which seems interesting, attractive, and charming in one's surroundings. The same impulse, when turned in the direction of art, inasmuch as this always involves the use of form, tends also to imitation. But an imitation of that which is interesting, attractive, and charming in form, especially in form communicating to mind and spirit the suggestions of a creative and divine impulse, is nothing more nor less than a reproduction of what men, when using the term in its highest sense, mean by beauty. What is there in beauty, however, that it should be used by the art-impulse when giving expression to the mental and spiritual? A review, which follows, of the history of opinion on the subject, reveals that the effects of beauty are well-nigh universally attributed—not always explicitly but certainly implicitly —in part to form, but in part also to significance suggested by the form. In other words, the charm exerted by beauty is exerted partly upon the senses, because the elements of the form harmonize with one another and with the physiological requirements of the ear or eye, and partly upon the mind, because the suggestions of these elements harmonize with psychological requirements. The consequent definition reached is, that "Beauty is a characteristic of any complex form of varied elements, producing apprehensible unity (*i. e.*, harmony or likeness) of effects

(1) upon the motive organs of sensation in the ear or eye, or (2) upon the emotive sources of imagination in the mind, or (3) upon both the one and the other." There are the best of reasons, therefore, why a creative and divine impulse tending to imitation should reproduce beauty, the mere existence of which alone may involve that appeal to the mental and spiritual nature which is made by what we term significance. But we must not forget that in art the mind may do more than represent significance as a secondary consideration, as would be the case did it do so merely because, by way of accident, as it were, a certain significance was necessarily suggested by the form used. The mind often represents thoughts and emotions as a primary consideration,—that is, it decides upon them first, and, afterwards, selects the forms through which to communicate them. We are obliged, therefore, to know something about the ways in which the mind communicates or represents thoughts or emotions through any forms whatever, irrespective of their being characterized by beauty. The remainder of the book shows how, at different stages of the influence exerted by precisely the same external phenomena, entirely different phases of conscious thoughts and emotions are aroused to activity. This activity is analyzed into that which primarily is instinctive or spontaneous, is reflective or responsive, or is a blending of both the others in what may be termed the instinctively reflective or the emotive. It is shown that for every phase of activity there is only one natural form of expression; and that it is this form and no other which, when artistically developed, *i. e.*, developed with reference to beauty, finds appropriate embodiment in one of the five arts of Music, Poetry, Painting, Sculpture, or Architecture.

In the volumes following " Art in Theory," the order of thought adopted in that book is reversed. Having begun the discussion of the general subject by observing forms as they have been produced by art, and drawing inferences from them, ending with the final inference that all are necessarily expressive of a certain significance, it seemed natural that the endeavor in subsequent volumes to determine how art should fulfil the requirements indicated in the introductory volume should start with significance, and work outward, showing what different conceptions it is possible to express in art, and how these determine its form. In pursuing this line of thought, the first thing to do, of course, was to examine the connection between significance and form in general. This subject was assigned to the volume of the series not yet published, and to be entitled " The Representative Significance of Form." The next thing to do was to examine the connection between significance and the possible forms of each of the different arts in particular. This was done in the volume entitled " Poetry as a Representative Art "; also in that part of the volume entitled "Rhythm and Harmony in Poetry and Music" which is devoted to the discussion of "Music as a Representative Art," as well as in the volume entitled " Painting, Sculpture, and Architecture as Representative Arts." Having examined the methods of representing significance through form in general, and in each class of forms in each different art in particular, the next thing to do was to examine form in itself, that is, as something which, though influenced by significance, and in practice always connected with significance, may, nevertheless, for the purposes of analytic study, be considered as existing apart from anything else, and as developing according to laws having to do mainly, if not solely, with that which pertains to the appeal to the senses. Here, in analogy to the course pursued when studying significance, attention was directed first to the sources, methods, and effects of form in general. This was done in the volume entitled "The Genesis of Art-Form." Next, what had been learned with reference to form in general was applied to form as manifested in each of the arts. This was done in the two concluding volumes of the series, "Rhythm and Harmony in Poetry and Music," and "Proportion and Harmony of Line and Color in Painting, Sculpture, and Architecture."

To describe the contents of the different volumes more in detail, "The Representative Significance of Form" begins with the presumption that form, even as it exists in nature, always represents some significance; and that it is from nature, therefore, that, directly or indirectly, a man derives, in the main, the conceptions which he embodies in art. The methods of deriving such conceptions are first considered, and then it is shown how each class of conceptions may be represented in each of the different arts. Advancing from that which is more elementary to that which is more complex, there are treated in this way the conceptions of space, time, existence, matter, movement, force, arrangement, operation, method of operation, organism, life, import, and, finally, of the infinite, the eternal, and the absolute, together with conceptions of truth in the abstract and in the concrete, as embodied either in formulæ or in action. In all cases it is shown that significance and form necessarily go together. After this, the different emphasis which the ways of blending the two give to the one or to the other is shown to distinguish artistic from religious truth, and also from scientific; and the various conditions, methods, and purposes are unfolded, in connection with which development and expression are given to each of the three. In

RECAPITULATION. 425

accordance with the distinctions thus made, it is then pointed out that, as manifested in art, the basic principle of the religious tendency prompts to the instinctive, spontaneous, spiritual subordination of form to significance, which we have in the sublime and the grand, the most artistic expression of which is in epic art; that the basic principle of the scientific tendency prompts to the reflective, responsive, materialistic equipoise of significance and form, found in the picturesque and the simple, the most artistic expression of which is in realistic art; and that the basic principle of the distinctively artistic tendency prompts to the instinctively reflective, emotive, and idealistic subordination of significance to form, found in the brilliant and the striking, the most artistic expression of which is in dramatic art. The same three respective tendencies, considered both in their tragic and their comic phases, are shown to be at the basis also of the more important subdivisions of epic, realistic, and dramatic art; after ample illustrations to exemplify and confirm which propositions, the book closes by finally indicating as developed from the same tendencies certain expressional differences, as well as correspondences, between the arts of Music, Poetry, Painting, Sculpture, and Architecture.

As has been intimated, the next thing in the order of the development of the thought was to apply the principles so far unfolded to each of the arts considered separately. In treating of these arts, the discussion is begun by showing that it is natural as well as necessary for a man to express his thoughts and emotions through audible or visible forms; and that a certain method of developing these forms causes them to be artistic. It is shown, besides, that, even before being thus developed, the forms are all of them methods of communicating thoughts and feelings through using, for this purpose, certain external factors which, in themselves, are devoid of thought or feeling; in other words, that artists, owing to an application of the principle of association or of comparison, reveal operations of the mind through employing, either by way of appropriation or reference, the physical phenomena of nature; and that, for this reason, we can understand the arts fully only so far as we consider them as representative, on the one hand, of mental conceptions, and, on the other, of material surroundings. In the volumes devoted to this subject, therefore, it is shown that it is possible for every natural method of expression to become thus representative, at times, both of the human mind and of external nature. The elementary factors of expression are shown to be, in the arts of sound, intonations and words, and, in the arts of sight, gestures, drawings, carvings, and other objects made by hand. From these primarily it is argued that form in representative art is developed. The ways in which it is developed are indicated, first, by analyzing the methods in which these factors are made to be expressive, and observing for what phase of representation, either mental or material, each phase of expression is fitted ; and later by observing the general effect of the representation produced when the methods and phases are combined in a completed art-form.

Expression is found to be produced through different methods of using, in the arts of sound, duration, force, pitch, and quality of tone, and—respectively corresponding to these, in the arts of sight—extension, strength of line, hue, and mixture of hues. It is from these methods that we derive and, as affected by instinctive, reflective, or emotive tendencies, that we appropriate for representative purposes such effects as those of movement, pause, accent, versification, metre, tune, tone, and other characteristics of rhythm and harmony of sound; and such effects as those of size, shape, shading, tinting, and other characteristics of proportion and harmony of line and color.

In the volume entitled "Poetry as a Representative Art," as well as in the essay on "Music as a Representative Art," it is shown, for instance,—to mention only a few particulars as illustrative of many more,—that, both by way of suggestion and of imitation, solemnity, gravity, and dignity are represented by long words and notes causing slowness of movement as contrasted with the opposite; that self-assertion and vehemence are represented by distinctness of accent and loudness of tone as contrasted with indistinctness and softness; that conclusiveness, decision, affirmation, and satisfaction are represented by downward as contrasted with upward movements either in the tunes of verse or of song; and also that feelings like fright, amazement, indignation, contempt, horror, awe, surprise, solicitude, delight, admiration, and determination are each represented by different qualities of tone, whether indicated in vowels and consonants or in musical instruments.

In the last halves of the essays, both on poetry and on music, the elements which are considered separately in the first halves are examined as representing mental conceptions or material surroundings when combined in completed art-products, the purpose being to bring out clearly, if possible, as applied to both theme and treatment, whether plain or figurative, the distinctions between the poetic and the prosaic, the musical and the merely sonorous.

In an exactly analogous way, the general subject is developed, as applied to the arts of sight, in the volume entitled "Painting, Sculpture, and Architecture as Representative Arts." First, through an analysis of the elements of visible representation, it is shown that large size or deep shading in certain features, when connected with the opposite in other features, suggests, whether in landscapes, figures, or buildings, either conceptions or surroundings characterized by such traits as heaviness, strength, immobility, influence, or nearness; and, again, that outlines formed by the continuity of curves, and also those manifesting irregularity, suggest the normal and natural in landscapes, and the free and unconstrained in figures, whereas straightness, angularity, and regularity suggest the abnormal and artificial, as in effects of volcanic action in nature, of self-conscious and constrained action in men, and of rectangularity in buildings and in most other human constructions. In unfolding this subject, the principles shown to underlie other forms of visible representation are applied to a complete system of expressing thoughts and emotions through the shapes, postures, gestures, and facial movements of the human body. Following this, comes a discussion of the representative significance of the different colors.

The concluding part of the book treats of the representation of mental conceptions and also of material surroundings in compositions as wholes; first, in landscape, portrait, genre, historic, allegoric, and symbolic painting and sculpture, and, after this, in architecture. In discussing this latter art, it is shown that the constructive conception, as well as the plan, can be represented in the interior and exterior of a building; and in a series of illustrations presenting side by side various huts and tents as constructed by the natural man, and columns, pediments, entablatures, arches, roofs, and spires of perfected art, it is shown that the latter are developed from the former through a picturesque and statuesque and, in this sense, representative motive.

Having observed now how each of the arts is expressive of significance, in that it is representative both of mental conceptions and of material surroundings, the next thing in order, as indicated on page 424, seemed to be to direct attention to the subject of form, considering this, first, as related to art in general, and next, to each art in particular. Form, as related to art in general, was treated in the volume entitled " The Genesis of Art-Form." Taking up the thread of thought where dropped in the previous volume, this opens by examining the very beginnings of form when representing significance. The necessity is pointed out of having inaudible and invisible thoughts or emotions, when they are to be imparted to another, communicated to him through some audible and visible medium. Then it is pointed out that the particular method in which they may be thus communicated in art is only one of many similar ways in which the mind is obliged to use material surroundings. It is recalled that all knowledge, and not only this, but all understanding and application of the laws of botany, mineralogy, psychology, or theology, depend upon the degree in which a man learns to separate certain plants, rocks, mental activities, or religious dogmas from others, and to unite and classify and name them; and that it is classification which enables him to have knowledge and understanding of the materials which nature furnishes, and to make an efficient use of them. It is maintained that, while science classifies facts, and philosophy theories, art classifies forms or appearances; and it is stated also that the general process in all cases is the same,—a process which involves an application of the same principles of association and comparison which are mentioned on page 426 as being at the basis of all earliest attempts at expression. This process in its elementary stages is a putting of like with like. If the factors be not actually alike in form the process involves gathering them into groups according to the principle of mental association; or, if they be alike in form, of doing the same according to the principle of comparison. The essay maintains, in short, that it is the endeavor to produce unity of impression out of the variety and complexity everywhere apparent in nature, as one is influenced sometimes by the requirements of the mind, sometimes by those of nature, and sometimes by both, that leads to the different methods adopted in art-construction, the whole of which methods, arranged in the order of their logical development, are indicated in the chart on page 3 of the present volume.

In the volume entitled "Rhythm and Harmony in Poetry and Music," as also in the present volume, this method of putting like with like, as modified by the conditions of variety everywhere characterizing the materials with which art has to work, is shown to be at the basis of all the different developments of form as form with which the art of our times is acquainted. Rhythm and proportion are traced to effects produced by a grouping, of which the mind is conscious, of like or allied measurements, or multiples of measurements, in time or space; and harmony, whether of spoken words, of musical notes, of outlines, or of colors, is traced to a grouping, of which the mind is not conscious, of like or allied measurements, or multiples of measurements, in vibratory movements. To exemplify the truth of this statement, as evinced in every detail of the forms of these arts, has necessitated much explanation and no little repetition. But these are excusable if they have suggested any important considerations not before recognized. For instance, the latest, and perhaps the best, book produced in our country which discusses poetic form, is developed from the same limited conception of it indicated in the definition of Poe in his essay on "The Poetic Principle," namely, "the rhythmical creation of beauty." No one would say that in "Rhythm and Harmony in Poetry and Music" there is any lack of thoroughness in the treatment of rhythm in poetry or of its various applications and possibilities,—to say nothing of the freshness of the treatment, owing to the circumstance that a year before the book was published, the scientific investigations that suggested, perhaps, the most important conclusions in it had not been made. At the same time, no one can read that book carefully and not recognize that harmony, too, as distinctly differentiated from rhythm, plays as noteworthy a part in the general effects of poetry as in those of music; that, different as are both factors and effects as used in poetic and in musical harmony, nevertheless, the methods of it in both arts illustrate identical principles. That an analogous fact is true, not only in these arts, but also in painting, sculpture, and architecture, has been shown in the present volume, concerning the line of thought in which, however, nothing need be added here.

To recapitulate: in these volumes, the effects of form in art have been traced to a single principle, and to the same principle have been traced the effects of whatever significance also may be expressed in each form. All art, in any of its manifestations, has been shown to be an emphasizing, through a method of elaboration, of factors taken from one's surroundings, which are used not only in art, but in every attempt at expression, for the purpose of representing, by way of association or comparison, sometimes these surroundings themselves, and sometimes the thoughts and emotions communicated through them. Moreover, whether we wish to emphasize the factors themselves, or the purpose for which the mind uses them, each end is best attained by putting, so far as possible, like with like in the sense of grouping features having either corresponding effects upon the mind, *i. e.*, like significance; or corresponding effects upon the senses, *i. e.*, like forms; or, as is frequently the case, corresponding effects upon both the mind and the senses. Stated thus, the principle may seem very simple and insignificant. But any one who has read the volumes of this series, and observed the applicability of the principle to all possible effects of form in all the arts, together with the way in which analogous effects in different arts have been correlated to one another; and who has observed also the applicability of the principle to the mental effects of art, whether produced by the grandest generalizations that can broaden thought, and the profoundest passions that can excite emotion, or only by the smallest specific accent of a syllable, the measuring of a tone, the shading of a line, or the turning of a little finger,—any one who has observed these facts, and is at all appreciative of the vastness and complexity of the subject, or is acquainted with the chaotic conditions in which the histories of opinions have left men's common conceptions of it, or is merely aware of that which, in general, is the distinctive aim of all philosophical analysis,—any such man will recognize the degree in which, when the elements investigated are made to seem single and simple, the comprehensiveness and importance of the discussion are enhanced.

In any study of art, however, it must always be borne in mind that to reach a philosophical result is not the sole or the chief aim. This aim is practical; and it was a practical aim that first suggested this series of volumes. At a time when their writer was an author and a teacher, looking for guidance and finding none, most of the criticism of the day, whether of poetry, painting, or architecture, revealed an absence of any standards of judgment, if not a disbelief in the possibility of their existence. Indeed, some of the foremost leaders in criticism took the ground that there are no such standards, an opinion virtually maintained, despite all protests to the contrary, in what are, perhaps, the freshest and most suggestive of the books on æsthetics that have been produced even very lately.

As a result of having or acknowledging no standard, about all that criticism can attempt is to observe a poem, a painting, or a building, and praise it, in case it resembles some other product of a like kind—say by a Tennyson, a Corot, or some Greek or Gothic builder—which has been previously praised by some other critic. Judgments formed according to this method either exalt imitation in production into artistic excellence, as well as imitation in opinion into critical acumen; or else, because there seems some defect in such conceptions, they confound in their search for the opposite of imitation the indications of mere eccentricity with those of genuine originality. Meantime, the art either imitative or eccentric that is developed by such conceptions continues to prove satisfactory to men so long only as the temporary fashion that occasions it continues in vogue. There is not a library, or picture gallery, or street, or campus of any size in this country, that is not filled almost to overflowing with modern compositions which were extravagantly praised by the foremost authorities of a few years ago, but which to-day are acknowledged to be well-nigh worthless as specimens of art; and the sorriest feature of the condition is that this race toward worthlessness is still going on between many upon whose works enormous sums of money, to say nothing of undeserved and misguiding laudations, are now being lavishly expended.

So long as the author of this series of volumes, upon the principle of "Live and let live," refrains, as he has always consistently done, from personal attacks upon artists and critics and patrons of art, to some of whom, in his own conceptions, he is now very definitely referring, he cannot be rightly accused of being willing to attain notoriety in that easiest way possible in our own age,—at the expense of others; even if he cannot expect to be recognized as one who, in all that he has written, has been mainly anxious to be helpful to them. But whatever they may think, he is certain that he will prove helpful in reality, in case he succeeds in doing no more than directing attention to the fact that the conditions of art that have just been described must always continue so long as opinion or performance is based upon the conception that there can be no approximately definite standards. And if this be so, it is not being theoretical but practical, to maintain that in art, as in all other departments of life, these standards can be discovered. We can find that upon which everything else on the earth's surface rests, if only we can get down deep enough. We can find the basic method of art, if only we can do the same. To find this, has been the object of these volumes. Nor is it assuming too much to hope that the physiological as well as the psychical investigations of the present day have been carried so far that no further discoveries, much as they may add by way of confirmation to the theories here unfolded, will necessitate any material change in their general trend.

Another thought is suggested. The tendencies to imitation on the one side and to eccentricity on the other, which have been said to characterize the developments of art where there is no belief in approximately definite standards, is connected with a false conception of what constitutes that originality which everybody acknowledges to be essential to great art. It is the conception that originality is a constituent of mere form. Originality of course is a characteristic of form, in which alone it can be manifested; but the artistic originality which men mean to applaud when they speak of it, is originality of form as expressive of significance, originality that is felt to be a manifestation of mental freshness and uniqueness, therefore of what we term—including in our conceptions both the intellectual and the spiritual—personal force. That it is this force issuing from the sources of the soul to which men mean to refer when praising originality, needs no further proof than that the trait which they praise is not always prevented by imitation of form, nor always helped by eccentricity of form. An actor can show his personal originality by imitating; and a very bashful man can entirely hide his by eccentricity. Notice, too, that the argument against the existence of standards of art founded on the supposition that they may interfere with originality has, for the reasons just stated, no basis in fact. To make external forms conform to a standard is not to interfere with the expression of the originality which is of the soul and mind. Through an application of identical methods, one may give an elocutionary education to two men, making the voices of both equally musical and their movements equally graceful. Yet the method as carried out in the forms manifested by the one may make him a great and original actor, and the personality behind the forms manifested by the other may result in no greatness or originality whatever. At the same time, the first man, with all the original bent of his genius, could not have become the great artist that he is, without learning to conform his representation to the standards of his art. Thus it is in all the arts. Criticism cannot produce personality, but can guide it to successful performance. It can prevent that total waste of ability which is invariably expended upon worthless products, where either imitation or eccentricity has led taste away from a recognition of standards which are as enduring as the ages, because rationally deduced from principles deeply seated in humanity and in nature. Rules of art cannot create artistic ability; but they can cultivate it. They cannot make a man a genius; but, if he have genius, they can enable him to give it vent in such ways that it will exert its due influence; and, if he live, as every man does, where he must accommodate his productions to the demands of those about him, the study of æsthetics can elevate conceptions and tastes so as to give a higher aim to the efforts which are directed to the satisfying of them. The born artist may be a ruler of humanity by divine right; but it is art, the requirements of which can be taught and learned, that alone can give him his government, army, palace, throne, crown, and sceptre, and not only these, but the subjects, too, who on account of their appreciation of the significance of these will acknowledge his authority.

That, in our times, these requirements of art need to be specially pointed out and dwelt upon, will be conceded without argument. The age is scientific, and the country's aims are directed toward material progress. Both facts cause us to emphasize the real rather than the ideal, the substance rather than the suggestion, that which is held in the hand rather than that which is conceived in the brain. In such conditions, the phase of the play-impulse that prompts to art cannot tend to give expression to its highest possibilities. A cowboy of the West could take little pleasure in the Seventh Symphony, the " Excursion," the " Sistine Madonna," the " Dying Gladiator," or Roslyn Chapel ; and, for this reason, no artist of the Western plains would be stimulated to produce its like. But taste in appreciation or production can be cultivated ; and, in the degree in which it is cultivated, a new realm of thought will open for a man, and with it a recognition, hitherto not experienced, of those almost infinite correspondences between spiritual and material relationships which every great product of art manifests. Thus gradually the mind will enter a region of thought in which the play-impulse, which, at first, is satisfied to expend its energies upon the merely apparent and superficial, will care for more than a fife and drum, a jingle of rhyme, a dash of color, a trick of chiselling, or an incongruous pile of stone and mortar. The mind will not be satisfied unless, at times and often, music, poetry, painting, sculpture, and architecture suggest the profound and the sublime ; in fact, unless the humanities have had their perfect work, and art has become humanizing in all of its relations.

To open such a region to the mind, has been the object of the work of which these volumes contain the records. The region has been explored before; but of late years has it been explored in the right way? Historic products, simply because they have come to fill a large space, have been supposed, though often only weeds and underbrush, to be the best that could be expected. To show that this is not so, it has been necessary to clear obstructions away from the plants of better promise whose progress had been checked, and to lay bare the soil where sunlight and nutriment can work as they should. To spend one's hours with axe and spade chopping down and rooting up is not wholly satisfactory, but at times it is essential; and this fact is a sufficient excuse for much that has made the records of this work dull and tedious, requiring often, no doubt, as much painstaking care to read them intelligently as to write them. But, perhaps, the student for whom the work has been done will prize the volumes the more for their own practical recognition of their limitations. One cannot catalogue the implements that aid the mechanism of technique without neglecting rhyme and rhythm. He cannot beat clear recognition into minds and senses steeled against it, without a deal of reiteration. That which was undertaken in these volumes did not seem to permit of a method that might have proved far more pleasurable both for author and for reader. How can one get down to the roots of anything, so long as he persists in making his chief aim the enjoyment of its flowers? Our libraries are full of treatises upon art appealing to the imagination. The series of volumes which this concludes has been intended to appeal to the understanding. We may exercise imagination and go astray, in case we fail to exercise the understanding also. But so long as we are really using the latter, whether as artists or critics, we are much less likely to go astray, however imaginative. To understand a subject completely, one must be led to analyze it, and to perceive its minutest details. Details that are minute require minuteness in presentation. Your small matter may be as effectually lost in generalities of style as a needle in a dust-heap. Or, as applied to considerations of a broader character, one cannot manifest the coolness needed in a philosophic presentation, through a manner aglow with the heat of fancy ; nor accurately balance principles in the scale of argument, when allowing either side of it to be borne up or down by a bias of sentiment. This work on æsthetics has been all work from the beginning. Not without much conscious expenditure of effort and constraint has the author been able to the very end to hold it strictly to its own province and purpose. He has not deviated from these, because he has believed that both for himself and his readers, both for the critic and the artist, both for the producer of art and its patron, this course would be the surest through which to secure the desired results. And not only the surest but the shortest. He soonest obtains leisure, who devotes himself most exclusively to labor in the hours of labor. He soonest enters into the enjoyment of the garden bright with its fragrant blossoms and the orchard laden with its ripening fruit, whose days of preparation are most scrupulously spent in clearing, weeding, planting, and grafting.

INDEX.

Abacus, considered in proportion as a part of entablature, 203, 210, 213, 215, 217, 221; defined, 185; depicted, 182; measurements related to breadth of column, 219–221; to other parts, 191–194, 195, 198, 203, 205, 208–211, 213–215, 217
Abruptness—Art-Method, 3; of line, 67; of color, 411, 412
Accent, 6, 7
Accuracy of measurements determining ratios in art not essential, 179–181, 184, 185, 202, 203
Acropolis, 178, 224, 252, 257; Restoration of west end of, 186
Acroterium, 183, 197
Ægina, temple of, 182, 186, 189, 192, 196, 204, 208–210, 212, 220, 221, 224; Temples of, and of Bassæ, 178, 196
Aërial Perspective, colors in, 321–324
Æsthetic, 283; the, vs. the ethical, 108
Æsthetics, outline of system of Comparative, 419–432; importance of study of, 436
After-Image, colored, in eye, 371, 372, 375–377, 380–384
Ageladas, 97
Aglaophon, 300
Agrigentum, 187, 191, 193, 195, 221
Aguilonius, 268
Alexander the Great, 301
Alexandrine Greek Art, 249

Alliteration, 232
Alteration—Art-Method, 3, 66; in color, 366
Alternation—Art-Method, 3, 66, 116, 127; in architecture, 148, 164–166, 168, 174; in color, 361, 369; in outline, 231
American Face, beauty and proportions of, 128, 129
Angelo, M., 302
Angles, like, as determining proportion, 66, 67
Animals, contours elliptical, 288, 289
Ankles, proportions of, 132–134
Anne, Queen, architecture, 227; poetry, 225
Antiquities of Athens, Stuart, 181
Aosta, Arch of Augustus, at, 153
Apelles, 92, 301
Apollodorus, 300
Apollo, Belvedere, 83, 84, 98, 123; Sauroctonos, 99, 104, 141; temple of, at Delos, 194, 221
Apparent effects, important in art, 243, 244, 258–264; in proportional measurements more important than real, iii., iv., 24, 25, 32, 34, 38, 151–161, 179, 180, 217. See Perspective.
Arcadia, of Pausanias, 26
Architectura, De, Vitruvius, 26, 64, 117, 120, 219, 256
Architectural Record, 243, 248.
Architecture, Antique, de la Sicile, Hittorf, 182; History of, Fergusson, 28; Principles of Athenian, Penrose, 29, 181, 248, 254, 262

441

Architecture, 5 ; colors in, and in pictures, 296 ; colors on exteriors, 189, 192, 194, 416-418 ; decoration in, 413-418 ; development and progress in, 227, 228, 415-418 ; Egyptian, 244, 249 ; entasis or curves in straight effects of, 234-265 ; Gothic, 64, 144-176, 226, 227, 252 ; Greek, 8, 36, 64, 177-228, 246-265 ; Greek *vs.* Roman, 222-225, 262, 263 ; how made artistic, 145-149 ; how made representative, 145-148 ; irregularities in Greek, 248-252 ; its relation to nature and to imitation, 144, 145 ; judged from distant effects, 35, 36, 179-181, 202, 203, 244, 246, 249, 251, 265 ; perspective in, 36, 234, 236-265 ; proportion in, 40-42 ; proportion in Gothic and modern, 56, 144-228 ; proportion in Greek, 177-228, 246-265 ; rhythm of, 42, 184

Architrave in Greek temple, 182 ; proportion to frieze, 191-198 ; to other members, 185, 186, 191, 192, 194-196, 203, 205, 207, 209

Aristodemus, 301

Aristophon, 300

Art, anticipates discoveries of science, 298, 299 ; connection between significance and form in, 104-108, 112, 128, 129, 139, 140, 420-432 ; creative and divine, 421, 422 ; develops with scientific discovery, 299-308 ; influence of criticism on 436, 437 ; not irresponsible but humanizing, 110-112 ; not useful but pleasurable, 421

Art-Composition, methods of, 2 ; with chart of, 3

Art : Its laws and the reasons for Them, Long, 368

Art in Theory, 2, 107, 129 ,297, 354, 362, 415, 420, 423 ; analysis of essay on, 420-422

Art of Painting, Fresnoy, 122 ; Reynolds, 367

Artemidorus, 301

Arts, as expressive of phases of mental action, 422 ; of time and space, 4 ; of sound and sight, 4-7

Association, as influencing conceptions of beauty, 104, 106, 107, 129, 290 ; principle of, uhderlying art-development, 426, 430, 432

Assonance, 232

Assyrian Square, type of, 35

Athenian Architecture. *See* Architecture.

Athens, temples at, 249

Atmosphere, colors of, 305, 306, 319-324 ; to be distinguished from local colors of objects, 377-383

Audran, 124

Augustus, Arch of, at Aosta, 153

Bacchus and Ariadne, Titian, 407

Backgrounds, near and distant, 271-275, 278-282, 292, 293 ; colors of, in relief, 387, 388

Bacon, 89

Balance—Art-Method, 3, 63, 65, 78 ; in architecture, 161, 171, 173-175 ; 231, 284 ; in color and painting, 358-361, 364, 366, 367, 406, 411

Barbizon-Fontainebleau Painters, 308

Bassæ. See Phygaleia.

Baudry, 308

Bavaria, 256

Beautiful in Nature, Life, and Art, The, Symington, 298

Beautiful, the, in art, 421

Beauty, ascribable to association, 104-108, 128, 290 ; to effects on mind, 107, 108, 318 ; to physical causes, 113, 114, 361, 362 ; connected with absence of visual effort, 282, 283 ; connected with proportion and harmony, 2 ; curve, the line of, 59-61, 135, 136, 282, 283, 286, 287 ; determined by both form and significance, 104-108, 112, 139, 140 ; discrepancies in standards of, 112, 113 ; meaning and office of, in art, 421, 422 ; models of, from nature as in Greek art, 88-102, 111, 140 ; of Ameri-

INDEX. 443

Beauty—*Continued.*
  can face, 128, 129; of face, 126–129; of human form, 71, 101, 104–108, 139, 140; vibrations at basis of, 113, 114
Beauty, Science of, Hay, 46
Belgian School of Painting, 304
Bellini, 303
Bezold, Von, ix., 333, 387, 390, 392, 401, 403, 404, 406
Binocular Vision, 266–295
Birds, elliptical contours of, 288, 289; proportions in, 78
Black and White, influence on complementary colors, 334, 335
Blanc, C., 376
Blouet, 182
Blue by lamplight, 315; color, in water and atmosphere, 318, 319. See Colors.
Bol, 305
Boldini, 308
Boris, Tower of, in Kremlin, Moscow, 173
Bouguereau, 308, 322
Bow Church Steeple, London, 171
Breadth, 366. See Massing.
Breton, J., 322, 354, 356, 360
Brewster, 274, 282
Brilliant, colors, objection to use of, in painting, 365, 385, 386; the, in art, 425. See Colors.
Brittany Washerwomen, Breton, 354, 356, 360
Broken Colors, 304, 312. See Colors
Brücke, 274, 275, 282
Buckhart, J., 255

Cabanel, 308, 322
Calf, proportions of human, 132–134
Camera, 21, 22
Canal, The, by Corot, 74–77
Canterbury Cathedral, 38
Capital, of column, as related to Greek proportion, 185, 186, 188–191, 195, 198, 203, 207–210, 212, 213, 217; considered as pendant of entablature, 203, 207, 210; Corinthian, 220; Doric, 183; Ionic, 204; of same measurement

in Greek temples as the cornice and stylobate, 188–191; proportional relationship to architrave, freize, upper width of column, and width of metopes and triglyphs, 191–195. See Abacus.
Caracci, 303
Caravaggio, 303
Carlo Dolci, 303
Cathedral, Canterbury, 38; Chichester, 41, Ely, 52–56
Central Congregational Church, Boston, 39
Central Point—Art-Method, 3, 64, 65; in color, 363, 368
Ceres, Temple of, Eleusis, 187, 194, 221
Cespedes, De, 304
Character. See Beauty, Face, Human Form, Significance.
Chares, 98
Château, de Randau, 51; Chenonceau, 53
Chaucer's Crystal Palace, 298, 299
Chemical action in nerves of seeing and hearing, 382
Chenonceau, château, 53
Chiaroscuro, 367. See Massing and Light and Shade.
Chiavavalle, Dome of, Italy, 174
Chichester Cathedral, 41
China, art of, 89
Church, an American, 163
Chlorophyl, 317
Cimabue, 302
Circles, as determining proportional measurements, 68–72; especially when intersecting, 136–139, 278–288, 291, 292. See Curves.
Circumferences, intersecting. See Circles.
Circumspective, as distinguished from perspective, 233
Claparède, 268
Classic *vs.* Romantic in Art, 420
Classification—Art-Method, 61, 429
Claude Lorraine, 305, 306
Clothing, ethical influence of, 108–112; proportional divisions of, 79–84
Cockerill, 19, 29, 44, 178, 181, 188,

Cockerill—*Continued*.
188, 189, 192, 196, 197, 204, 205, 220, 248
Cold Colors, 303, 304, 313, 320–324, 384–388, 407, 408; in aërial perspective, 321–324; in backgrounds and reliefs, 387, 388; in complementaries, 335, 336, 384–388, 407, 408; in-doors and out, 320, 321; in shadows at different times of day, 319–321
Cologne Cathedral, 153, 155, 156, 180, 207
Colors, action of eye in recognizing, 378–383; actual and apparent, 24, 243, 244, 318; actual of natural objects, 317–321; as illumined by other colors, 314–322; as imitated from nature in painting, 243, 244, 296–298, 389, 390, 414; as representing distance, 321–324; as used by Egyptian, Greek, and later painters, 300–304; at different times of night and day, 314–322; balance of, 358–361, 364, 366, 367; bright and brilliant, 365, 374, 385, 386; broken, 304, 312; complication in, 369; congruity in, 361, 362, 368; consonance in, 370–405; continuity in, 361, 369; cold, 302–304, 313, 319–324, 335, 336, 384–388, 407, 408; dark, 311, 312, 384–388; dull, 374; effect of distance on, 243, 244, 321–324, 328, 371; effect of light and darkness on, 311–313, 410; effect on one another when side by side, 371, 372, 384–396; English School of Water, 305; full, 312; gradation in, 302, 303, 305, 306, 308, 406–412; harmony of, 27, 326, 327, 353, 355–418; high, 312, 374; in painting *vs.* decoration as in architecture, 296, 298, 389, 390, 413–415; light, 311, 312, 384–388; local, 312, 313, 325, 377–383; low, 374; mixing in eye, 307, 337, 371; neutral, 313, 385, 386; on exteriors of buildings, 189, 192, 194, 416–418; pale, 304, 312; pitch of, 6, 374; positive, 313; primary,

313, 326; production of, from light illustrated, 309–311, 329–331; production of from pigments, 311, 332, 333; quality of, 6; scientific study of, necessary, 298–308; secondary, 313, 326; selected, used in art, 297, 312, 352; shades of, 312; shadows of, 300, 303, 304, 319, 320, 358, 361, 365–368, 376, 378–380, 384–388, 390, 391, 408–412; theories of harmony of, 326, 327, 352–354, 391–405; tints of, 312; tone of, 6, 308, 312, 327, 355–358; transmit and reflect colors like their own, 314–317; used in painting for color's sake, 296, 297; varied in painting, 355, 356, 365; vibrations of retina, coalescing to form harmony of, 347–351, 353, 354, 356, 373–375, 377–383, 404, 405; warm, 302–304, 313, 319–324, 327, 336, 384–388, 407, 408; waves determining each of the, 402; waves of, in the ether, 349, 350, 373–375, 377–383
Color Scale, 389–405; chart of, 333–336, 390–393, 398, 402, 414
Colossus of Rhodes, 98
Columbus, vi
Columns of Greek Temple, 184, 187; breadth to height, 219; curves in, 260, 261, 262; flutings, 264, 265; height of, less than apparent, 151, 152, 202, 203; inter-spacing of, 195, 248, 263, 264; leaning of, 257, 258, 259; lower diameter of, 196; proportion of height of, as related to entablature, pediment, tympanum, and stylobate, 201–217; sizes of, 248, 263; upper diameter of, 191–196; tapering of, 257, 259–263
Common Multiple for Vibrations causing harmony in eye or ear, 340, 343, 347, 353, 357
Common Sense as applied to art subjects, 112
Comparative Æsthetics, sketch of system of, 419–432
Comparison, applied to measurement of spaces, 10, 11, 14, 24, etc.;

INDEX. 445

Comparison—*Continued.*
Art-Method, 3, 10, 61–64, 68;
basis of color-harmony, 314–317,
327–330, 354–360, 362, 364–368;
basis of proportion, 14, 15, 19,
23, 24, 28–43, 50, 52–56, 64,
88, 116, 124, 134, 146, 162, 184;
basis of rhythm, 19, 23, 24, etc.;
principle of, underlying art-development, 426–430, 432
Complement—Art-Method, 3; in
color, 297, 327–329, 354, 355, 412;
in proportion, 63, 68, 78, 173, 412
Complementary Colors, basis of consonance, 370–377; basis of harmony, 353–356; harmony not
always produced by, 335; numbers
of, practically infinite, 335, 397,
398; production of, from construction of the eye, viii., 380–383;
from light, vii., illustrated, 328–336; from pigments, 332, 333;
from light waves, 375–380. See
Contrast.
Complexity—Art-Method, 3, 18, 61,
146, 430; in color, 328, 362; in
proportion, 18, 61, 146; of architecture, 170, 171, 213, 216
Complication—Art-Method, 3, 66; in
color, 369; in proportion, 170, 171
Comprehensiveness—Art-Method,
3; in color, 362, 363; in proportion, 64
Concord, temple at Agrigentum,
187, 193, 221
Cones and rods in the eye, viii., 349,
350, 380–383
Confusion—Art-Method, 3, 62; in
color, 328
Congruity—Art-Method, 3; in architecture, 146–148; in color, 361,
362, 368; in proportion, 64, 104;
in the human figure, 115, 116
Conscious, action of the eye in perceiving outlines of different shapes
at different distances, 271–283;
mental action when making measurements of rhythm and proportion, iv., v., 23–27, 50, 64, 65,
178, 179, 343, 344, 430, 431. See
Unconscious.

Consonance—Art-Method, vii., 3,
64, 66; in architecture, 148, 166,
168; in color, vii., 351, 363, 370–405, 410, 412; in outline, 231; result of proportional ratios in vibrations, 343, 344, 394–405; similarly
produced in ear and eye, 372–377,
394–405. See Harmony, Ratios,
and Vibrations.
Constable, 305
Continuity—Art-Method, 3, 66; in
color, 361, 369
Contour of human form, 59, 68–72,
85–87, 135–143, 290–295. See
Elliptical, Human Form and
Shape.
Contrast—Art-Method, 3, 63, 68,
412; in color, 328, 329, 354–366;
in relief from background of color,
387, 388; simultaneous in color,
376, 383, 386; successive, or consecutive in color, 371, 372, 375–377, 383; analogue of successive
in sound, 372–374. See Complementary Colors.
Conversations, Eckermann's, 376
Corinth, temple at, 195, 203, 255
Corinthian Order, 203, 220
Cornelius, 306
Cornice, 183, 186–196, 198, 201–207, 209, 212, 215; like measurement of, and of Greek capital and
stylobate, 188–191
Corona, 182, 185–187, 190, 198, 203,
205, 207–209, 213–215
Corot, 308, 322, 433
Correggio, 303, 304, 367
Correspondence between, arts of
sound and sight, 1–7, 10; proportion and harmony, 27, 31, 64–66,
430, 431; proportion and perspective, 20–31; proportion and
rhythm, iv., v., vi., 2, 3, 7, 10,
13–19, 23–26; 74, 115–117, 179,
430, 431; speech and proportion
in painting, 13–15, 74, 114–116;
speech-harmony and harmony of
outline, 229–232, 431; speech-rhythm and proportion, 13–15,
74, 114–116. See Consonance,
Harmony, and Proportion.

Corti's Rods, 347
Countenance. See Face.
Counteraction—Art-Method, 3, 62; in color, 328, 392.
Cranach, 306
Creative periods early in art-history, 222
Criticism, influence of, on art and originality, 436, 437
Crystal Palace of Chaucer, 298, 299.
Culture, influence of, on art and originality, 436, 437
Curvalinear. See Curves.
Curvature as related to proportion, 141, 142. See Curves.
Curved lines. See Curves.
Curves, 266-295; causing ease of vision, 277-295; comparative measurements of, in columns, 202; exemplifying gradation, 59-61, 291-295; in human bodies, 58-60, 69-72, 134-142, 290-295; in architectural straight lines, Egyptian and Greek, 246-265; in horizontal straight lines, 234-237, 239, 240, 243, 257, 258; in vertical straight lines, 237-239; like, as determining proportion, 58, 59, 62, 63, 66-72, 78, 87, 134-142; the lines of beauty, 282, 283
Cymatium, 183, 191, 197, 198, 201-203, 206, 207, 212-214, 216
Cyma Recta, 183-185

Dædalus, 89, 97
Damophilus, 300
Dark Colors, 311, 312, 385-388
Daubigny, 322
David, 306
De Architectura, Vitruvius, 26, 64, 117, 120, 219, 256
Decamps, 322
Decline in Art after periods of progress, 222
Decorative Painting, 296, 298, 389, 390, 413-418; character of mediæval, 301; distinguished from pictorial, 296-298, 309, 390, 425
Delacroix, 306, 370
Delagardetta, 181
Delaroche, 306

Delos, temple of Apollo at, 194 221
De Nittis, 322
Descent from the Cross, the, Rubens, 358, 367; picture, 359
Diadumenos, 95, 97
Diana, temple of, at Eleusis, 191, 193, 221
Diaz, 308
Diseases of the Eye, Noyes, 21
Discobolus, 96, 97
Dissonance—Art-Method, 3, in proportion, 66; in colors, 406

Distance, as represented in color, 243, 244, 321-324, 366, 411; effect of, on eyes, 233, 234; proportions of buildings to be judged from, iii., 35, 180, 202, 244, 246, 249, 251, 265; were judged thus by Greeks and Egyptians, 244-259. See Perspective.
Dolci, C, 303
Domenichino, 303
Donaldson, 248
Doric Architecture, 181, 211, 219, 220
Dorotheus, 301
Douw, 305
Dove, 274, 275, 282
Dramatic Art, 425
DuPiles, 122, 124
Duration—Art-Method, 4-6, 16, 19
Dürer, 306
Dusseldorf School of Painting, 306
Dutch Painters, 304
Dyck, Van, 304
Dyke, Van, 365
Dying Galatian, or Gladiator, 437

Ease of eyes' action in perceiving outlines, 139, 140, 230-233, 268-295
Eccentricity, cultivated when there are no standard of taste, 433, 434; *versus* originality, 435, 436
Eckermann, 376
Ediou, 249
Effect of **distance on magnitude**, light, **contrast, and detail**, Stimson, 235

Effects, general, as from distance, 251, 252; optical. See Distance and Illusions.
Egyptian, painting, 300; temples, 244, 246, 249
Elements, of Art Criticism, Samson, 117; of Drawing, Ruskin, 368
Eleusis, temple of Ceres at, 194; of Diana at, 191, 193, 221
Elgin, Lord, 248
Elizabeth, Architectural Style of, 227
Ellipse, 280-291; as determining proportional measurements, 68, 69; in form of vases, plants, birds, beasts, fishes, 283-290; in human forms, 137, 138, 290, 291, 295; illustrated, 287, 289; its extensive use in art, 283; its outline, the line of beauty, 282, 283
Elliptical. See Ellipse.
Ellipticlanceolate shape, why used in art, 280-291; illustrated. 58, 59, 70-72, 136, 137, 138, 280, 283-285, 289
Ellis, 101
Ely Cathedral, interior, 52-56
English, School of Water Colors, 305
Entablature, in Greek temple, 183, 187, 189, 192, 194-196, 198, 201-217, 221, 224, 245-252, 254-259; curves in, 245-248, 254-259; height as proportioned to that of columns, pediment, stylobate and tympanum, 201-222; leaning forward of, 245-250, 255-258. See Like with Like, Proportion, and Ratios.
Entasis, 246-265. See Curves.
Entombment, The, Titian, 366
Epic Art, 425
Erectheum, 262
Esculapius, 193
Ethical in art-effects, 108
Etty, 305
Euphranor, 301
Eupompus, 91, 300
Eycks, Van, 304
Excursion, Wordsworth, 437
Experiment at basis, of Gothic architectural proportion, 252, 253; of Greek, 252, 253, 265

Expression, elements of, in art, 426-429; in human figure as a whole, 93, 104-114, 128, 129, 139, 140. See Beauty, Face, Human Form Significance.
Extension—Art-Method, 4-7, 19
Exteriors of Buildings, colors of, 189, 192, 194, 415-418
Eyes, action of, in seeing, 139, 140, 231-238, 257, 261, 263, 264, 286, 291-295; binocular vision of, 267-295; cavity of, 22; conscious and unconscious action of, in perceiving outlines and relief, 271-275, 280-282; Diseases of, 21; field of view of both, and of one eye, 267-271, 276-286; effect on perspective of rotation of, 237, 238; formation of image in, 22; mixing of colors in, 307, 337, 371; organism perceiving color, 349, 350, 380-383; what secures ease of action of, in perceiving outlines, 139, 140, 230-233, 268-295

Fabius, 301
Fabullus, 301
Face, American, 128, 129; beauty and character in, 105, 106, 128; conventional character of Greek, 92-95; curvilinear measurements of, 134,135; expression in, 94, 105, 106, 128, 129; Greek, 92-95, 125, 126, 128, 129; proportions of, 85-87, 105, 106, 125-129; rectilinear measurements of, 85-87, 125-128
Faun of Praxiteles, 97, 99
Feet, poetic, 16. See Measures.
Fergusson, J., 28
Field-theory of color-harmony, 353, 354, 392
Fillets, Architectural, 187, 189, 203
Finger behind another as seen by one and both eyes, 269
Fishes, elliptical contours of, 288, 289; proportions of, 78
Flemish, Correggio, 304; School of Painters, 304, 305
Florence, Academy of, 306
Foliage, real colors of, 317, 318

Fontainebleau - Barbizon, School of Painters, 308
Force—Art-Method, 5–7
Form in art, considered in itself, 429–432; two effects of: communication and imitation, 420–422; *versus* significance, 104–108, 112, 128, 129, 139, 140, 158, 420–432. See Contour, Elliptic, Human Form, Outline, and Shape.
Fortuny, 308, 355, 365
Foster, M., 267, 276, 345, 346, 347, 349
Foundation. See Stylobate.
Frère, 322
Fresnoy, 122, 123
Frieze, Greek, 182, 185, 186, 191–196, 205; as related to architrave, column, pediment, and tympanum, 191–198
Fromentin, 322
Full colors, 312

Gainsborough, 305
Ganymede, statue of, 103
Genesis of Art-Form, The, 1, 61, 63, 64, 66, 67, 104, 117, 120, 146, 168, 176, 232, 237, 286, 303, 328, 329, 348, 358, 369, 415, 424, 429; analysis of argument in essay on, 429, 430
Gentile, 302
Geometric, æsthetics, 295; designs, 286, 287
Geometry in proportion, 141
German Painting, 306
Gérôme, 308, 322
Ghent, street and belfry at, 172
Giants, temple of, at Agrigentum, 191, 195, 221
Giorgione, 303
Giotto, 302
Gladiator, or Galatian, Dying, 437
Glycon, 97
Goethe, 92, 376
Golden Section, as determining proportion, 27
Good, The, in art, 425
Goodyear, W. H., 243, 248, 249, 255, 265
Gorgasus, 300

Gossip, painting by C. Marr, 355
Gothic, art, 227; cathedral, 64; experiments in building, 252, 253; proportion in, 52–56; revival in architecture, 226
Gradation—Art-Method, 3, 61, 67, 408; in architecture, 148, 171–173; in color, 302, 303, 305, 306, 308, 406–412; in human face and form, 138–140, 292–295; phonetic, 233
Grammar of Painting and Engraving, Blanc, 376
Granet, 355
Green Color, by lamplight, 315; difficult to paint because of many complementaries, 335, 336; living, in landscapes, 318
Greek, architectural proportions, 117–228; architecture as contrasted with Roman, 262, 263; conception of proportion, 26–30, 44; conventional face, 92–95, 125, 126, 128, 129, 134, 135; entasis, 246–265; experiments in methods of constructing temples, 252, 253; fret, 12; measurement in proportion apparent not real, 179–181; painting, 300, 301; painting of exteriors of temples, 189, 192, 194, 416–418; proportions of human form, 117, 118, 120–124; study of nature in producing human form, 90–102; study of posture, 141, 142; temples, 8, 64, etc.
Greuze, 306
Gros, 306
Grouping—Art-Method, 3; in proportion, 61, 62, 67; in color, 328
Guido, 303
Gwilt, Joseph, iii., 120, 198

Hadrian, 97
Hals, Franz, 305
Hansen, 182
Harmony, Greek use of term, 26, 27
Harmony of Color, 2, 7, 325–412; a human invention, 297, 352, 353; and of music, similarly conditioned, 338–347, 372–377, 394–405; and of sound analogous vii., 2, 7, 25–27,

Harmony of Color—*Continued.*
343-345; as related to consonance vii., 351, 371; as tone, 327, 355-358; balance in, 360, 361; connection of, with all art-methods, 3, 327-329, 357-359, 406-412; correspondence between causes of, and of rhythm and proportion, 27, 31, 65, 66, 343, 344, 430, 431; determined by ratios between rates of vibrations, 347, 348, 373-375, 377-383, 394-405; determined by vibrations coalescing in retina, 347-351, 354, 356, 373-375, 377-383, 404, 405; groups of two, three, and four colors producing, 391-405; organs of eye recognizing, 349, 350, 380-383; physiological basis of, iv., v., 338, 347, 349-351, 353-358, 378-383, 391-407, 430, 431; psychical causes connected with, 344, 360, 375, 376, 406-408; theories of, 326, 327, 352-354, 391-405; two phases of, 350-351; scales of, 389-412; unconscious action of mind in judging of, iv., v., 23-27, 64, 65, 343-345, 404, 405

Harmony of Outline, 23-26, 229-295; correspondence to harmony of speech, as used in poetry, 229-232

Harmony of Sound, 2, 7, 23; and of speech, 26, 229, 230, 326; determined by ratios between rates of vibrations, and physiological basis of, iv., v., 23-26, 229-232, 338-348, 356-360, 398-400, 403, 430

Hay, D. R., 28, 46, 49, 68, 137, 256-258

Heat, relation of, to chemical action, to color, and to nerve-perception of particular sounds and colors, 382

Hellquist, 363, 364, 366, 369
Helmholtz, vii., 332, 340
Hercules, statue of, 94, 97
Hermes, statue of, 97, 100
Hermogenes, 301
High colors, 312, 374

Hilarius, 301
Historic method of art-study not always the best, 437, 438
History of Painting, brief, 300-308
Hittorf, 182, 187-190, 193, 194, 197, 208, 220
Hofer, 248
Hogarth, 305
Holbein, 306
Horizontal, cornice in Greek architecture as related to proportion, 188, 189, 197, 203, 205-209, 215; level in perspective, 234-237, 239, 240, 255, 256; lines in perspective, 234, 236, 238-243, 255, 256; made æsthetically effective by means of curves, 234-237, 239, 240, 243, 257, 258
Horopter, 268, 269
House of Fame, Chaucer, 298
How to judge of a picture, Van Dyke, 365
Hues, 312. See Colors.
Human Face. See Beauty, Face, and Human Form.
Human Form, beauty of, as dependent on association and significance, 92-108, 112-114, 128, 129, 139, 140; on likeness in measurements, when clothed or unclothed, 78-88, 115-143; on likeness in vibrations, 113, 114; on taste, 113, 114, 128, 129; curvilinear outlines of, as in segments of ellipses and circles, 58-60, 68-72, 87, 134-143, 290-295; Greek measurements and proportions of, 120-130, 133, 134; proportions as dependent on congruity or fitness, 115, 116; on curvilinear measurements, 58-60, 63-72, 87, 135-143; on rectilinear measurements, 78-88; 115-135
Illusions, optical, in connection with sizes of columns, 263, 264; with straight lines, triangles, and cross lines, 240-249, 257, 258
Image on the retina, 21, 23; formation of this, 22; measurements of, determine measurements of proportion, 23, 24, 34

29

450 *INDEX.*

Imitation, of architecture, 224; of nature in color, 296-298, 352, 414, 433, 434; in criticism and art-production, 433-436
Impressionism, extremes of, 307
Incongruity—Art-Method, 3, 64; in color, 362
Individual experience and experiment in art-methods, 252, 253
Induction, method of practiced before time of Bacon, 89
Inherent Colors, 312, 313, 325
Inness, 322
Interchange—Art-Method, 3, 67; in architecture, 148, 166-168, 170, 171; in outline, 231; in color, 406-408, 411
Interspersion—Art-Method, 3, 16; in color, 368, 369
Ionian capital and order of architecture, 203, 204, 219, 220
Irregularity in Greek temple-measurements, 248-250, 262, 263
Israels, 322
Italy, painting of, 302, 306

Japan, art of, 89, 90; knowledge of human form, 90; lack of nude art, 110; morality of, 110
Jules Breton, 354, 356
Juno Lucina, temple of, at Agrigentum, 187, 193
Jupiter, at Nemea, temple of, 191, 194, 221; at Olympia, temple of, 190, 194, 221; Olympus, temple of, 250, 262

Kaffir Station, Africa, 34
Karnack, temple at, 249
Kaulbach, 306
Keynote, in music and color, 357, 358, 374
Kuttenberg, spire at, 171

Landscape, proportion in, 13, 14, 73-78
Laocoön, 98
Lawrence, 305
Le Conte, ix., 21, 238 268, 272-275, 282, 349

Leg and Foot, proportions of, 132-134
Legh, Peter, 27, 150
Lens of Eye, 22; adjusted to different backgrounds, 273
Leonardo da Vinci, 299, 302, 306
Lerolle, H., 322, 361
Lessing, 306
Lesueur, 306
Liberty, Thompson, 219
Life, colors of, in nature, 317-319
Light and Shade, abruptness in, 412; as represented by early and later painters, 301-304; as represented in different colors at different times of night and day, 314-316, 319-324; balance produced by, 358-361; complementary color of in the shadow, 376, 378-380, 384-388, 390, 391; gradation in, 408-411; massing in, 366-369
Light colors, 311, 312, 384-388; light tint of light-color put with dark shade of dark color, and *vice versa*, 410
Light in general, as in atmosphere, distinguished from local color, 377-383
Like with Like, basis of artistic classification, 61-67 note, 430-432; basis of proportion, v., 8, 10-19, 39-43; 52-56, 59, 60, 62-64, 68-84, 87, 88, 116, 117, 120-143, 184, 222; basis of harmonious coloring, 314-317, 325-328, 361, 362, 364-366, 368-370; in measurements of Greek abacus, corona, and other mouldings, 185-188; of Greek capital, cornice, and stylobate, 188-191, 221; of Greek architrave frieze, combined raking cornice and cymatium, upper diameter of columns, and of metopes and triglyphs, 191-195, 221; of Greek entablature, tympanum, and upper space between columns, 195-199, 221; of Greek entablature with capital and pediment, 198, 201, 202, 204-212, 221; of human

INDEX. 451

Like with Like—*Continued.*
    face, 85-87, 105, 106, 125-129; of human form, 58-61, 68-72, 78-88, 115-135; of modern architecture, 51-58, 116, 117, 149-176, 225, 226; of landscapes, 13, 14, 73-78; of Greek architecture, 185-226; of rhythm, 16-18, 64, 65, etc.; illustrated in poetry and music, 16-18, 230, 231, 232; in ornamentation, 11-13; in rectilinear and curvilinear outlines, 39-42, 52-59, 61, 64, 68-72; not inconsistent with alternation, 116, 117, 127; not inconsistent with variety, 62 note, etc. See Harmony, Proportion, Ratios, and Vibrations.
Lines, curved, indicating likeness and proportion, 58, 59, 62, 63, 66-72, 78, 87, 134-142; imaginary, indicating proportional measurements, 85-88; poetic, rhythm of, 18; straight, indicating proportion, 6, 7, 58, 68, 79, 80. See Curves, Horizontal, Perspective, Proportion, and Vertical.
Lippi, 302
Lloyd's, W. W., Appendix to Works of Penrose and Cockerill, 19, 29, 44, 183, 194, 196, 201, 202, 211, 218
Local color, 312, 313, 325; as distinguished from atmosphere, 377-383; as perceived by eye, 377-383
Locksley Hall, Tennyson, 18
Long, S. P., 368
Loomis, E. H., ix.
Lorraine, 305
Ludwig I., 256
Luxor, 249
Lysippus, 91, 97, 98

Maas, 305
Maison Carrée, 245-247, 249; illustration of, 245, 247
Manner or style as related to matter, 438, 439
Maori Festival, 33
Marquand, A., ix

Marr, C., 355
Marriage at Cana, Paul Veronese, 360
Masaccio, 302
Massing—Art-Method, 3, 66; in color, 364, 366-369, 408
Measures in music, 16-18; in poetry, 16-19
Measurements, accuracy of, not essential in art, 179-181, 184, 185, 202, 203; apparent not actual at basis of proportion, iii., iv., 24, 25, 32, 34, 38, 39, 151, 179; conscious of, in effects of rhythm and proportion, iv., v., 23-27, 50, 179; different schemes of, in different parts of forms, 116, 117, 127; natural tendency to make, 10, 11, 14; to join like with like, 10, 11, 14; unconscious of, in effects of harmony of color or sound, iv., v., 23, 26, 27, 343-345, 404, 405. See Like with Like, Ratios, and Proportion.
Mediæval Castle, 36
Medinet Habou, 246, 249
Meleagros, statue of, 102
Memling, H.; 304
Memoir on The Systems of Proportion, etc., Lloyd, 19, 44
Memorabilia, 91
Mengs, R., 306
Mephistopheles, 106
Metopes, 12, 192-195, 214
Michael Angelo, 302
Micon, 300
Middle Ages, art of, 89
Millet, J. F., 308, 322
Milton, 211
Mixing of colors in eye, 307, 337, 371; in pigments, 311, 332, 333
Minerva, statue of, 97; temple of, at Sunium, 193, 221; at Syracuse, 193
Models in art, need of, 88-102, 111, 140, 141, 144, 145; used by Greeks, 88-102, 111
Modern Chromatics, Rood, ix., 315, 321, 386, 393, 396, 409
Modern Painters, Ruskin, 59
Monks in Oratory, Granet, 355

452   INDEX.

Moorish Art, 227
Moscow, Tower of Boris, Kremlin, at, 173
Mouldings, architectural, 187, 191, 192, 197, 198, 208, 209 ; coloring in Greek, 192
Müller, 268
Munich, School of Painting, 306
Murillo, 304
Music 16, 17. See Consonance Harmony, Rhythm, and Proportion.
Music of the Eye, Legh, 27, 150
Myron, 97

Natural History, Pliny, 91, 92, 301
Nature, Greek study of, in human figure, 82-102, 111 ; imitation of, in coloring, 243, 244, 296-298, 389, 390, 414 ; necessity of study of, 82-102, 111, 140, 141, 144, 145 ; proportion in, 13, 14, 74-79 ; real colors of objects in, 317-322
Nausica, figure from Poynter, 142
Nemea, temple of Jupiter at, 191, 194, 203
Nemesis, temple of, at Rhamnus, 187, 193, 221
Neptune, temple of, at Pæstum, 187, 193, 221
Netherlands, painters of the, 303, 386, 388
Neutral Colors, 313, 385, 386
Newton, 309
Nicias, 301
Nicomachus, 301
Nimes, France, 245-249
Niobe, Statue, Group of, 98, 101
Notes, ratios of, in music, 16 ; see Harmony, Ratios, Vibrations.
Noyes, H. D., 21
Nude Art, 109-112

Olympia, temple of Jupiter at, 190, 194, 221
Olympus, temple of Jupiter, 250, 262
On the Law of Proportion which Rules all Nature, Zeising, 27
Opera House, Paris, 167, 170, etc.
Opie, 305

Orcagna, 302
Order—Art-Method, 3 ; in proportion, 62, 116 ; in color, 328
Organic Form—Art-Method, 3, 63, 146 ; in color, 358, 360, 363
Organ Recital, Lerolle, 361
Originality, not inconsistent with standards of art and criticism, 433, 435, 436
Ornamental Geometric Designs, etc., Hay, 286
Ornamentation, based on principle of putting like with like, 11-13
Outline, effect of, analogous to that of pauses, 4, 5, 7 ; harmony of, 229-295 ; suggestively indicating proportion, 50-59, 76-81
Ovolo, of capital in Greek architecture, 182, 185-189, 191, 198, 205. See Like with Like, Proportion, and Ratios.

Pæstum, temple at, 187, 193, 221, 255
Painting,5 ; brief history of,300-308 ; Egyptian, 300 ; Greek, 300 ; imitation of nature in, 243, 244, 296-298, 389, 390, 414 ; on Greek exteriors of buildings, 189, 192, 194, 416-418 ; decorative or architectural versus pictorial, 296, 298, 389, 390, 413-415. See Colors.
Painting, Sculpture, and Architecture as Representative Arts ; 64, 102, 128, 145, 146, 148, 158, 323, 361, 415, 416, 423 ; analysis of the essay on, 428
Pale Colors, 304, 312.
Pallas of Velletri Statue, 97
Pamphilus, 300
Pantheon, illustration of, 223 ; proportions of, 224
Parallelism—Art-Method, 3, 65, 78 ; in color, 361, 363
Parallel Lines in Perspective, horizontal, 233-238 ; vertical, 237-240
Parrhasius, 301
Parthenon, 28, 29, 35, 97, 151, 186, 190, 193, 194, 196, 197, 201, 202,

Parthenon—*Continued.*
220, 222, 245, 250-252, 256-258, 262, 263, 416, 418; illustration of, 190; proportions of 211-218; stylobate and columns of, as photographed, 251
Partial effects in art alike, 340-343; tones in music, 372-375, 398-404
Pausanias, 26
Pausias, 301
Pediment, Greek, difficulty of calculating its height from below, 215-217; its height, same apparently as that of the entablature added to a part of the column's capital, 198, 201, 202, 204-212, 221; ratio between this height and the height and breadth of other features of the Greek temple, 200-222; unsatisfactory measurements of, 197
Pennethorne, John, 246, 249
Penrose, F. C., 29, 181, 183, 194, 196, 197, 201, 202, 211, 220, 248, 249, 250, 254, 255, 262, 263
Pericles, 300
Perspective, aërial, 321-324
Perspective, linear, effects of, as distinguished from those of proportion, iii, iv, 25-31, 35-38, 65, 178, 179, 244, 246, 251-253; effects of, considered in itself, 232-265; in architecture, especially Greek, 36, 245-248, 255-258; in causing optical illusions, 240-246; in differentiating actual from apparent measurements, iii, 24, 25, 32, 34; in curving and leaning forward of Greek entablature, 245-250, 255-258; in horizontal lines, 233-238; in landscape, 237-239; in vertical lines, 237-239
Perugino, 302
Pheidias, 97, 300
Phigaleia, temple of, 186, 187, 190, 194, 201, 208, 210, 218, 221, 219, 220
Phrase, rhythm of musical, 18
Phryne, 92
Physical, or

Physiological cause of gradation in color, 410, 411; of harmony of color, iv., v., vii., 338, 347, 349-351, 353-358, 378-383, 391-407; of outline, 23-26, 229-243; of music, iv., v., 23-26, 338-348, 356-358, 398-400, 403
Physical Characteristics of the Athlete, Sargent, 88; Development of Women, Sargent, 88
Physiology, Text-Book of, Foster, 267, 276, 345
Pictures. See Painting.
Picturesque, The, in art, 425
Pigments, colors produced by mixing, 311; producing complementaries, 332, 333; study of, in art and science, 300-308
Piloty, K., 364, 366
Pinus, 301
Pitch, of color, 5-7, 374; of sound, 5-7
Plato, 26
Pliny, 91, 92, 300, 301
Plutarch, 300, 301
Poetic Principle, The, Poe, 431
Poetry as a Representative Art, 5, 423; analysis of essay on, 427
Poetry, measures and ratios of, 16-18
Polycleitus, 95, 97
Polygnotus, 300
Positive Colors, 313
Posture, grace of, determined by curved lines, 290; Greek study of, 141, 142
Poussin, 305
Praxiteles, 92, 97-100
Prévost, 268, 274, 282
Primary Colors, 313, 326
Principality — Art-Method, 3, 63, 116; in architecture, 284; in painting, 355, 356-358, 367, 368
Principles of Athenian Architecture, The, 181, 248, 254, 262. See Penrose.
Progress—Art-Method, 3, 61, 67; in color, 412
Proportion, analogue of rhythm rather than harmony, iv., v., vi., 2, 3, 7, 10, 13-19, 23-26, 74,

Proportion—*Continued.*
115–117, 179, 430, 431; apparent not actual measurements considered in, iii., iv., 24, 25, 32, 34, 38, 151, 179, 180; architectural, 34–42, 51–58, 116 144–228; as developed by all the art-methods, 61–67 note, 148; beauty dependent on, 2; based on putting like measurements with like, v., 8, 10–19, 39–43, 52–56, 59, 60, 62–64, 68–84, 88, 116, 117, 120–143, 184, 222; characterizing natural forms, 13, 14, 73–78; complexity of, 15; confounded with linear perspective and so misunderstood, iv., v., 25–31, 35–38, 178, 179, 244, 246, 251–253; conscious, not unconscious, action of the mind in judging of, iv., v., 23–27, 50, 178, 179, 430, 431; correspondences between effects of and of harmony, 27, 31, 64–66, 430, 431; curvilinear indications of, 58–61, 68–72, 88–135, 142, 291; dependence of, on fitness or congruity, iii., 115, 116, 146–148; distinguished from harmony, iv., v., 25, 26, 430; effects less physical than psychological, iv., v., 24, 25, 50; effects of, not always distinguishable from those of contour, 148, 149, 173; facial, 85–87, 105, 106, 125–130; Greek architectural, 177–228; Greek conception of, v., vi., 26–30, 36–38; Greek, of human face and form, 120–130, 133, 134; judged from distance, iii., 35, 36, 180; judged from parts not wholes of bodies or buildings, v., 152–154, 222; importance of, 2, 14, 15; in birds, fishes, quadrupeds, trees, etc., 77, 78; in clothing, 79–82; indicated by imaginary lines, 85–87; indicated by marks of like subdivision, 43–47, 152–161; in human figures, 9, 58–60, 68–72, 78–87, 115–143; in or between irregular figures, indicated by inscribing them in square or curved regular figures, 48–74; in landscapes, 13, 14, 73–77; in stained glass, 78, 79; of Parthenon, 211–218; of rooms, 150, 151; rectangular and rectilinear, 44–58, 68; that objects are characterized by, a statement of fact, 10; theories concerning, 25–31. See Like with Like, Measurement, and Ratios.

Proportions of Typical Man, Sargent, D. A., 88

Propylæa, temple, 186, 190, 196, 210, 218

Protogenes, 301

Psychical or mental effects in connection with harmony of color, 344, 360, 375, 376, 406–408; with proportion, iv., v., 23–27, 50, 343–345, 430, 431. See Harmony and Proportion.

Pyreicus, 301

Pythagoras, vii.; his system of tone-harmony, 338

Quality of sound and color, 5–7

Radiation in color, 363, 408

Raeburn, 305

Raking Cornice, over the tympanum in Greek temple, 183, 185–189, 191, 197, 198, 203, 206, 207, 213, 214, 216; for proportions and measurements of, see Like with Like and Ratios.

Randau, Château de, 51

Raphael, 92, 180, 302

Ratios, 9; as used by Greeks were simple and of small numbers, 19, 39, 40; between alternating members the numbers need not be apparent, 117, 127, 165, 166; between architectural members in Greek temples, as the abacus, corona, etc., and the capital, cornice, and stylobate, 188–191; between these three and the architrave, the frieze, the combined raking cornice and cymatium, the upper diameter of columns, and width of the metopes and the

INDEX. 455

Ratios—*Continued.*
triglyphs, 191-195, 221; between these six and the entablature, the tympanum, and the upper space between columns, 195-199, 221; between these spaces and also between the entablature with capital and the pediment and the height of columns with or without capitals, 198, 201, 202, 204-214, 221; in poetry and music, 16-18; not apparent to consciousness when causing harmony of sound or color, iv., v., 23-27, 343-345, 353, 354, 404, 405; not invariably apparent when causing proportion or rhythm, 19; of no practical value to art when their meaning not understood, 29, 30; operative in both rhythm and proportion and in harmony of sound and color, iv., 31, 64-66, 430, 431, recognized in the degree of fulfilling art principle of putting like with like, v., 8, 10-19, 39-43, 52-56, 59, 60, 116, 117, 120-143, 184, 222, 347-351, 354, 356, 373-375, 377-383, 404, 405; similar in harmony of sound and of color, 338-347, 372-377, 394-404; to be of use, they must be of small numbers, v., 19, 39-42, 44, 117, 143, 149. See Harmony, Like with Like, and Proportion.
Realistic art, 425
Red color by lamp-light, 315; in foliage, 317, 318
Regensburg, Bavaria, 256
Regularity, lack of in Greek measurements of temples, 248, 250, 262, 263
Relief, colors in backgrounds of, 387, 388
Rembrandt, 304, 367, 412
Renaissance, painting before and after the, 301; revival in architecture, 226, 227
Representation of nature and mind in art, 420, 426-429. See Beauty and Significance.
Representative Significance of Form,

The, 423, 424; analysis of essay on, 424, 425
Repetition—Art-Method, 3, 61, 64, 66; in architecture, 148-151, 162-164, 168; in color, 364-366, 368, 410; in human figure, 116, 117; in measurements at the basis of proportion, 162, 164, 175, 184; importance of, 14; of shape, 164, 175; of tone-harmony and that of outline, 231, 232. See Harmony, Like with Like, and Proportion.
Republic, The, of Plato, 26
Resonators of Helmholtz, 340
Retina, 21, 22; illustrated, 350, 380, 381; organs of, recognizing color, viii., 349, 350, 378-383; vibratory action of organs of, in perceiving color, 349, 350, 353, 354, 356, 360, 374, 377-383, 404, 405, 411, 412. See Vibrations.
Reynolds, Sir J., 122, 305, 367, 407
Rhamnus, temple at, 153, 187, 219, 221
Rhodian School of Sculpture, 98
Rhyme, 230, 232
Rhythm and Harmony in Poetry and Music, 2, 13, 16, 23, 230, 232, 233, 325, 328, 338, 342, 349, 373, 397, 400, 403, 406, 411, 414, 423, 424; analysis of essay on, 430, 431
Rhythm, analogue of proportion, iv., v., vi., 2, 3, 7, 10, 13-19, 23-26, 74, 114-117, 179, 430, 431; connection between, and harmony of sound, 27, 31, 63-66, 343, 344, 430, 431
Rico, 308, 365
Richelieu Pavilion, Paris, 150
Rings of Ovola, 187
Rods and Cones of the Eye, viii., 349, 350, 380-383
Romanesque Architecture, 227
Romantic *vs.* Classic Art, 420
Romney, 305
Rood, O. N., ix., 315, 321, 393, 396, 409
Room, proportions of a, 150, 151
Rosa, S., 303
Roslyn Chapel, 437

456　　　　　　　INDEX.

Ross, 181
Rotation of eyes and effect on perspective, 237, 238
Rousseau, 308
Rubens, 304, 358, 359, 367, 376
Ruskin, 59, 286, 368, 409
Ruysbrack, 99
Ruysdael, 305

Samson, G., W., 117
Sandby, 305
Sargent, D. A., 88
Scales, color, 389-405; of color and music, 357, 358, 374, 375, 389-405; Von Bezold's color chart of, 333-336, 390-393, 398, 402, 404
Schadow, 306
Schaubert, 181, 248
Science of Beauty and Laws of Geometric Proportion, Hay, 46
Scientific study of color necessary to artists, 298-308
Scopas, 98
Scourging of Christ, The, Titian, 324
"Scribner's Magazine," 88
Sculpture, excellence of Greek, 91; Greek face of, conventional, 92-95, 126, 128; Greek, modelled upon nature, 89-101; posture in Greek, 141, 142; proportions in Greek, 83, 84, 89-101, 118-134, 141, 142; styles of different in Greek, 96-101
Secondary colors, 313, 326
Segesta, temple at, 193, 221
Selinus, temple at, 187, 190, 193, 195, 221
Septimius Severus, Arch of, 152, 207
Setting—Art-Method, 3, 65, 363
Shade. See Colors and Light and Shade.
Shades, 312; and tints that go together, 410. See Colors.
Shadows. See Colors, and Light and Shade.
Shakespeare, 92, 180
Shape, and measurement connected in effect, 148, 163, 164, 172, 173;

beautiful, when its outlines are all perceived together with the least conscious visual effort, 278-287, 293-295; horizontally, 279; vertically, 279-287. See Contour, Curves, Ellipse, Human Form, and Proportion.
Sight, Le Conte, ix., 21, 238, 349, 268, 272, 273
Sight, arts of, 4-7; binocular, 266-295; field of, for one and both eyes, 267-278
Significance in beauty, 104-108, 112, 139, 140; of human face, 104-106, 128; of human form, 92-108, 112-114, 128, 129, 139, 140; vs. form in art, 104-108, 112, 128, 129, 139, 140, 158, 423-432
Significance, The Representative, of Form, analysis of essay on, 424, 425
Simplicity of proportion and rhythm, 14, 15, 20
Sistine Madonna, 437
Socrates, 91
Sonnävater and Knut Entering Stockholm, Hellquist, 363, 364, 366, 369
Sound, arts of 4,-7. See Harmony of Sound.
Space, arts of, 4; tendency to divide into like subdivisions, 10-13, 28; correspondence between arts of, and of time, 4-7, 10, 28
Spanish Lady, by Fortuny, 355
Spanish-Roman School of Painting, 365
Spectrum, 297, 298, 310, 311, 314, 329-331
Speech-harmony, compared to effects of harmony of outline, 229-232, 431
Speech-rhythm, an adaptation from nature, 74, 90; compared to effect of proportion, 74, 90, 112, 114-116
Stained-glass windows, proportion of human figures in, 78, 79
Standards, of art-judgment, and their influence on production,

INDEX. 457

Standards—*Continued.*
433-437; of measurement in human form, 116, 118; when a complex is compared with a simple figure, rectangular, and curvilinear, 48-72, 87, 134-143; or is crossed by straight lines, 57, 58, 67, 68, 78-87, 125-129
Steps of Greek temple, 188-190, 194
Stereoscopy, principle of, 270-276
St. Étienne du Mont, Paris, 167-169
Stimson, J. W., 235
St. Mark's, Venice, 237
St. Paul's, Covent Garden, London, 224, 225; illustration of, 225
Straight lines, increase apparent length in their own direction, 151, 152, 202; indicate proportions when at equal distances, drawn really, 57, 58, 67, 68, 78-87, 125-129; or imaginatively, 85-87; or suggestively, 56; parallel, vertical, and horizontal, how brought together and curved by perspective, 233-265
St. Stephens, Caen, 37, 154, 170
St. Sophia, Constantinople, illustration of, 226
St. Sulpice, 154, 156, 157, 160
Stuart, 181, 248
Stylobate of Greek temple, 183, 188-190, 194, 196, 201, 206, 208, 209, 213, 214, 217, 250; as related to other members, 200-222. See Like with Like and Ratios.
Sublime, The, in art, 425
Subordination—Art-Method, 3, 63; in color, 355, 358, 408
Sunium, temple at, 187, 193, 219, 221
Sydney, Australia, university at, 147
Symington, A. J., 298, 299
Symphony, Seventh, 437
Symmetry—Art-Method, 3, 66; in outline, 249; in color, 361, 411
Syracuse, temple at, 193
System of Geometric Proportion, A. Hay, 28

Taste, discrepancies in, 112, 113; can be cultivated, 437; standards of, not inconsistent with originality and genius, 433-437
Temperaments, human, represented by different schemes of proportion, 116
Temples, Greek, 8, 12, 29, 30, 35, 36, 44, 56, 116, 117, 248-264, 417, 418
Temples of Ægina and Bassæ, Cockerill, 19, 29, 44, 178, 181, etc.
Tenniers, 304
Tennyson, 18, 433
Texture, color of, 317
Thebes, temple at, 246
Themis, temple of, at Rhamnus, 187, 193, 221
Theory of Color, Von Bezold, ix., 333, 387
Theory, right, necessary to right art-methods, 49, 140, 141, 253
Theseum or Theseus, temple of, 36, 156, 187, 189, 193, 196, 201, 210, 211, 218-221, 224, 250, 252, 262
Theseus, statue of, 97, 98
Thiersch, 243
Thompson, 219
Timæus, Plato, 27
Time, arts of, 4; correspondence between arts of, and of space, 4-7, 10, 28
Tintoretto, 303
Titian, 92, 299, 302, 303, 324, 366, 367, 407
Tone, the term as used both for colors and sounds, 6; in color, 308, 312, 327, 355-358. See Harmony.
Tones, partial, in music, 372-374, 398-404
Transition—Art-Method, 3; in outline, 61, 67, 148; in color, 412
True, The, in art, 424
Triglyphs, 12, 192
Tryon, 308, 322
Turner, 305
Turpilius, 301
Tympanum of Greek temple, 183, 195-198, 201, 204, 206, 207, 209, 210, 213, 214; as related to en-

Tympanum—*Continued.*
tablature and column-height, 201–222; same height as entablature and upper space between columns, 195–199, 221; unusual height in Parthenon, 215–217

Unity—Art-Method, 3, 16; in architecture and outline, 18, 19, 61, 63, 116, 284; in color, 314, 325–328, 354, 355–358, 363, 368, 369, 400

Unconscious action of mind in recognizing effects of measurements causing harmonic ratios in sound and color, iv., v., 23–26, 64, 65, 343–345, 404, 405

Van Dyck, 304
Van Dyke, J. C., 365
Van der Velde, 305
Van Eycks, 304
Vanishing point in perspective, 233
Vase, the elliptical outlines of, among all people, 283, 284, 287, 288; illustrated, 283, 285
Variety—Art-Method, 3, 18, 61, 62, 64; in architecture, 164; in color, 328, 354–358, 364, 366, 369, 400, 406, 430–432; in human form, 116; not inconsistent with effects of tone in paintings, 355–358
Velasquez, 303, 307
Venetian School of Painters, 302, 304, 386
Venus, Anadyomene, 92; ascribed to style of Praxiteles, 105; de' Medici, 92, 97, 123
Vernet, H., 306; J., 306
Veronese, Paul, 303, 360, 376
Vertical lines as affected by perspective, 237–239; 257–262. See Curves and Perspective.
Vibrations, in organs of sight or hearing, as distinguished from waves of light or sound, 313, 378, note; as influencing conceptions of beauty in general, 112–114; common multiple for, and ratios of, determining harmony in music, 28, 65, 66, 338–347, 372, 375, 398–401; determining harmony in color, 347, 348, 373–375, 377–383, 394–405; differences between those producing sound and color, 372–377; numbers of, causing each of the colors, 402; physiological effects of, causing harmony of color when coalescing in retina, 349, 350, 353, 354, 356, 360, 377–383, 404, 405, 410, 411; similarity of ratios of, in harmony of sound and of color, 372–377, 394–405; similarity of those producing harmony of sound and of color to the beats and outlines producing effects of rhythm and proportion, 27, 31, 64–66, 343, 344, 430, 431; size, rate, and form of, determining musical harmony and quality, 338–347; unconsciousness of the mind of the causes of, when producing effects of harmony of sound or color, iv., v., 23–26, 27, 64, 65, 343–345, 404, 405

Villegas, 308
Vinci, Leonardo da, 302
Violet color by lamp-light, 315
Vitruvian Scroll, 12
Vitruvius, M. P., 26, 64, 117–120, 122, 141, 150, 219, 222, 224, 246, 251, 252, 256, 258, 261–264; his trustworthiness, 120, 262, 263; The Architecture of, 198
Von Bezold, ix., 333, 387, 390, 392, 401, 403, 404, 406
Von Klenze, 256

Wagner, 211
Walhalla, The, 256
Walker Museum, Chicago University, 54
Warm Colors, 303, 304, 313, 320–324, 384–388, 407, 408; in aërial perspective, 321–324; in backgrounds and relief, 387, 388; in causing harmony by preponderance, 327, 396, note; in complementaries, 335, 336, 384–388, 407, 408; indoors and out, 320, 321; in shadows and not at different times of day, 319–321; quiet, un-

Warm Colors—*Continued*.
  obtrusive effects of color obtained through using, 385
Waves, producing sound and color, distinguished from the internal vibrations experienced in the ear and eye, 313, 378, note; occasioning color, their action, 349, 350, 373–375, 377–383; occasioning sound, 344, 349, 373, 374; size, rate, and shape of, and of vibrations determining musical harmony and quality, 338–347; their shape when compound illustrated, 340. See Vibrations.
Wedge, shape of man's form, 138–140
Wheatstone, 274, 282

White, and black as complementaries, 334, 335; light containing all the colors, 309–311, 329–331
Wiener Bauzeitung, 248
Wilkie, 305
Willesden Church, 40, 154
Window, stained glass of, indicating proportion, 78, 79
Winckelmann, 306
Wouvermanns, 305

Yellow color, by lamp-light, 315
Young, Sir T., 402, 403

Zamaçois, 308, 365
Zeising, A., 27
Zeuxis, 301

OTHER WORKS BY PROF. GEO. L. RAYMOND

The Essentials of Æsthetics. 8vo. Illustrated . . Net, $2.50

This work, which is mainly a compendium of the author's system of Comparative Æsthetics, previously published in seven volumes, was prepared, by request, for a textbook, and for readers whose time is too limited to study the minutiæ of the subject.

"We consider Professor Raymond to possess something like an ideal equipment. . . . His own poetry is genuine and delicately constructed, his appreciations are true to high ideals, and his power of scientific analysis is unquestionable." . . . "After graduating in this country, he went through a course of æsthetics with Professor Vischer of the University of Tübingen, and also with Professor Curtius at the time when that historian of Greece was spending several hours a week with his pupils among the marbles of the Berlin Museum. Subsequently, believing that all the arts are, primarily, developments of different forms of expression through the tones and movements of the body, Professor Raymond made a thorough study, chiefly in Paris, of methods of cultivating and using the voice in both singing and speaking, and of representing thought and emotion through postures and gestures. It is a result of these studies that he afterwards developed, first, into his methods of teaching elocution and literature (as embodied in his 'Orator's Manual' and 'The Writer') and later into his æsthetic system. . . . A Princeton man has said of him that he has as keen a sense for a false poetic element as a bank expert for a counterfeit note; and a New York model who posed for him, when preparing illustrations for one of his books, said that he was the only man that he had ever met who could invariably, without experiment, tell him at once what posture to assume in order to represent any required sentiment."—*New York Times.*

A Life in Song. 16°, cloth extra, gilt top $1.25

"Mr. Raymond is a poet, with all that the name implies. He has the true fire—there is no disputing that. There is thought of an elevated character, the diction is pure, the versification is true, the meter correct, and . . . affords innumerable quotations to fortify and instruct one for the struggles of life.'—*Hartford Post.*

Ballads, and Other Poems. 16°, cloth extra, gilt top . . $1.25

"A work of true genius, brimful of imagination and sweet humanity."—*The Fireside* (London).

"Fine and strong, its thought original and suggestive, while its expression is the very perfection of narrative style."—*The N. Y. Critic.*

"Proves beyond doubt that Mr. Raymond is the possessor of a poetic faculty which is worthy of the most careful and conscientious cultivation."—*N. Y. Evening Post.*

The Aztec God and Other Dramas. 16°, cloth extra, gilt top . $1.25

"The three dramas included in this volume represent a felicitous, intense, and melodious expression of art both from the artistic and poetic point of view. . . . Mr. Raymond's power is above all that of psychologist, and added thereto are the richest products of the imagination both in form and spirit. The book clearly discloses the work of a man possessed of an extremely refined critical poise, of a culture pure and classical, and a sensitive conception of what is sweetest and most ravishing in tone-quality. The most delicately perceptive ear could not detect a flaw in the mellow and rich music of the blank verse."—*Public Opinion.*

Dante and Collected Verse. 16°, cloth extra, gilt top . . $1.25

"The book, in its adaptation of modern ideas and of metrical accomplishment to old world themes, is a characteristic product of American culture and refinement."
Edinburgh (Scotland) Scotsman.

"Brother Jonathan cannot claim many great poets, but we think he has 'struck oil' in Professor Raymond."—*Western (England) Morning News.*

"This brilliant composition . . . gathers up and concentrates for the reader more of the reality of the great Italian than is readily gleaned from the author of the Inferno himself."—*Oakland Enquirer.*

The Writer (with POST WHEELER), a concise and complete Rhetoric.
12° . . . . Net, $1.00

"Of great value not only in the schoolroom but in the library."—*Education.*

The Orator's Manual. A Text-book of Vocal-culture, Emphasis, Gesture, and the Subject-matter of Public Address. 12 Net, $1.20

"It is undoubtedly the most complete and thorough treatise on oratory for the practical student ever published."—*The Educational Weekly, Chicago.*

G. P. PUTNAM'S SONS, New York and London

www.ingramcontent.com/pod-product-compliance
Lightning Source LLC
Chambersburg PA
CBHW021419300426
44114CB00010B/556